Clinical Supervision Activities for

# Increasing Competence and Self-Awareness

# Clinical Supervision Activities for

# Increasing Competence and Self-Awareness

Edited by

Roy A. Bean
Sean D. Davis
Maureen P. Davey

WILEY

Cover Design: Wiley
Cover Image: © iStockphoto/Terryfic3D

This book is printed on acid-free paper.⊗

Copyright ©2014 by John Wiley & Sons, Inc. All rights reserved.

Published by John Wiley & Sons, Inc., Hoboken, New Jersey.
Published simultaneously in Canada.

Limit of Liability/Disclaimer of Warranty: While the publisher and author have used their best efforts in preparing this book, they make no representations or warranties with respect to the accuracy or completeness of the contents of this book and specifically disclaim any implied warranties of merchantability or fitness for a particular purpose. No warranty may be created or extended by sales representatives or written sales materials. The advice and strategies contained herein may not be suitable for your situation. You should consult with a professional where appropriate. Neither the publisher nor author shall be liable for any loss of profit or any other commercial damages, including but not limited to special, incidental, consequential, or other damages.

This publication is designed to provide accurate and authoritative information in regard to the subject matter covered. It is sold with the understanding that the publisher is not engaged in rendering professional services. If legal, accounting, medical, psychological or any other expert assistance is required, the services of a competent professional person should be sought.

Designations used by companies to distinguish their products are often claimed as trademarks. In all instances where John Wiley & Sons, Inc. is aware of a claim, the product names appear in initial capital or all capital letters. Readers, however, should contact the appropriate companies for more complete information regarding trademarks and registration.

For general information on our other products and services please contact our Customer Care Department within the United States at (800) 762-2974, outside the United States at (317) 572-3993 or fax (317) 572-4002.

Wiley publishes in a variety of print and electronic formats and by print-on-demand. Some material included with standard print versions of this book may not be included in e-books or in print-on-demand. If this book refers to media such as a CD or DVD that is not included in the version you purchased, you may download this material at http://booksupport.wiley.com. For more information about Wiley products, visit www.wiley.com.

*Library of Congress Cataloging-in-Publication Data:*

Clinical supervision activities for increasing competence and self-awareness / edited by Roy A. Bean, Sean D. Davis, Maureen P. Davey.
     pages cm
  Includes bibliographical references and index.
  ISBN 978-1-118-63752-4 (pbk. : alk. paper); ISBN 978-1-118-65336-4 (ebk); ISBN 978-1-118-82791-8 (ebk) 1. Psychotherapy.
2. Empathy. I. Bean, Roy A., editor of compilation.
  RC480.C563 2014
  616.89'14–dc23
                                                                              2013042744

Printed in the United States of America

10 9 8 7 6 5 4 3 2 1

# CONTENTS

# PREFACE

Across all mental health professions, practitioners have long been focused on providing competent and effective treatment to their clients. Countless empirical studies and theoretical papers have been published in an attempt to improve the quality of clinical treatments. More recently, this collective investment in quality clinical education and treatment has been reflected in outcome-focused educational accreditation principles, more stringent measures of therapeutic success, and explicit measures of clinical competence and treatment efficacy.

In most instances, the practice of clinical training has been advanced, as exemplified by standardized educational curriculums designed to help clinicians meet outcome-based criteria for graduation and licensure. Unfortunately, a primary or unbalanced devotion to outcome-based education can be limiting in at least two ways. First, it can turn the supervisor's focus to the assessment of clinician outcomes in lieu of being actively engaged in the training process and the current experiences of the clinicians-in-training. Second, it can emphasize supervisory attention to clinician factors that are more easily observed (e.g., knowledge acquisition, skill development) rather than therapist awareness and competencies in the more subtle areas, such as overcoming personal biases or developing intuition, empathy, and perspective taking.

One of the key characteristics of a competent and emotionally stable clinician is self-awareness. In fact, regardless of the mental health specialization (e.g., professional counselor, psychologist, clinical social worker, marriage and family therapist, psychiatrist, chemical dependence counselor), all psychotherapists need to be aware of their own biases and personal limitations. As supervisors and educators work to assess and foster competence and self-awareness, they serve an important gatekeeping function by guarding access to the profession and, more importantly, by protecting clients from inadequate and/or unethical clinical care. A greater level of self-awareness can help clinicians avoid many problems and, when needed, can facilitate the resolution of training issues. Competent clinicians who have greater self-awareness are also able to more easily keep professional boundaries and to avoid dangerous levels of countertransference and enmeshment with clients. Similarly, clinicians who have been well-trained at this level are more often able to avoid burnout and are more likely to genuinely and professionally connect to their clients.

In order to better facilitate the training process, this edited book includes a collection of tried-and-tested best practices designed to help students and new clinicians develop greater competence and self-awareness. This book is designed to help clinicians be better prepared to work with increasingly diverse client populations and challenging clinical issues. Given the self-directed nature of post-licensure professional growth and continuing education, this book is also designed to help experienced clinicians "check for blind spots" and continue their own development.

The training activities presented here are designed to create an experientially based learning opportunity for clinicians, as directed by a facilitator (typically a clinical instructor or supervisor). The activities should be used as a supplement to high-quality, attentive clinical supervision and not as a replacement. After all, the experience of supervision and education is a big part of what prepares clinicians for the experience of face-to-face work with clients.

The book chapters are divided into two sections: Core Clinical Competence and Self-Awareness and Diversity-Focused Competence and Self-Awareness. These categories are not mutually exclusive, as both types of activities are seen as necessary for optimal clinical development. The training exercises can be introduced as a supervision requirement, class assignment, implemented as part of a supervisee's remediation requirement, or self-assigned to facilitate personal growth.

# Core Clinical Competence and Self-Awareness

It has been said that in couples therapy, three sessions are going on at once—the one the therapist is experiencing and the one each partner is experiencing (Helmeke & Sprenkle, 2000). The same can be said for individual, group, and family therapy. Each person in therapy filters what is happening in the room through a complex web of life experiences, cultural influences, biases, current life stressors, and family backgrounds, just to name a few. Successfully navigating this web is part of what can make therapy challenging and exciting, because it requires clinicians to develop the ability to:

- Observe him- or herself conducting therapy
- Observe each client observing him- or herself
- Observe each client observing other family members
- Observe each client observing the clinician/self

Not surprisingly, the degree to which therapists are attuned to clients' experiences in therapy, and therapists' level of willingness and ability to change course in session accordingly, is a well-documented common factor of effective therapy (Sprenkle, Davis, & Lebow, 2009).

This awareness involves therapists' ability to see and understand their biases, assumptions, personal well-being, and general issues. More importantly, clinicians need to be able to evaluate how these issues impact the therapeutic process (Blow, Sprenkle, & Davis, 2007). While the ability to do this is a skill, we believe it is deeper than that. A skill is something you can turn on and off, whereas we submit that truly competent clinicians incorporate this skill into who they are—it becomes an integral part of them as they gain experience.

As a whole, the first half of the book presents experiential activities designed to help therapists develop greater self-awareness and clinical competence. Presented first are two chapters by noted author and educator Harry Aponte, who with his colleagues describes activities centered on their "person-of-the-therapist" model. The first activity involves writing and then rewriting a paper designed to foster awareness. The second activity involves completing an instrument designed to complement and deepen personal insights gained in the paper. Aponte and colleagues set the stage for the book by pointing out that personal issues are unavoidable and can be a source of strength in therapy if a therapist is aware of them.

The next seven chapters focus from various angles on the foundational therapeutic attribute of empathy. Clinicians enjoy much greater influence when they understand and validate their client's reality. Being deeply and nonjudgmentally understood can be immensely healing, yet this foundational skill can be one of the most difficult for new clinicians to learn and for seasoned clinicians to retain. Unexamined assumptions and judgments often get in the way of empathy for new clinicians, whereas routine and burnout are often the enemies of empathy for experienced clinicians.

Parker and Blackburn outline an "empathy game," in which therapists gain empathy for clients by watching clips of recorded sessions. Schneider has developed a process through which clinicians learn to appreciate different perspectives through process recording and videotapes. Cravens and Whiting describe an activity designed to increase mindfulness and a nonjudgmental attitude. Burke and Hohman discuss a reflective listening exercise. Esmiol and Partridge outline an instrument and activity that can help clinicians seek and nondefensively accept client feedback. Banford and Tambling outline a group exercise in which therapists reflexively share themes they notice in themselves and each other. Mirick encourages therapists to gain empathy for clients by picking one of their bad habits and discussing it with a colleague.

Just as clinicians need empathy for their clients, they also need empathy for themselves. It has been said that water cannot be drawn from an empty well. If a clinician cannot identify and respond appropriately to his or her own needs, it will be difficult to do the same for his or her clients. Therefore, the next three chapters focus on self-care and developing resiliency. Bohlinger, Wahlig, and Trudeau-Hern outline a mindfulness-based meditation exercise for developing self-compassion. Gillespie and O'Reilly invite clinicians into a mindfulness and narrative-based contemplative dialogue with their colleagues, in which clinicians reconnect with their initial desires to enter the field. Akyil, Pham, and Cunningham present their "concerns of a beginning therapist" questionnaire, which is designed to help beginning therapists and their supervisors articulate growth areas and track developmental progress.

The next three chapters focus on helping clinicians understand how early life experiences with their family and peers impact their clinical work. Davis and Gonzalez-Cort outline an interview with a clinician's family of origin designed to help clinicians gain insight into their emotional triggers so they can be less reactive in therapy. Similarly, Roberts-Pittman and Viviani have therapists construct a genogram to explore their conflict styles and the effect these may have on being a therapist. Williams and Banks have therapists journal about early life experiences related to self-concept. Hall describes an activity designed to increase safety and deepen experiencing in group therapy.

Several clinical settings present unique challenges requiring specialized knowledge. The first three chapters in this section deal with trauma. Hass-Cohen, Veeman, Chandler-Ziegler, and Brimhall outline a fascinating approach to helping clinicians gain empathy for the experiences of international clients who have experienced traumas such as war and natural disasters with which the clinician may be unfamiliar. Then Hass-Cohen and Chandler-Ziegler outline an activity designed to help clinicians cope with vicarious trauma. Similarly, Schwerdtfeger discusses an approach to helping clinicians practice self-care when working with trauma. Next, Steiner and Cox describe an activity to help clinicians find alignment between their work culture and personal values.

This section closes with two chapters dealing with clinicians working in medical settings. Couden Hernandez and Kim discuss a reflecting team exercise designed to help physicians and clinicians deliver bad news compassionately in a medical setting. Mendenhall and Trudeau-Kern help clinicians prepare for the challenges of working in a medical setting by completing a "health genogram" to help clinicians understand their experiences with health-related experiences in their family.

# Diversity-Focused Competence and Self-Awareness

A culturally sensitive approach to care is essential among all clinical providers because it has been linked to provider–client engagement, treatment adherence, and the quality of mental healthcare (Langer, 1999; Núñez, 2003, 2009; U.S. Department of Health and Human Services, 2001). The client–provider relationship is built on the ability of providers to show interest in and knowledge about the client as a whole person. Yet clients' previous experiences of biased care or discrimination by others in the healthcare system, or society in general, can lead to guardedness and mistrust toward individual clinical providers and mental health institutions (U.S. Department of Health and Human Services, 2001). In addition, clinical providers may hold unconscious biases toward diverse clients. The relationship between providers and clients, therefore, is a crucial one. Trust in clinical providers is fundamental to improving clinical outcomes, especially among historically marginalized client populations in the United States.

It is important for healthcare providers to learn how to be effective with diverse patient populations where neither the culture of the provider nor the client is favored and "gain an understanding of the impact of their own culture and also a broader appreciation of interactions among cultures, rather than just memorizing characteristics of certain broad groups" (Nuñez, 2003, p. 1072).

In order to promote cultural sensitivity and self-awareness in the area of diversity competence, 21 tried-and-tested activities are presented. The authors developed these activities to help student trainees and new clinicians develop greater self-awareness and to help clinical supervisors train supervisees to be better prepared to work with increasingly diverse client populations in the United States. Chapters were developed to challenge narrow-mindedness, to encourage self-discovery, and to identify providers' own prejudices and limitations. The topics presented in this section include the following: multicultural awareness, white privilege, gender-based privilege and oppression, culture-based privilege and oppression, class-based privilege and oppression, disability/ability awareness, deaf awareness, immigrant client and immigrant therapist awareness, sexual orientation–based privilege and oppression, co-victims of rape awareness, weight and body awareness, addiction and recovery awareness, ageism, and finally, death and grief awareness.

The first two chapters cover activities that promote general multicultural awareness. Caldwell and Galiardi describe a cultural card group activity that facilitates the discussion of oppression and privilege in relation to a range of multicultural issues (e.g., gender, age, body size, ethnic/racial background, family constellation, sexual orientation, ability/disability, educational background, religion, and socioeconomic status). Bean, Hsieh, and Clark next describe an activity where clinicians explore a change in one key aspect of their identities (e.g., gender, sexual orientation, ethnicity/race) to encourage them to develop greater perspective-taking abilities and to improve awareness of factors that can influence their own life experiences as providers.

Carter, Swanke, and Brown describe an activity to increase awareness about the power imbalances during clinical encounters. Renowned author and presenter Peggy McIntosh describes a self-awareness group exercise to help providers better understand White privilege. Newman, Pettigrew, Trujillo, and Smock Jordan, as well as Banks and Williams, describe activities that increase awareness about social class, ethnicity, and resource disadvantages, help to uncover personal biases, and encourage more empathic approaches with vulnerable clients. Nash and Hufnell each describe experiential activities to help increase understanding and cultural effectiveness with clients who have a diverse range of abilities. Additionally, DeGraff, Sorenson, Atchley, and Smock Jordan provide readers with an opportunity for increased awareness about clients who present with substance abuse problems and co-occuring mental/physical disabilities.

In three separate chapters, Akakpo, Lasley, and Zeytinoglu and colleagues focus on immigrant clients and training foreign-born therapists in the United States. Akakpo describes a strategic game to increase self-awareness and understanding of culturally sensitive interventions for recent immigrants from Africa. Lasley describes an experiential exercise to help increase clinicians' cultural sensitivity with immigrant clients in the United States. Zeytinoglu and colleagues describe an activity for clinical supervisors to use with their foreign-born supervisees to better attend to the effect of acculturation on immigrant therapists who are seeing clients in the United States.

Walker and Hernandez and Luna, Heath, Andrews, Smock Jordan, and Higgins describe activities to help providers and student trainees develop more self-awareness and cultural sensitivity while working with lesbian, gay, bisexual, transgender/gender-nonconforming, and queer clients (LGBTQ). Merchant and Whiting describe an exercise that encourages the discovery of compassion for victims of domestic violence, and Rich describes an activity to help providers develop empathy for co-victims of rape. Pratt and Craven describe an exercise to promote greater awareness of weight and body issues experienced by clients. Piercy and Palit describe reflexive learning activities to help providers work with clients in addiction and in recovery, and Bradford, Ketring, and Smith also describe an experiential exercise to improve empathy for clients experiencing addiction and recovery from substance abuse. Schade describes an activity designed to increase knowledge about common stereotypes about older clients, and finally Humble, Pilkinton, Brodie, and Johnson describe a learning activity using a simulated role-play of a client who receives a terminal diagnosis from a physician to help providers develop skills to practice effectively in the context of end-of-life issues.

As satisfied as we are with this book and its contents, we also have to recognize that more can and should be written on the topic of experiential-based clinical training. Awareness and competency trainings can be extended to a great many more general clinician attributes and several additional clinical populations. In particular, we note the need for additional training activities to help clinicians develop greater competence and awareness in the areas of religiosity and spirituality, working with children and adolescents, and helping families cope with severe mental illnesses. Other topics of interest (to us and to the larger training field) include working with non-English-speaking clients (and translators) and ways to partner with community leaders to reach underserved minority populations where stigmas may prevent mental health treatment.

Clinical competence and awareness are neither easily developed nor quickly mastered and an hour-long activity will not be sufficient to bring about lasting change. Regular supervision and mentoring by professional colleagues are the most direct and reliable ways to continue to grow and develop as clinicians. The reader is invited to engage students, supervisees, and/or professional associates in conversations on these topics, using these activities as part of the experience, but not the end of it.

# References

Blow, A. J., Sprenkle, D. H., & Davis, S. D. (2007). Is who delivers the treatment more important than the treatment itself? The role of the therapist in common factors. *Journal of Marital and Family Therapy, 33,* 298–317.

Helmeke, K. B., & Sprenkle, D. H. (2000). Clients' perceptions of pivotal moments in couples therapy: A qualitative study of change in therapy. *Journal of Marital and Family Therapy, 26,* 469–483.

Langer, N. (1999). Culturally competent professionals in therapeutic alliance enhance patient compliance. *Journal of Health Care for the Poor and Underserved, 10,* 19–26. PMID: 9989004.

Núñez, A. E. (2003). *Looking within to see the outside better: A course on enhancing effectiveness in cross-cultural care.* Philadelphia, PA: Hahnemann University. (Cited in 2001 Institute of Medicine Report as an example of curricular excellence.)

Núñez, A. (Assoc. Ed.). (2009). In L. A. Hark & H. M. DeLisser (Eds.-in-Chief), *Achieving cultural competency: A case-based approach to training health professionals.* Oxford, UK: Wiley Blackwell.

Sprenkle, D. H., Davis, S. D., & Lebow, J. (2009). *Common factors in couple and family therapy: The overlooked foundation for effective practice.* New York, NY: Guilford Press.

U.S. Department of Health and Human Services. (2001). *Mental health: Culture, race and ethnicity.* A supplement to *Mental health: A report of the Surgeon General.* Washington, DC: Author.

# ACKNOWLEDGMENTS

The process of developing an idea into a book is usually challenging and enjoyable, and this project is no exception. We are so very grateful for the help and support of our editor at Wiley, Rachel Livsey. We couldn't have done this without her, and all of these great ideas and wonderful training activities would have remained underutilized if not for her belief in the book. We are also very appreciative of the assistance received from Amanda Orenstein at Wiley, who helped us immensely to stay organized and on time.

We are also grateful for the wonderful editing team at the BYU Faculty Editing Service and all of their work to prepare each chapter for publication. In particular, we are indebted to Jenn McDaniel, as their valiant leader and editing supervisor, who helped us shape so much of the book and its contents. We are appreciative of the generosity of our contributors, their willingness to share great ideas with other professionals and to give up "trade secrets" for the greater good of clinical training. We look forward to seeing how far our influence extends as future generations of clinicians are prepared, professionally and personally, using these training activities.

I would also like to acknowledge the following reviewers for their thoughtful comments and feedback: Laura Simpson, PhD, LPC-S, Walden University, Germantown, TN; Linda Homeyer, PhD, Texas State University, San Marcos, TX; Jeannie Falkner, PhD, Walden University, Oxford, MS; Ann Goelitz, LCSW, Northern Westchester Hospital, Ridgefield, CT; Phil Rich, EdD, MSW, Director of Clinical Program Development at the Stetson School, Amherst, MA; Pasquale Giordano, LPC, Director of Home-Based Services at Bridges, Hamden, CT; Philip H. Brown, MSW, LCSW, Northeast Psychotherapy Associates, LLC, Plainfield, CT; and Stephen A. Giunta, PhD, Program Coordinator, Counseling and Psychology, Troy University, Tampa, FL.

For my part, I am especially thankful for the loving support of my wife, who patiently endured the whole process from the initial pitch of the book concept to the final moments of meeting revision deadlines. You are the best, Tracey, the best! Our children (Victoria, Sydney, and Andrew) have had to share me with this book over the past year, and that hasn't always been easy or convenient—my apologies and my thanks to you. I am appreciative of my co-editors, Sean and Maureen, who started as my friends and ended up as better friends. I could not have done this without you, thank you.

*R. Bean*

Big projects like this do not come to fruition without collective sacrifice. I would like to thank those who sacrificed the most to help me complete this project, namely my wife, Elizabeth, and my children, Andrew, Hannah, Rachel, and William. I wish to thank my colleagues and graduate students at Alliant International University for encouraging me as I disappeared into another book project; I could not ask for a more supportive university culture. I also thank the authors of the chapters in this book, as well as those that were not published. Many excellent chapters were cut simply because of space limitations. Lastly, I wish to acknowledge my co-editors Roy Bean and Maureen Davey. Your kindness, support, and teamwork made this book seem like far less work that it actually was.

*S. Davis*

I would like to thank and acknowledge a great many people who helped to make this book possible. I wish to offer sincere thanks to my spouse, Adam, and my daughter, Gabriela, for helping me carve out the time necessary for editing this book. My graduate students and colleagues provided input and plenty of constructive criticism along the way. I also want to acknowledge and thank the many graduate students and scholars who wrote chapters for our book; we could not have done this project without your hard work and dedication. Finally, I wish to acknowledge the steady support and encouragement of my co-editors Roy Bean and Sean Davis, and our publisher Wiley, who helped bring this project to fruition.

*M. Davey*

Clinical Supervision Activities for

# Increasing Competence and Self-Awareness

# PART I

# CORE CLINICAL COMPETENCE AND SELF-AWARENESS

# CHAPTER 1

# FACILITATING CLINICIAN DEVELOPMENT USING THEMES OF PERSONAL ISSUES

Karni Kissil, Alba Niño, and Harry J. Aponte

## Introduction

The quality of the therapeutic relationship has been presented in the literature as a pivotal factor linked to better therapeutic outcomes (Grencravage & Norcross, 1990; Sprenkle, Davis, & Lebow, 2009). This chapter draws from the Person-of-the-Therapist Training model (POTT; Aponte & Winter, 2000) and demonstrates the use of an instrument with the goal of increasing clinicians' awareness and acceptance of their personal issues as a way of facilitating deeper connections with their clients. The richer the relationship is with the client, the greater the clinician's capacity is to effectively assess and intervene. This chapter is the first of two and introduces the reader to the concept of the *signature theme*. In the subsequent chapter, the application of signature themes to clinical work is discussed (see "Exploring the Person-of-the-Therapist for Better Joining, Assessment, and Intervention" in this volume).

## Rationale

Most self-of-the-therapist approaches to training clinicians view *resolution* of personal issues as a necessary means of change and growth that frees clinicians to become more effective professionals (e.g., Bowen, 1972; Kerr, 1981; Satir, 2000). Although the goal of reaching resolution seems appropriate, it can be a lifelong endeavor, and possibly even an unachievable goal, as we might never fully resolve all of our emotional and relational issues. Our clients get who we are as people and clinicians *in the present*, not who we would like to be. Because of this, the POTT approach emphasizes learning the intentional use of self *as-is*. We all carry our personal struggles into our therapeutic encounters, and they color our thinking, emotional reactions, and behavior with our clients. However, our personal issues and our struggles can be used to relate to our clients and their issues. The POTT model adopts the concept of the "wounded healer" (Nouwen, 1972), stating that we can empathize with and relate to the woundedness of others through our own woundedness. Thus, our wounds can be powerful tools allowing us to feel our clients' pain, understand their life struggles, and speak to their will to change. In order to be able to intentionally use our brokenness to connect with our clients, we must be able to consciously reach into our own wounded places and use what we find to understand and intuit where our clients may be.

POTT pivots on the concept of clinicians' *signature themes*—the lifelong, ongoing issues that run through the struggles of their personal journeys. Increased awareness and acceptance of the signature themes and continuous reflection on how they manifest themselves in therapeutic encounters translate into a clinician being able to take conscious responsibility for what he or she brings to the therapeutic engagement with a client, and result in an enhanced ability to connect purposefully and effectively with clients around therapeutic tasks.

# Activity Instructions

The exercise described as follows is intended to be the starting point of a journey of self-discovery and learning. It can be used in the context of a clinician's supervision or training, or as part of an informal mentoring/supervision group. The POTT initial exercise has three steps:

1.  Writing a reflection paper addressing the topics described in the guide (see below)
2.  Meeting with a mentor for personal support and to discuss the topics addressed in the reflection paper
3.  Rewriting of the reflection paper, incorporating the insights gained during the discussion with the mentor

Unlike the more reflective activities in this book, it would be difficult to conduct this activity on a self-assigned basis; this journey requires the support and guidance of a seasoned clinician who serves as a mentor for the new clinician, as well as a safe and caring environment where the clinician can openly talk about his or her own family history, experiences of hurt, shortcomings, and struggles. Therefore, the instructions are written specifically for the mentors or supervisors conducting the activity.

It is important for mentors to note that the essential element in any context for this POTT exercise is that they provide the safety and support of a relationship with the student or supervisee that allows for follow-up with personal issues of the clinician that require special attention. Attending to personal issues usually brings to the surface painful memories and uncomfortable thoughts and feelings for the clinician. Thus, the environment in which the exercises are done has to be continuously supportive and stable, where the clinician knows that he or she will not be left alone to deal with the emotional aftermath of the POTT experience.

Consistent with the POTT approach, the initial reflection paper should deal with several key points. Detailed instructions for writing each part are included here:

- **Your Signature Theme.** Describe what you believe to be the personal issue that has been most dominant in your life. This is the hang-up of yours that has vexed and continues to vex you, affecting many or all areas of your life.

- **Your Genogram.** Attach a three-generational genogram of your family, with comments that may help your mentor understand who the characters are and their relationships to one another.

- **Your Family History.** Provide a history of your family as you believe it relates to your signature theme. This is your hypothesis about the contributions your family members and their relationships may have made to the origin and perpetuation of your signature theme.

- **Your Struggle With Your Signature Theme.** Speak to how you deal with your signature theme. Describe where you handle it poorly and where you deal with it most effectively. Identify who in your life is most helpful in wrestling with it and how you make good use of this person's help.

- **Your Clinical Work.** Add your thoughts regarding how you believe your signature theme has affected or may affect your relationship with clients and your work with their issues—negatively and positively.

The clinician's openness and willingness to be vulnerable are necessary when writing the reflection paper. Once the paper is finished, it is shared with the mentor prior to and in preparation for the face-to-face discussion. The meeting with the mentor serves as an opportunity to explore the thoughts addressed in the written exercise, illuminate blind spots, and carry the introspection to a deeper level. Also, the mentor is expected to assist the clinician in connecting

Example 5

the personal and professional realms by helping the clinician see how the signature theme might manifest itself in the clinician's work. Because the discussion of the reflection paper with the mentor can be an emotionally charged experience where the clinician might feel overwhelmed, it is important for the mentor to maintain a supportive relationship with the clinician throughout this process.

After the discussion, the clinician-in-training should write a new and updated version of the reflection paper. This updated reflection should distill the insights derived from the discussion with the mentor into a coherent narrative, allowing the clinician to give closure to this stage in the POTT journey and return to it as a point of reference as needed. It is highly recommended that the discussion with the mentor be recorded either in audio or video format, as many important issues can be discussed in a short and emotionally charged period of time, and the student may not be able to remember them completely or accurately. Students who have viewed the video-tapes of this experience have frequently reported that they either missed or forgot parts of the discussion with the mentor. Students also found it very helpful when the trainer provided them with specific written feedback on their initial papers that they could refer to in the writing of the second version.

# Example

A. K. was a first-year master's-level student who attended a POTT class as part of her training as a marriage and family therapist. Each student was required to complete the initial reflection paper, e-mail it to the POTT trainers and classmates before class, and then discuss it in class with the trainers while the other students observed and provided feedback at the end. In her paper, A. K. wrote about the process of defining her signature theme:

*I didn't think it would be possible for me to group all the painful events in my life into just one category and call it my signature theme. However, as I began the reflection process, I started dissecting each experience one by one, and amazingly I began to see how it was all connected. I came to the realization that the experiences may have been different, but the underlying theme was always the same: the need to meet others' expectations.*

A. K. then went on to tie her signature theme to significant events in her history, such as needing to protect her mother from her father's abusiveness, getting frequent messages that she was the only source of pride and joy for her mother and grandmother, and feeling intense pressure to meet the resultant expectations. She also connected her theme to current difficulties in her relationships, stating:

*This need to meet others' expectations has led to a number of personal challenges that I have been on a journey to overcome, including insecurity, passivity, and uncertainty. I've been so consumed with meeting others' expectations that it has been very difficult for me to live life on my own terms.*

Regarding the way her signature theme might manifest in her therapeutic work, A. K. wrote:

*I know that there will be some clients who have expectations beyond my capabilities, and no matter how hard I try, I will not be able to meet their expectations. This will be a struggle for me because I will feel like I failed them.*

In the discussion, the trainers helped A. K. understand that her signature theme made sense considering the circumstances of her upbringing. She was also able to see the huge emotional price she was paying for working so hard to conform to others' expectations and hiding her true self (which she perceived as defective). She described feeling exhausted and drained. When discussing the way her signature theme could play out in her work with clients, A. K. was able to expand her thinking and see how her need to conform could interfere with her ability to challenge clients, but it could also be an asset by allowing her to better empathize with and understand clients with similar struggles. At the end of the exercise, A. K. had a clear idea of how she could use this particular issue—one that she has struggled with her entire life—to help her be a more effective clinician.

# Measuring Progress

To measure progress in self-awareness, it is necessary to remember that the primary purpose of this exercise in the POTT model is greater effectiveness in performance as a clinician. The proving ground to measure the effects of self-awareness in the POTT model is the actual therapeutic process, because the goal of this self-awareness is to be able to become more empathic in relating, more intuitive in assessing, and more efficacious in intervening with the client. In practical terms, this means using a variety of supervision modalities, such as live supervision and videotapes of sessions, along with the POTT's "supervision instrument" (Aponte & Carlsen, 2009), for two purposes: (1) observing the clinician's performance in clinical sessions, and (2) assessing his or her ability to articulate the conscious and purposeful use of self in working with clients.

Also, because this type of work is emotionally demanding, it is not recommended for clinicians who are in the midst of life crises or seriously unsettling life transitions. A clinician in a turbulent process of separating from home may need to seek personal therapy before he or she is expected to be reflective about internal emotional processes when working with a conflicted parent–child relationship. A clinician who is tenuously managing his or her emotions about the sexual abuse he or she suffered at home may need to do some personal work before addressing issues of intimacy with a married couple. There needs to be recognition of when the clinician's needs exceed the limits of the support a trainer, supervisor, or group can offer. In such cases, supervisors may need to refer clinicians for focused counseling to help them deal with these issues.

# Conclusion

It is integral to the concept of the POTT model to continue to work on the person-of-the-therapist by linking the conclusions of this exercise with the clinician's clinical work. In our case, we have used this instrument at the beginning of a POTT class in a couple and family therapy program with first-year master's-level students. After following the three steps of the activity described in this chapter, students have participated in mock therapy sessions where they could receive direct clinical feedback through live supervision while focusing on their signature themes. Other options for continuity of this work are to have it as a point of reference for supervisory work, by exploring how the signature theme is triggered by a client or how the theme can be used actively and purposefully to advance a therapeutic goal. Depending on the work context and supervisory relationship, supervisees may or may not choose to share with their supervisors their reflection papers with all of their family history. However, they should be prepared to speak about their signature themes, as these relate to the cases being supervised. It would be helpful for any trainer or supervisor mentoring within the POTT model to undergo training in working with supervisees' signature themes, which begins with learning to utilize their own signature themes in their own therapy practice.

The person-of-the-therapist reflection paper exercise attempts to bring our humanity back to the profession and to promote a way of thinking in which clinicians are not expected to be perfect and free of struggles in order to be considered effective. Rather, this exercise reminds us that this human vulnerability allows us to see more deeply into our clients and relate to them more sensitively.

# Additional Resources

Aponte, H. J. (1992). Training the person of the therapist in structural family therapy. *Journal of Marital and Family Therapy, 18*(3), 269–281.

Aponte, H. J. (1994). How personal can training get? *Journal of Marital and Family Therapy, 20*(1), 3–15.

Aponte, H. J. (1996). Political bias, moral values, and spirituality in the training of psychotherapists. *Bulletin of the Menninger Clinic, 60*(4), 488–502.

Aponte, H. J., & Kissil, K. (2012). "If I can grapple with this I can truly be of use in the therapy room": Using the therapist's own emotional struggles to facilitate effective therapy. *Journal of Marital and Family Therapy*. Published online December 17, 2012. doi: 10.1111/jmft .12011.

Bowen, M. (1972). Toward a differentiation of a self in one's family. In James L. Framo (Ed.), *Family interaction* (pp. 111–173). New York, NY: Springer.

Simon, G. M. (2006). The heart of the matter: A proposal for placing the self of the therapist at the center of family therapy research and training. *Family Process*, *45*, 331–344.

Watson, M. (1993). Supervising the person of the therapist: Issues, challenges, and dilemmas. *Contemporary Family Therapy*, *15*, 21–31.

# References

Aponte, H. J., & Carlsen, C. J. (2009). An instrument for person-of-the-therapist supervision. *Journal of Marital and Family Therapy*, *35*, 395–405.

Aponte, H. J., & Winter, J. E. (2000). The person and practice of the therapist: Treatment and training. In M. Baldwin (Ed.), *The use of self in therapy* (2nd ed., pp. 127–165). New York, NY: Routledge.

Bowen, M. (1972). Toward a differentiation of a self in one's family. In James L. Framo (Ed.), *Family interaction* (pp. 111–173). New York, NY: Springer.

Grencavage, L. M., & Norcross, J. C. (1990). Where are the commonalities among the therapeutic common factors? *Professional Psychology: Research and Practice*, *32*, 372–378.

Kerr, M. E. (1981). Family systems theory and therapy. In A. S. Gurman & D. P. Kniskern (Eds.), *Handbook of family therapy* (pp. 226–264). New York, NY: Brunner/Mazel.

Nouwen, H. J. M. (1972). *The wounded healer*. New York, NY: Doubleday.

Satir, V. (2000). The therapist story. In M. Baldwin (Ed.), *The use of self in therapy* (2nd ed., pp. 17–28). New York, NY: Haworth.

Sprenkle, D. H., Davis, S. D., & Lebow, J. L. (2009). *Common factors in couple and family therapy: The overlooked foundation for effective practice*. New York, NY: Guilford Press.

# CHAPTER 2

# Exploring the Person-of-the-Therapist for Better Joining, Assessment, and Intervention

Alba Niño, Karni Kissil, and Harry J. Aponte

## Introduction

The central tenet of the Person-of-the-Therapist Training model (POTT; Aponte & Winter, 2000) is to help clinicians to *intentionally* use the depth of their human experience to promote deeper and more genuine connections with their clients—helping them to maximize their effectiveness in all aspects of their clinical work, including the assessment and intervention processes. In Chapter 1, we presented the first step in the POTT training: an instrument to help clinicians increase their awareness and acceptance of their personal issues and struggles (known in this model as *signature themes*). In this chapter, we present the next step in this journey: the *clinical case instrument*. This tool helps clinicians focus their attention on how signature themes and other personal factors manifest themselves in their clinical work in three areas: connection with clients, assessment, and intervention.

## Rationale

The clinical case instrument is part of the POTT model (Aponte & Winter, 2000) and is a modified version of the supervisory instrument described in Aponte and Carlsen (2009). For a brief description of the rationale of the POTT model, we direct the reader to the chapter in this volume titled "Facilitating Clinician Development Using Themes of Personal Issues."

Through the use of the POTT clinical case instrument, clinicians can increase their awareness of how personal factors play out in their relationships with specific clients and around specific issues. From the POTT model perspective, all clinicians have to accomplish three main technical tasks in their therapeutic work: (1) Establish a therapeutic relationship with the clients; (2) assess the clients' current states (e.g., what the presenting problem is, what resources clients have, clients' readiness for change); and (3) make the necessary interventions to promote therapeutic change. Clinicians are the main instruments of therapeutic work, and all of these professional tasks are carried out through the person that the clinicians are at the moment they engage with their clients in the therapeutic process.

For this reason, it is essential for clinicians to understand how personal factors, including signature themes (personal core issues), play a role in their work. Reaching this level of understanding helps clinicians take responsibility for what they bring to the therapeutic process. More importantly, this heightened level of self-knowledge and self-awareness allows clinicians to more consciously and purposefully use themselves to potentiate therapeutic outcomes. The type of information that the clinical case instrument asks for and the type of reflection that these questions generate allow clinicians to better understand the characteristics of the case, the quality of the therapeutic process, and the personal and technical challenges that clinicians face with specific clients around specific issues.

# Activity Instructions

The POTT clinical case instrument is best suited for training and supervisory contexts. While individuals can benefit from addressing the prompts included in the activities related to the implementation of the instrument, much of the clinician's growth in these activities comes through discussion with a trusted mentor or supervisor. The activity instructions are therefore directed primarily to clinicians who have a mentor or supervisor. Clinicians who take part in case consultations, peer supervision, or other types of clinical groups can also use this instrument to organize their ideas for formal or informal case discussions. This way, discussions can be more targeted, and clinicians' challenges can be better identified and more directly addressed. Before using the clinical case instrument, clinicians should reach some level of awareness of their signature themes and the way these themes might affect their therapeutic work. The instrument presented in Chapter 1 will assist clinicians in the beginning stage of this process. Once this groundwork is established, clinicians can move to examine specific cases, clients, and presenting problems.

The application of the clinical case instrument follows three steps:

1. Answering each of the prompts listed in the POTT Clinical Case Instrument Outline (see Table 2.1)

2. Meeting with a mentor, supervisor, or fellow clinician to discuss the topics addressed in the document

3. Rewriting the POTT Clinical Case Instrument Outline to incorporate the insights gained during the discussion

It is important for the mentor, supervisor, or peer to have a copy of the clinician's completed outline in advance in order to have a preliminary understanding of the case and the challenges the clinician is facing. Receiving an advance copy also helps mentors and supervisors to better prepare to guide the session, allowing them to tailor it to the clinician's needs. As stated in Chapter 1, we strongly recommend for this meeting or discussion to be recorded, preferably on video. This recording can be reviewed by the clinician in preparation for future sessions with the client.

**Table 2.1  POTT Clinical Case Instrument Outline**

1. State your current understanding of your signature theme.

2. Provide general information about the client(s), including pseudonym(s), age(s), gender(s), occupation(s), etc.

3. Attach the client(s)' genogram.

4. State the agreed-upon issue that brought the client(s) to therapy and note anything in it that carries personal meaning for you, especially in relation to your signature theme.

5. Identify other agencies and professionals involved with the client(s). Describe their relationship to the case and to your clinical work.

6. Describe your personal reactions to your client(s) and the client(s)' reactions to you, attending in particular to how your signature theme may be triggered by the relationship or clinical material.

7. Address your cultural or spiritual values that may be causing you to view the issues the client(s) are presenting differently from the client(s)' perspectives.

8. Identify how the differences and similarities in social locations between you and your client(s) may be affecting your relationship with your client(s) and your understanding of the case.

9. Explicate your hypotheses about the roots and dynamics of the client(s)' issue.

10. Explain your therapeutic strategy with the case and how you would use yourself to carry out your therapeutic tasks (connecting, assessing, and intervening).

11. Identify your personal challenges working with the client(s) around the focal issue, noting especially if and how your signature theme plays a part in the nature of the challenge.

12. Identify what technical and personal issues you wish to discuss in today's session.

Example

11

Finally, because this type of work demands that clinicians open themselves to their own experiences and vulnerabilities, it is important for clinicians to embark on this journey in a context where they feel safe and supported. The support and guidance of a mentor, supervisor, or experienced peer is highly recommended to establish a safe emotional environment in which the clinical case instrument can be utilized to its full potential.

# Example

J. L., a student in a marriage and family therapy master's program, looked for assistance using the clinical case instrument in relation to a client. J. L.'s client was a woman who had recently been diagnosed with a severe illness. This client was undergoing an invasive treatment while also facing multiple stressors, including lack of support from friends and family, financial instability, and depressive symptoms. The client reported that the illness had been very difficult for her, not only because of the severity of her diagnosis, but also because she felt compelled to make the painful decision of interrupting her pregnancy. J. L.'s client, who had been very proud of herself and her accomplishments, was now feeling sad and lonely. At the beginning of the therapeutic process, J. L. was deeply saddened by her client's story and her daily suffering. J. L. was therefore actively working on finding sources of social support and additional financial assistance for her client.

It then happened that through conversations with other professionals involved in her client's treatment, J. L. learned that her client had lied to her. As J. L. looked deeper into the matter, she learned that the client's story about how she had received her diagnosis was not true. In addition, she learned that her client did, in fact, have family members and friends who were willing to support her. For J. L., realizing that her client had been lying made her feel betrayed and confused as to how to proceed therapeutically. She felt emotionally disconnected from her client and was unable to move beyond the fact that the client had deceived her.

To better understand and cope with her feelings of distrust and betrayal, J. L. used the clinical case instrument. The prompts helped J. L. connect her visceral emotional reaction with one of her signature themes. J. L. had been emotionally neglected by her caregivers. The longing for love and acceptance made her vulnerable to relationships characterized by lies, abuse, and betrayal. J. L.'s constant battle was to not allow herself to be deceived and abused in relationships for the sake of a little love and attention. She realized that being lied to by her client made her relive the pain of feeling disrespected and taken advantage of in the past and made her question her capacity to read people and protect herself. Overwhelmed by her own pain, J. L. became angry and distrustful toward the client.

Where writing the clinical case instrument helped J. L. identify the roots of her struggle with her client, the discussion of the instrument with her mentor helped J. L. use her own struggles to better understand her client's situation and to change her approach to the case. In discussing the answers in her initial write-up with her mentor, J. L. was able to more clearly see her own contribution to the impasse and to take responsibility for her part. Thus, in the second writing of the clinical case instrument, J. L. expressed, "I realize I was seeing the worst in [my client], having felt wronged and betrayed. I now know that her lying to me was not an effort to deceive me, but more so a combination of me not asking the right questions and an effort on her part to save face." Before, J. L. had taken her client's actions personally. After the exercise, she was better equipped to adopt a professional perspective.

With the mentor's guidance and support, J. L. was able to generate new hypotheses about the case that were more centered on the client's struggles and less focused on J. L.'s need to protect herself. J. L. knew from her personal experience that wanting love and craving human connection can lead a person to use unhealthy strategies to satisfy such a personal need, including taking part in destructive relationships. This knowledge helped J. L. generate new hypotheses about her client. Thus, in her rewriting of the clinical case instrument, J. L. wondered if maybe her client was "so scared of not being loved that she creates situations to evoke sympathy [and] to create compassion." Being able to generate new ways of understanding, J. L. was able to take a less self-protective and more empathic stance, which in turn opened the door for her to consider new possible goals in treating her client. As stated by J. L. in the rewriting of the clinical case instrument, "I want to help [the client] realize she is worthy of love."

# Measuring Progress

The POTT clinical case instrument is meant to further the clinician's use of self in the therapeutic process. While the focus is on the work in a specific case, the instrument is constructed to heighten the clinician's mastery of self in therapy—from management of self in the relationship to the process of assessment and the implementation of strategies and interventions. The following is a brief summation of a clinician's growth that should ideally happen if the instrument were used as prescribed. Clinicians who consistently use this instrument should:

- Feel more personally grounded in their work with clients as a result of increased awareness of themselves throughout the therapeutic process (including emotional reactions, personal biases, and personal vulnerabilities).

- Feel more personally in command of themselves in the therapeutic process, because the clinicians are better connected to themselves (what they are experiencing and what they are projecting within the relationship with clients).

- Feel more in touch with what is happening between them and their clients by instinctively being able to perceive and interpret what is taking place overtly and subliminally in the therapeutic relationship.

- Be better able to distinguish between what they and the clients are contributing to the therapeutic process. In so doing, clinicians can self-monitor and take responsibility for how they are using themselves to carry out the therapeutic tasks, while simultaneously being able to track the client within the framework of that therapeutic process.

- Be better able to identify how they relate to their clients, enabling them to be more responsive to the clinicians' inquiries and interventions. This way, clinicians can better determine what to draw from themselves and their history to potentiate personal instrumentality in carrying out their therapeutic efforts.

- Be better able to self-correct in the therapeutic process.

- Be better able to ask for what they need from their supervisors/mentors.

# Conclusion

The POTT clinical case instrument naturally follows the initial work of identifying the clinician's signature themes. This follow-up tool teaches clinicians how to apply their new self-knowledge and awareness in a clinical setting. It enables clinicians to become more aware of how their personal struggles and life experiences play out in their clinical work. Clinicians can use this awareness to foster a deeper and more genuine connection to their clients, to feel where their clients are in the therapeutic process, and to intuit how to intervene more effectively.

# Additional Resources

Aponte, H. J. (1992). Training the person of the therapist in structural family therapy. *Journal of Marital and Family Therapy, 18*, 269–281.

Aponte, H. J. (1994). How personal can training get? *Journal of Marital and Family Therapy, 20*, 3–15.

Aponte, H. J. (1996). Political bias, moral values, and spirituality in the training of psychotherapists. *Bulletin of the Menninger Clinic, 60*(4), 488–502.

Bowen, M. (1972). Toward a differentiation of a self in one's family. In James L. Framo (Ed.), *Family Interaction* (pp. 111–173). New York, NY: Springer.

Simon, G. M. (2006). The heart of the matter: A proposal for placing the self of the therapist at the center of family therapy research and training. *Family Process, 45*, 331–344.

Watson, M. (1993). Supervising the person of the therapist: Issues, challenges, and dilemmas. *Contemporary Family Therapy, 15*, 21–31.

# References

Aponte, H. J. & Carlsen, C. J. (2009). An instrument for person-of-the-therapist supervision. *Journal of Marital and Family Therapy, 35*, 395–405.

Aponte, H. J., & Winter, J. E. (2000). The person and practice of the therapist: Treatment and training. In M. Baldwin (Ed.), *The use of self in therapy* (2nd ed., pp. 127–165). New York, NY: Routledge.

# CHAPTER 3

# THE EMPATHY GAME

## Trent S. Parker and Kristyn M. Blackburn

# Introduction

Empathy is not only an important skill for clinicians, but it is also one of the common factors of major models of therapy (Blow & Sprenkle, 2001). Ways in which clinicians develop empathic responses are therefore important to consider. The purpose of this activity is to help clinicians develop the ability to put themselves in another's position and respond from this new perspective. Although this activity works best in a group setting, it can also be used on an individual basis or with dyads.

# Rationale

Since Rogers (1957) suggested that empathy is one of six conditions necessary for therapeutic change to occur, empathy has been demonstrated to be an essential component for therapy, regardless of the model used (Feller & Cottone, 2003). In fact, in a recent meta-analysis, Elliott, Bohart, Watson, and Greenberg (2011) found that empathy is a moderately strong predictor of therapy outcome. The challenge in researching and teaching empathy is creating a definition that encompasses what everyone "knows" empathy means. Batson (2009) identified eight distinct concepts of empathy: (1) knowing another person's internal state, including his or her thoughts and feelings; (2) adopting the posture or matching the neural responses of an observed other; (3) coming to feel as another person feels; (4) intuiting or studying oneself into another's situation; (5) imagining how another is thinking and feeling; (6) imagining how one would think and feel in the other's place; (7) feeling distress at witnessing another person's suffering; and (8) feeling sorry for another person who is suffering.

These eight concepts can be grouped into two general empathic processes: *cognitive empathy* and *affective empathy* (Reniers, Corcoran, Drake, Shryane, & Völlm, 2011). Cognitive empathy is the ability to understand what another person is experiencing. It has been suggested that it is rare for empathy to exist without a cognitive component (Kerem, Fishman, & Josselson, 2001). Generally, the cognitive component includes the understanding of why other people may be feeling the way they do and involves an intellectual or imaginative process to arrive at another's emotional state. Affective empathy involves being able to vicariously experience the emotional experience of others (Reniers et al., 2011). In the literature, this is also referred to as *emotional contagion*, or the ability to automatically mimic the emotional expression of another person and to converge emotionally (Hatfield, Cacioppo, & Rapson, 1994).

Cognitive and affective empathy have been widely researched, though more in the area of interpersonal relationships than in therapeutic relationships. Within the area of therapy, both processes of empathy have been shown to be related to session depth (Duan & Kivlighan, 2002). In their meta-analysis of empathy's role in therapy, Elliott et al. (2011) recommend that the clinician demonstrate empathy regardless of theoretical orientation, treatment format, or the severity of clients' presenting problems. They further conclude that it is important to make efforts to understand and empathize with clients and to demonstrate this understanding. Interestingly, the clinician does not need to have a similar experience as the client in order to demonstrate empathy or understanding (DeGeorge & Constantino, 2012).

This activity is designed to develop both processes of empathy in order to increase clinicians' ability to not only empathize with their clients but to demonstrate this empathy as well. Being able to see things from everyone's perspective can be challenging, especially when each family member has his or her own way of perceiving the situation. The overall goal is to encourage the clinician to empathize with all clients in the room.

# Activity Instructions

This activity focuses on developing the empathic responses that clinicians provide to clients. Although clinicians at any level can participate in and benefit from the activity, it is particularly helpful for clinicians who have been working with clients for less than four years and are receiving supervision. This activity is best completed in supervision, either in individual or in groups less than 10.

To conduct this activity, it is helpful to have some form of recorded client–therapist interactions from a therapy session. Although it would be possible to use the empathy game without video or audio, it may present challenges for everyone to get a sense of the context. If this type of in-session recording is not available, it is important for the presenting clinician to provide additional details about the case. The following list is a step-by-step set of instructions for conducting the activity:

1. **The presenting clinician provides basic information about the case.** Client demographics, including ages, occupations (if any), and who lives in the household, are often helpful. The presenting problem should also be provided, as well as any other problems that have emerged through the process of therapy up to that point.

2. **If available, a clip of a therapy session, either audio or video, can be presented.** At the beginning, particularly when focusing more on cognitive empathy, a longer video clip may be helpful (e.g., 3 to 5 minutes) in order to allow clinicians to consider the situation and think about how they would feel. This time frame is particularly helpful when working on affective empathy.

3. **After the video clip has been shown, clinicians take turns talking about the empathy they have gathered from the clip.** If a couple or family has been presented, it is helpful to talk about each member separately (e.g., having everyone talk about the father before moving on to the mother or child). As it becomes easier for clinicians to identify the feelings clients are experiencing, it is helpful to have them think of a time when they experienced something similar. This begins the transition to affective empathy. It is not necessary to talk about details, but it is important for the clinicians to eventually start to feel similar to the clients, rather than just thinking about the emotion.

4. **When moving into affective empathy, it is helpful to use shorter video clips.** This facilitates the clinicians' ability to rely less on cognitive empathy and more on the emotional reaction they have as they listen to and experience with the clients. The chief difference when working on affective empathy is that the clinicians should talk about the experience of the emotion while experiencing the emotion themselves. Clinicians can and should talk about it as though they were talking with the client. This facilitates their ability to use affective empathy with their own clients and provides several examples for the presenting clinicians to use with the case they are presenting.

The personal nature of this activity creates two important points. First, supervisors must remain clear about the boundary between supervision and therapy, because it is possible that a clinician may experience traumatic emotions or begin to talk about unresolved issues during this activity. Should this happen, appropriate referrals should be made. Second, although a solid supervisor–clinician relationship is essential, it is also important for the relationships among clinicians (in group settings) to be strong and built on trust. This type of relationship is often easier to build in groups less than 10. However, the activity can be conducted with a larger group depending on the relationships among its members.

It is also possible for supervisors to follow up with clinicians either through discussions or written assignments in the form of reflective statements. Questions that can spur reflection include: "What challenges did you have when empathizing with this client?" or "What was it like for you when you were able to emotionally connect with the client?" or "How does your

Example 17

relationship with the client change when you empathize with him or her? How does it remain the same?" Group discussions can follow similar questions as the group processes the experience.

# Example

The following is an example of the activity occurring in a group supervision setting. For the purpose of this example, the participating clinicians can be assumed to be at a level in which they are capable of experiencing both cognitive and affective empathy. This example demonstrates how the activity works with clinicians focusing on one family member at a time.

**Presenting clinician (PC):** "I have been working with this family for six weeks. Michael and Sarah brought their 15-year-old son, Ben, to therapy because of disobedience at home. Michael and Sarah have both expressed frustration, but it seems like Sarah is the parent who has the most difficulty with Ben. Over the past few weeks, I have observed that Michael is often dismissive of Sarah in session in front of Ben. I am unsure of what direction I should be going with the family."

The presenting clinician then shows a clip where Sarah is discussing her most recent argument with Ben. She states that Ben broke curfew while Michael was out of town last week. Sarah explains that Ben did not provide her with an explanation and told her that she had no power over him and stormed off. Sarah is visibly upset while retelling this story, sitting with her head downcast and her hands clasped in her lap. Michael abruptly ends the story and states that he is angry with Sarah for not telling him about this incident earlier.

**Supervisor (S) (speaking to the supervisees):** "I would like for each of you to tell me what you think Sarah is thinking and feeling while she was telling her story."

**Clinician 1 (C1):** "I think that Sarah was embarrassed. She is obviously disrespected by her son at home, and she is also disrespected in public, in the therapy room. She was unable to look anyone in the eye when she was talking. She looked down at her lap and cried the entire time."

**S:** "Are you able to think of a time in your life when you experienced that level, or depth, of embarrassment?"

**C1:** "I wanted to curl up and hide myself from the world. I walked around with this feeling of helplessness and humiliation. I thought that I was going to get sick at any moment because my stomach was so nervous and upset. It was hard for me, like it is for Sarah, I think, because the embarrassment happened at the hands of someone who was supposed to be supportive of me."

**S:** "I also want to know some other thoughts about what may be going on for Sarah."

**Clinician 2 (C2):** "What came across to me while I was listening to and watching Sarah was a sense of defeat, of absolute helplessness. It seems like she is unsure of where to start to improve the situation."

**S:** "Have you ever felt defeated?"

**C2:** "Maybe not at the level that Sarah is experiencing with her family, but I have."

**S:** "How did you experience that feeling of defeat?"

**C2:** "I went into a self-protective mode. I felt like the only person I could trust or rely upon was myself, so I turned away from a lot of other relationships that were important to me. In the end, I felt isolated. I felt like, even if I wanted to, I could not reach out to anyone for support. It was a hard period of time for me."

| | |
|---|---|
| **S (directed to the presenting clinician):** | "What are your thoughts listening to these perspectives?" |
| **PC:** | "I think that I have been caught up in the urgency of the situation, which made me unable to see just how much Sarah is hurting right now. It is hard to imagine feeling that unsupported and disrespected by your own family. I'm not even sure if Michael and Ben see Sarah's hurt. It is something that I want to bring to their attention." |
| **S:** | "Let's turn the tables for a moment and focus on Michael. What do you think he is thinking and feeling in this clip?" |
| **C2:** | "He seems to be at the end of his rope. I think that he was so abrupt with Sarah because he feels so out of control. I am sure that it is hard for him to feel that as a man." |
| **S:** | "What do you mean by that?" |
| **C2:** | "Men are supposed to be in control. They are supposed to be able to feel like they are protecting their families. As a man, I understand the pressure associated with that responsibility." |
| **S:** | "So what does it feel like to be a man and be out of control?" |
| **C2:** | "I know that it is humiliating when I feel out of control. I have moments where I question my worthiness, especially when I see my wife hurting." |
| **S (directed to presenting clinician):** | "What are your thoughts about Michael after hearing these comments?" |
| **PC:** | "I always assumed that Michael was just an angry man and that he put all of the blame on Sarah. After listening to our discussion, I understand that it may be more about humiliation and a feeling of failure than anger. I think that Michael and Sarah are experiencing a lot of the same feelings and don't even realize it." |

Most clinicians who have participated in the empathy game report it to be an important part of their clinical training. One supervisee commented, "I think that the empathy game was the most influential aspect of my training. I view empathy and connecting with people as the most critical part of the therapy process, and the empathy game helped to teach me about human connection." In general, the process is intended to help supervisees connect to similar emotions within themselves in order to better understand their clients. This understanding often helps supervisees to connect to clients they once thought of as difficult to connect to. Another supervisee commented, "The empathy game helped me to relate to clients that I would not normally be able to understand." In general, this is possible, as one supervisee put it, because "it helps to see how others empathize, and I learned a lot from witnessing the other [supervisees] empathize with a certain emotion."

It should be noted that supervisees also comment that the empathy game challenges them emotionally. One supervisee commented, "[The empathy game] was a catalyst for self-reflection and, therefore, a tool for simultaneous personal and professional growth, which is an integral part of a therapist's training." During the course of the game, supervisees are often able to become aware that their personal feelings can get in the way of how they view and interact with their clients. They also learn how, as one supervisee said, "to better use my own experience to fully relate to another person and understand what it is like to be in their shoes."

# Measuring Progress

The ability to cognitively and affectively empathize with another individual is a process that requires time and refinement. The clinicians participating in this activity must be willing to experience the thoughts and feelings that the clients are experiencing in the discussed sessions, which is often unpleasant and sometimes painful. Clinicians must be patient with themselves while developing their ability to empathize, just as they must be patient with their clients as they experience these thoughts and feelings.

Progress is typically indicated first by clinicians being able to empathize with all clients in the room and to resist the temptation to side with one over the others. The clinician's ability to pay attention to personal reactions and biases allows for the recognition and acceptance of every client's experience. The principle of multipartiality will also become evident as the clinician will be able to take the perspective of every client in the room. Second, progress is also indicated by an ability to identify emotions, even those that are not expressed verbally. This means that the clinician is aware of the emotional climate of the therapy room, as well as the emotions, body language, and microexpressions of each client. A third indication of progress is being able to express affective empathy with clients. In other words, the clinician is able to explore clients' emotions and reflect those emotions while vicariously experiencing the emotions.

Supervisors can facilitate a clinician's growth by attending to patterns of clients, situations, or emotions with which the clinician tends to struggle. Talking about these patterns and even empathizing with the clinician can increase the clinician's comfort level in working with clients. Additionally, talking about these patterns can help the clinician to move away from wanting to prevent others from feeling uncomfortable emotions to seeing them in the bigger picture: that they are only a part of the human experience and can add just as much meaning as the more comfortable emotions.

# Conclusion

We have found that some beginning clinicians have a difficult time seeing the situation from the perspective of all clients in the system. One of the advantages of the empathy game is the practice of doing so from both a cognitive and affective empathic stance. In addition, when the empathy game is used with another clinician or in a group, it has the additional advantage of offering multiple ways of viewing clients' situations and emotions. It is likely that each clinician in the activity will have a different way of perceiving and connecting to the situation. This offers several choices for the clinician to proceed when working with the presented client.

We often talk about empathy in the supervisory context and sometimes assume that clinicians know how to empathize. This exercise allows them to develop empathic skills. Additionally, the empathy game allows clinicians the opportunity to actually experience empathy within the safety of the supervisory relationship and prepares them to empathize with clients in session.

# Additional Resources

Block-Lerner, J., Adair, C., Plumb, J. C., Rhatigan, D. L., & Orsillo, S. M. (2007). The case for mindfulness-based approaches in the cultivation of empathy: Does nonjudgmental, present-moment awareness increase capacity for perspective-taking and empathic concern? *Journal of Marital and Family Therapy, 33*, 501–516.

Bohart, A. C. (2004). How do clients make empathy work? *Person-Centered and Experiential Psychotherapies, 3*, 102–116.

Giblin, P. (1996). Empathy: The essence of marriage and family therapy? *The Family Journal: Counseling and Therapy for Couples and Families, 4*, 229–235.

# References

Batson, C. D. (2009). These things called empathy: Eight related but distinct phenomena. In J. Decety & W. Ickes (Eds.), *The social neuroscience of empathy* (pp. 3–17). Boston, MA: MIT Press.

Blow, A. J., & Sprenkle, D. H. (2001). Common factors across theories of marriage and family therapy: A modified Delphi study. *Journal of Marital and Family Therapy, 27,* 385–401.

DeGeorge, J., & Constantino, M. J. (2012). Perceptions of analogue therapist empathy as a function of salient experience similarity. *Journal of Psychotherapy Integration, 22,* 52–59.

Duan, C., & Kivlighan, D. R. (2002). Relationships among therapist presession mood, therapist empathy, and session evaluation. *Psychotherapy Research, 12,* 23–37.

Elliott, R., Bohart, A. C., Watson, J. C., & Greenberg, L. S. (2011). Empathy. *Psychotherapy: Theory, Research, and Practice, 48,* 43–49.

Feller, C. P., & Cottone, R. R. (2003). The importance of empathy in the therapeutic alliance. *Journal of Humanistic Counseling, Education, and Development, 42,* 53–61.

Hatfield, E., Cacioppo, J., & Rapson, R. (1994). *Emotional contagion.* New York, NY: Cambridge University Press.

Kerem, E., Fishman, N., & Josselson, R. (2001). The experience of empathy in everyday relationships: Cognitive and affective elements. *Journal of Social & Personal Relationships, 18,* 709–730.

Reniers, R. L., Corcoran, R., Drake, R., Shryane, N. M., & Völlm, B. A. (2011). The QCAE: A questionnaire of cognitive and affective empathy. *Journal of Personality Assessment, 93,* 84–95.

Rogers, C. R. (1957). The necessary and sufficient conditions of therapeutic personality change. *Journal of Consulting Psychology, 21,* 95–103.

# CHAPTER 4

# SEEING THROUGH THE EYES OF THE OTHER USING PROCESS RECORDINGS

Dana A. Schneider, Elizabeth Rodriguez-Keyes, and Elizabeth King Keenan

## Introduction

This chapter describes a two-step process including videotaping and process-recording activities to facilitate self-awareness and the expression of empathy and acceptance toward other points of view. These activities are designed for beginning student clinicians who are currently completing their coursework and their first clinical internship. The first step of videotaping helps clinicians become more aware of their inner thoughts, feelings, beliefs, and personal values. The intentional focus on their own inner experiences helps clinicians identify and respond appropriately to their intense feelings, thoughts, biases, and other negative perceptions of clients and their problems, which in turn improves their ability to listen to and express acceptance and empathy toward clients. This first step also helps participating clinicians become more aware of their nonverbal communication with clients, helping them assess how their internal experiences of empathy and acceptance match what is being conveyed nonverbally to their clients. The second step of the activity, process recording, helps clinicians reflect on their ability to use self-awareness to analyze their inner experiences and their outer expressions of empathy and acceptance (both verbal and nonverbal) while still being attuned to their clients' communication.

## Rationale

This chapter describes two types of self-awareness: (1) self-awareness of inner thoughts, feelings, beliefs, and personal values regarding clients and the presenting problems, and (2) self-awareness of one's own nonverbal and verbal communication of empathy and acceptance. Lessened clinical awareness of inner thoughts, feelings, beliefs, and personal values can result in a judgmental attitude; an inability to listen to a client; undue persuasion encouraging a client to pursue a particular change; and communication (verbal or nonverbal) that conveys disapproval, disappointment, frustration, or other negative attitudes. Failure to become aware of and attend to these types of negative thoughts, intense affect, or personal biases is referred to as *countertransference*. Prior research suggests it is important to identify and to address clinicians' verbal and nonverbal reactions to clients, because the regulation of countertransference can improve the clinical process (Gelso & Hayes, 2002; Norcross, 2010).

Preoccupation with intense emotions, judgments, and other thoughts can also interfere with clinicians' ability to be more attuned to and responsive to clients, an ability that is associated with more positive clinical outcomes (Norcross, 2010). Furthermore, prior research has suggested that clients have consistently identified listening to clients and avoiding critical or pejorative comments as efficacious factors during clinical encounters (Norcross, 2010).

Additionally, studies have consistently reported that clinicians' engagement (versus detachment), expressive attunement, and affective attitude and self-congruence (genuineness) are all associated with positive therapeutic outcomes (Orlinsky, Ronnestad, & Willutzki, 2004). It is also suggested that therapist qualities such as warmth, empathy, care, and acceptance are associated with positive outcomes, and clients report feeling more connected to clinicians who express these qualities (Sparks & Duncan, 2010). These qualities are also consistently associated with positive clinical outcomes (Elliott, Greenberg & Lietaer, 2004) and are most accurately measured by the client's perceptions of the clinician's expressions of empathy and positive regard (Norcross, 2010).

Activities that promote self-awareness, such as written process recordings, have been criticized because of the possibility of inaccuracies, the amount of time they take, and supervisors' lack of knowledge about using them effectively. In this chapter, we address these criticisms and demonstrate how process recordings, in conjunction with videotaping, can provide a rich source of information regarding clinical exchanges between therapists and clients.

# Activity Instructions

In this activity, clinicians have many opportunities to examine their inner thoughts and reactions to clients and their ability to foster a positive relationship and express empathy to clients during clinical encounters. This activity is designed to be implemented over the course of a two-year training program across the different stages of training. These activities can be easily adapted for ongoing supervision and are also appropriate for licensed clinicians who want to enhance their self-awareness in order to improve their clinical work. To ensure client confidentiality, clinicians should review the policies within their clinical settings regarding videotaping clients and digitally storing videotapes and must always receive written consent from clients prior to videotaping sessions. Although some student clinicians report that this activity and process recordings are time consuming, training programs can reinforce their importance by providing the required time during the internship to complete them.

Formatted into four columns (see Figure 4.1), process recordings typically include a written account of the dialogue between the client and clinician; the clinician's identification of his or her inner thoughts, feelings, and reactions at specific points of the dialogue; and supervisory comments. The dialogue is written from the clinician's recollection of what was said in the session and resembles a script from a play.

Process recordings may also include the clinician's evaluation of his or her clinical skills, more lengthy reflections describing his or her observations, or other key aspects related to that specific clinical encounter. In order to protect the confidentiality of clients, all names and identifying information should be removed from the recordings.

Clinicians begin the activity by analyzing process recordings of more experienced trainees. Next, clinicians learn how to develop their own process recordings by first transcribing portions of videotaped interviews they conducted with people of their choosing.

For their first videotaped interview assignment, clinicians are instructed to interview an acquaintance and ask the following assessment questions: (a) "Who is important in your life?" (b) "What stressors are you currently experiencing?" and (c) "How are you coping with these stressors?" Clinicians then transcribe five pages of the videotaped interview dialogue using a process-recording format (see Figure 4.1). The trainee is instructed to choose and transcribe a segment that seems significant and then describe why that particular segment of the clinical

| Dialogue and Observations of Nonverbal Communication | Internal Feelings/ Reactions | Strategies/Skills Used | Supervisor Comments |
|---|---|---|---|
|  |  |  |  |

**Figure 4.1**/Process Recording Outline

encounter was chosen. The instructor is privy to the entire interaction, as he or she reviews both the actual videotape and process recording.

For the process recording, the dialogue is written out in the first column. In the second column, clinicians will note when they were focused on what the interviewee was saying and when they were distracted. They will also identify skills or strategies that they used during the session. In the third column, clinicians describe their internal reactions, including how genuine they felt while interacting with the interviewee, if they experienced a sense of connection or disconnection with the interviewee, and why they think a disconnection may have occurred (e.g., personal biases, cultural differences, taboo topics, differences in values). Clinicians also describe if they were able to demonstrate acceptance of the interviewee and his or her experience and express empathy for what it must be like to be that person. In the third column, they identify skills or strategies that they used during the session; and the fourth column is reserved for supervisory comments.

During the second semester of the first year of the program, clinicians are matched with other trainees whom they do not know and are instructed to meet with them on two different occasions to conduct videotaped interviews. Following the second interview, clinicians write another process recording, this time breaking the entire dialogue into three different sections—the beginning, middle, and end. During this second process-recording assignment, clinicians write the dialogue in the first column. In the second column, the participants write what they were feeling and thinking during specific parts of the conversation and whether their inner feelings and thoughts affected their ability to listen or to respond at a particular moment. In the third column, clinicians also describe their thinking processes associated with their actions. They describe what they reflected on, how they determined what to do, the clinical strategy they facilitated, and the skills they used. In a separate narrative that is handed in with this assignment, participants reflect on what it was like to hear interviewees talk about their culture, community, and family, as well as overall reflection questions.

Finally, clinicians assess their ability to be accepting, genuine, and empathic during the conversation by reflecting on their own inner experiences, reviewing the videotape again, and listening to feedback from the interviewee. Beginning clinicians initially need encouragement to be more self-reflexive and track all of their responses to an interviewee, especially if they are concerned that their responses are inappropriate or unusual. Validating clinicians' efforts in developing self-awareness and self-reflexivity encourages more ongoing honest appraisal during future clinical encounters.

The use of this training exercise can continue beyond the clinicians' first year in a training program. We require student clinicians to submit process recordings throughout the year. These process recordings are based on clinicians' recall of what was said during conversations with clients (not verbatim dialogue), along with their reflections about their inner thoughts and reactions. To assist with their recall of the clinical encounter, student clinicians are encouraged to take notes after client interactions and to use their own observations of both the content and process of the session. During the final semester of the second year, student clinicians conduct a case presentation during their seminar class that resembles an agency case consultation. During the presentation, student clinicians read their process recordings aloud and use them to guide the seminar discussion.

It is easy for supervision time to be taken up with the discussion of tasks, with little or no reflection on the process of relationship building, engagement, empathy, countertransference, development, and the use of a professional sense of self. We also encourage supervisors to take time to write down their own reflections and questions regarding student clinicians' work to enable them to review and consider their ideas after a supervisory meeting.

# Examples

Student clinicians have shared with us how they have used videotaping and process recordings to evaluate their own progress. A student clinician in her final year noted:

> *I feel like process recordings were very useful to self-evaluation and reflection. They take a long time and are annoying to do but are worth it.*

In the words of another trainee:

*The process recordings are very beneficial to our learning process as clinical trainees. It is extremely important we be able to reflect on what was said between ourselves and a client [whom] we encounter in our placement.*

Although initially self-conscious about videotaping themselves, student clinicians report positive experiences after seeing themselves conduct interviews. One student clinician reported:

*The videotapes were a huge help in assessing my own self-awareness. I was able to watch how I interacted with clients and then process how I was feeling after to see what I did right and what I needed to improve upon.*

Another trainee shared:

*I was able to replay the video and notice areas I could improve in.*

Another trainee remarked:

*At first I found the videotape assignments very challenging, and watching myself speak with others was hard. But in the end, it did help me realize what I do in conversation. Without watching myself, I probably would have never known how my body language affects my communication.*

Another trainee noted:

*It was very weird to see myself on camera talking to a "client," but throughout the semester there was noticeable improvement in dialogue, body language, and other skills when comparing the last videotape process recording to the first. This process was definitely helpful.*

Some student clinicians preferred videotaping to process recordings. One student clinician said:

*The videotapes were more helpful than the process recordings ever could be! It allowed me to really see what was taking place in the room, to truly reflect on the events of the session. The tape also allowed me to become more comfortable in future sessions as I was able to see what worked and didn't work and where improvements were needed.*

When videotapes and process recordings are used together, student clinicians note the importance of being able to review their work. One student clinician remarked:

*The process recordings allow us to not only practice our skills using the facilitation method but also go back and think about what we did correctly and what skills might need improvement.*

Encouraging student clinicians to engage in this level of self-awareness and reflection also guides them in how to begin the important process of monitoring and evaluating their own progress. One student clinician shared:

*While completing process recordings, I find it very helpful to go back and reflect on what I said in a conversation. While in conversation, I do not really think about what is said and do not realize where I could have improved or where I did well until going back and observing what I said. It also greatly helps to have the opinion of someone else, either a professor or MSW supervisor, and be provided with constructive criticism. I learn from what I said in one conversation and proceed to use it in future conversations.*

One student clinician noted the importance of integrating feedback into ongoing work:

*As the year has progressed, I have taken many of the suggestions that my supervisor has provided in my process recordings and used the feedback in the field. While conversing with clients, I am more aware of what I am saying to clients and how even the simplest of comments can be either harmful or helpful. A comment that I may think is unimportant may change the whole direction of a conversation.*

# Measuring Progress

Over time, the use of videotaping and process recordings can enhance student clinicians' self-awareness and ultimately their ability to use this self-awareness to better understand clients and to measure their own progress. The following questions can help supervisors assess and enhance the level and depth of student clinicians' self-awareness:

- Are student clinicians able to identify their internal feelings and thoughts about the content and process of an interview?

- Can student clinicians identify how internal reactions may be unconsciously and non-verbally expressed through their interactions with their clients (through the questions asked, the choice of what client material to respond to, and their ways of responding to this material)?

- Can student clinicians identify where their own internal responses may indicate the emergence of bias, differing value systems, or taboo topics?

- Do student clinicians demonstrate an ability to suspend judgment with regard to their own internal reactions and value their reactions as an important source of information?

- Do student clinicians demonstrate the ability to catch internal reactions and make an informed choice of how to proceed in the moment?

- Are student clinicians receptive to feedback that may expand on their own self-awareness?

# Conclusion

We suggest that process recordings can help both supervisors and student clinicians develop more insight about potential blind spots and enhance their self-awareness and understanding of their clinical work. Moreover, while student clinicians are required to have some degree of self-awareness while writing their process recordings, their awareness can be augmented by the verbal and written reflections of their supervisors.

Based on our experiences with student trainees, videotaped interviews and process recordings support the development of enhanced self-awareness and the ability to critically monitor and examine relationships with clients. By pairing the process recording with videotaping, we believe we have addressed the critique that process recordings may not provide as accurate an account of the client–clinician interaction as an audiotape (Graybeal & Ruff, 1995). With this combination of visual and written reflection at the beginning of their training, student clinicians begin to appreciate some of the limits of process recordings when verbatim transcription is not feasible. At the same time, we have found that student clinicians' reconstruction of a clinical session through a process recording guides their ongoing self-reflexivity as they relate to specific moments of client dialogue and provides insight about their conscious and unconscious experience of the interaction. These skills benefit both student clinicians and more experienced licensed practitioners by fostering lifelong professional development and reinforcing self-awareness of inner experiences and their ability to respond to moments of challenge during clinical encounters.

# Additional Resources

Aveline, M. (1992). The use of audio and videotape recordings of therapy sessions in the supervision and practice of dynamic psychotherapy. *British Journal of Psychotherapy, 8*(4), 347–358.

Haggerty, G., & Hilsenroth, M. J. (2011). The use of video in psychotherapy supervision. *British Journal of Psychotherapy, 27*(2), 193–210.

Walsh, T. C. (2002). Structured process recording: A comprehensive model that incorporates the strengths perspective. *Social Work Education, 21*(1), 23–34.

# References

Elliott, R., Greenberg, L. S., & Lietaer, G. (2004). Research on experiential psychotherapies. In M. J. Lambert (Ed.), *Bergin and Garfield's handbook of psychotherapy and behavior change* (5th ed., pp. 493–539). Hoboken, NJ: John Wiley & Sons.

Gelso, C. J., & Hayes, J. A. (2002). The management of countertransference. In J. C. Norcross (Ed.), *Psychotherapy relationships that work: Therapist contributions and responsiveness to patients* (pp. 267–283). New York, NY: Oxford University Press.

Graybeal, C. T., & Ruff, E. (1995). Process recording: It's more than you think. *Journal of Social Work Education, 31*(2), 169–181.

Norcross, J. C. (2010). The therapeutic relationship. In B. L. Duncan, S. D. Miller, B. E. Wampold, & M. A. Hubble (Eds.), *The heart and soul of change* (2nd ed., pp. 113–141). Washington, DC: American Psychological Association.

Orlinsky, D. E., Ronnestad, M. H., & Willutzki, U. (2004). Fifty years of psychotherapy process-outcome research: Continuity and change. In M. J. Lambert (Ed.), *Bergin and Garfield's handbook of psychotherapy and behavior change* (5th ed., pp. 307–389). Hoboken, NJ: John Wiley & Sons.

Sparks, J. A., & Duncan, B. L. (2010). Common factors in couple and family therapy: Must all have prizes? In B. L. Duncan, S. D. Miller, B. E. Wampold, & M. A. Hubble (Eds.), *The heart and soul of change* (2nd ed., pp. 357–391). Washington, DC: American Psychological Association.

# CHAPTER 5

# DISCOVERING ACCEPTANCE AND NONJUDGMENT THROUGH MINDFULNESS

Jaclyn D. Cravens and Jason B. Whiting

## Introduction

Mindfulness has been integrated into the mental health field as a means to help clinicians be more present, open, and attentive with their clients. This state of being can be adopted by clinicians regardless of their theory of change and can enhance the therapeutic relationship between clinician and client. The purpose of this chapter is to introduce an activity that teaches both novice and experienced clinicians to be more mindfully present with themselves and their clients and to cultivate acceptance and nonjudgment in their practice.

## Rationale

The therapeutic relationship has been identified as one of the most powerful predictors of positive outcomes in therapy, more so than any specific therapeutic model (Norcross, Beutler, & Levant, 2005). One factor that enhances the therapeutic relationship is therapeutic presence, which is a quality of *being* more than it is *doing* (Gehart, 2012). Therapeutic presence can be understood as being empathetic, compassionate, nonjudgmental, accepting, and patient toward clients. In recent years, the practice of mindfulness has been integrated into a wide range of psychotherapeutic models (e.g., cognitive-behavioral, family systems, postmodern approaches), with a more recent focus on how the practice of mindfulness can be used to develop the therapeutic relationship (Gehart & McCollum, 2007).

Mindfulness is a quality of consciousness that has been promoted by several philosophical and spiritual contemplative traditions for thousands of years, but it has only recently been integrated into Western health professions. It has been shown to have positive effects, including reduced stress, increased personal health, improved pain management, and better relationships (Hayes & Smith, 2005; Kabat-Zinn, 1990). *Mindfulness* can be defined as intentionally focusing attention on moment-to-moment experience without judgment (Kabat-Zinn, 1995). Mindfulness is nondeliberative in nature, in that it involves simple observation without thinking about or evaluating events and experiences (Grossman, Niemann, Schmidt, & Walach, 2004).

The most widely accepted theory concerning why mindfulness works comes from Shapiro, Carlson, Astin, and Freedman (2006). They posit that mindfulness practice leads to a shift in perspective termed *reperceiving*, or the capacity to dispassionately observe or witness the contents of one's consciousness. Through the process of reperceiving, the clinician is able to practice nonjudgment toward clients or their presenting problems and create room for enhanced acceptance in the therapeutic relationship. When clinicians engage clients in an open, caring, and nonjudgmental way, they enable clients to "sit with" and deeply experience the problem and therefore transform their relationship with it (Gehart, 2012).

Through the process of mindfulness, a person is able to disidentify from the contents of consciousness (i.e., thoughts, emotions, value judgments) and view her or his moment-by-moment experience with greater clarity and objectivity. Shapiro et al. (2006) define this process as reperceiving because it involves a fundamental shift in perspective. Rather than being immersed in the drama of one's personal narrative or life story, a person is able to stand back and simply witness it. As Goleman (1980) suggested, the first realization in meditation is that the phenomena contemplated are distinct from the mind contemplating them.

# Activity Instructions

The purpose of this activity is to help clinicians integrate the principles of mindfulness into their clinical work, which will assist them in being more present in session, and to help them cultivate a stance of acceptance and nonjudgment. Clinicians who are struggling with reactivity toward clients in their practice can benefit from this activity. This activity is well-suited for graduate student clinicians who have begun seeing clients, although clinicians at any level of experience can benefit from the activity. Although no prior knowledge of mindfulness philosophy is necessary to complete the activity, supervisors wishing to use this activity should have knowledge of basic mindfulness principles and techniques.

The mindfulness and acceptance activity is divided into two parts that are to be conducted together. Clinical supervisors should make handouts of both exercises to assist clinicians in completing the activity. After clinicians have completed both parts of the activity, the supervisor should discuss the activity by using the provided process questions. Supervisors should allow clinicians privacy where desired, especially in the second exercise. They can focus on the process-level questions and less on the specific content of the problem. Clinicians can decide how much information they divulge with the supervisor about their problems.

## Exercise 1: Vignettes on Client Change

For the first exercise, supervisors should pass out the Exercise 1 handout containing the following instructions: Carefully read over the vignette and pay attention to any initial reactions or first impressions you have of the clients. Be curious about the reactions you have and try to reflect on these reactions in a nonjudgmental way. Record your reactions and first impressions.

*Andrew and Elise present for therapy at your office after calling to schedule marital counseling. Their presenting problem is "communication." After exploring with the couple about how they currently communicate and what areas they would like to improve, the couple reveals that arguments tend to escalate to volatile levels and that at times Andrew has become so angry that he has grabbed, pushed, and slapped Elise. Andrew is quick to state that he has never really physically hurt her, and Elise backs him up by responding that he has never bruised her or caused her to go to the hospital. Andrew also states, "I do wish that we could work on Elise not getting me so angry so that we can stop fighting like this." Andrew goes on to share that he does not really see the point in being present for therapy because Elise is the one who needs to work on her behavior, the root of what he sees as being their problem. Elise shares that she is willing to do anything to be a better wife and that she only wants to make him happy.*

Supervisors should allow clinicians as much time as needed to complete the first exercise. In past presentations of this activity, clinicians required between 10 and 15 minutes to read the vignette and record their initial reactions. After the clinicians have completed Exercise 1, the supervisor should have clinicians transition into the second exercise, waiting to process Exercise 1 until both exercises have been completed.

## Exercise 2: Person-of-Clinician Mindfulness Activity

The second exercise handout should contain the following information: For this activity you should think of a problem that has created significant difficulty in your life or your relationships. This problem may be one with which you have struggled to find a solution, that has personally challenged you, or that has had some consequence on you or your relationships. While considering your response to the two questions below, cultivate nonjudgmental awareness of any physical or emotional responses that are evoked. You may choose to write down these physiological responses. If you find it difficult to recall the experiences associated with this problem, it may be helpful to get in a comfortable position, close your eyes, and try to bring yourself back to that time. As you consider this problem, remain curious and nonjudgmental about it and your response to it. Be open to what the problem is and how you have been affected by it. You do not

Example                                                                                      29

need to decide what should or should not have happened; just examine it as it is. Remember to try and just accept the problem in all of its various ways and consider the different ways you have managed or accepted the problem.

- Name the problem that has created significant difficulty in your life or relationships.
- In what ways has the problem been a teacher for you? How have you changed or grown because of the problem?

The supervisor should allow as much time as needed for the clinicians to complete the second exercise. Past presentations of Exercise 2 varied in the amount of time that clinicians needed to finish the activity. It is important that clinicians do not feel rushed and that they are allowed to sit with their problem, being fully present in the moment. Once all clinicians have finished the second exercise, the supervisor should lead a discussion based on the process questions provided.

After the two exercises have been completed, the supervisor should use the following questions to discuss the activity with clinicians. It is important that the supervisor be aware that some clinicians may not feel comfortable sharing the second exercise, because it deals with more personal, self-of-clinician information. The supervisor should inform clinicians that they do not have to share Exercise 2 as a group. For clinicians who wish not to process Exercise 2 as a group, the supervisor can allow them to process the exercise in individual supervision. Regardless of the format selected by the clinician, the following questions should be presented and discussed:

**Process Questions**

- What was it like for you to consider your own relationship with a problem? Was it difficult to remain nonjudgmental? Were you able to avoid becoming reactive or anxious?
- After completing both exercises, did you find that you were more judgmental or reactive toward yourself than you were with the clients in the vignette?
- Have there been particular client populations or presenting problems where you have noted more difficulty refraining from judgment or reactivity? If so, how did you manage those reactions?
- After completing the self-of-the-therapist portion of this activity, would you change anything about your responses to the client vignettes?
- Why is it important to be able to remain nonjudgmental and accepting of your client(s)?
- How have you handled reactivity or judgmental feelings toward the clients with whom you have worked in the past?
- What have you learned about yourself and therapeutic acceptance as a result of these activities?

During the group process portion of the activity, supervisors should pay particular attention to any responses that reflect a reactive or judgmental stance toward either the clients in the vignette (Exercise 1) or clinicians' own selected problem (Exercise 2). Additionally, supervisors should try to draw out information about particular client populations or presenting problems that may pose more difficulty for clinicians to remain nonjudgmental or hold a stance of acceptance with (e.g., domestic violence, child abuse). For those clinicians who demonstrate reactivity or a judgmental stance during either or both exercises, the supervisor can recommend that the clinician read from the additional resources list provided in this chapter or the Gehart and McCollum (2007) article. To conclude the activity, supervisors may choose to lead clinicians in a mindfulness practice, such as deep breathing, guided imagery, or progressive muscle relaxation.

# Example

Exercise 2 of this activity has been used with a graduate course on mindfulness, geared toward master's and doctoral students. Both authors had success utilizing the activity and offer the following examples to demonstrate common themes of student clinician reactions.

While processing the activity with the class, students shared how they were able to move themselves from a place of anxiety and reactivity to a more mindful approach of acceptance and nonjudgment. A common reaction to the activity was that it was difficult to mindfully consider the problem. Many students stated that just thinking about a problem in their life made them feel anxious and guilty for the problem's existence. For example, one student stated, "I can remain nonjudgmental of the client because their problems are not mine to control, but I should be in control of my problems, so I found myself being judgmental and reactive towards my own issues." Another student shared that he struggled to even consider his own problem, stating, "In order to make it through this semester, I have just had to put up a wall between myself and the problem; I am not sure how I can accept this problem for what it is at this time." Students were asked to consider whether they believed their clients have similar experiences in the therapy room.

Several students noted that they had to focus on applying the mindfulness techniques they had learned over the course of the semester to move beyond their initial judgmental reactions. This process of moving away from their anxiety included deep breathing, becoming more aware of their physiological responses, and focusing on just sitting with the problem. The next question posed to the class was how comfortable they felt in leading clients through mindfulness activities. Some students discussed their concerns with how the client might react to such activities, whereas other students pointed out that the mindfulness techniques helped them better consider the role the problem has played in their life. A recommendation given to the class was to practice leading their peers in mindfulness techniques, which will help them gain confidence in using deep breathing in sessions; clients will be more comfortable with the techniques if the students present them more confidently.

Overall, students reported that it was helpful to apply the concepts of acceptance and nonjudgment to their own lives and that it made them better appreciate the important role mindfulness can play in helping their clients lessen their reactivity to or judgment of their own presenting problems. After finishing the activities, one supervisee noted the following:

> *I always thought that I was able to maintain a nonjudgmental and accepting stance with my clients. Through these activities I realized that although I maintain this stance in session, after some of my more challenging sessions end, I become reactive about some of the things that my clients shared in session. It is clear that I need to consider how this post-session reactivity may impact my future sessions. Using mindfulness techniques may help keep me from becoming judgmental when I reflect back on a case.*

# Measuring Progress

The supervisor is able to measure clinicians' progress based on the process questions provided to accompany the activities, which are designed to assist clinical understanding of the importance of acceptance as an integral piece of the therapeutic relationship. Signs of progress are largely qualitative in nature and include statements that demonstrate a stance of acceptance, nonjudgment, and the ability to reflect on any initial reactions the clinician has toward self or client. Any indication of continued reactivity or judgment from the clinician would indicate a lack of progress.

In addition to the progress measured through the process questions, supervisors should recognize a decrease in clinicians being judgmental or reactive toward clients. If clinicians continue to find themselves being judgmental of specific cases or clients, then supervisors should follow up with each clinician. Individual supervisors should concentrate on addressing clinician reactivity or judgment. Supervisors should revisit the process questions and focus on helping clinicians to develop an awareness of and explore the origins of their reactivity. Supervisors can then instruct clinicians to engage in some simple mindfulness techniques (e.g., deep breathing, guided imagery) to assist them in becoming more open and accepting.

# Conclusion

The purpose of this activity is to help clinicians integrate mindfulness techniques into their clinical work, facilitating greater acceptance and nonjudgment of their clients. By completing this activity, clinicians will develop mindfulness techniques that can enhance the therapeutic relationship and help clinicians better appreciate the difficulties their clients face when they come to clinics for help with their problems.

# Additional Resources

Brown, K. W., & Ryan, R. M. (2003). The benefits of being present: Mindfulness and its role in psychological well-being. *Journal of Personality and Social Psychology, 84*, 822–848.

Siegel, D. J. (2010). *The mindful therapist: A clinician's guide to mindsight and neural integration.* New York, NY: W. W. Norton.

# References

Gehart, D. R. (2012). *Mindfulness and acceptance in couple and family therapy.* New York, NY: Springer Press.

Gehart, D., & McCollum, E. (2007). Engaging suffering: Towards a mindful re-visioning of marriage and family therapy practice. *Journal of Marital and Family Therapy, 33*, 214–226.

Goleman, D. (1980). A map for inner space. In R. N. Walsh & F. Vaughan (Eds.), *Beyond ego* (pp. 141–150). Los Angeles, CA: Tarcher.

Grossman, P., Niemann, L., Schmidt, S., & Walach, H. (2004). Mindfulness-based stress reduction and health benefits: A meta-analysis. *Journal of Psychosomatic Research, 57*, 35–43.

Hayes, S. C., & Smith, S. (2005). *Get out of your mind and into your life: The new acceptance and commitment therapy.* Oakland, CA: New Harbinger.

Kabat-Zinn, J. (1990). *Full catastrophe living: Using the wisdom of your body and mind in everyday life.* New York, NY: Delacorte.

Kabat-Zinn, J. (1995). *Wherever you go, there you are.* New York, NY: Hyperion.

Norcross, J., Beutler, L., & Levant, R. (2005). *Evidence-based practices in mental health: Debate and dialogue on the fundamental questions.* Oxford, England: Oxford University Press.

Shapiro, S. L., Carlson, L. E., Astin, J. A., & Freedman, B. (2006). Mechanisms of mindfulness. *Journal of Clinical Psychology, 62*, 373–386.

# CHAPTER 6

# ENCOURAGING SELF-REFLECTION IN THE REFLECTIVE LISTENING PROCESS

Paul Burke and Melinda Hohman

## Introduction

The exercise on self-reflection presented in this chapter is based on person-centered therapy and reflects an adaptation of an exercise commonly used in the training of motivational interviewing (MI). While expertise in MI or person-centered methods is not necessary, an understanding of some of the underlying concepts of MI work will assist those undertaking this exercise.

MI is a collaborative, goal-oriented style of communication that, when practiced with fidelity, strengthens clients' personal or intrinsic motivation for pursuing changes related to a specific concern (Lundahl, Kunz, Tollefson, Brownell, & Burke, 2010; Miller & Rollnick, 2013). The guidelines, skills, and theoretical assumptions that shape the practice of those who facilitate MI conversations encourage an operant clinician-client climate (often referred to as the "MI Spirit") composed of four interacting behaviors: (1) collaborative intention and practice, (2) clinician acceptance of a number of person-centered and strengths-focused values, (3) compassion, communicated through a clear focus on the best interest of the client, and (4) evocation, or "drawing out" from clients their desires, confidence, reasons, abilities, and capacities that might support eventual commitment to a particular change. At the core of all person-centered practice is developing accurate empathy through skillful use of reflective listening (Cain, 2013). While working to empathize with clients, clinicians reflect on their clients' points of view, realities, and ultimately, understandings of the situation that brought them to the therapeutic setting. Additionally, skillful reflective listening requires clinicians to examine the extent to which they are hearing personal biases, judgments, thoughts, feelings, and hopes for the client while attempting to listen to clients.

Helping clinicians to consider how and what they are choosing to reflect upon is useful in clinical supervision (Bennett et al., 2007). This has been referred to as reflexive practice (Schon, 1987). In this process, it is important for clinicians to understand their reactions to client thoughts, feelings, and perceptions. Additionally, clinicians should examine the consequences of their own reflective responses. These are important tasks in clinical supervision and skill coaching. The purpose of this chapter is to describe an activity that can help supervisors encourage reflexivity (reflecting on reflections and their effect) during a training exercise. This learning exercise is designed to help clinicians improve their skills in developing accurate empathy with clients, explore various personal projections, and process contaminants that thwart empathic engagement.

## Rationale

Empathy involves clinicians sensing and articulating the clients' inner realities precisely and accurately, and it evolves through the clinicians' skillful formation of deep and accurate reflections of meaning in the client's own personalized context (Miller & Rollnick, 2013; Rogers, 1965). When working within the person-centered approach, achieving accurate empathy is essential in facilitating therapeutic conversational processes, the foundation of which involves establishing active engagement with the client's perspective on the key topic of the discussion. Helpful conversation requires first seeking to understand the client's frame of reference and the logic that drives the client's thoughts, feelings, and behaviors. Still, the clinicians' capacity to empathize while simultaneously containing personal thoughts, feelings, suggestions, and hopes for the client requires practice, feedback, and self-reflection. Without such containment, establishing empathy can be difficult. A failure of empathy caused by listening to self-generated thoughts rather than to client-generated perspectives can prevent clinicians from engaging with the client's point of view, which is a precursor to mutual engagement.

Reflective listening involves much more than repeating or even going beyond what the client has said. Skillful reflective listening statements begin with self-reflection. Competent reflective listening requires self-reflecting on what the client says and then decoding such statements to determine what the client thinks, feels, and means (Hohman, 2012). Importantly, it also requires disciplined reflection on how the "self" of the clinician could be influencing, interpreting, judging, evaluating, appraising, or otherwise altering the accuracy of the client's point of view.

Clinician thoughts and behaviors that interfere with effective communication and distort understanding of the accuracy of client perspectives can be considered "communication traps" (Miller & Rollnick, 2013). They are termed "traps" because these behaviors often contaminate the integrity and objectivity of the listening and reflection practices that should build engagement and, ultimately, help clients reflect upon, clarify, and strengthen their wants, reasons, needs, and plans for change. These traps hamper the conversation, holding it back from an otherwise more helpful trajectory. A few examples of communication traps are listed here:

- The "Premature Focus Trap": Identifying a core focus for the discussion regarding what ought to be changed before the client has articulated a specific area of concern and engaged in a collaborative relationship with the clinician.

- The "Expert Trap": Assuming that the client's relative lack of expertise with the issue of concern is the primary obstacle and that, accordingly, the clinician must rely primarily on personal "expertise" and install advice, education, and suggestions into the client to provide the benefit of more expertise.

- The "Question-Answer Trap": Relying on expertise to form questions that might yield diagnostic or assessment information that would allow the clinician to identify the key problem and thus formulate possible solutions and prescriptions in order to solve the problem before the engagement process has been achieved.

It can be difficult for clinicians to focus on what clients *say* without filtering that important information through what they *think* clients say. This is particularly problematic in the early part of communication exchanges because the primary goal should be conversational and relationship engagement but the tendency is to engage in self-centered (as opposed to person-centered) assessment and personalized interpretation of client statements. Engaging with clients requires that clinicians be capable of situating early discussions within the frame of reference of the client as evidenced by accuracy in reflection and avoidance of bias and self-contamination (Miller & Rollnick, 2013). When given opportunities for guided self-reflection, some clinicians indicate that it is this filtering that enervates communication traps and interferes with bona fide mutual engagement in helping conversations.

Skillful reflective listening helps clients hear themselves speak their thoughts, make adjustments as required, and make decisions about what they think and feel they ought to change. It helps them begin to form an internalized argument for a specified and targeted positive change. Keeping one's self out of the client's point of view, while nurturing engagement in a change conversation, is a necessary and difficult discipline to master. For clinicians, such discipline is essential if they intend to hear their clients and help their clients hear themselves.

# Activity Instructions

This 30- to 45-minute self-reflection exercise can be conducted with supervised groups of 6 to 20 participants who have had previous training and experience with producing reflective statements during the early phases of counseling interviews. This activity's purpose is to help clinicians identify various communication traps that may interfere with their ability to develop accurate empathy and engagement with clients in the initial stages of therapeutic conversations.

The supervisor typically assumes the role of the client. Each group member is given one or more opportunities to practice acting as the clinician by responding through simple and complex reflections of the client's content and meaning. For this exercise, participants need to be willing to make a few mistakes in order to learn. Therefore, supervisors should establish a learning environment that supports and normalizes mistake-making in order to invite clinician self-disclosure and engagement.

Before beginning the activity, the supervisor constructs a scenario that indicates a client problem or concern that could be addressed within the scope of practice of the group participants. The scenario should be complex enough to require at least 20 minutes of conversation to obtain good understanding of the issue's dynamics and of the client's logic and concerns related to the issue. The supervisor should also select which common communication traps to discuss with the group and should create a poster, slide, or handout for clinicians to reference throughout the activity. Traps to discuss include: (a) the premature focus trap, (b) the assessment trap, (c) the expert trap, (d) the labeling trap, (e) the blaming trap, (f) the chat trap, (g) the taking sides trap. For a more in-depth description of these traps, see resources by Miller and Rollnick (2002; 2013).

As the activity begins, the supervisor should review the following information with the participant group:

- The purpose of reflective listening in the engaging process.

- The common communication traps (presented in poster, handout, or slide).

- Reflective listening skills and types of reflective responses, simple and complex.

- The relationship between reflective listening and developing therapeutic empathy.

Next, the facilitator should explain that he/she will act as the client and will speak to the entire group as if the group were the treating clinician. In this role-play, the focus is on an issue or concern that requires clarification and exploration. The first group member to act as the clinician will begin the role-play with the following script: "Hi, [client name]. Thanks for coming in to talk with me. Tell me a little bit about what made you decide to come here today." When there is a pause in the conversation and in those instances when a clinical reflection would be appropriate, a volunteer from the group should respond with a reflective statement. Afterward, the client reacts to the reflection and continues the conversation as would be typical in the scenario's context. When another such pause occurs, this process repeats but with the reflective statement voiced by a different participant. This back-and-forth process between client discussion of a concern and participant reflection of client meaning and content will continue until all participants have injected at least one reflection into the conversation. (Supervisors should note that participants can either be assigned a numerical order for offering reflections or be encouraged to "jump in" when they feel ready and when it is appropriate. Participants can provide one interaction or several before moving on.)

The only "rule of engagement" for the role-play is that when participants are reflecting as the clinician, they must respond with simple or complex reflections to client statements. Asking questions, educating, giving information, or dispensing advice or suggestions is prohibited. This can be challenging as many clinicians struggle to stay with the required sustained reflections. Participants may also become stuck with how to offer a reflective response to a particular statement. In such cases, participants or the supervisor may call for a pause in the interview.

During pauses in the interview, the supervisor interviews the clinicians/participants about their urge to probe, provide information or advice, or fall into other "traps" that impede engagement. With the intention of engaging participants further in the process, the facilitator can ask one or more of the following self-reflection prompts:

- *From what this client has already said, what do I need to say back again to show that I understand what the client is saying, feeling, thinking, or meaning?*

- *Would reflecting such an understanding lead me closer to or further away from mutual engagement in the conversation?*
- *Why do I want to make this reflection? Is it one of the following reasons?*
  - *I want the client to see things the same way that I do.*
  - *I want to verify what I think the assessment may indicate here.*
  - *I know the problem that needs to be addressed and the client isn't seeing it my way.*
  - *I know what the focus of this conversation should be and I want the client to understand my perspective on this.*

Participants who struggle to sustain reflective listening throughout the exercise are encouraged to identify internal thoughts, assumptions, feelings, needs, and other obstacles to sustained reflection. They are then invited to share such insights with the group. This quickly makes it apparent that a clinician's internal dialogue and motivation to prematurely change the client can interfere with that clinician's capacity to join with the logic and the phenomenology of the client and to develop empathy.

Participants then begin a self-exploration process, leading to enhanced understanding of the motive(s) behind their desire to probe, educate, assess, or offer solutions instead of reflections. When participants stop reflectively listening, they often discover a hidden, possibly unconscious, motive to "change the client" or "identify/fix the problem." Through such self-reflection, clinicians can gain insight into their need to prematurely discuss change with the client during the engaging process or to prematurely identify and plan for solutions to the client's initial concern(s).

When participants have developed some insight into their struggle to stay with and reflect the client's perspective, the supervisor can ask them to consult the provided reference list of communication traps. As the exercise continues and participants have multiple opportunities to experience communication traps, participants should be able to identify one or more obstacles that underlie their problematic need to prematurely influence the client rather than to achieve solid engagement. Clinicians may also be asked to comment on possible origins for the development of various traps within themselves that are exposed during this exercise's self-reflection work.

Once the clinicians' concerns have been addressed, supervisors should resume the role-play. The exercise should continue until each participant has had only one or more turns as the clinician. Most groups are able to attend well for about 30 minutes.

Following the role-play, supervisors should conduct a 5- to 10-minute debriefing with the clinician group using discussion prompts such as:

- What do you think you did that worked well? What seemed most helpful for your client?
- What did you learn about yourself as an "empathic listener" or as an "empathic reflector" in this exercise?
- Which, if any, common communication traps seem to affect you most? Why might this be?
- What is one thing you could work on to make yourself more skilled at obtaining engagement through accurate reflection?

# Example

The supervisor created the following scenario to discuss with the class:

*The client, Devon, is a 24-year-old white male who has been court-ordered to attend mental health counseling. He is on probation for assaulting his mother when she confronted him about getting a job and not being at home all of the time. He has been evaluated by a psychiatrist and diagnosed with major depression and substance dependence on marijuana. Devon does not feel that he has these problems. He just wants everyone to leave him alone. Devon refuses to take the medication prescribed by the psychiatrist, even though he wants to get off probation.*

Example                                                                    37

When the activity begins, the supervisor asked participants to summarize what they knew about reflective listening and communication traps, described the activity, and explained that a very conscientious attempt to nurture mutual engagement is this session's intent. The role-play then begins.

**Volunteer #1:** Hi, Devon. Thanks for coming in to talk with me. Tell me a little bit about what made you decide to come here today. [opening script]

**Devon (supervisor):** I don't know why I need to come see you. This is such a waste of time—my time and your time.

**Volunteer #1:** You see this as a fairly useless exercise. [simple reflection]

**Devon:** Yep. Pretty much.

**Volunteer #2:** Right now there are better ways that you could be spending your time. [complex reflection]

**Devon:** [shrugs] Sure, and I bet you would rather work with someone who actually wanted help.

**Volunteer #3:** You are really frustrated, and you imagine that I am too. [complex reflection]

**Devon:** Yes, this is all just so stupid. Just because I got into a fight with my mother! She called the cops! Then I go to jail, and the doctor there tells me this all happened because I am depressed and maybe smoke too much dope. What does he know! Then they tell me I have to see you because I won't take my meds. They think that if I talk to someone then things will be better. Shows what they know.

**Volunteer #4:** You're thinking that this all seems so totally overblown. [complex reflection]

**Devon:** Yes! It's my mother who has the problem. She nags me constantly. "Devon, get a job." "Devon, everyone else works, why can't you?" "Devon, you need to get out of your room and act like an adult!" Like, she thinks all I want to do is sit around. I have plans, too, you know. I just am not doing it like she wants me to.

**Volunteer #5:** Well, why don't you just move out then? Then you wouldn't have to listen to her nag? [question asking and advice/suggestion giving]

**Supervisor:** Let's take a timeout! What just happened here? Let's discuss what happened that stopped the reflective listening.

**Volunteer #5:** It was hard to keep reflecting. He was being so negative, blaming his mother for his problems. I wanted him to see that if she is the problem, then why doesn't he just move out? That way he could get away from her nagging. [Motive = implanting insight. Trap = taking sides]

**Supervisor:** You wanted him to start to take some responsibility. [complex reflection]

**Volunteer #5:** Exactly! He was blaming his mother when it is really his own behavior. But I see what I did; instead of reflecting what was going on with him, I gave him advice. I wanted to push him into admitting that it wasn't about his mother—it was about him.

**Supervisor:** As a clinician, where do you think this came from in you? [open question, to explore motive]

**Volunteer #5:** I was getting frustrated and wanted to move things along. [Motive = skip past the engaging process and into problem solving]

**Supervisor:** What do you think the client may have been feeling while you were feeling frustrated in that way? [open question]

**Volunteer #5:** Well, I suppose he was probably pretty frustrated with all the conflict between him and his mom. I guess I could have reflected his frustration—you know, stayed with his feelings and not reacted so much to my own.

**Supervisor:** What communication traps did you fall into? [open question]

**Volunteer #5:** I could see how I "became the expert"—giving him ideas about what to do—and I was also sort of siding with his mother a little bit, I think.

|   |   |
|---|---|
| | I think my biggest problem was his refusal to take responsibility, and I wanted to push him into admitting that he couldn't move out because he has no job and no money. His being stuck is of his own making, even if he does have depression. Maybe I was even trying to shame or embarrass him, just to get him unstuck in his blaming. Maybe if he saw the need he would begin to change, to take his meds, feel better, look for work, get a job, save money. Just like you have on the wall there, I was in a hurry and wanted to implant some awareness. |
| **Supervisor:** | What might you do differently, if you were to keep reflecting to engage him? [open question] |
| **Volunteer #5:** | I don't know. I was getting stuck in my own frustration. |
| **Supervisor:** | What are some ideas from the group? [open question, solicits from the group] |
| **Volunteer #6:** | Maybe you could reflect something like, "This is frustrating for you because you have your own goals and ideas for your life." Get him to talk about those things. |
| **Supervisor:** | That might work well. Let's resume the role-play. Would someone be willing to jump in now and try out some additional reflections in order to deepen the engagement here. |
| **Volunteer #6:** | So, Devon, neither you nor your mother like the idea of you sitting around the house all the time. You've got some plans for your life and it seems like your mom is not aware of them, or at least she's not as focused on those as you are. [complex reflection] |
| **Devon:** | Well, I haven't really talked to her much about my plans, I guess. |

The role-play then continued with new participants volunteering to compose and offer reflections in response to client statements, with the supervisor allowing participants to falter and break out of their reflective listening mode occasionally in order to examine the motives and traps underlying such breaks. At the conclusion of the role-play, participants were asked to offer observations and insights about what they have learned about their own biases and internal processes:

- "It was hard for me to wait for the client to catch up with where I was at in terms of understanding the problem. I had figured it out long before the client did—and then I wanted to ask questions to guide them to my conclusion." (Premature Focus Trap)

- "It was amazing to me how much I wanted to respond with a question to so much of what the client said. At first I just thought it was my style of letting my client know that I was following her. I discovered, though, that I was trying to gather information from her that would help me to assess the situation, to figure it out." (The Question/Answer Trap)

- "I learned that in reflective listening, we don't just want the client to hear what they say, we want to help the client think about what they say." (Insight into the value of self-reflection in reflective listening)

# Measuring Progress

One quantitative way to measure the progress of reflective listening skills is through having an independent observer code and provide feedback on audiotaped sessions with clients (Miller, Yahne, Moyers, Martinez, & Pirritano, 2004). Clinicians could then review audiotaped sessions on their own and use a journaling method to answer the exercise's questions. Such notes could then be reviewed in supervision. Qualitative signs of progress include the ability to sustain reflections with increased engagement from clients and to avoid common communication traps that hinder the engaging process.

# Conclusion

Reflective listening is a difficult skill to learn (Matulich, 2013). Although it looks easy from the outside, clinicians who wish to use this skill find that both practicing it and reflecting on choices made when practicing it are important in establishing engaged relationships with clients. Helping clinicians analyze their reflective listening skills will encourage them to reduce projection of their personal biases and prejudices and minimize communication contamination. This exercise may also help clinicians increase their mindfulness of the tendency to persuade, manipulate, or coerce clients into change, thus increasing engagement with clients.

# Additional Resources

Arkowitz, H., Westra, H. A., Miller, W. R., & Rollnick, S. (2008). *Motivational interviewing in the treatment of psychological problems*. New York: Guilford Press.

Hay, J. (2007). *Reflective practice and supervision for coaches*. Berkshire, England: Open University Press.

Rosengren, D. B. (2009). *Building motivational interviewing skills: A practitioner workbook*. New York: Guilford Press.

# References

Bennett, G. A., Moore, J., Vaughan, T., Rouse, L., Gibbins, J. A., Thomas, P., … Gower, P. (2007). Strengthening motivational interviewing skills following initial training: A randomized trial of workplace-based reflective practice. *Addictive Behaviors, 32*, 2963–2975.

Cain, D. J. (2013). Person-centered therapy. In J. Frew & M. Spiegler (Eds.), *Contemporary psychotherapies for a diverse world*. (pp. 165–213). New York, NY: Routledge.

Hohman, M. (2012). *Motivational interviewing in social work practice*. New York, NY: Guilford Press.

Lundahl, B., Kunz, C., Tollefson, D., Brownell, C., & Burke, B. L. (2010). Meta-analysis of motivational interviewing: Twenty-five years of research. *Research on Social Work Practice, 20*, 137–160.

Matulich, W. (2013). *How to do motivational interviewing* (2nd ed.). San Diego, CA: Author.

Miller, W. R., & Rollnick, S. (2002). *Motivational interviewing: Preparing people for change* (2nd ed.). New York, NY: Guilford Press.

Miller, W. R., & Rollnick, S. (2013). *Motivational interviewing: Helping people change* (3rd ed.). New York, NY: Guilford Press.

Miller, W. R., Yahne, C. E., Moyers, T. B., Martinez, J., & Pirritano, M. (2004). A randomized trial of methods to help clinicians learning motivational interviewing. *Journal of Consulting and Clinical Psychology, 72* (8), 1050–1062.

Rogers, C. (1965). *Client-centered therapy*. New York, NY: Houghton Mifflin.

Schon, D. (1987). *Educating the reflexive practitioner*. San Francisco, CA: Jossey-Bass.

# CHAPTER 7

# ENHANCING SELF-AWARENESS USING FEEDBACK REFLECTION

Elisabeth Esmiol and Rebecca Partridge

## Introduction

The purpose of this chapter is to provide a tool to help clinicians increase their self-awareness by intentionally reflecting on client feedback. Increasing clinician self-awareness is both a goal in itself and a factor in effectively integrating client feedback, which in turn can improve the therapeutic relationship and the effectiveness of the therapy (Duncan et al., 2003). Self-awareness is essential to processing client feedback, as clinicians' ability to remain self-aware by accurately self-assessing and self-evaluating impacts their effectiveness in responding to client feedback and improving therapeutic outcomes (Sparks, Kisler, Adams, & Blumen, 2011). Client feedback is critical to clinical effectiveness, as a client's subjective experience of the early therapeutic alliance and of meaningful change in the first few sessions predicts final treatment outcomes (Miller, Duncan, Brown, Sorrell, & Chalk, 2006). When clinicians value and respond to formal, real-time feedback from clients regarding the process and outcome of therapy, there are significant improvements in both client retention and therapeutic outcomes (Miller et al., 2006; Hafkenscheid, Duncan, & Miller, 2010). In this chapter, clinicians will learn to use the Feedback Reflection Exercise (FRE) to enhance self-awareness and better respond to client feedback, thus helping clinicians improve the effectiveness of the therapy they provide as well as their therapeutic relationships.

## Rationale

Feedback-informed treatment requires clinicians to elicit feedback from clients, reflect on the feedback, and then modify therapy accordingly (Duncan et al., 2003). The benefits of using client feedback to modify the course of therapy and thereby improve therapeutic alliance and effectiveness are well documented (Duncan, Miller, & Hubble, 2007; Miller et al., 2006; Miller, Hubble, & Duncan, 2007). However, the process of learning how to elicit client feedback and then process and respond to that feedback is less studied (Sparks et al., 2011). Self-awareness seems to be an important factor in learning how to effectively utilize client feedback. In processing client feedback, clinicians must be able to evaluate not only client reactions and responses but also themselves and their own ability to effectively build rapport and deliver interventions (Sparks et al., 2011).

The ability to successfully ask for client feedback, receive and process that feedback, and then make appropriate changes in the therapy process requires clinicians to have a considerable amount of self-awareness. Having an open conversation about a client's negative feedback can be uncomfortable for both clinician and client; however, self-awareness can greatly aid such difficult conversations. Nutt-Williams and Hill (1996) found that when novice clinicians engaged in negative self-talk about themselves in session, they also reported feeling more negative about their overall therapeutic effectiveness and about their client reactions. To counter this destructive tendency, Nutt-Williams and Hill recommend that clinicians increase self-awareness. This implies that if clinicians are aware of their tendency toward negative self-talk, then they are more prepared to distinguish between self-criticism and negative client feedback. Self-awareness can then aid in evaluating negative client feedback as clinicians examine treatment progress and the therapeutic relationship without the hindrances of negative self-talk.

Whether consulting with a colleague, supervisor, or personal therapist, seeking consultation appears to help increase clinician self-awareness (Lutz & Irizarry, 2009). Consultation has been linked to increasing self-awareness of personal triggers, areas of weakness and strength (Blow, Sprenkle, & Davis, 2007), power dynamics, and clinician bias (Esmiol, Knudson-Martin, & Delgado, 2012). Seeking consultation also appears linked to improving self-awareness during the process of receiving and responding to client feedback (Sparks et al., 2011). Receiving feedback can be difficult, and the process of proactively responding to constructive feedback from clients can be an especially daunting process for clinicians, even those who are seasoned (Duncan et al., 2007).

Nevertheless, consultation can help trainees understand that negative feedback is one of many different types of difficult conversations we engage in as clinicians and as people. The attitude with which we enter these difficult conversations sets the tone not only for the shared experience but also for the future course of the relationship and a mutual opportunity for growth. The FRE enables clinicians to increase their self-awareness about client feedback in a format that is especially suitable to consultation and supervision groups. Because it is not easy "holding up the mirror of feedback and taking a look," Sparks et al. (2011) recommend the mantra "There is no negative feedback, only negative responses to it" (p. 464). By utilizing the FRE in the context of supportive consultation relationships, clinicians have the opportunity to further grow in self-awareness and more effectively respond to client feedback.

# Activity Instructions

The FRE is an intentional self-reflection and action-planning exercise to be completed by clinicians in conjunction with administering Miller et al.'s (2006) Outcome Rating Scale (ORS) and Session Rating Scale (SRS) to clients. The FRE helps clinicians reflect on in-session dialogue, alternative ways to approach client feedback, and reflective writing to determine how they are eliciting, processing, and responding to feedback. By using the FRE to regularly reflect on the process of eliciting and responding to client feedback, clinicians gain greater self-awareness about their impact on clients and can modify the course of therapy as needed.

The FRE is a two-part activity consisting of (1) reflecting on how clinicians are eliciting constructive feedback and (2) engaging in the deliberate practice of reflecting, thinking, and acting in response to feedback. The first part of the FRE helps clinicians focus on actual client feedback and ways clinicians can ask for more productive feedback from clients. The second part of the FRE helps clinicians increase self-awareness regarding how they respond to client feedback. Clinicians are encouraged to reflect on client feedback, think about how it impacts the clinician, and create an action plan for the following week based on client feedback. Reflecting on client feedback aids clinician self-awareness and increases clinician understanding of personal reactions, biases, and triggers that they may not have been previously aware of prior to the FRE.

## Directions for Clinicians

To use the FRE, clinicians should ask clients to complete the ORS at the beginning of each session and the SRS at the end of each session. The four-question ORS rates how clients are doing individually, interpersonally, socially, and overall (Miller, Duncan, Brown, Sparks, & Claud, 2003). The four-question SRS rates the degree to which clients (a) felt heard, understood, and respected; (b) worked on and talked about what they wanted to; (c) felt the clinician's approach was a good fit; and (d) felt nothing was missing in session (Duncan et al., 2003). We recommend clinicians administer the SRS to clients with a short rationale, such as, "I want you to get the most out of therapy and would appreciate your honest feedback so I can better meet your needs." After administering the SRS, clinicians engage in a brief conversation with clients in which they practice eliciting specific, nuanced feedback focused on their client's lowest-scored question on the SRS. For example, if clients scored lowest on feeling heard and respected, clinicians could ask, "What could I have done differently today to help you feel more heard or respected?" The purpose of this conversation is to help clinicians understand how they need to adapt or change their style of therapy (Duncan et al., 2003).

To improve clinician self-awareness, we recommend clinicians complete the FRE at least once each week, either tracking a difficult case or a new case. In Part 1 of the FRE, clinicians report the actual feedback-eliciting conversation they had at the end of a session and then generate an alternative hypothetical conversation in which they imagine finding a new way to ask for small, concrete, contextually driven details that make clients feel cared for. In Part 2 of the FRE, clinicians are asked to increase self-awareness by (a) reflecting on the personal experience of eliciting client feedback, (b) thinking about how they are processing and integrating this feedback, and (c) planning a specific action for the next session that addresses the feedback or lack of feedback. This process helps clinicians increase their self-awareness through reflecting on their degree of openness or defensiveness toward client feedback. The aim of the FRE is to enhance self-awareness both in and out of the therapy room, as clinicians are asked such questions as "Where else do I see this issue impacting my life and relationships?"

**Directions for Supervision and Case Consultation**

Clinicians are encouraged to further increase self-awareness by using the FRE as part of a regular practice of clinical supervision, self-supervision, or case consultation. During regular supervision or consultation, clinicians can individually reflect on or collectively discuss the FRE and share their experience of receiving in-session feedback from both the SRS and from clients' verbal feedback. By regularly reflecting on or discussing the FRE, clinicians are held accountable for becoming more aware of how they start a session and whether there is a clear plan that meets the clients' needs and responds to any prior or ongoing client feedback. Using the FRE also helps clinicians evaluate how they end sessions and their degree of curiosity in drawing out and understanding client feedback. Regularly using the FRE can also help clinicians process any personal issues triggered in session or brought to light by clients themselves that may be interfering with responding to client feedback and facilitating change.

Additionally, discussing the FRE in supervision and consultation groups enables clinicians to receive input from supervisors or colleagues in evaluating multiple aspects of clinical competency. Using the FRE helps structure discussion around the important competencies of self-reflection and eliciting and attending to client feedback. Insights from supervisors and colleagues can assist both novice and experienced clinicians in focusing on areas they may not be fully aware of in their therapeutic practice and increasing the potential for improved self-awareness.

# Examples

Clinicians who regularly use the FRE describe the process as both challenging and helpful in improving therapeutic alliance and self-awareness. For student clinicians, challenges were mainly a result of difficulty in processing client feedback. One student stated:

> It isn't always easy to hear feedback from clients, especially when that feedback seems to be brutally honest; however, this type of feedback promotes the most growth for me, and I have come to appreciate it so much.

Despite these challenges, the majority of student clinicians found the FRE helpful in their developmental process of understanding personal strengths and weaknesses and building client rapport. For example, a student clinician stated:

> By getting negative feedback we can understand how we can better meet the needs of our clients and really work on what is important to them and tailor how we are in the room with the clients.

For this student clinician, the self-awareness to tailor her own behavior to client needs emerged from using the FRE to reflect on client feedback. Another student clinician's summary of her experience captures the essence of how the FRE fosters self-awareness:

> I personally do not believe I have yet to become more matched to these clients' needs and sociocultural contexts. I very much need to build up more courage in addressing these matters. I am thankful [the FRE] has taught me to go there rather than avoid it.

Table 7.1 is an example of the FRE completed by a clinician in training during her first practicum providing therapy. Her exercise was chosen as an example because of her ability to

**Table 7.1 Completed Feedback Reflection Exercise Form**

### FEEDBACK REFLECTION EXERCISE

| Clinician Name: | Date: | Client Code: | ORS/SRS: |
|---|---|---|---|
| Joanne | October 10, 2012 | XXX | 22/40, 30/40 |

*Did you follow last week's action plan?*      x Yes ☐ No ☐ Didn't see client(s)

#### Part 1: Eliciting Constructive Feedback

***Actual Clinical Conversation:*** *Write what you said this week to elicit constructive client feedback, followed by how the client responded and your follow-up response.*

| | |
|---|---|
| Actual Clinician Question | Was there anything I could have done to make you feel more comfortable this week? |
| Actual Client Response | From male partner: No. When I came in I was worried that you wouldn't believe my side of it, since Melissa is so competitive in the personality department. |
| Actual Clinician Response | And now, at the end of the session, <u>do you still feel like I won't believe you</u>? |

***Alternative Clinical Conversation:*** *Write alternative responses you could have given that may have elicited more specific feedback.*

| | |
|---|---|
| Alternative Clinician Question | Was there something that I did in the previous session to give you the impression that I wasn't going to believe you? |
| Alternative Hypothetical Client Response | Well, Melissa talks much more than me, and I felt like you spent more time asking her about her side than me about mine. |
| Alternative Clinician Response | <u>Thank you for bringing that up.</u> It's really important to me that both of you have a chance to feel heard in this room. <u>What can I do differently to make you feel heard</u>? |

#### Part 2: Deliberate Practice: Reflect, Think, Act

***Reflect:*** *Research indicates that receiving negative feedback early on actually yields better treatment results!*

| | |
|---|---|
| What specific, nuanced, context-driven feedback did you receive? | He felt like I wasn't going to believe him this session. Even though he said, "That's just me; I don't trust people," I felt like I had given him the impression that somehow I didn't believe his "side" of the story. Particularly because the issue is surrounding an event that depends on whose side of the story you choose. Additionally, Melissa is the louder, more talkative one, so <u>I find it easy to let her go on and on.</u> |

Table 7.1 (continued)

| | |
|---|---|
| What was your gut response to that feedback? | I understand why he felt that way. Seeing couples individually <u>sometimes does feel like we are asking for both sides to the story so we can judge who is "right."</u> However, I felt that we had a really good session together and that I joined with him pretty strongly during the one-on-one time, so I was interested to see if he felt that we connected also. |
| **Think:** Remember, as you reflect on client feedback, take responsibility instead of burden shifting! | |
| How am I processing this information? (Am I open, defensive, hurt, ignoring it, embarrassed?) | I kind of ignored it, attributing it to his statement "It's just me; I don't trust people or let people in." This is a way of not fully owning up to my responsibility to make him feel heard. It also makes me worry a little bit that what I talked about in my last reflection paper (about not being able to juggle both voices in the room equally) was something that he picked up on last session also. I didn't ask him about this though. |
| Where else do I see this issue impacting my life and relationships? | Generally, I don't think I tend to ignore things; however, since I've started seeing clients, I've definitely tended toward ignoring issues in my personal life—mostly because I am aware of the effort it takes to clearly and honestly communicate and to listen to the other person, and at the end of the day after concentrating so intently on my clients' communication, I feel lazy and tired and don't want to put the work in that is required in some of my own relationships. |
| **Act:** Plan out what you will do and say next session. | |
| What will I do differently next session regarding this specific piece of feedback? | At the end of the session, I will ask both partners if they feel I am giving them equal space to share and be heard. |
| Next Session Planned Clinician Question | "Something I would like to do now is just check in with both of you to see how you are feeling about the balance of the session and whether you feel that you are getting an equal chance to get to say what you need to in the session." |
| Next Session Hypothetical Client Response | From male partner: "I guess I'm getting more of a chance to talk." |
| Next Session Planned Clinician Response | "What would you need from me and from our sessions for you to respond 'I'm getting an equal chance to talk'?" |

elicit constructive feedback and openly reflect on her role in the therapy session. All names have been changed, and particularly noteworthy comments have been underlined.

# Measuring Progress

Clinicians will know they are increasing their self-awareness and improving their ability to elicit client feedback through the process of regularly completing and discussing the FRE with supervisors or colleagues. Specific signs of progress include the following:

- Increased awareness of discrepancies between clinician and client perceptions of the therapeutic work and process
- Increased recognition of personal shortcomings and areas of needed growth as a clinician
- Increased appreciation for client feedback in the therapeutic process and relationship
- Increased willingness to try new therapeutic responses in place of typical clinician actions and statements
- Increased commitment to eliciting and responding to client feedback despite discomfort
- Improved client outcomes and client–clinician relationships as reported by clients

Using the example of the completed FRE, we can see the student clinician demonstrating these six signs of progress. Beginning with the first sign, notice how the student clinician showed awareness of a possible discrepancy in her experience of having "a really good session together" and wondering if the client "felt that we connected also." This seems to show the student clinician shifting from assuming the client felt joined to being aware that the client may have felt unheard. The second sign of progress is evident in the student's awareness of "not fully owning up to my responsibility to make him feel heard" and writing "I find it easy to let her go on and on." This student's openness and nondefensiveness to her own need for improvement seems linked to the third sign of progress and her belief in the value of client feedback in building a strong therapeutic relationship.

After using the FRE weekly during her first clinical practicum, this student clinician stated she was still learning to use client feedback to develop therapeutic alliance but had "developed the skill to be able to just sit in the room as [clients] were giving me the feedback and listen to what they were saying without trying to make it better immediately." The student clinician demonstrated the fourth sign of progress as she responded with a new action, suggesting regular check-ins to see if the couple felt they were "getting an equal chance" to speak. The fifth sign of progress is apparent in her revising her actual response from "Do you still feel like I won't believe you?" to an alternative response in which she thanked the client for his feedback and asked, "What can I do differently to make you feel heard?" This seems to demonstrate her ability and commitment to elicit more nuanced feedback despite her initial discomfort and temptation to ignore the feedback. A supervisor could point out the strength of this alternative, open-ended response and help the student clinician generate additional ways to better attend to her client's needs. If a clinician had trouble generating a more effective alternative conversation, a supervisor or colleague could discuss and possibly role-play alternatives with the clinician. Finally, regarding the sixth sign of progress, both the clinician and her supervisor noted that as the student clinician continued to attend to client feedback, the client's positive feedback increased.

# Conclusion

Research indicates that the therapy process can benefit from clinicians increasing self-awareness (Axelrod, 2012; Williams, 2008) and utilizing client feedback (Duncan et al., 2007; Miller et al., 2006). The Feedback Reflection Exercise (FRE) is designed to help clinicians measure self-awareness specifically around using client feedback to strengthen the client–clinician relationship, ultimately toward improving client outcome. This therapeutic "alliance has been shown to be robustly predictive of outcome across treatments" (Wampold, Imel, & Miller, 2009, p. 151). By making specific client feedback the focus of self-reflection, the FRE enables clinicians to directly increase their self-awareness and improve the effectiveness of their therapy and the therapeutic relationship while attending to the specific requests of clients.

# Additional Resources

Duncan, B. L. (2012). *On becoming a better therapist*. Washington, DC: American Psychological Association.

Duncan, B. L., Miller, S. D., Wampold, B. E., & Hubble, M. A. (2009). *The heart and soul of change: Delivering what works in therapy*. Washington, DC: American Psychological Association.

Sprenkle, D. H., Davis, S. D., & Lebow, J. L. (2009). *Common factors in couple and family therapy: The overlooked foundation for effective practice*. New York, NY: Guilford Press.

# References

Axelrod, S. D. (2012). Self-awareness: At the interface of executive development and psychoanalytic therapy. *Psychoanalytic Inquiry*, *32*, 340–357.

Blow, A. J., Sprenkle, D. H., & Davis, S. D. (2007). Is who delivers the treatment more important than the treatment itself? The role of the therapist in common factors. *Journal of Marital and Family Therapy*, *33*(3), 298–317.

Duncan, B. L., Miller, S. D., & Hubble, M. (2007). How being bad can make you better. *Psychotherapy Networker*, November/December, 36–57.

Duncan, B. L., Miller, S. D., Sparks, J. A., Claud, D. A., Reynolds, L. R., Brown, J., & Johnson, L. D. (2003). The session rating scale: Preliminary psychometric properties of a "working" alliance measure. *Journal of Brief Therapy*, *3*(1), 3–12.

Esmiol, E., Knudson-Martin, C., & Delgado, S. (2012). Developing a contextual consciousness: Learning to address gender, power, and culture in clinical practice. *Journal of Marital and Family Therapy*, *38*(4), 573–588.

Hafkenscheid, A., Duncan, B. L., & Miller, S. D. (2010). The outcome and session rating scales: A cross-cultural examination of the psychometric properties of the Dutch translation. *Journal of Brief Therapy*, *7*(1&2), 1–12.

Lutz, L., & Irizarry, S. S. (2009). Reflections of two trainees: Person-of-the-therapist training for marriage and family therapists. *Journal of Marital and Family Therapy*, *35*(4), 370–380.

Miller, S. D., Duncan, B. L., Brown, J., Sorrell, R., & Chalk, M. B. (2006). Using formal client feedback to improve retention and outcome: Making ongoing, real-time assessment feasible. *Journal of Brief Therapy*, *5*(1), 5–22.

Miller, S. D., Duncan, B. L., Brown, J., Sparks, J. A., & Claud, D. A. (2003). The outcome rating scale: A preliminary study of the reliability, validity, and feasibility of brief visual analog measure. *Journal of Brief Therapy*, *2*(2), 91–100.

Miller, S. D., Hubble, M., & Duncan, B. L. (2007). Super shrinks: Who are they? What can we learn from them? *Psychotherapy Networker*, November/December, 27–36.

Nutt-Williams, E., & Hill, C. E. (1996). The relationship between self-talk and therapy process variables for novice therapists. *Journal of Counseling Psychology*, *43*(2), 170–177.

Sparks, J. A., Kisler, T. S., Adams, J. F., & Blumen, D. G. (2011). Teaching accountability: Using client feedback to train effective family therapists. *Journal of Marital and Family Therapy*, *37*(4), 452–467.

Wampold, B. E., Imel, Z. E., & Miller, S. D. (2009). Barriers to the dissemination of empirically supported treatments: Matching messages to evidence. *The Behavior Therapist*, *32*(7), 144–155.

Williams, E. N. (2008). A psychotherapy researcher's perspective on therapist self-awareness and self-focused attention after a decade of research. *Psychotherapy Research*, *18*(2), 139–146.

CHAPTER 8

# Exploring Personal Roles and Themes in Clinical Training

Alyssa Banford and Rachel Tambling

## Introduction

This chapter introduces an experiential supervision exercise that provides a dynamic self and group exploration for participants. The exercise, inspired by the work of Virginia Satir (1967), Papp and Imber-Black (1996), and Aponte et al. (2009), is an experiential learning exercise that meets three primary objectives. First, student clinicians will be able to engage in an experience similar to what their clients experience in family therapy, exploring the roles, themes, and patterns of a significant and meaningful group: their cohort group. Ideally, clinicians-in-training will be able to heighten their sensitivity to what it is like to be in a client role through experiential supervision activities as they mindfully monitor their own reactions to the experience of describing roles and themes within this meaningful group. Second, student clinicians will be able to observe, learn, and duplicate similar experiences with their own clients to foster exploration of roles and themes in other meaningful groups, such as families. We are hopeful that trainees will use this experiential activity as a model for the successful exploration of group dynamics with others. Finally, through this exercise, student clinicians will be offered a heightened degree of insight as to how their clinical work and demeanor are perceived by those around them, including their instructor(s) and peers, who are meaningful partners in the training environment. In other words, the activity can work as a mirror of sorts, held up to clinicians-in-training to allow them to see their clinical selves as their clients see them. Such a vision of the reflected self-of-the-therapist could create opportunities for the developing therapist to explore and develop congruence between their self-perceived versus other-perceived personae.

## Rationale

The process of training requires that student clinicians be able to comment and reflect on their own reactions, behaviors, and thought processes, as well as those of their colleagues in training (Aponte et al., 2009). In our training program, understanding, developing, and utilizing the self-of-the-therapist is heavily emphasized throughout the curriculum. Through their shared experiences in practicum settings, the student clinicians create a group dynamic that is central to the training process as they observe one another's clinical work and concurrent class work and spend time together outside of practicum. Because of their knowledge of one another personally and professionally, the use of peer feedback, as orchestrated in group supervision, is one avenue utilized for students learning about self.

It is a common belief that the process of supervision runs parallel with the process of therapy (Aponte et al., 2009). We think this is especially the case in supervision modalities where the development and exploration of the self-of-the-therapist is emphasized because of the personal examination and scrutiny required in such an approach. In other words, we see a marked parallel in exploring family life in the clinical setting and exploring the group life and inner world of the developing clinician and his or her cohort group in the supervision setting. As such, the inspiration for the following activity was taken from a clinical article discussing the concept of capturing central themes within a group as a means of therapeutic interaction (Papp & Imber-Black, 1996).

Papp and Imber-Black (1996) discuss the power of identifying, expanding, and examining the themes that underlie client experience in order to foster interaction with the themes and allow for different possibilities in the way that clients experience their lives and relationships and make sense of them. The power in the intervention lies in harnessing intangible themes that have real power in governing family/group dynamics and creating a way for clients to interact with the ephemeral by translating these dynamics into symbols. This allows the clinicians heightened ability to identify what assumptions inform behavior and interactions and invites the clinicians to further investigate, explore, and perhaps confront formerly accepted ways of being and relating.

Experiential therapies and the work of theorists such as Virginia Satir have been influential in the development of understanding both the themes of family interaction and the roles that family members occupy. Some well-known examples of common family roles identified by Satir include the "placator" and the "blamer" (Satir, 1967; Woods & Martin, 1984). David Kantor and colleagues (Duhl, Kantor, & Duhl, 1973) asked clients to experience and even physically enact the roles they carry that inform the way they relate to others. Others have used family sculpting as a way to enact themes and draw attention to psychological distance and role (e.g., Marchetti-Mercer & Cleaver, 2000; Simon, 1972). Attention to roles and themes has resulted in rich theoretical contributions to the way clinicians and supervisors alike communicate and operate (Aponte et al., 2009; Imber-Black, Roberts, & Whiting, 2003). When clinicians work in the therapy room and in supervision to identify roles and themes, it represents progress in translating vague forces in human relationships into concrete, observable patterns through labels. Labeling roles and themes provides a map of understanding and organizes how internal assumptions and experiences connect with outside manifestations of relational dynamics (Satir, 1967).

We have observed that, as with families, marriage and family therapy (MFT) training cohorts can invoke various members of the group to occupy or enact certain roles within the group or even within specific interactions. The roles that group members enact are often powerful and emotionally significant in terms of each member's internal experiences, outside manifestations, and group experiences. Although the nature of cohorts and supervision groups are temporary in their organization and are perhaps not as emotionally compelling as family relationships, we believe that they offer a naturally occurring set of role and theme dynamics that can be observed, explored, labeled, and thematically understood.

Furthermore, some clinicians may have limited awareness of the themes that organize their clinical work and the roles that inform their relationship to training peers and their clients. In such cases, clinicians-in-training may be hesitant to receive feedback about their clinical work and may struggle in relation to their peers in training. Satir advocated for genuine transparency in her work with clients: "I give myself permission to be totally clear and in touch with myself. I also give myself full permission to share my views, as well as permission to see if my views have validity for the people with whom I am working" (Satir, 1987, p. 24). We see great value in giving voice to roles and themes that are observed within supervision and cohort relationships. Such a process can be accomplished through this activity and is useful in combating a lack of self-awareness of patterns and themes of relating.

# Activity Instructions

We have used this exercise with a variety of clinicians at various stages of development and personal circumstances, but we would like to stress the importance of applying clinical judgment in administering this exercise. This activity is best used in a group with a high level of honesty and transparency with one another and where a strong focus on the self-of-the-therapist has been emphasized from the outset of training. In cases when group dynamics of transparency have not been a focus, an individual adaptation of this type of experiential exploration might be more appropriate.

Ideally, this activity should be completed with graduate student clinicians in their second year of schooling, regardless if they have begun seeing clients. Although this activity may be modified for a seminar or other activity, it works best when conducted by a seasoned supervisor who has a high level of familiarity with the activity participants and when the activity participants have a good deal of familiarity with one another. These instructions are therefore directed to the activity supervisors. It is important to note that a supervisor should carefully consider the emotional maturity of potential participants and the availability of the group to self-reflection and scrutiny. Prior to the activity, it may be helpful for supervisors to familiarize themselves with the article "Family Themes: Transmission and Transformation," by Papp and Imber-Black (1996).

In this activity, student clinicians take turns identifying, commenting on, and receiving feedback on a central or important theme of their clinical activity. To begin, the supervisor selects a trainee from the group and asks him or her to think about and identify a predominant theme in his or her work with clients or an interaction with others in the program. At the same time, the rest of the trainees are asked to consider their colleague and to also identify a theme in the work and interactions of their classmate. All trainees are asked to write down the themes, and the supervisor does so as well. The themes and any associated behaviors are reflected on and noted privately. Next, each member of the group selects some portion of their notes to share with the group aloud. Clinicians-in-training are encouraged to share the themes as nonjudgmentally as possible, and then each classmate and the supervisor share themes they noted.

After each classmate and the supervisor have shared their impressions of themes with the selected trainee, the trainee is given space to respond, discuss, and share his or her thoughts about two distinct experiences: (1) the experience of selecting a theme for describing his or her own clinical stance, and (2) the experience of hearing the themes identified by the instructor and colleagues in training. The interaction among peers, the supervisor, and the selected trainee should assist the trainee in exploring and expanding on themes and behaviors identified. The selected trainee may also wish to discuss his or her internal experience of and thoughts about the exercise.

Themes may be experiential in nature and reflect a common theme displayed in behaviors. For example, one trainee's theme was "live out loud," representing the fact that she accomplished much of her processing verbally and had a strong voice within the group and often operated as a spokesperson for her training cohort. Exploration of this theme gave the group an opportunity to discuss and process the times when this trainee speaking for the group was preferable and times when it was not.

Some themes are more relational and describe reactions or common outcomes to seemingly repeated situations. For instance, another trainee had an identified theme of "If I'm not heard, I will go away" to capture her process of removing herself when feeling silenced. Identifying this theme opened a space for the cohort to discuss, along with the trainee, how the group experienced her perception of silence and "going away."

Finally, some other themes were indicative of a role the trainee played in relation to others in the group. For example, one student selected his theme to be that of a "protector." The group processed how this role played out and was activated in instances when he perceived another member of his cohort to be vulnerable or upset.

Ideally, this activity works well in groups with 6 to 10 trainees. In groups larger than 10 trainees, we recommend doing the exercise in partnerships or in small groups and then coming together as a large group to reflect on general impressions of the activity. This adaptation should only be made when the trainees are familiar with one another and feel comfortable sharing the themes of their work. A verbal consent for the activity should be obtained from trainees, and trainees should be free to restrict their sharing or to stop the discussion at any point that the trainee feels unsupported. This activity can also be done in individual supervision or in paired supervision as well.

Students and supervisors will be best prepared if they are familiar with Papp and Imber-Black's (1996) article and Aponte et al.'s (2009) article about themes in training. The activity has been predominantly carried out in the self-of-the-therapist course, which is held two hours each week. We have traditionally gone through the themes of five to six students in one class session and used one-and-a-half to two classes to explore the themes in tandem with the readings. At the end of the activity, the supervisor should take responsibility to consolidate the experience by thanking the students for the degree of transparency they chose to exhibit and for the sharing everyone participated in. The point should be reiterated that altering the themes is less important than awareness of them; by sharing the expanding themes we broaden the possibilities of changing themes that feel oppressive or incongruent and allow for greater awareness as a mental health professional. The supervisor should consistently make him- or herself available for follow-up conversations and to facilitate questions or comments that students wish to make privately. As a follow-up after the exercise, students can be prompted to write their reactions as a personal journal entry, which can be submitted to the supervisor as a forum for private communication or kept as a personal reflection for the trainee's own benefit.

# Examples

We have noted several outcomes as we have conducted these activities with trainees. First, for many of the clinicians-in-training, this is an emotional experience in which they felt very seen and understood by those in the group. Many student clinicians remark that their classmates seem to understand them and to see the central themes in their lives based on the behaviors they have observed. Furthermore, many student clinicians are able to make critical connections between their within-cohort themes and the larger themes operating within their lives. It comes as no surprise to us as supervisors that themes tend to be isomorphic, and the illustration of themes within a safe group—the cohort or supervision group—can facilitate the exploration of similar themes in other relationships.

Student clinicians generally describe this exercise as a positive experience that fostered self-understanding and connection with the group. Many clinicians report feeling heard and honored for their roles in the group. For instance, one of the trainees was nicknamed "a tuning fork" for her ability to detect and to emotionally resonate with subtle emotions and to accurately reflect and join with a broad range of emotional experiences with her clients. We discussed as a group and reflected with this trainee how this facet of her work was an advantage but also left her susceptible to feeling overwhelmed or burned out and thus requiring extra elements of self-care and support at certain times.

Others trainees experienced their themes differently but were able to see new sides of a theme. This is particularly true among student clinicians who believe that their role or theme is "bad" or "less than" in some way. For example, one trainee had the theme of "friendship with clients." The trainee indicated that he embodied that theme in his work but fully acknowledged that his ability to create rapport with his clients was not enough—that "just being a friend" was an indication that he was not being therapeutic and skillful. As a group we processed this experience with the trainee and shared a more textured view of the skill we had observed in this trainee's development of "friendship" with clients. For example, we talked about this trainee's particular ability to suspend his own beliefs to make room for the experiences of others, thereby causing them to feel truly seen. We also shared our own personal reactions with this trainee of having experienced the skills utilized in his ability to develop "friendship."

By interacting with others around their themes, student clinicians can see the ways in which their own theme functions and contributes to group dynamics, both positive and negative. For instance, with the clinician whose theme was related to being a "hero" and "protector," we processed how at times he might block an interaction or conflict between other cohort members. We were able to openly discuss what is hard for this trainee to witness when others have conflict and how his "protection" can be helpful but at times a hindrance.

For many student clinicians, this process provides some psychic distance from the theme so that it can be examined with less judgment and more compassion. Finally, this exercise provides student clinicians with a new emotional experience and the opportunity to relate to others in unique ways around a powerful theme. When clinicians-in-training feel heard and seen, and when they can interact with the themes in nonjudgmental ways, new interaction potential is fostered. For example, student clinicians who experience themselves as protectors may feel relief when they hear from the group that the associated behaviors are appreciated but not needed. This can free them to continue to enact the role in typical ways or to experiment with other behaviors or other roles.

# Measuring Progress

Clinicians will note progress in their self-awareness as they are able to identify roles that they take on in their supervision group and themes across their cases. Supervisors utilizing this activity should engage their supervisee clinicians in conversation in both individual and group meetings that are centered on themes and roles they are noticing in themselves and others. For many supervisees, the themes and behaviors identified in the exercise can become open topics of conversation in subsequent group and individual supervision sessions. Through continued exploration of the central themes, supervisees can learn to more effectively identify themes at work, can objectively evaluate the behaviors associated with the themes, and can act with more awareness and control in interpersonal situations. Progress is measured in this activity through increased attention to themes and improvement in the clinician's ability to interact thoughtfully around the theme.

Typically, progress in ability to identify and process themes is assessed informally in individual supervision and in the seminar course where the use of the self-of-the-therapist is covered. We have used this exercise in the last semester of our training program as a capstone. However, another way to measure progress is to complete this exercise at different points in the training process and ask trainees to keep a record of the themes identified at different points. The overall intention of the activity is to induce greater flexibility in trainees to consciously select their demeanor as clinicians, supervisees, and group members. By increasing attention to themes that permeate and transcend a case, trainees will be able to skillfully and nonjudgmentally observe their own emotional reactions and alter them.

# Conclusion

This group-supervision experience is designed to be an overt investigation of covert roles in training cohorts and supervision groups about themes across cases. We find that experiential activities like this one allow clinicians to develop heightened sensitivity to themes within interpersonal relationships. Furthermore, the exploration of interacting themes within meaningful groups enables clinicians-in-training to think systemically about the ways in which themes and associated behaviors might be managed, altered, or selectively enacted to serve treatment goals with clients. Finally, the process of exploring often-unspoken themes within a group setting can be a powerful opportunity for personal growth and for exploration consistent with a self-of-the-therapist training exercise.

# Additional Resource

Satir, V. (1988). *The new peoplemaking*. Palo Alto, CA: Science and Behavior Books.

# References

Aponte, H. J., Powell, F. D., Brooks, S., Watson, M. F., Litzke, C., Lawless, J., & Johnson, E. (2009). Training the person of the therapist in an academic setting. *Journal of Marital and Family Therapy, 35*(4), 381–394.

Duhl, F. J., Kantor, D., & Duhl, B. S. (1973). Learning space, and action in family therapy: A primer of sculpture. *Seminars in Psychiatry, 5*(2), 167–183.

Imber-Black, E., Roberts, J., & Whiting, R. A. (Eds.). (2003). *Rituals in families and family therapy*. New York, NY: W. W. Norton.

Marchetti-Mercer, M. C., & Cleaver, G. (2000). Genograms and family sculpting: An aid to cross-cultural understanding in the training of psychology students in South Africa. *The Counseling Psychologist, 28*(1), 61–80.

Papp, P., & Imber-Black, E. (1996). Family themes: Transmission and transformation. *Family Process, 35*(1), 5–20.

Satir, V. (1967). Family systems and approaches to family therapy. *Journal of the Fort Logan Mental Health Center, 4*(2), 81–93.

Satir, V. (1987). The therapist story. *Journal of Psychotherapy and the Family, 3*(1), 17–25.

Simon, R. M. (1972). Sculpting the family. *Family Process, 11*(1), 49–57.

Woods, M. D., & Martin, D. (1984). The work of Virginia Satir: Understanding her theory and technique. *The American Journal of Family Therapy, 12*(4), 3–11.

# CHAPTER 9

# ADDRESSING RESISTANCE
# TO BEHAVIOR CHANGE

Rebecca Mirick

## Introduction

Clinicians commonly encounter resistance, especially when working with mandated clients or when therapy focuses on difficult presenting issues such as child welfare or substance abuse (R.H. Rooney, 2009). Resistant clients can present challenges for clinicians. Resistance can manifest in behaviors such as anger, frustration, aggression, or refusal to participate, and unsurprisingly, resistance has been shown to negatively impact the development of the working alliance (Smith, 2008). Resistant clients often do not do as well as other clients; high levels of resistance are linked with poor client outcomes (Karno, Beutler, & Harwood, 2002; Piper, McCallum, Joyce, Azim, & Ogrodniczuk, 1999).

Due to the negative consequences of resistance, it is important that clinicians learn to effectively develop a positive alliance with resistant clients, engaging them in treatment. The first step in this process is for clinicians to replace some or all of the frustration and anger they might feel toward resistant clients with empathy, a core component of a positive working alliance and effective work (Feller & Cottone, 2003). Normalizing resistance, or reframing it as a normal, expected, universal reaction to being asked to change (Brehm, 1966), versus a pathological response, can support clinicians in the development of empathy (Miller & Rollnick, 2002; R. H. Rooney, 2009). The following experiential activity creates an opportunity for clinicians to experience resistance, develop an awareness of their own capacity for resistance, consider resistance from the clients' perspective, and reflect on their own reactions to resistance in others.

## Rationale

Clients may express resistance through many difficult behaviors, including anger, defensiveness, aggression, arguing, interrupting or ignoring the clinician, blaming others, making excuses for behaviors, minimizing the problem, being unwilling to make changes, arriving late to counseling, or not attending counseling at all (Miller & Rollnick, 2002; R. H. Rooney, 2009). Clinicians working with resistant clients often assume this behavior is linked to motivation to change (Altman, 2008; Reich, 2005), although research with clients has not supported this assumption (Altman, 2008; Smith, 2008). Clinicians often use confrontational techniques to increase client compliance (Altman, 2008; Reich, 2005; Smith, 2008), which in fact can increase resistance (G. D. Rooney, 2009; Smith, 2008). High levels of resistance are linked with poor client outcomes (Karno et al., 2002; Piper et al., 1999), and involuntary clients may experience serious legal consequences as well (e.g., the loss of custody of a child through the child welfare system; Atkinson & Butler, 1996; Reich, 2005).

R. H. Rooney (2009) has suggested that the technique of normalizing resistant behavior can increase clinicians' effectiveness with resistant clients. Miller and Rollnick (2002), in their motivational interviewing approach, have used similar ideas and reframed resistance from an individual issue to a manifestation of the interactions between the clinician and client—a sign that something is amiss in those interactions. The following experiential activity is developed from this theoretical framework. I have frequently used this activity while teaching graduate students in advanced clinical practice classes, but it could also be used effectively as an exercise in a supervision group, field education group, or continuing education training. The instructions are written for a supervisor or training leader.

This activity is designed to facilitate the development of self-awareness of resistance while also providing a space to practice simple motivational interviewing techniques of conducting an interview while managing the resistance. This experience allows the clinician to experience the process of resistance from both the clinician and the client perspective, creating opportunities to observe resistance as stemming from the interaction rather than from individual characteristics of the client (Miller & Rollnick, 2002).

It is common, especially for newer clinicians, to identify resistance as an individual internal client issue, being unaware of how clinician behavior also plays a role in client resistance (Miller & Rollnick, 2002; R. H. Rooney, 2009). For clinicians, the lack of awareness of the process of resistance and their own role in its development can lead to instances where the clinician actually increases the client's resistance with his or her actions, although his or her intent was the opposite (G. D. Rooney, 2009). For example, by taking a directive or confrontational approach or increasing the use of the power and authority inherent in his or her position, the clinician can inadvertently increase resistance (Berg & Kelly, 2000; Karno et al., 2002; R. H. Rooney, 2009). Clinicians who pathologize resistant clients, lack empathy toward them, or believe resistance indicates a reduced motivation for change exhibit signs that they could benefit from increased awareness of this clinical issue. Although this exercise was designed for student clinicians or newer clinicians, any clinician could participate in this experiential exercise; there is no rule-out criteria.

Taking on the role of client, even briefly as in this activity, provides clinicians with an opportunity to clarify how their own behaviors and communication can create resistance in clients. Increasing clinicians' awareness of their own resistance normalizes resistance because they, too, have experienced it. They can develop a deeper understanding for what resistance feels like, how it manifests, and what strategies can be effective to address it. Participants also learn how client resistance can be distinct from client motivation (for change), given that resistance is related to a natural, expected ambivalence around changing a behavior (Miller & Rollnick, 2002). Most importantly, this experience of being a client and feeling resistance, even around a minor behavior, increases empathy, which is a core component of the alliance and crucial for effective work (Feller & Cottone, 2003) with clients who are often addressing much larger issues than the clinicians in this exercise. Thus, the empathy gained through this activity may represent an important first step toward working effectively and respectfully with resistant clients.

# Activity Instructions

In preparation for the exercise, clinicians are asked to choose an insignificant bad habit that they are willing to discuss in the group (e.g., arriving late to work, drinking too much coffee, biting one's nails, or eating too much junk food). The instructor emphasizes the choice of an *insignificant* habit; clinicians should refrain from picking a behavior that is too serious or personal. Topics such as alcohol or drug problems, sexual issues, or eating-disorder behaviors are inappropriate and should not be used. Instead of helping clinicians understand resistance, these serious problems have the potential to generate so much resistance that clinicians cannot objectively learn from the experience, instead being overwhelmed by negative affect. Material that is too personal may also cause their partners to experience discomfort, making them unable to fully participate in the exercise.

The steps of this experiential activity are outlined as follows:

1. Before the exercise begins, clinicians should complete assigned readings on resistance (R. H. Rooney, 2009) and motivational interviewing techniques for using with a client while addressing resistance when it is encountered (e.g., "rolling with the resistance" [Miller & Rollnick, 2002]). Clinicians think of an insignificant bad habit that they are willing to discuss with a partner and with the class. Examples are given to them (e.g., drinking too much coffee, not exercising enough, or eating too many sweets).

2. To begin the activity, clinicians break into pairs. One clinician is assigned the role of client and the other the role of clinician. The clinician interviews the client about the

bad habit the client has chosen. The clinician's tasks are to use active listening and to avoid offering suggestions, opinions, or interventions, all behaviors that risk triggering resistance. Clinicians listen for resistance and change their interviewing approach in response to any resistance. The client's assignment is to answer the questions naturally. Both the clinician and the client are asked to attend to feelings of resistance or defensiveness in the client role and to consider how and why those feelings persist or subside. The fact that these are real conversations versus role-plays has two benefits: (1) decreasing the self-consciousness and discomfort that can arise with role-playing and (2) increasing the likelihood that the client will experience resistance.

3. After 15 minutes, the clinician and client pair switch roles and complete step 2 again.

4. The pair debriefs after the exercise is complete. This debriefing starts with clinicians discussing their experience in the client role, focusing on times when they felt resistance, their experience of resistance (e.g., Did your resistance feel rational? If not, did this realization decrease your resistance? How did it feel? What increased or decreased your resistance?), their understanding of why the resistance occurred (e.g., Was it in response to something the clinician said? Did the clinician push too hard for change? Did you feel judged?), and their responses to this internal feeling of resistance (e.g., Did you pretend compliance? Get irritated? Try to change the subject?).

5. After each partner has had a chance to talk about the experience in the client role, partners then discuss being in the clinician role, including their experiences with the client's feelings of resistance (e.g., Could you tell when the client was resisting? How did it make you feel?) and their responses (e.g., What did you do? Was it successful? Why or why not? How could you tell if it was successful or not?).

6. After debriefing, the pairs return to the larger group and discuss the activity all together. The group pays attention to experiences that were universal, normalizing resistance and exploring how it was experienced from the position of both the clinician and the client. All participants identify triggers for resistance and how resistance felt for both clinician and client, as well as how the clinicians can take what they have learned in this exercise and apply it to their work.

The purpose of this activity is twofold. First, it provides clinicians with practice interviewing an involuntary client about a problem behavior while being attuned to resistance, and an opportunity to get feedback on this process both from their partner and the group leader. Second, each clinician experiences resistance, normalizing the reaction and increasing awareness about resistance. Even clinicians with experience using techniques incorporating these sorts of skills, such as motivational interviewing, report this as a challenging exercise and often request more time to practice these skills.

# Examples

Most clinicians reported positive experiences with this exercise. Although the exercise is purposely designed to feel less artificial than many traditional role-playing exercises, many clinicians still initially felt self-conscious, stopping the interview to make a comment or to get feedback on how to proceed because they felt stuck. Once they overcame these initial feelings, most clinicians expressed appreciation for the opportunity to practice interviewing skills and experience resistance. Even clinicians who use these skills regularly felt they benefited from the practice exercise, particularly because of the opportunity to get feedback from both the instructor and their peers. Listening to the client and reflecting the client role seems to be particularly challenging for clinicians; many default to offering solutions, suggestions, or advice. Even with feedback from the instructor or partners, this remained a challenging task for many clinicians. Discussing this issue in the group format has been effective.

Although developing interviewing skills for work with resistant clients is an important skill, the primary learning experience of this exercise is self-awareness: to experience firsthand some of the feelings, reactions, and thoughts that clients have when they discuss a problem behavior.

Participants described feeling reluctant, angry, and defensive when their partners asked them about the problem, suggested a way to stop the behavior, or pushed them to make a change in their behavior. Even as role-playing clients, they recognized these feelings as irrational because they believed they should stop the behavior. Clinicians expressed surprise at how intensely they felt emotions, including reluctance to change, even knowing that this was only a class activity.

Clinicians who picked behaviors that were important to them or were deeply ingrained in their lives (e.g., eating sweets, arriving late, or texting too much) responded to the interview with more resistance than those who picked behaviors to which they did not have any strong attachment (e.g., packing lunches more often, biting nails). This was particularly true when the behavior was one that the clinician had decided must change (e.g., remembering to take her birth control) versus when the behavior was one that the clinician thought should change or had been told to change (e.g., eating less junk food, not texting while talking to people), without internal motivation to quit. When the behavior was a serious problem (e.g., smoking), the exercise was less effective because the clinician's resistance to the discussion was so strong that it overpowered the exercise. In one particular pair, a clinician who chose to talk about her smoking became quite angry at the discussion, so much that she was not able to have an intellectual discussion about the experience of resistance and anger—the intensity of her emotion was too overwhelming.

During the exercise, many pairs spiraled into a sequence of the clinician making suggestions and the client refusing them, saying that the proposed solutions "don't work" or that they have "tried everything." This mirrors experiences many clinicians have had with clients and feels familiar to clinicians. In the group discussion, we reflect on how common this process is and explore ways to understand this now that the clinicians have experienced resistance themselves. Many clinicians commented that they had not realized how often they give advice or make suggestions until they were sitting in the role of client, saying things like "I've tried that and it hasn't worked."

After the activity was completed, the majority of clinicians reported that this brief exercise increased their awareness of resistance both in themselves and in others, changing the frame from resistance as pathological to resistance as a normal, expected reaction. A lot of feedback focused on how challenging the activity was when the clinician stayed attuned to resistance; it often appeared subtly, but when they were looking for it, they noticed it more often. Many clinicians talked about how surprised they were at their own resistance to discussing a self-selected, fairly inconsequential behavior. When I have used this activity, it has been one component of a 14-week class. Weeks later, on the written evaluation, this activity is frequently named by clinicians as one of the most useful components of the class.

# Measuring Progress

The goals of this activity were twofold: (1) provide clinicians with practice interviewing an involuntary client about a problem behavior while being attuned to resistance, and (2) create an opportunity for each clinician to experience resistance, normalizing the reaction and increasing awareness about resistance. The first goal is easily accomplished, and the majority of the clinicians agreed enthusiastically that this exercise was a useful tool in increasing their confidence at interviewing and working with resistant clients. The second goal, which is more experiential, is more difficult to assess.

To measure the effectiveness of this activity, I assess clinicians through observation during the exercise by spending a few minutes with each group, listening to the conversation and observing the interactions, and through the evaluations and comments of the clinicians in the group discussion that follows the activity. During the exercise, if a group is struggling (e.g., falling out of the role, struggling with the conversation, not responding to clear signs of resistance), I offer suggestions or briefly role-play the role of clinician myself. Clinicians who have a good understanding of the exercise actively adjust their approach in response to resistance.

The group discussion is an important component of this activity both for developing self-awareness and evaluating the effectiveness of the exercise. During the group discussion, the instructor can engage in an informal evaluation of the activity by having clinicians report back on these goals and share what they have learned from the experience, and what they will take with them into their practice. The instructor's role is to help clinicians place their reactions and feelings into a theoretical framework of resistance and discover effective ways to decrease resistance. To assess the effectiveness of the exercise in the discussion, the instructor should look for an understanding of the universal nature of resistance, an increased awareness of resistance (e.g., "I had no idea that I was so resistant to changing this behavior" or "Every time I offered a suggestion to change, the other person seemed not to like it"), and a thoughtful discussion of ways to approach it as a clinician (e.g., "I'd like to practice these skills more" or "I keep getting stuck with the client") versus a client-blaming approach (e.g., "I think that the person really didn't want to change"). A follow-up written evaluation is also helpful in securing the clinicians' responses to the exercise several weeks after it was done and determining how much of the learning is retained long-term.

# Conclusion

Clinicians encounter resistance in work with many types of clients. Resistance is linked to negative outcomes partly because of assumptions about the relationship between resistance and lack of motivation. Learning how to effectively engage and work with resistant clients is an important aspect of clinicians' training. This brief experiential activity offers clinicians the opportunity to reflect on resistance, experience it for themselves both in the clinician and client role, and deepen their awareness of the phenomenon of resistance.

# Additional Resources

Berg, I. K., & Kelly, S. (2000). *Building solutions in child protective services*. New York, NY: Norton.

Chovanec, M. (2008). Innovations applied to the classrooms for involuntary groups: Implications for social work education. *Journal of Teaching in Social Work*, *28*(1–2), 209–225.

Miller, R. M., & Rollnick, S. P. (2002). *Motivational interviewing: Preparing people for change*. New York, NY: Guilford Press.

Mirick, R. (2012). Reactance and the child welfare client: Interpreting child welfare parents' resistance to services through the lens of reactance theory. *Families in Society*, *93*, 165–172.

Rooney, R. H. (2009). *Strategies for work with involuntary clients* (2nd ed.). New York, NY: Columbia University Press.

# References

Altman, J. (2008). Engaging families in child welfare services: Worker versus client perspectives. *Child Welfare*, *87*(3), 41–61.

Atkinson, L., & Butler, S. (1996). Court-ordered assessment: Impact of maternal noncompliance in child maltreatment cases. *Child Abuse & Neglect*, *20*, 185–190. doi: 10.1016/S0145-2131(95)00146-8

Berg, I. K., & Kelly, S. (2000). *Building solutions in child protective services*. New York, NY: Norton.

Brehm, J. (1966). *A theory of psychological reactance*. New York, NY: Academic Press.

Feller, C. P., & Cottone, R. R. (2003). The importance of empathy in the therapeutic alliance. *The Journal of Humanistic Counseling, Education and Development*, *42*, 53–61. doi: 10.1002/j.2164-490X.2003.tb00168.x

Karno, M. P., Beutler, L. E., & Harwood, T. M. (2002). Interactions between psychotherapy process and patient attributes that predict alcohol treatment and effectiveness: A preliminary report. *Addictive Behaviors*, *27*, 779–797.

Miller, R. M., & Rollnick, S. P. (2002). *Motivational interviewing: Preparing people for change*. New York, NY: Guilford Press.

Piper, W. E., McCallum, M., Joyce, A. S., Azim, H. F., & Ogrodniczuk, J. S. (1999). Follow-up findings for interpretive and supportive forms of psychotherapy and patient personality variables. *Journal of Consulting and Clinical Psychology, 67*, 267–273.

Reich, J. A. (2005). *Fixing families: Parents, power and the child welfare system.* New York, NY: Routledge.

Rooney, G. D. (2009). Oppression and involuntary status. In R. H. Rooney (Ed.), *Strategies for work with involuntary clients* (pp. 349–387). New York, NY: Columbia University Press.

Rooney, R. H. (2009). *Strategies for work with involuntary clients* (2nd ed.). New York, NY: Columbia University Press.

Smith, B. D. (2008). Child welfare service plan compliance: Perceptions of parents and caseworkers. *Families and Society, 89*, 521–533. doi: 10.1606/1044-3894.3818.

# CHAPTER 10

# TEACHING SELF-COMPASSION TO DECREASE PERFORMANCE ANXIETY IN CLINICIANS

Anna I. Bohlinger, Jeni L. Wahlig,
and Stephanie Trudeau-Hern

## Introduction

The purpose of this activity is to have clinicians examine their own experiences of self-compassion through a mindfulness activity. This allows clinicians to focus on and support kindness toward self, a sense of common humanity, and mindfulness in the presence of unpleasant emotions. This activity may be particularly useful for early-career clinicians, who may learn to lessen performance anxiety and enhance empathy for clients' experiences through supported self-compassion activities. By teaching and supporting self-compassion in early-career clinicians, supervisors can help to decrease performance anxiety in their trainees.

## Rationale

Theory suggests that clinician self-awareness facilitates a more positive therapeutic experience for both clients and clinicians (Bowen, 1978; Minuchin, Lee, & Simon, 2006). Part of self-awareness is the ability and willingness to see oneself accurately in terms of both strengths and weaknesses. A common temptation for early-career clinicians is to evaluate themselves only in terms of achieving levels of "expert" (Skovholt & Ronnestad, 2003), which can lead to skewed self-evaluations, especially in response to real or perceived mistakes. High performance expectations may create feelings of anxiety, failure, or lowered self-esteem. Managing performance anxiety with kindness, rather than criticism, may be supported by using self-compassion (Leary, Tate, Adams, Allen, & Hancock, 2007).

Self-compassion may be a more appropriate fit for managing anxiety, beyond the construct of self-esteem. *Self-esteem* is defined as having a strong and positive sense of self that remains fairly stable throughout various contexts and over time (Burns, 1979). Among the potential problems with simply working to improve clinical self-esteem is that clinicians develop a false sense of competence and can blame clients or contexts for any deficiencies in growth areas (Doherty, 2012). A construct that would improve therapist development and performance would have to both allow for and accept growth areas as a normal part of development and encourage the space to improve. This construct has been developed and is embodied in the idea of self-compassion.

Based on Buddhist psychology, *self-compassion* is a construct that includes being kind to self in the face of failure, experiencing a sense of common humanity, and being mindful in the presence of painful feelings (Neff, 2003; Neff, Hsieh, & Dijitterat, 2005). Self-compassion is different from self-esteem; where self-esteem is about having positive feelings toward oneself, self-compassion is about self-care (Leary et al., 2007). Unlike self-esteem, promoting self-compassion has not been linked to increased narcissistic attitudes or distorted self-concepts (Damon, 1995; Leary et al., 2007; Seligman, 1995). Instead, by generating feelings of compassion, it is believed that one who practices self-compassion will feel more compassion toward negative emotions as they arise, increase positive emotions, and gain insight into the nature of these emotions (Hofmann, Grossman, & Hinton, 2011).

Given the high degree of stress that mental health professionals face on a daily basis (Figley, 2002) and the common anxiety that new clinicians feel about performance (Skovholt & Ronnestad, 2003), the development of mindfulness skills such as self-compassion can be a helpful internal resource (Cohn & Fredrickson, 2010). Existing research supports the development of these skills and their overall value to the training process (Leary et al., 2007; Neff, 2003; Shapiro, Brown, & Biegel, 2007; Shapiro, Astin, Bishop, & Cordova, 2007).

The loving-kindness meditation described in the activity is derived from Buddhist practices and is particularly well suited for creating the internal experience of self-awareness and positive emotions such as self-compassion (Cohn & Fredrickson, 2010; Hofmann et al., 2011). Echoing the support of self-awareness and compassion studies, research has found evidence that loving-kindness and compassion meditations were related to increases in positive emotions, mental health, and physical health. Additionally, the same meditations were associated with decreases in stress and negative emotions, such as anxiety and mood symptoms (Cohn & Fredrickson, 2010; Hofmann et al., 2011). A follow-up study of participants who had learned the loving-kindness meditation found that they maintained the benefits even if they did not continue the meditative practice (Cohn & Fredrickson, 2010).

# Activity Instructions

The loving-kindness meditation can be practiced at any time, at any place, or in any posture (Hofmann et al., 2011). In its most basic form, this meditation consists of directing feelings of loving and kind concern for the well-being first of self, then of specific others, and finally of all beings and the entire universe. The following exercise is a modification of the loving-kindness meditation, with the specific intention of helping new clinicians to generate self-compassion in managing performance anxiety. It can be read aloud to students and trainees by their supervisor, or it can be used by beginning clinicians as a guide for their own self-reflective practice.

If the activity is to be implemented in a class or supervision setting, the supervisor should keep in mind the following recommendations:

- Students should feel free to sit comfortably in their chairs, lie down on the floor or mats, or find another position that is comfortable.

- They should be encouraged to close their eyes if they feel comfortable doing so. If they choose to leave their eyes open, the supervisor should encourage them to pick a place to focus their vision and soften their gaze.

- Give them time to settle into getting comfortable before beginning the meditation. It may be helpful to suggest that students take a deep breath before beginning.

- Supervisors should dedicate 10 to 15 minutes to practice this meditation, and, after the supervisor has read the meditation, students should be given a few moments to come out of the meditation as they are ready.

- The meditation should be read slowly and with compassion, giving students ample time to feel their connection with others throughout the journey.

Although it is not necessary for supervisors to have their own mindfulness practice in order to effectively lead this activity, we recommend that supervisors read over the meditation multiple times, getting familiar with the flow, noting places to pause or emphasize particular words, and perhaps modifying the language to fit the supervisee/class before leading it with trainees. If desired, you may give students time to journal or otherwise reflect on their experience after the guided meditation has finished.

Example 63

*Find a comfortable time, place, and posture in which you can relax and turn inward. Let your eyes close and focus on your breath. It is often helpful to count with your inhales and exhales, keeping them even. Feel yourself relax. If your mind wanders, simply notice your thoughts without critique, and gently bring your attention back to your breath.*

*When you feel ready, turn your attention to the place in your chest where you experience caring, compassion, and empathy. Imagine a little white light there—your compassion, turning and pulsing and available to you. Now, recall an important person in your life—someone toward whom you feel warmth, love, and appreciation. Let those feelings fill you. Feel the warm, white light of compassion growing and pulsing in your chest as you think of that person. Grow that light bigger with your love, appreciation, and compassion for that person until you are glowing with it. Now, turn your attention to just the feeling, and hold it. Feel the power of your own compassion pulsing within and around you, wrapping you up, and holding you tight. Embrace yourself with this warm light of compassion.*

*Now grow it bigger, and radiate this light of compassion to others. Send it to those you know well—your family, your friends. Radiate this light to new clinicians who are learning alongside you, and grow it to touch and warm your supervisors and your clients. Imagine that your white light can reach in and touch their fears, their disappointments, their self-criticism, their hurt, their mistakes—whatever it is that is troubling these people on their own human journeys, your light of compassion now touches. Imagine that, on some level, for even just a brief moment, they experience some relief, a glimmer of hope, forgiveness, empathy, and compassion for themselves.*

*With each person you touch, repeat a statement slowly and silently to yourself, as a gift to that person. It can be any statement that touches your heart, as long as it connects with your compassion. Some examples include "May you find peace," "May you be happy," "May you know forgiveness," or "May you grow from your mistakes."*

*When you have radiated your love to those closest to you and to those with whom you are sharing your growth as a clinician, continue to grow your light of compassion even larger. Grow it to wrap up your town and send your light and words of compassion to everyone there. Grow it to wrap up your state. Imagine all people in all their experiences, their joys and sorrows, struggles and triumphs, mistakes and successes. Wrap them with compassion and silently leave them with your words. Take your time, and grow your light bigger—big enough to wrap your country, big enough to wrap your continent. Spread your love across oceans until it wraps up the world—all humanity, every creature, every landscape. Send your compassion out to the universe, across space and time. For all mistakes that have been made in the past and all that will be made in the future, send your compassion.*

*Then, when you are ready, slowly bring your white light of compassion back—back to the earth, back across the oceans, your continent, your country, and your state, back to your town and to the people close to you, and then back to yourself. Imagine putting whatever has been troubling you into a box and sending your warm light to it. Wrap it up, and cherish this experience with the compassion you might feel for a newborn child. Then, leave it wrapped up in compassion, glowing with warmth and light, and imagine releasing it to the universe, to join with the other boxes of troubles that are shared in our human experience. Wrap yourself one last time in the love and light of your compassion, and then bring it back inside your chest, where it will remain available, pulsing and glowing and infinitely abundant, for whenever you need it next.*

# Example

In the following example, Jeni, a novice clinician, describes her experience in using the loving-kindness meditation in connection with treating a difficult client:

> *In my first year of clinical training, I (JLW) struggled terribly with one of my clients. He was a concerned father, who often came in with his 13-year-old son, the identified patient. I felt frustrated and angry with the man. I believed that he was not taking any responsibility for what was going on in his family system. I also believed that, despite his commitment to therapy, most of what he said and did was contributing to the "problem" more than it was helping. I dreaded our appointments, and I often left sessions feeling helpless and upset. I didn't want to be this guy's therapist; I was no good at helping him anyway.*

*Not surprisingly, my supervisor became very familiar with this case. We processed it from many different angles—case reporting, case presentation, live and video supervision, journaling, reflective questions—but I just couldn't get past my feelings. With each session, I felt myself becoming more and more frustrated, and I blamed myself even more than I blamed him. I was stuck, and my only hope was graduation or sudden termination by the client system. Then one day, my supervisor asked me a very simple question: "What do you think you need to do in order to work with this client?" The answer came to me out of nowhere: "I need to love him."*

*It was then that I recalled the loving-kindness meditation, which I had stumbled upon several years earlier. Before my next session with this client, I took 10 minutes in an empty room to engage in this practice. I found my heart swelling with compassion. I began to see this man as a father in pain—worried and feeling helpless and guilty about what his son was going through. Then I began to see that his struggles were the struggles of humanity. He was coping with pain, loss, and fear, and he was doing the best he knew how—like everyone, like me. Underneath my frustration was a deep concern accompanied by a fear that I wasn't good enough to help. As my compassion and love grew for this client and his journey, it also grew for myself and mine.*

*My heart felt swollen with love and acceptance, and at that session, I knew I was different. I had shifted cognitively and emotionally. I was more present, more compassionate, and more committed to being with and supporting this client system. I was also more confident in and compassionate toward myself.*

*The loving kindness-meditation has since become a resource that I use regularly for myself as I work with clients. I have also used this meditation with my clients, walking them through the process in their search for compassion toward self and others. Additionally, I have offered the loving-kindness meditation to supervisees as a tool that they might use when they need it. I wouldn't hesitate to guide a beginning clinician through this journey of compassion should the opportunity arise. Speaking from experience, it can be transformative.*

# Measuring Progress

Measuring progress toward self-compassion is something that can be accomplished in several different ways. Qualitative measures, such as the reflective awareness reported previously, and formal quantitative measures, appropriate for use in supervision or research settings, can be used to measure progress. For example, journaling at multiple points on particular aspects of self-compassion, such as common humanity, may demonstrate qualitative changes in how particular trainees evolve in their evaluations of these aspects. From a quantitative perspective, several scales for the measurement of self-compassion have been developed (e.g., Neff, 2003).

# Conclusion

Performance anxiety is an unavoidable part of development of the clinician. Use of the loving-kindness meditation to increase self-compassion in the face of performance anxiety is a skill that may be beneficial for many clinicians and clinicians-in-training. Some participants may struggle with this exercise, especially if a meditation practice is not currently a part of their lives. In those situations, participants should be encouraged to simply observe their difficulty without attachment to the results. Observation without judgment is one of the essential skills for mindfulness; practicing this *is* a form of mindfulness in itself. Finally, both mindfulness and self-compassion are skills, and, as with any skill, the best way to learn it is through regular practice.

# Additional Resources

Germer, C. K. (2009). *The mindful path to self-compassion: Freeing yourself from destructive thoughts and emotions*. New York, NY: Guilford Press.

Neff, K. (2009). "Self-compassion: Test how self-compassionate you are." Retrieved from http://www.self-compassion.org/test-your-self-compassion-level.html

Neff, K. (2011). *Self-compassion: Stop beating yourself up and leave insecurity behind*. New York, NY: HarperCollins.

Salzberg, S. (2002). *Lovingkindness: The revolutionary act of happiness*. Boston, MA: Shambhala.

# References

Bowen, M. (1978). *Family therapy in clinical practice*. New York, NY: Jason Aronson.

Burns, R. B. (1979). *The self concept in theory, measurement, development and behavior*. New York, NY: Longman.

Cohn, M. A., & Fredrickson, B. L. (2010). In search of durable positive psychology interventions: Predictors and consequences of long-term positive behavior change. *Journal of Positive Psychology*, *5*(5), 355–366. doi: 10.1080/17439760.2010.508883

Damon, W. (1995). *Greater expectations: Overcoming the culture of indulgence in America's homes and schools*. New York, NY: Free Press.

Doherty, W. (2012). One brick at a time: Therapy is more craft than art or science. *Psychotherapy Networker*, *36*(5), 23–28, 59–60.

Figley, C. (2002). Compassion fatigue: Psychotherapists' chronic lack of self care. *Journal of Clinical Psychology*, *58*(11), 1433–1441. doi: 10.1002/jclp.10090

Hofmann, S. G., Grossman, P., & Hinton, D. E. (2011). Loving-kindness and compassion meditation: Potential for psychological interventions. *Clinical Psychology Review*, *31*(7), 1126–1132. doi: 10.1016/j.cpr.2011.07.003

Leary, M. R., Tate, E. B., Adams, C. E., Allen, A. B., & Hancock, J. (2007). Self-compassion and reactions to unpleasant self-relevant events: The implications of treating oneself kindly. *Journal of Personality and Social Psychology*, *92*, 887–904.

Minuchen, S., Lee, W. Y., & Simon, G. M. (2006). *Mastering family therapy: Journeys of growth and transformation* (2nd ed.). Hoboken, NJ: Wiley.

Neff, K. D. (2003). The development and validation of a scale to measure self-compassion. *Self and Identity*, *2*, 223–250.

Neff, K. D., Hsieh, Y. P., & Dijitterat, K. (2005). Self-compassion, achievement goals and coping with academic failure. *Self and Identity*, *4*, 263–287.

Seligman, M. E. (1995). *The optimistic child*. Boston, MA: Houghton Mifflin.

Shapiro, S. L., Brown, K. W., & Biegel, G. M. (2007). Teaching self-care to caregivers: Effects of mindfulness-based stress reduction on the mental health of therapists in training. *Training and Education in Professional Psychology*, *1*(2), 105–115.

Shapiro, S. L., Astin, J. A., Bishop, S. R., & Cordova, M. (2007). Mindfulness-based stress reduction for health care professionals: Results from a randomized trial. *International Journal of Stress Management*, *12*(2), 164–176.

Skovholt, T. M., & Ronnestad, M. H. (2003). Struggles of the novice counselor and therapist. *Journal of Career Development*, *30*(1), 45–58.

# CHAPTER 11

# RECONNECTING WITH THE MOTIVATION TO BECOME A CLINICIAN

Bob Gillespie and Julia O'Reilly

## Introduction

This chapter will present a five-part, one-hour self-awareness exercise integrating mindfulness practice (Kabat-Zinn, 1990) and contemplative dialogue featuring questions drawn from narrative therapy (Madsen, 2007). Mindfulness practice cultivates an open space for contemplation of many of the taken-for-granted aspects of being a clinician. Questions drawn from narrative therapy are introduced as a method of inquiry to reflect on clinicians' motivations to enter the field of mental health. This exercise reconnects clinicians with their original motivation to become clinicians and serves as a meaningful compass on their professional journey.

## Rationale

One powerful tool for cultivating self-awareness is the practice of mindfulness. A secular, experiential approach to regulating attention, *mindfulness* is an intentional way of directly connecting to the present moment with an attitude of nonjudgment, receptivity, and curiosity (Kabat-Zinn, 1990). Clinical training programs are beginning to integrate mindfulness practice into their curricula as a method of developing therapeutic presence and strengthening trainees' abilities to nurture therapeutic relationships (Gehart & McCollum, 2008). In addition, preliminary research suggests some positive outcomes for clinicians who practice mindfulness (compared to those who do not). These outcomes include better therapeutic outcomes, increased empathy, and reduced burnout and anxiety (Grepmair et al., 2007; Krasner et al., 2009).

The journey of a mental health professional can sometimes obscure and marginalize the valuable resources and personal experiences that all clinicians have brought to the field. For some trainees, the pace and rigor of an academic training program may be overwhelming with the breadth of clinical models, ethics, and professional expectations. Beginning clinicians can place tremendous pressure on themselves to generate client progress immediately, causing them to embark on a fruitless chase to find the magic intervention that solves a client's problem on the spot. As a result of their striving to appear competent, many trainees carefully hide their feelings of inadequacy and neglect their primary reason for entering the field of mental health. Experienced clinicians can also fall prey to the assembly-line demands of meeting monthly clinical quotas. These challenging financial and organizational concerns can disconnect clinicians from sustaining practices, causing them to lose touch with their motivation to become clinicians. This exercise seeks to reconnect clinicians with their original motivation for entering the mental health field and to provide a deepened sense of purpose for their clinical practice.

Questions drawn from narrative therapy offer an effective means for clinicians to reflect on their professional identity (White, 1997). Narrative therapy emphasizes how identity is constantly evolving and constructed through social interactions (Freedman & Combs, 1996).

In the instructions presented as follows, clinicians are asked to both identify their motivation to become clinicians and contemplate the meaning of this development in their lives. Specifically in the *mindful dyad dialogue* section, a type of narrative therapy question called an *externalizing question* is used. These externalizing questions feature a shift in language that portrays the quality of Motivation (signified by a capital letter) as a distinct and separate entity. This shift provides an opening for clinicians to explicitly reflect on their ongoing relationship with Motivation and trace its development over time. By helping clinicians inquire into their original motivation to become clinicians, externalizing questions increase the possibility of intentionally including this Motivation in their present work and expanding it into their future work.

# Activity Instructions

The following activity instructions are directed to a supervisor for leading a group supervision exercise with either beginning or experienced clinicians. Prior to guiding the activity, the supervisor must take the time to personally develop an intimate connection to the mindfulness practice. Neither the supervisor nor the activity participants need any prior knowledge of narrative therapy in order to engage with the questions in the activity.

The group supervisor opens this one-hour exercise by stating that the daily stress and pressure of clinicians' professional lives can obscure their original motivation to be clinicians. To help participants slow down and shift from their autopilot mode of being busy, the supervisor introduces the practice of mindfulness as a guiding thread throughout the exercise, consistently providing participants with reminders to return to direct sensory experience. The supervisor may state the following as an orientation to mindfulness:

> *Mindfulness practice is a way of making friends with ourselves, a way of becoming familiar with who we are. It is not about trying to rid ourselves of qualities or experiences we wish were not there, nor is it an attempt to reach some special, relaxed state of nonthought. Mindfulness is simply being present with our experience with an attitude of receptivity and acceptance.*

## Opening Mindfulness Practice

To begin, the supervisor guides participants in a 5- to 10-minute awareness of breathing mindfulness practice to establish a foundation of being present (see instructions later). Ringing meditation bells may be used to signal the beginning and ending of formal practice sessions as well as transitions throughout the exercise. The supervisor may also inquire about any previous mindfulness experience in the group and tailor the practice to meet the specific needs of the participants. When facilitating mindfulness practice and narrative inquiry, the supervisor should frequently and consistently check in with participants about their experience at each stage of the exercise. The supervisor may use the following *awareness of breathing* mindfulness meditation instructions as a guide to leading the participants:

- **Posture.** In a chair, take an upright, dignified posture with a strong back and a relaxed, open front. Adopt an intentional posture that communicates to your mind that you are practicing being awake. Hands can rest gently on your thighs or your lap, and feet can be placed flat on the floor. Close your eyes or gaze softly on the ground about six feet in front of you. Notice any unnecessary effort in the body—especially in the shoulders, neck, jaw, or lower back—and remind yourself to feel as comfortable and at ease as is possible for you.

- **Breath.** Now, become aware that you are breathing and investigate with curiosity where you feel the breath most vividly in your body—potential areas include the nostrils, the chest, or the abdomen. Choose to rest your attention in one part of the body and feel the movement of the breath there. Attend to when you are breathing in and when you are breathing out, noticing the pause between each cycle of the breath. Allow the breath to breathe itself.

- **Coming back.** Whenever you notice that your attention has wandered and is no longer on the breath, gently but firmly escort your attention back to the breath. This is the key moment. *Having thoughts* is not a sign that you are not doing it right; in fact, the simple act of returning over and over again to the breath is the practice. You may notice a waterfall of thoughts or you may feel very relaxed. Either outcome is okay, because you are not trying to achieve any ideal state. Keep coming back to feeling the breath in the body, resting your attention, breath by breath.

The supervisor needs to be aware that sustained mindfulness practice may occasionally have a temporary destabilizing effect on practitioners. If the awareness of breathing practice feels overwhelming, the object of attention can be shifted to a more distal focus—like the awareness of sounds—or to neutral body sensations such as the soles of the feet or the hands. Other stabilizing practices are opening the eyes, feeling the points of contact of the body with the chair and floor, or shifting attention to the immediate sensory experience in the room.

## Individual Contemplation

The foundation of attention established in the opening mindfulness practice fosters a contemplative environment that promotes insight. Therefore, the supervisor seamlessly transitions the participants from the opening mindfulness practice into the second part of the activity—contemplation—by instructing participants to shift their attention from their breathing to a series of questions that they contemplate in silence. Contemplation is a way of chewing on topics of importance and digesting what they mean to us (Mipham, 2003). To loosen any constraining expectations, the supervisor might also share that while insight and clarity may be the results of the contemplation, confusion or distraction are also acceptable outcomes.

The supervisor reads the following narrative therapy questions (adapted from Madsen, 2007) sequentially, leaving about one minute between each question for silent contemplation (5 minutes for contemplation, 10 minutes for group reflection):

- What does it mean to you to be a clinician?
- What word or phrase would capture the spirit of your decision to train as a clinician?
- As the person you are today, what meaning does this contemplation bring forward for you at this time?

After contemplating this third question, the supervisor signals the end of formal practice (verbally or with meditation bells if available). The supervisor provides some silent transition time (about 30 seconds) and then asks the participants what they noticed during their practice. Together, the participants may reflect on any difficulties or insights that emerged during the contemplation. To nurture the processes of mindfulness and reflection, open spaces of silence during the group dialogue are also included.

## Mindful Dyad Dialogue

Following the group reflection, the practice of mindfulness is then taken a step further and expanded into the interpersonal dimension through mindful dialogue in pairs (20 to 25 minutes). This dyad portion of the exercise is inspired by training exercises from the teacher training curriculum for mindfulness-based stress reduction (Blacker & Stahl, 2008). The dyad provides the opportunity for each participant to express her or his own motivation and to connect with a colleague's motivation. Handouts featuring the narrative therapy externalizing questions (adapted from Madsen, 2007), listed as follows, are passed out to each participant as a reference for the dialogue:

- What specific situations or feelings brought the Motivation to become a clinician into your life?
- How were you able to act on that Motivation to bring yourself to where you are now?
- If you look into your present life as a clinician, where might you find that Motivation still urging you on?
- What does that Motivation look like in your life?
- As you continue on this path as a clinician, what might follow next as you reconnect with this original Motivation to be a clinician?
- What would be the next little step you could take to honor your relationship to this Motivation?

To provide clarity, the supervisor asks for a volunteer and offers a demonstration of the mindful dyad dialogue by giving the following setup instructions:

*This exercise features a unique seating position in which partners sit in chairs next to each other, but face opposite directions (e.g., with partners sitting side by side with one partner's right shoulder next to the other partner's right shoulder). Partners can decide together if they would like the option of interlocking their arms. This shoulder-to-shoulder seating position is a way of creating connection and proximity without the intensity of sustained direct eye contact, allowing you to tune into your experience with more freedom and less distraction. Considering the number of people in the room, you are encouraged to speak softly and deliberately. One benefit of the shoulder-to-shoulder seating position is the close proximity of the speaker's voice to the listener's ear.*

*During the mindful dyad dialogue, there will be two roles—a giver of questions and a receiver of questions. We will switch roles halfway through the exercise, so each of you will have about 10 minutes to experience each role. A brief awareness of breathing practice will follow each transition. On the handout, there is a list of six externalizing questions drawn from narrative therapy that can be used as a method of mindful inquiry.*

*The giver of questions asks her or his partner one of the questions and then is a witness—being mindful of sounds, body sensations, thoughts, and emotions. Listening is an embodied mindfulness practice, and returning to the sound of your partner's voice is a way of being present. Each time the receiver of questions finishes answering a question, no additional response is offered from the giver except for saying, "Thank you." When to ask the questions, how long to pause, and whether to ask a question again are up to the person in the giver role. You may not get through all the questions, and you may decide to repeat one question a few times. Allow the wisdom of the present moment to guide you.*

*The receiver of questions will be answering the questions from the giver. The practice of mindfulness of speech is knowing what you are saying as you are saying it and listening to yourself speaking. You may pause as much as you feel is necessary to stay embodied in your experience as you speak. The receiver also has the option to answer with "I don't know," "Pass," "I'm not sure," or "Could you please repeat the question?"*

After offering these instructions, the supervisor then briefly demonstrates the exercise by being the receiver of questions while the partner asks the supervisor a few questions from the handout. It is very important that the supervisor models mindfulness of speech, pauses frequently, and provides genuine and personal answers. Once the demonstration is complete (about 5 minutes), the supervisor determines if the participants have any questions, asks them to find a partner using only minimal speech, and requests that the pairs arrange themselves into the shoulder-to-shoulder seating position. If there is an odd number of participants, the supervisor can also function as a partner.

To begin the mindful dyad dialogue, the supervisor guides the participants through a brief awareness of breathing mindfulness practice (like the opening mindfulness practice) lasting 30 seconds to 1 minute and then signals that participants may begin the dialogue. The supervisor is responsible for timekeeping and also signals the participants to exchange roles at the halfway point of the exercise. In our experience, 10 minutes is an effective amount of time to experience each role. To help participants pause and cultivate a sense of presence during points of transition, the supervisor also guides a brief awareness of breathing practice at the halfway point and conclusion of the dyad practice.

## Group Reflection

Following the mindful dyad dialogue, the entire group gathers to discuss this training experience and to process any resonances, surprises, or challenges (5 to 10 minutes). This group reflection is a critical feedback loop and also helps the participants voice their takeaways from the exercise. The narrative therapy questions listed as follows (adapted from Madsen, 2007) may be used to facilitate group reflection:

- What from this exercise captured your attention?
- What images were evoked in the process?
- What insights from this exercise do you want to carry back into your own work?

The closing mindfulness practice is a bookend to the opening practice and reinforces the importance of being present (3 to 5 minutes). It is an opportunity for participants to integrate their experiences and set their intentions moving forward as clinicians.

# Example

This exercise was incorporated into group supervision for a master's-level clinical training program. Nine students and recent graduates participated in the exercise outlined previously and shared their experiences in the final group discussion. The following three key themes emerged from the participants: compassion for self and others, the pressure of measuring up, and the value of mindfulness.

Many of the participants shared that their motivation to become clinicians was inspired by their efforts to find meaning in their own suffering. One student tearfully expressed how his own recovery propelled him to help others. The surfacing of this vulnerability from their personal lives led to group expressions of compassion for themselves, their fellow students, and their clients. The participants' feeling of shared humanity and their ability to connect to clients' suffering through their own personal suffering demonstrated the cultivation of compassion.

The participants articulated that a common obstacle to connecting with this compassion and motivation was the pressure of trying to measure up to some ideal standard of the perfect clinician. Through the dyads and group reflection, participants began to identify their shared struggle of "doing too much" in the hopes of appearing competent to clients, colleagues, and supervisors. A poignant truth dawned for the participants: Everyone else does not have it all together either.

The value of mindfulness practice resonated as a potential antidote to this self-doubt by offering the participants the possibility of connecting with and trusting their experience. Several members confessed how the mindfulness practice was challenging but that the sustained practice during the exercise provided opportunities to progressively settle into their present experience. One student remarked, "At first, staying with my breath felt impossible. But as we continued practicing, I began to feel more present and alive!" In addition, several participants voiced that the mindful dyad dialogue was the highlight of the exercise because they experienced an expanded sense of being present while interacting with another person.

# Measuring Progress

Signs of increased self-awareness in clinicians include experiencing a greater sense of purpose in their clinical work and feeling more present in their daily activities. Activities such as writing a letter to themselves as a clinician or journaling with the narrative therapy questions in this exercise can provide tangible documents that facilitate an ongoing connection with their motivation to become clinicians. A contemplative environment can be fostered through opening and closing mindfulness practices in group supervision, weekly mindfulness practice groups, or brief mindfulness practices before and/or after clinical sessions. The Five Facet Mindfulness Questionnaire (Baer, Smith, Hopkins, Krietemeyer, & Toney, 2006) is a well-researched instrument that can be used to assess clinicians' mindfulness over time through 39 self-report items that measure five different mindfulness skills: observing, describing, acting with awareness, nonreactivity to inner experience, and nonjudging of inner experience.

# Conclusion

This group supervision exercise integrating mindfulness practice and narrative therapy questions has been effectively adapted for experienced clinicians, for individual supervision, and for focusing on positive clinical experiences. Mindfulness practice and narrative inquiry are complementary paths offering insights into how clinicians relate to their experiences as professionals and human beings (Gehart & Pare, 2008). Connecting with their original motivation to become clinicians provides sustenance in challenging clinical environments and clarifies their primary purpose for meeting with clients. Our hope is that this exercise benefits all clinicians in cultivating a deep, meaningful motivation for their work.

# Additional Resource

Hick, S. F., & Bien, T. (Eds.). (2008). *Mindfulness and the therapeutic relationship.* New York, NY: Guilford Press.

# References

Baer, R. A., Smith, G. T., Hopkins, J., Krietemeyer, J., & Toney, L. (2006). Using self-report assessment methods to explore facets of mindfulness. *Assessment, 13,* 27–45. doi: 10.1177/1073191105283504

Blacker, M., & Stahl, R. (2008, April). *Dying to this moment: Joys and obstacles in the teaching of mindfulness-based interventions.* Presentation at the Sixth Annual International Scientific Conference for Clinicians, Researchers and Educators, The Center for Mindfulness, Health Care, and Society, Worcester, MA.

Freedman, J., & Combs, G. (1996). *Narrative therapy: The social construction of preferred realities.* New York, NY: W. W. Norton.

Gehart, D., & McCollum, E. E. (2008). Inviting therapeutic presence. In S. F. Hick & T. Bien (Eds.), *Mindfulness and the therapeutic relationship* (pp. 176–194). New York, NY: Guilford Press.

Gehart, D. R., & Pare, D. (2008). Suffering and the relationship with the problem in postmodern therapies: A Buddhist re-visioning. *Journal of Family Psychotherapy, 19,* 299–319. doi: 10.1080/08975350802475049

Grepmair, L., Mitterlehner, F., Loew, T., Bachler, E., Rother, W., & Nickel, M. (2007). Promoting mindfulness in psychotherapists in training influences the treatment results of their patients: A randomized, double-blind, controlled study. *Psychotherapy and Psychosomatics, 76,* 332–338. doi: 10.1159/000107560

Kabat-Zinn, J. (1990). *Full catastrophe living: Using the wisdom of your body and mind to face stress, pain and illness.* New York, NY: Delacorte.

Krasner, M. S., Epstein, R. M., Beckman, H., Suchman, A. L., Chapman, B., Mooney, C. J., & Quill, T. E. (2009). Association of an educational program in mindful communication with burnout, empathy, and attitudes among primary care physicians. *Journal of the American Medical Association, 302,* 1284–1293. doi: 10.1001/jama.2009.1384

Madsen, W. C. (2007). *Collaborative therapy with multi-stressed families* (2nd ed.). New York, NY: Guilford Press.

Mipham, S. (2003). *Turning the mind into an ally.* New York, NY: Riverhead Books.

White, M. (1997). *Narratives of therapists' lives.* Adelaide, Australia: Dulwich Centre Publications.

# Chapter 12

# Giving a Voice to Clinicians-in-Training About Their Concerns

Yudum Akyil, Binh Pham, and Norja Cunningham

## Introduction

The Concerns of a Beginning Therapist (COBT) questionnaire is a newly developed tool based on the experiences of three doctoral students and their faculty supervisor. The purpose of this tool is to aid supervisees in gaining awareness of their concerns as beginning clinicians by ranking their clinical skills. This questionnaire is designed to help beginning clinicians generate conversations with their supervisor about their personal concerns in seeing clients. In addition, supervisors will be able to use this questionnaire to track beginning clinicians' progress and development during their supervision sessions. This tool is used as a strength-based intervention to encourage clinicians to explore concerns, to discuss these concerns with supervisors, and to eventually develop self-confidence in providing therapy to clients.

## Rationale

Research shows that new clinicians have high rates of anxiety and depression about being good therapists (Bischoff, 1997; Bischoff, Barton, Thober, & Hawley, 2002). Although many new clinicians recall believing that they were equipped to be therapists, they sometimes feel challenged by not having all the answers when they finally encounter clients. Bischoff (1997) wrote about this process, in which beginning clinicians deal with feelings of inadequacy, calling it the "imposter syndrome," where clinicians believe that clients expect them to be experts, and if they do not have the answers, the clients will find them to be frauds. These beliefs can create high levels of anxiety and doubt, which can inhibit clinicians' ability to communicate concerns to their supervisor. This internal dialogue about clinicians' anxiety and concerns is often not addressed in supervision sessions in a formal manner and is likely to create feelings of shame; therefore, clinicians are less likely to discuss these issues with their supervisor.

Qualitative research studies of novice marriage and family therapy (MFT) students revealed that the student clinicians felt a lack of self-confidence during their first three months of seeing clients (Bischoff, 1997; Bischoff et al., 2002). They reported feeling inadequate in the therapy room when interventions did not work, which led to mild to severe somatic symptoms (Bischoff, 1997; Bischoff et al., 2002). In the first four to eight weeks of clinical contact, clinicians reported crying spells, sleeplessness, decreased appetite, and gastrointestinal problems (Bischoff, 1997). Although there is a dearth of studies of clinicians from other cultures, it is reasonable to suggest that this experience is nearly universal.

In the literature, the origins of clinicians' concerns and anxiety have been explored using family genograms (McGoldrick, Gerson, & Petry, 2008), cultural genograms (Hardy & Laszloffy, 1995), and the person-of-the therapist model (Aponte, 1982). The use of genograms has helped beginning clinicians explore themes in their family of origin. Supervisors are able to assist novice clinicians to be aware of triggers, unresolved issues in the family, beliefs and values, and areas of growth and resiliency in clinicians' families (Hardy & Laszloffy, 1995; McGoldrick et al., 2008).

The person-of-the-therapist model is utilized for supervisors and clinicians to understand the origins of clinicians' concerns and anxieties by asking new clinicians to explore family-of-origin patterns, internal dialogues, and personal experiences that may influence their work as clinicians (Aponte, 1982).

As a supplement to these other assessment and intervention approaches, the COBT questionnaire was developed to help beginning clinicians increase their level of understanding of the specific nature of their concerns about their clinical skills. The majority of clinical programs screen clinical students for quality of self-reflection and the ability to conceptualize client cases. However, very few attempt to assess and address the level of concern that student clinicians have about doing therapy. This is unfortunate, because understanding their concerns and allowing student clinicians to voice them through the supervisor–clinician relationship enhances the relationship, as well as the overall experience for the student clinicians (Murphy & Wright, 2005). Individual supervision also mitigates compassion fatigue, which clinicians are more susceptible to in the first year of clinical work (Figley, 2002).

This tool may also reduce the incidence of supervisors abusing their power. Allowing student clinicians space to share their concerns intrinsically tells them their thoughts matter. This collaborative approach to supervision is more respectful and relationally astute (Murphy & Wright, 2005). It also allows the student clinicians to choose what to disclose to their supervisors. Thus, the supervisors are not violating any boundaries associated with the power they hold, and the student clinicians are given power over their own thoughts, feelings, and self-disclosures (Murphy & Wright, 2005).

# Activity Instructions

Because the relationship between the supervisor and the clinician is a necessary component of this activity, instructions are directed to the supervisors. The instructions lay out how supervisors are to deliver the COBT questionnaire. Ideally, the COBT questionnaire (see Table 12.1) is assigned to first-semester master's-level MFT students to initiate conversations regarding primary concerns and anxieties as beginning clinicians. It is a flexible tool that can be adapted to different models of supervision.

The initial exercise associated with the COBT questionnaire has the following steps:

1. The supervisor will administer this questionnaire to supervisees as a group. Supervisees will rate the 15 items from 1 (not a concern) to 5 (a big concern) and rank order their top five concerns. They can add any concerns that were not listed in the COBT questionnaire.

2. The student clinicians will share their top five concerns with their supervision group and tell a personal family story that relates to one of those concerns.

**Table 12.1 Concerns of a Beginning Therapist Questionnaire**

|  | No Concern |  |  |  | Big Concern |
| --- | --- | --- | --- | --- | --- |
| Being ineffective | 1 | 2 | 3 | 4 | 5 |
| Having difficulty with joining | 1 | 2 | 3 | 4 | 5 |
| Being unable to deal with clients' emotions | 1 | 2 | 3 | 4 | 5 |
| Not knowing the next step | 1 | 2 | 3 | 4 | 5 |
| Feeling closer to one member of the family | 1 | 2 | 3 | 4 | 5 |
| Paperwork | 1 | 2 | 3 | 4 | 5 |
| Not knowing how to implement a model | 1 | 2 | 3 | 4 | 5 |
| Being unable to control the room | 1 | 2 | 3 | 4 | 5 |
| Being unable to deal with own emotions | 1 | 2 | 3 | 4 | 5 |
| Being self-conscious | 1 | 2 | 3 | 4 | 5 |
| Making a mistake | 1 | 2 | 3 | 4 | 5 |
| Being unable to decide which model to use | 1 | 2 | 3 | 4 | 5 |
| Feeling incompetent | 1 | 2 | 3 | 4 | 5 |
| Setting too-high expectations for myself | 1 | 2 | 3 | 4 | 5 |
| Not being able to deal with crisis situations | 1 | 2 | 3 | 4 | 5 |

Example 75

3. After ranking the concerns and having the class discussion, the supervisees will reframe their top five concerns in a positive manner to come up with their learning objectives. For example, a concern such as "not knowing the next step" could be changed to an objective of "finding effective questions."

4. It is a good idea for supervisors to talk over the ratings in individual meetings with supervisees. Supervisees are also instructed to make one- to two-page weekly reflective journal entries. These journal entries will allow trainees to reflect on their experiences in sessions or classes. The journal entries will be shared in individual supervision with their supervisors. These journals will assist the supervisor and supervisee in tracking the internal processes of student clinicians' growth and development.

5. Supervisees will use their list of concerns (from step 3) as a reference for themselves in individual supervision and for each other in group supervision. For example, when observing a classmate's therapy session, trainees can give feedback referring back to the student clinician's top-rated concerns.

6. At the end of the semester, supervisees will rescore themselves, talk about their improvements or areas of growth, and give each other feedback regarding their progress. Finally, they can meet with their supervisor to evaluate their progress.

# Example

This tool was used with first-year master's-level MFT students in both the United States and Turkey. The trainees filled out the COBT questionnaire in the first class (e.g., pre-practicum 110 or professional seminar 110 course) before they started seeing clients in the therapy room. Both courses started with class discussions and involved role-plays, which helped prepare students to provide therapy to clients. The supervisor introduced this tool in the first class and continued using it in individual and group supervision sessions. The supervisor asked the student clinicians whether they felt different in terms of their top concerns after role-playing and later on after their real sessions. Using the COBT, the student clinicians also gave feedback to each other about their progress. Lastly, the supervisor used the COBT to respond to student clinicians' reflective journals, which reflected on their experiences in their sessions or classes. Using the COBT questionnaire, the supervisor was able to refer to the student clinicians' concerns and objectives, making it easier to focus on certain areas that are crucial for the student clinicians' development.

Throughout the COBT questionnaire, the supervisees were able to think about each session and determine the ranking of their concerns on the questionnaire. The supervisees were assigned to find evidence for and against specific dimensions highlighted in the COBT questionnaire. When they did not come up with any examples for progress, the classmates or supervisor recalled related incidents from an observed therapy session. During the last class, the supervisees rescored their concerns and saw significant changes. They reflected on their progress and areas of growth. One student said, "I realized where I improved, and this relaxed me. I also faced my ongoing worries and realized what areas I need to focus on." Another student said, "When I look back, I see myself as much more effective and confident. I know I still need to improve as a clinician. Filling out this form has led me to look closely to my development as a therapist and gives me hope for the future."

In addition to assessing therapy outcomes, this tool gave the student clinicians an outline to help them form their learning objectives for the semester. The process of thinking about where they wanted to see themselves at the end of the semester helped them to identify and verbalize their strengths and areas of growth. Discussions regarding each item helped to deconstruct their concerns and goals.

Another example of how to use the COBT questionnaire is to brainstorm the multiple perspectives that can be reflected in answering the questionnaire. For example, while one of the common goals was "being an effective clinician," prior to the supervision group discussion, all of the supervisees had only a vague idea about what "effective" meant. The COBT questionnaire helped open discussions about multiple interpretations of effectiveness. For some, it meant the clients verbalize they benefited from therapy, and for others it meant making the clients happy. This illumination gave trainees an opportunity to discuss how the concept of "effectiveness" is different for each clinician, for each member in the client's family, and for the client's family as a whole unit. The supervisor also discussed situations in which effectiveness is unknown, because of no-shows or premature terminations. This supervisor normalized the beginning clinicians' reactions to no-shows or premature terminations by introducing the subject prior to them seeing clients.

In other instances, delicate issues were brought up in group supervision discussions, such as being too concerned about physical appearance or trying to be the superhero for the client. One student clinician shared his personal family story regarding his role of saving others in his family, and he was concerned about how this would play out in his clinical work. In group supervision session, his colleagues (other beginning clinicians) gave him insightful feedback. This sharing enhanced the group's cohesion and opened up space for others who may have been hesitant to share family stories in group supervision discussions before this session.

The COBT activity also led a beginning clinician group to share a concern about making mistakes when conducting the initial assessment with clients. Trainees were anxious about what to do next in generating a hypothesis based on this initial assessment. In addressing this concern, this supervisor helped student clinicians recognize the importance of this first session in the therapeutic relationship and its purpose in gaining clients' trust and building rapport. As this group began to accrue more hours of therapy experience, they felt more relaxed about the initial assessment phase and began to pay attention to "being there" with their clients. One student said, "Once I started to see clients, I realized that it is more important to be able to build the alliance with the client and create motivation and hope in them rather than focusing solely on which model to implement."

# Measuring Progress

The goal of the COBT tool is to increase student clinicians' openness in discussing their concerns about being new clinicians, which promotes reflection, sharing, and normalization—all important components of person-of-the-therapist work. This tool may enhance the supervisees' self-awareness and acceptance as beginning clinicians, which would eventually reflect on their performance as clinicians. Thus, the effects of this tool on supervisees can be measured by assessing their progress as effective clinicians. Supervisors may evaluate the difference between student clinicians' pre-semester and post-semester concerns and have a discussion about the progress. The supervisor may also use the Basic Skills Evaluation tool (Nelson & Johnson, 1999) to evaluate supervisees' progress throughout the semester. Moreover, the student clinicians' own reflections regarding the impact of this tool on their therapeutic competence would provide important data to measure their progress.

Significant themes emerging from student clinicians' responses may also be used as feedback for the supervisors or the program to evaluate their effectiveness in terms of different MFT competencies. In our study, these supervisors saw significant changes in student clinicians' ability to manage their own emotional state (i.e., anxiety, self-doubt). For example, using the COBT tool, the supervisor realized that the student clinicians' concerns regarding the executive components of therapy, such as controlling the room or completing paperwork, decreased once they started to see clients. In contrast, some student clinicians did not experience any improvement in conceptualizing and implementing family models during their first semester. This supervisor utilized the COBT tool in assessing a clinician's anxiety and concern about implementation of a specific family therapy model, and focused on this student clinician's implementation of the model for the next three semesters through role-plays, in session feedback, and discussion after sessions. Although this would be a general developmental issue, the supervisor used this theme as feedback and shared it with her colleagues and program as a way to meet individual student clinicians' needs and help them reach their potential.

# Conclusion

Beginning clinicians likely will have concerns before seeing clients for the first time, which diminish with more experience. Many clinicians are not given the opportunity to reflect on their clinical process and development. This tool encourages clinicians to become more aware of their learning process and person-of-the-therapist development, recognize the meaning of challenges, accept their strengths and areas of growth, find ways to reduce their anxiety related to their concerns, and observe their progress as a beginning clinician. Moreover, using this tool aids supervisors to gain a better understanding of their supervisees' concerns. Isomorphically, supervisees who are in tune with their supervisors will be able to be more in tune with their clients.

# Additional Resources

Gehart, D. (2013). *Mastering competencies in family therapy: A practical approach to therapy and clinical case documentation* (2nd ed.). Springer Grover, CA: Brooks/Cole.

Kottler, J. (2010). *On being a therapist* (2nd ed.). San Francisco, CA: Jossey-Bass.

Kottler, J. A. (2011). *The therapist's workbook: Self-assessment, self-care, and self-improvement exercises for mental health professionals* (2nd ed.). New York, NY: Jossey-Bass.

Patterson, J., Williams, L., Edwards, T., & Charnow, L. (2009). *Essential skills in family therapy* (2nd ed.). New York, NY: Guilford Press.

# References

Aponte, H. J. (1982). The person of the clinician: The cornerstone of therapy. *Family Therapy Networker, 46*, 19–21.

Bischoff, R. (1997). Themes in clinician development during the first three months of clinical experience. *Contemporary Family Therapy, 19*(4), 563–580.

Bischoff, R., Barton, M., Thober, J., & Hawley, R. (2002). Events and experiences impacting the development of clinical self confidence: A study of the first year of client contact. *Journal of Marital Family Therapy, 28*(3), 371–382.

Figley, C. R. (2002). *Treating compassion fatigue*. New York, NY: Brunner-Routledge.

Hardy, K., & Laszloffy, T. (1995). The cultural genogram: Key to training culturally competent family clinicians. *Journal of Marriage and Family Counseling, 21*(3), 227–237.

McGoldrick, M., Gerson, R., & Petry, S. (2008). *Genograms: Assessment and intervention* (3rd ed.). New York, NY, US: W. W. Norton & Co.

Murphy, M. J., & Wright, D. W. (2005). Supervisees' perspectives of power use in supervision. *Journal of Marital and Family Therapy, 31*, 283–295.

Nelson, T. S., & Johnson, L. N. (1999). The basic skills evaluation device. *Journal of Marital and Family Therapy, 25*(1), 15–30.

# CHAPTER 13

# A New Experience With the Family of Origin

Sean D. Davis and Armando Gonzalez-Cort

## Introduction

The family-of-origin interview activity has several key purposes. First, it can expose clinicians to Bowen's concept of differentiation experientially when they explore their own family of origin issues (Anonymous, 1972). Second, it can help clinicians better understand what types of individuals or family interactions might trigger emotional responses, how they typically respond to these triggers, and what clinical implications this reactivity may have. Third, through the activity, clinicians begin experiencing and processing these triggers *before* they are surprised by them in the therapy room. Fourth, it helps increase awareness of any cultural values that may differ from their own family values. Finally, the activity pushes clinicians to find out more about their own families, which allows for more empathy for their clients when they are asked to discuss sensitive family matters in therapy.

## Rationale

Given that the clinician's own level of emotional stability is a key element of successful therapy (Blow, Sprenkle, & Davis, 2007), it is important to consider that clinicians will likely provide services to clients who bear similarities to the therapist's own family members or other significant parties. When faced with this type of client or client system, clinicians may automatically slip back to previously learned ways of interacting, which may not be therapeutic. The less aware clinicians are of these personal triggers, the more likely it is that their therapeutic maneuverability will be constrained by these previously learned responses, and the therapeutic process could suffer as a result.

Kerr and Bowen (1988) described this type of clinician as having low differentiation from his or her family of origin. *Differentiation* refers to the ability to disentangle thinking and feeling states and consciously balance both when deciding how to respond in an anxiety-provoking situation. Clinicians with poorer differentiation often will limit their clinical repertoire to whatever does not make anyone in the room (including themselves) anxious and, consequently, the core issues—those driving the client's anxiety—will not be addressed fully. As clinicians become more differentiated, they are better able to make clear, intentional choices in the presence of intense emotions—their own and those of clients (Davis, 2005).

Because theories or techniques are ineffective if a clinician is too anxious to be able to apply them at the right moment, Bowen considered a well-differentiated clinician to be the most important predictor of successful therapy (Kerr & Bowen, 1988). Consequently, a central training goal is to help a clinician-in-training to become aware of and increase his or her level of differentiation. A person's baseline level of differentiation is acquired in his or her family of origin, so direct interaction with his or her own family is the most productive place to begin the journey of increasing differentiation, as described in the following activity.

# Activity Instructions

This activity is designed to help clinicians begin the process of purposefully increasing differentiation. It is typically assigned during the first semester of master's-level coursework in the interviewing skills or pre-practicum courses, although it can be adapted to use for clinicians of any professional orientation and developmental level. However, while portions of the activity may be undertaken on a self-assigned basis, much of the growth in this activity comes when clinicians are working under the guidance of an experienced supervisor; these instructions, therefore, are directed specifically to the activity supervisor.

Prior to the activity, the clinician should be familiar with the major concepts related to the activity, including family-of-origin work, family genograms, differentiation, and basic interviewing skills. When assigning the activity, the supervisor should provide a brief explanation of the rationale for the assignment. Afterward, clinicians are instructed to interview each family member and ask the following three questions:

1. If our family went to counseling, what would it be for?

2. In what ways might our family be different if counseling were successful?

3. In what ways might our family be the same if counseling were successful?

These three questions are used to start the interview, and clinicians are encouraged to use basic interviewing skills to expand each interview as it unfolds. "Family member" includes all members of a clinician's biological family, as well as any other individuals he or she considers to be "family." Clinicians can only omit a family member if interviewing him or her would put anyone at risk of physical or emotional harm (e.g., an estranged or abusive parent), if they are unreachable (e.g., in the military or incarcerated), if the clinician does not consider anyone "family" (e.g., being raised in the foster care system), or if cultural norms would preclude such an interview. In these instances, clinicians should be given an alternative assignment that is tailored to their unique situation and designed to achieve the same objectives, such as visualizing the interview or conducting the interview with each family member imaginarily placed in an empty chair.

In order to get the most from this experience, interviews should be conducted in person, over the telephone, or through a video calling platform such as Skype. Written interviews through mail or e-mail are discouraged, as the intensity of the contact and subsequent personal insights are usually weaker.

Student clinicians' personal responses are the central focus of this assignment, rather than their family members' responses to their questions. During and after the interview, student clinicians are encouraged to notice and document their emotional, behavioral, and cognitive responses. Many clinicians-in-training are understandably reluctant to complete this very personal assignment. Instructors should explain that this assignment is *designed* to raise their anxiety; the objectives of the assignment could not be met otherwise. It is one thing to discuss differentiation in the abstract, but it is another to experience it directly with one's own family. Once clinicians understand the rationale behind this assignment, most agree to participate.

Some family members express strong reservations about participating in the assignment. Clinicians are encouraged to explain that aliases will be used in the paper, nonessential identifying information will be changed, and all papers are held in strict confidence and are returned to the student clinicians in person as soon as possible. If a family member is still reluctant to participate, clinicians are not required to share that family member's responses in the paper. If the family member is still reluctant, the clinician does not have to interview that person because it would be unfair to penalize the clinician for something outside of his or her control.

Once they have completed the interviews and documented their responses, clinicians are required to write a minimum 12-page paper addressing the following areas:

- *Genogram/Family Background* (two-page minimum). The purpose of this section is to orient the supervisor to who is in the clinicians' families. Clinicians should discuss the following points:

Example                                                                                          81

- What are the names (pseudonyms) and ages of your family members?
- What are major family themes?
- What was it like for you to grow up in this family?
- Is there any other information the supervisor should know in order to understand family interview responses?

   Also, note that this genogram should only go back one generation in order to allow clinicians to adequately discuss their interview experience without the paper becoming too lengthy.

- *Family Interview Responses* (two-page minimum). Clinicians should list each family member's responses to the interview questions. Responses do not have to be verbatim; they can be summarized. Following this, clinicians should present their own responses to the questions in this section. Although clinicians are not required to share their responses with family if they do not wish, they are required to write about the process that led to that decision.

- *Your Reaction* (four-page minimum). Clinicians should discuss the emotional, cognitive, and behavioral reactions they had to the interviews. Clinicians should explore questions such as:

  - What were my fears as I prepared for these interviews?
  - To whom did I most, and least, want to talk?
  - Was I tempted to not ask some family members certain questions that I asked others? If so, why? Which responses surprised me?
  - What, if anything, did I learn about my family? How did I handle that information?
  - What did I find myself thinking and feeling during the interview?
  - Did I notice myself doing anything out of the ordinary during the interview (e.g., wanting to leave, laughing more than usual, fidgeting)? If so, what might that say about me in that situation?
  - With which family members did I feel most/least comfortable? Why? What might that say about specific clients I may see in a helping situation and how I experience them during therapeutic encounters?

- *Clinical Implications* (four-page minimum). Clinicians should discuss the implications of the insights gained in the reaction section for their own clinical work—both strengths and weaknesses. Clinicians should consider discussing topics such as:

  - What types of clients might the clinician be good at working with?
  - What attributes did the clinician develop in his or her family that may be clinically beneficial?
  - Did certain types of individuals invite certain responses, and what implications does that have for the clinician? (For example, perhaps a clinician learned from the interview that he or she tends to shut down around aggressive people. What impact might that have on the clinician's therapy with an aggressive client? Or perhaps the clinician really wanted the approval of a disapproving family member, so the clinician downplayed this project when interviewing him or her. How might therapy be different if the clinician has a client who is similar to that family member?)

# Example

One clinician describes his story as follows, after completing this activity with his own family:

*Without hesitation, I (AGC) can say that the first year of my master's program in marriage and family therapy yielded the greatest opportunities for me to gain a deeper level of self-awareness. Conducting the family interviews and developing my family's genogram for this assignment shifted so much for me. Throughout the interviews, pieces of context emerged that I previously never imagined existed, while the genogram showed me patterns and themes within my family that I had never seen before.*

*Growing up as an only child with my mother created many opportunities for us to engage in deep, reflective conversations about my family's past. In many ways, being open and transparent has been a significant family value for my mom and me, but something about approaching this conversation from within the framework of this assignment created an entirely different type of dialogue for us. My mother's transparency helped to move our interview into some profoundly deep and raw areas, in which she talked candidly about the experiences she had had as a single parent and mother. I found myself more willing to ask questions that I might not otherwise have asked, and I was very aware of my own emotional responses while processing the personal information she shared. What emerged were stories that I had never heard and parts of our family history that I had never imagined.*

*I can recall hanging up the telephone that evening in a minor state of shock and awe—blown away by all of the information that had emerged. I knew then that this conversation was a major game changer for how I made sense of my own family; consequently, this shift has had a profound impact on my own sense of self. In processing this information, I began to see the origins of pieces of myself that had developed in both positive and negative ways. I realized that many of my refined listening skills and deeper curiosity for the evolution of relationships came from growing up around more adults than children in my childhood. While this likely helped to create some personal assets for my career as a clinician, it also meant that I might need to pay closer attention to the developmental expectations I have for children and parents that I encounter in sessions. Having this new insight, which in some ways was overwhelming to me, gave me a strange sense of peace because I developed a deeper understanding of myself. However, this conversation with my mother was just the beginning.*

*While not required, I was so intrigued by what I was learning that I decided to also interview my extended family. The next day I found myself seated next to my maternal grandmother on her couch, scribbling notes in a flurry as she rattled off stories about her upbringing. What emerged was both startling and fascinating at the same time. I began to look at my grandmother in a whole new light. I no longer just saw the maternal matriarch of my mother's family—I began to see a woman with more dimensions than I ever knew existed. Moreover, I began to see just how many similarities there were between my mother's and grandmother's lives. One by one, conversations continued to unfold with my maternal grandfather, cousins, and a family friend whom I had considered to be a father figure to me.*

*This activity helped me develop a greater sense of compassion and understanding for each of my family members. Through the process of personal reflection, I started to see how family dynamics and history contributed to the development of particular intergenerational themes and realized the larger context behind the important values my family has fought to uphold. Once I developed this insight, I was better able to understand the impact they had on my own developing identity. I also realized that what I did not know was just as telling as what I had discovered.*

*Even after completing this assignment, the momentum to discover more about my family remained. This assignment clarified just how little I knew about my father's side of the family. My father was born and raised in Mexico and lived in the United States only briefly, returning to Mexico after my parents' divorce when I was just three years old. Before he passed away, my father made many efforts to help me get to know his side of the family. Yet, for years after his death, I made little effort to go back to Mexico and connect with his family members. Sometime during this assignment, I began to realize that what I was really avoiding was not simply connecting with my father's family but continuing my healing from my father's passing. Reconnecting with his family would not only provide me with an opportunity to get to know this part of my family but also an opportunity to continue to heal as his son.*

*Months after the assignment, I traveled to Mexico for my paternal grandmother's eightieth birthday celebration and experienced a trip that truly changed my life. Not surprisingly, the conversations that had begun with my mother's side of the family eventually spilled over to conversations*

*I had with the uncles, aunts, cousins, and my grandmother on my father's side. When it was time to head home from my trip, I stepped onto the plane a changed man. The tales exchanged during those talks with my father's family taught me so much about my father and his family—something that I thought I would never have. For the first time in my life, I felt connected to my own Mexican heritage and finally felt complete.*

*Prior to this assignment, I worried that not growing up in a traditional nuclear household might imply that I would have trouble recognizing ideal family structures. I now realize that every set of adverse circumstances presents an opportunity to put a family's resourcefulness to use. For my family, it took a village to raise me. However, not having my father around hardly meant that I would forever remain blind to the qualities that encompassed a good father. Fortunately for me, those qualities came packaged in a close family friend and in my grandfather.*

*I have no doubt that I would not have been so willing to engage in, or even seek out, these conversations with my family members from both sides had it not been for this required assignment. The lessons of self-awareness that I gained from conducting these interviews made me more aware of the pieces of myself that I bring into sessions as a clinician. Taking ownership of these different pieces and the impact they have on therapy has allowed me to take greater responsibility for my work. It also has taught me that even my own personal limitations have a context, and often that context must first be honored before ownership and subsequent efforts to change can be made—a concept that now serves as a key guiding principle in my clinical work.*

*We all have blind spots, areas that trigger more intense emotional responses, but I do not believe these areas constitute our weaknesses. In my eyes, these only become weaknesses when we choose to ignore or bury them rather than to heal from them. Sometimes awareness is the greatest intervention for our clients, and as clinicians we are not immune to this same principle of change. In so many ways, I believe this assignment truly mirrors the journeys we often take with our clients—a journey to discover pieces of ourselves embedded in the histories and stories of those loved ones surrounding us.*

# Measuring Progress

Several quantitative measures of differentiation could be used to chart student clinicians' progress—including Haber's Level of Differentiation of Self Scale (Haber, 1993) and Skowron's Differentiation of Self Inventory (Skowron & Friedlander, 1998), both of which have adequate internal reliability—but qualitative measures may be more appropriate for this activity. Increasing differentiation through self-discovery is a lifelong process, and this assignment can continue to affect student clinicians for a long time after its completion. This is why it is important to make the assignment emotionally intense: The more intense the assignment is, the further its effects will ripple out. Furthermore, student clinicians' progress will be maximized if they continue to be supported in their journeys of self-discovery in supervision and/or mentoring contexts. Supervisors could read the self-reflection paper in order to familiarize themselves with the student clinicians' central areas of strength and areas for growth. Supervisors can help clinicians learn how to untangle themselves from their own personal triggers in the therapy room and use their reactions as therapeutic tools and assets rather than as something to be feared.

It is recommended that supervisors meet with clinicians as needed subsequent to their completing the assignment. Increasing differentiation is a lifelong journey in which this assignment can provide a boost. Continuing supervision can "hold" clinicians in the anxiety created by this assignment, thus further reinforcing gains in differentiation. Supervisors can review major themes uncovered during the interview and discuss how these themes are playing out in therapy and/or with the clinicians' family of origin. As an instructor, I (SDD) have watched hundreds of graduate and undergraduate students complete this exercise. Despite being initially reluctant, most students ultimately share that it was one of the most powerful exercises they have ever completed. Most note that they gained new, freeing insights about their families and that they experienced their own personal awareness and levels of differentiation start to shift. In some cases, students have contacted me years later to share the personal change this assignment initiated.

# Conclusion

Through the course of a clinician's career, it is nearly impossible to predict the variety of different clinical scenarios a clinician might encounter. Yet, one element a clinician can examine and account for are the common responses they have when faced with the relational dynamics within his or her own family of origin. Identifying potential relational or emotional triggers facilitates the development of self-awareness, which then accelerates the development of increased differentiation. By engaging in this assignment, students are provided with an opportunity to develop greater introspection, and they are given the chance to empathize with the challenge that clients face in working toward greater differentiation.

# Additional Resources

Gilbert, R. M. (1992). *Extraordinary relationships: A new way of thinking about human interactions*. New York, NY: Wiley.

Gilbert, R. M. (2006). *The eight concepts of Bowen theory*. Falls Church, VA: Leading Systems Press.

McGoldrick, M., Gerson, R., & Petry, S. (2008). *Genograms: Assessment and intervention* (3rd ed.). New York, NY: W. W. Norton.

# References

Anonymous. (1972). Toward the differentiation of a self in one's own family. In J. Framo (Ed.), *Family interaction* (pp. 111–173). New York, NY: Springer.

Blow, A. J., Sprenkle, D. S., & Davis, S. D. (2007). Is who delivers the treatment more important than the treatment itself?: The role of the therapist in common factors. *Journal of Marital and Family Therapy*, *33*, 298–317.

Davis, S. D. (2005). Beyond technique: An autoethnographic exploration of how I learned to show love towards my father. *The Qualitative Report*, *10*(3), 532–541.

Haber, J. E. (1993). A construct validity study of a differentiation of self scale. *Scholarly Inquiry for Nursing Practice*, *7*, 165–178.

Kerr, M. E., & Bowen, M. (1988). *Family evaluation: The role of the family as an emotional unit that governs individual behavior and development*. New York, NY: W. W. Norton.

Skowron, E. A., & Friedlander, M. L. (1998). The differentiation of self inventory: Development and initial validation. *Journal of Counseling Psychology*, *45*, 235–246.

# CHAPTER 14

# EXPLORING CONFLICT AND ITS IMPORTANCE TO CLINICIAN DEVELOPMENT

Bridget Roberts-Pittman and Anna M. Viviani

## Introduction

Supervision serves as an essential element to clinical training because it serves multiple functions, including providing a safe place for student clinicians to develop professional boundaries and self-awareness. As part of this self-awareness, clinicians must learn to recognize their personal "hot spots," such as how they manage conflict both in their personal and professional lives. All clinicians will deal with conflict at some point in their careers; therefore, it is imperative that they learn to manage conflict as part of their clinical development. Not only is self-awareness necessary for successful conflict resolution, but it is also essential for preventing or resolving countertransference. Conflict and countertransference can occur at any point in a clinician's career, making ongoing self-reflection an essential part of every clinician's wellness toolkit. This chapter uses a genogram and personal reflection exercise specific to conflict to encourage self-reflection and personal growth throughout a clinician's career.

This chapter is designed to start closing a significant gap in the supervision and training literature, in which conflict is addressed sparingly. In more than two decades of literature, only a handful of scholarly works address conflict, focusing specifically on competition and conflict in group supervision (Bogo, Globerman, & Sussman, 2004), conflict resolution and training clinical supervisors (Johnson & Stewart, 2000), using contracts to minimize or avoid potential conflict (Storm, Todd, Sprenkle, & Morgan, 2001), and interpersonal conflict and parallel process (Ellis & Douce, 1994). Although these articles address conflict in terms of supervision (e.g., between supervisee and supervisor and in group supervision) or interpersonal conflict (e.g., within the workplace), they do not address conflict in terms of developing clinicians' awareness of skills related to managing conflict in their clinical work. The activity described in this chapter emphasizes the importance of clinicians examining their own views and experiences with conflict in order to enhance their development and increase their confidence in effectively managing conflict when it arises during clinical encounters.

## Rationale

Thomas (1976) was the first to define five primary styles of conflict management. In the first style, *accommodating*, one person places high value on the relationship with the other person and concedes to the other party's wants/needs at the expense of his or her own wants/needs. In the second style, *avoiding*, each party circumvents the situation entirely. In the third style, *compromising*, both parties reach a place of agreement, yet neither one obtains his or her original goal. In the fourth style, *competing*, one party is successful in reaching his or her goal at the expense of the other party. In the fifth style, *collaborating*, both parties join together in meaningful dialogue in an environment of trust, each party recognizing and valuing the relationship between the two of them as one central component. A mutually desired outcome is obtained through problem solving. The activity presented in this chapter allows student clinicians to better understand their own styles of conflict management and to apply that knowledge to the supervision relationship first and then more broadly to their client relationships.

Supervision serves two primary purposes. First, supervision provides a rich learning environment because it is a safe place for clinicians to learn professional boundaries and to develop self-awareness skills. Stoltenberg and McNeill (2010) assert that this development comes through "self-preoccupation, awareness of the client's world and enlightened self-awareness" (p. 23) and suggest that such development is ongoing throughout clinicians' careers. Second, supervision protects the client by allowing clinicians to process issues related to countertransference. The debate continues as to whether the supervisor's primary responsibility is the supervisee or the client (Bernard & Goodyear, 2008). Yet if we accept that the supervisee and client are equally important, then the issue of countertransference comes clearly into focus as a supervision issue that must be explored. Supervisors have the opportunity to guide clinicians through a journey of self-discovery and to help them collect the tools necessary to navigate their future as professionals. Supervision should occur in a safe environment that provides opportunities for clinicians to learn self-reflective skills, explore strengths, build resiliency, and examine family-of-origin patterns.

Conflict often appears in our work with beginning supervisees. The supervisory relationship mirrors how conflict is experienced in other aspects of clinicians' lives. For example, when a client's presenting concern closely resembles a family issue currently being experienced by a beginning clinician, some relevant issues emerge that must be addressed in supervision. First, beginning clinicians have little experience in separating their personal experiences from the client's personal experiences. Second, beginning clinicians may struggle to recognize, appreciate, or distinguish the unique lived experiences of the client as separate from their own experiences.

From the perspective of conflict-management style, the supervisor may choose to address the concept of competing values and/or outcomes since those relate to treatment goals and objectives. The optimal outcome of supervision is to help student clinicians evaluate which conflict-management style they are utilizing, while assisting them in moving toward a style that is most similar to collaboration. For example, if a student clinician highly values the relationship with the client and uses the accommodation style of conflict management, then the supervisor could discuss the importance of collaboration and model the collaborative style. Again, within the supervisory relationship, trust and safety are essential, allowing the student clinician to explore and practice new skills, such as assertiveness, and eventually reach a level of mastery with those skills.

The genogram can be used with any of the standard models of supervision to elicit individual clinician self-awareness and professional growth at any point in the clinician's career. Marlin (1989) states, "The point of doing your genogram is to affirm yourself within the context of your family history. The process starts with family examination and ends with self-discovery and self-validation" (p. 8). A genogram helps clinicians explore numerous aspects of their history that might contribute to countertransference with clients. If the clinician is willing, this activity can be done privately or with a trusted supervisor, allowing the clinician to explore and process potential unresolved feelings. The beauty of the genogram is that it can be repeated indefinitely throughout a clinician's career, focusing on different aspects of the clinician's life and thus allowing for continual self-discovery. The active use of a genogram allows the clinician to create a self-evaluative, self-correcting system. This chapter offers a genogram assignment specific to a student clinician's self-awareness relative to conflict. Such an assignment could have utility at many points in a clinician's development and career; however, this chapter has a deliberate focus on student clinicians at the beginning of their graduate training in a mental health field.

# Activity Instructions

Clinicians struggle at various points in their development, and specific clients can often elicit emotional responses in beginning clinicians. Maintaining a dialogue about the student clinicians' own experiences and how they are experiencing counseling relationships with particular clients fosters the needed personal and professional development. Furthermore, this dialogue is useful when offering corrective feedback and when a student clinician is struggling to implement treatment that moves the client, couple, or family forward. This activity, which sets a base for that dialogue, is typically utilized as a required course assignment for graduate-level student clinicians who are providing direct counseling services under live supervision in a university-based clinic. The activity involves two specific elements: (a) the construction of a family genogram depicting three generations of the student clinician's family and (b) the completion of a reflection paper, answering deliberate and targeted questions that can be used as a self-assessment guide. Facilitators should share the following instructions with clinical trainees to prepare them for creating a family genogram and writing a personal reflection paper:

*For this assignment, you will construct your own family genogram and write a reflection paper. Genograms are the structural illustration of individuals and their relationships to each other as well as the mapping of contextual features. The 2008 textbook by McGoldrick, Gerson, and Shellenberger titled* Genograms: Assessment and Intervention *will serve as your main resource for this assignment. No other prior experience with genograms is necessary.*

*Genograms must contain a minimum of three generations (i.e., you and your siblings, your parents and stepparents, and your grandparents). You may choose to include aunts, uncles, cousins, and step- or half-siblings if they are important to your reflection (e.g., your maternal aunt was your primary caregiver).*

*Your genogram must contain the following information:*

- *Structure of individuals*
- *Relationship lines (i.e., close, conflictual, too close/fused) from you to other members of your family. It is not expected that you would have relationship lines to each person, only to those who are most salient to you.*

*Along with creating the genogram, you will write a paper reflecting on your family experience as well as on your experience with this assignment. The paper should include a title page, but no references are expected. No specific page length is required; however, a comprehensive reflection is expected. In other words, it would be impossible to benefit from this experience if you write only a few pages. Your reflection should answer the following questions:*

- *What is your family like? Give an overview of family members and their relationships to you.*
- *Would you describe your family-of-origin as overtly conflictual?*
- *Would you describe your family-of-origin as silently conflictual?*
- *How did you experience conflict between your parents or guardians growing up?*
- *How did you observe conflict to be handled between your parents or guardians growing up?*
- *How did you experience conflict between you and your siblings growing up?*
- *How did you observe conflict to be handled between you and your siblings growing up?*
- *What is your birth order? How has your birth order had an influence on you? Did your sibling position change?*
- *What are the birth orders of your parents?*
- *If you are in a relationship, what is your spouse's or partner's birth order?*
- *What are the important/meaningful aspects of your genogram (i.e., patterns, events)? Please describe.*
- *Families are complex with contextual factors (e.g., triangulations, cut-off relationships). What are some significant influences from your family context?*
- *What aspects of your family-of-origin have influenced your decision to pursue your specific career (i.e., the helping profession)? How so?*
- *Of the five styles of conflict management (accommodate, avoid, compromise, compete, and collaborate), with which one or ones do you most closely identify?*
- *What did you learn about your family's style of conflict resolution and your response to it?*

- *How would you describe your style of conflict management (i.e., in your interpersonal or romantic relationships) today?*
- *How do you see yourself handling conflict when it arises in a therapy session?*
- *What did you learn about yourself personally and as a clinician as a result of this experience?*

# Examples

Student clinicians entering the counseling field will have had their own personal experiences with overt conflict, or the lack thereof, which will highly influence their initial comfort level with conflict. Their personal experiences will also influence the ways in which and degrees to which they intervene in session. For example, Clinician A, from a "silent family," who never observed overt family conflict, might say, "I never saw my parents raise their voices at each other." On the other hand, Clinician B, from a highly conflictual family, might say, "You knew you were loved when you were being yelled at." Many other student clinicians entering the counseling field have had family experiences that fall somewhere between the two ends of this continuum. In terms of clinical intervention, Clinician A may be very uncomfortable at the first sign of conflict and may be quick to intervene and diffuse the situation with clients. However, Clinician B will be more comfortable with conflict and may allow the tension and dialogue to continue for a bit before intervening. Both of these student clinicians have the same potential to develop into exceptional clinicians. Learning how their own personal experiences influence them will contribute significantly to their development.

Furthermore, student clinicians may become anxious when they learn that conflict in session is inevitable and unavoidable yet ultimately useful. This assignment has great utility in terms of clinician development and can be used at various points in student clinicians' training programs or later as student clinicians enter their professional careers. It also serves as a pivotal starting point for various forms of supervision: live, video recording, or case-note supervision. In our experience, this assignment is a central component of supervision for our students during live and videotape supervision.

The following case example illustrates the implementation of this assignment and its utility. Tim, a second-year student clinician, was struggling to connect with two particular clients, a couple dealing with relationship issues. The male partner appeared to be more expressive, while the female partner was more passive. Tim was struggling to address particular aspects of their relationship for fear of evoking conflict. Tim met with his supervisor to discuss the client issue and was able to verbalize that a "disconnect" existed, but he was not able to articulate reasons for this lack of connection. Together, he and his supervisor explored possible reasons for the disconnect, but none seemed to resonate as an authentic explanation with Tim. Tim had completed the genogram activity as part of a required course, and its outcome became a focus of the supervision session. Tim was asked to reflect on his own experiences and then report back on how they were influencing his work with these particular clients. Within the week, Tim came to his supervisor and commented that the activity challenged him to look at his hesitancy in the treatment room. Tim stated during supervision, "My own family was dysfunctional, and conflict was a part of daily life." For Tim, his hesitation came from not wanting to evoke conflict because of the fear it created for him. During supervision, Tim and his supervisor discussed ways to progressively move the couple toward change, which included the potential risk of evoking conflict in the process. They identified possible ways conflict could arise and potential ways for Tim to intervene, enabling him to articulate the direction he hoped to go in the session and pinpoint specific areas in which he wanted feedback from the supervisor.

During live supervision of the next session, Tim implemented his plan for the session and slight conflict emerged. Because of his participation in this activity and prior planning with his supervisor, Tim maintained his composure, experienced the conflict without fear or apprehension, and utilized the conflict to evoke more dialogue from the female partner. He expressed that he could feel a true connection with his clients and could see how conflict can be useful in session. He also asserted in his reflection paper: "This assignment let me see what a vehicle

I can be for my clients. Conflict is not something to be feared but to be worked through." With ongoing supervision and his own self-exploration, Tim was able to work successfully with the couple and assist them in meeting their treatment goals, fostering further development for Tim as a beginning clinician.

With its intentional focus on conflict, this assignment offers a safe forum for student clinicians to express their thoughts and feelings about their own lived experiences. The purpose is to assist student clinicians in developing into competent clinicians with the awareness and skills necessary to deal with the inevitability of conflict in clinical practice.

# Measuring Progress

As previously explained, this activity asks student clinicians to construct their own genograms along with writing a reflective self-assessment paper; however, the completion of the assignment is only the beginning. Development as a clinician is a continual and an ongoing journey of personal growth, and an assignment such as this one represents the beginning of that journey. This is only one tool supervisors may choose to implement to foster personal growth and awareness relative to conflict-management styles. We suggest utilizing this activity early in the student clinicians' training program and then repeating it closer to the conclusion of the program as a way of self-evaluating personal growth. Student clinicians may begin to recognize how their experiences influence who they are as clinicians and the importance of self-reflection. Supervisors may wish to complement this activity with a more quantitative measure of the student clinicians' conflict-management styles, such as the Dealing with Conflict Instrument developed by Alexander Hiam (2005).

From the supervisor's perspective, progress may be subtle or dramatic. In Tim's case, the supervisor witnessed a dramatic shift in clinician self-awareness. The student clinician was struggling with significant anxiety and countertransference issues with two particular clients. Other forms of intervention to draw the student clinician's awareness to the issue were attempted but did not produce the results needed for Tim's development. Reflecting back on the genogram assignment provided that growth. After completing the genogram, Tim was able to self-identify areas of concern and take self-directed steps to modify his counseling behaviors. He was visibly changed by the activity, and the intervention took less time and effort from the supervisor than any of the other interventions attempted. That self-guided transformation significantly impacted the client relationship and improved the overall clinical functioning of the student clinician.

# Conclusion

Conflict has been discussed in the supervision and training literature in terms of group supervision, supervisee–supervisor relationships, and interpersonal conflict; however, very little can be found that speaks to the importance of effectively assisting student clinicians in exploring their own experiences and comfort levels with conflict. Conflict is an inevitable part of the counseling experience, and exploring their own views on conflict is vital to beginning clinicians' development. The activity presented in this chapter is useful at the beginning of a training program and is intended to assist students in recognizing and managing challenging situations that mirror their own experiences. The benefits for students include greater self-awareness, increased ability to be in the "here and now" with their clients, and greater recognition of the importance of continual self-reflection.

# Additional Resources

Aasheim, L. (2012). *Practical supervision for counselors: An experiential guide*. New York, NY: Springer.

Kaiser, L. T. (1997). *Supervisory relationships: Exploring the human element*. Pacific Grove, CA: Brooks/Cole.

# References

Bernard, J. M., & Goodyear, R. K. (2008). *Fundamentals of clinical supervision* (4th ed.). Boston, MA: Pearson Education.

Bogo, M., Globerman, J., & Sussman, T. (2004). The field instructor as group worker: Managing trust and competition in group supervision. *Journal of Social Work Education, 40*, 13–26.

Ellis, M., & Douce, L. (1994). Group supervision of novice clinical supervisors: Eight recurring issues. *Journal of Counseling and Development, 27*, 520–525.

Hiam, A. W. (2005). *Dealing with conflict instrument: Leader's guide*. Amherst, MA: HRD Press.

Johnson, E., & Stewart, D. (2000). Clinical supervision in Canadian academic and service settings: The importance of education, training, and workplace support for supervisor development. *Canadian Psychology, 41*, 124–130.

Marlin, E. (1989). *Genograms: The new tool for exploring the personality, career, and love patterns you inherit*. Chicago, IL: Contemporary Books.

McGoldrick, M., Gerson, R., & Shellenberger, S. (2008). *Genograms: Assessment and intervention* (3rd ed.). New York, NY: W. W. Norton.

Stoltenberg, C. D., & McNeill, B. W. (2010). *IDM Supervision: An integrative developmental model for supervising counselors and therapists* (3rd ed.). New York, NY: Routledge.

Storm, C., Todd, T., Sprenkle, D., & Morgan, M. (2001). Gaps between MFT supervision assumptions and common practice: Suggested best practices. *Journal of Marital and Family Therapy, 27*, 227–239.

Thomas, K. (1976). Conflict and conflict management. In M. D. Dunnette (Ed.), *Handbook of industrial/organizational psychology* (pp. 900–902). Chicago, IL: Rand McNally.

# CHAPTER 15

# Examining the Source of Negative Self-Beliefs

## Larry D. Williams and Andrae Banks

# Introduction

The literature demonstrates that, in Western cultures, notions of the self are shaped from personal life experiences and socioenvironmental factors. Among the dominant agents contributing to one's concept of self are authoritative figures and social media. Authority figures such as parents and teachers may repeatedly compliment or criticize a child based on his or her appearance or behavior, leading the child to believe that he or she is good or bad based on these comments. Similarly, social media and advertising consistently reinforce the idea that our jobs and possessions determine our worth. When subjected to life's unexpected changes, these individuated concepts of self are often short-lived, creating a need for people to constantly reassert who they are according to their environmental circumstances and societal expectations (Chestang, 1996). The process of constantly evaluating one's self in an attempt to meet environmental circumstances and societal expectations may result in feelings of a depreciated self-worth. This may ultimately manifest itself in confusion and the individual engaging in destructive behaviors to self and society.

# Rationale

According to many scholars, our self-concept includes a variety of self-representations that can vary in structure and function depending on the context (Arnd-Caddigan & Pozzuto, 2008; Dewane, 2006; Mikami, Gregory, Pianta, & Lun, 2011; Nyarko, 2012). The way people view themselves can have a powerful impact (both positive and negative) on how they view the world and their relationships. On the positive side, healthy self-concepts allow people to organize their beliefs about behaviors and experiences that are then reflected in expectations and predictions about the future (Sloan, 2007; Ying, 2011). Thus, the structure of the self helps individuals make meaning out of life, which can enhance their experiences both personally and professionally.

When clinicians have a positive, nurturing self-representation, it can serve as a model for clients who are struggling with a negative self-concept. Additionally, our sense of self serves as a motivational function that permits individuals to identify goals and standards for performing selected behaviors. Ultimately, a positive self-representation—one that affirms and nurtures the individual's self-worth—can safeguard one against many of the challenges of daily living.

In contrast, individuals who experience negative self-evaluations or abusive treatment from unhealthy family members can have self-representations that marginalize or devalue their self-worth (Ganzer, 2007). Moreover, the concept of self-worth is connected to health-related behaviors that may be either life-enhancing or life-threatening. For example, some scholars suggest that a connection exists between a diminished self-worth and suicidal ideations in adolescents (Harter, 1999). This self-representation results from individuals measuring their worth in relation to standards established by their peers, popular culture, or personal experiences. However, these standards may be in conflict with the individual's own views of his or her self (Francis & Skelton, 2008; Reid, 2007; Sadi & Uyar, 2013; Unal, 2012). This disparity therefore exists between the individual's real self-defined self and the individual's perceived self, which is adopted to conform to the pressures imposed by external forces.

The following experiential activity is based on Marcia's (1980) theory on identity-status development in adolescents and on Grotevant's (1997) theory on the dimension of processes. Marcia's theory originated with the concept of *ego identity* and *identity diffusion* or confusion, and suggests that adolescent identity formation evolves through the process of individuals making a commitment to find their own unique and enduring identities, followed by an intense internal exploration and personal inventory of their own development. The exercise is intended for second-year clinical students in a children and family concentration. The exercise must be conducted under the guidance of an experienced therapist who has significant knowledge of group and counseling techniques, because the process involves intense self-exploration that can sometimes elicit past traumatic experiences. Ideally, the exercises should be conducted in groups of between 15 and 20 students in order to maximize the experience.

Marcia outlined four stages in the commitment and exploration process, beginning with the lowest level of identity formation and progressing to the highest level of achievement. These stages include (a) identity diffusion, (b) moratorium, (c) foreclosure, and (d) identity achievement. *Identity diffusion* is the initial stage in which an individual has no fixed identity and is not examining other possibilities for a more developed identity. During the *moratorium* stage, the individual experiences intense intrapersonal crisis and exploration and struggles to develop values and goals that are consistent with a self-defined self. The third stage, *foreclosure*, refers to the level in which an individual makes a commitment to a particular identity without undergoing a period of intense self-exploration, thus forfeiting a possible positive self-concept that may have been damaged or strongly influenced by a childhood trauma characterized by a dysfunctional family environment or negative peer influences. During the final stage, *identity achievement*, the individual makes a firm commitment to a particular positive self-concept after a period of deep introspection.

The second aspect of the activity is informed by Grotevant's (1997) dimension of process. Two vital components of this model are ability and orientation. *Ability* refers to a person's capacity to think critically, to solve problems, and to formulate a point of view. *Orientation* refers to attitudes that influence a person's willingness to engage in a process of exploration. In this context, exploration is viewed as utilizing information about oneself and his or her environments—physical environments (neighborhoods, communities, schools) and social environments (families, peer networks, and culture)—to make rational choices. This process is critical in the adolescent's construction of a positive self-representation (Rew, 2005).

## Activity Instructions

This exercise was implemented with second-year student clinicians in a children and family concentration to help them explore their own personal and professional identities. Before the exercise begins, the supervisor should assign readings on identity development from seminal identity theorists, including Bolby, Cooley, Erikson, Freud, Marcia, and Piaget. The activity is then communicated to participants in accordance with the steps noted here.

First, the supervisor should instruct student clinicians to keep a journal documenting what they learned about identity development from the assigned readings. The journal should include the date and heading, followed by a descriptive and reflective paragraph or two of the topic the writer is reflecting upon. In addition, the journal should describe the influence the event may have had on their self-development. Furthermore, students should describe the social setting in which the event is undertaken, the level of peer involvement, family participation, and any cultural practices or assumptions shaping this activity.

Second, after journaling, the supervisor should ask the student clinicians to list adjectives that they feel best describe them (e.g., smart, compassionate, self-reliant). This should be listed at the end of each journal entry.

Third, the supervisor should ask student clinicians to share their self-identifying descriptors with their peers and supervisor for open discussion and feedback. Feedback from group members should include whether they agree or disagree with the individual self-assessments and descriptions.

Fourth, the supervisor should ask clinicians to begin the process of exploring the evolution of their definition of self. This requires an intense period of self-exploration. The process includes examining parental and family influences and childhood experiences and talking with family members and close friends. In addition, clinicians should also examine cultural factors that may have influenced their identities.

Next, the supervisor should ask student clinicians to make a commitment to adopt a new identity without becoming immersed in a process of intense self-examination. This process involves selecting an identity without the influence of social, cultural, and economic factors that may have been instrumental in the development of their original self-identity. For example, cultural education, social institutions, and experiences consistently provide individuals with justification for perceiving themselves in ways that diminish their self-worth. Moreover, a large body of research has been published on the relationship between racial identity schemas and self-limiting beliefs. One of the more popular theories based on genetic inferiority has been used as an explanation for high rates of poverty, crime, and disease among many Hispanics and African Americans. Many African Americans believe that they are doomed to repeat this intergenerational cycle of poverty and low academic achievement. However, some individuals reject the limitations of cultural, institutional, and social boundaries and develop a set of beliefs about themselves that is positive, life affirming, and free of deeply ingrained social boundaries (Karger & Stoesz, 2014).

Finally, based on the information gathered from the processes outlined previously, the supervisor should ask student clinicians to make a commitment to a particular self-identity with a new awareness of external influences, including socially prescribed gender roles and identity, peer relations, religious customs and beliefs, family traditions, popular culture, and community factors in order to establish if those external factors were actually relevant to their self-defined self. The activity is followed by a discussion wherein all members relate what they have learned about the process, receive feedback from the group facilitator and peers, and plan how they will implement what they have learned to create what I call the *self-defined self*.

# Examples

At the end of the semester, student clinicians were asked to share their experiences with the group. Many student clinicians reported that they gained valuable insights about the source of their self-representations. Some student clinicians attributed their self-conceptualization to cultural factors, such as culturally derived gender roles, racial stereotyping, religious beliefs, social customs, and family patterns, whereas others emanated from peer influences and popular culture. For example, one student (A. H.), an African American, was the first in his family to attend college. According to A. H., he was discouraged from pursuing a degree in social work by high school counselors and schoolteachers even after he was accepted into the program. Although he maintained the required grade-point average for completion, he continued to doubt his abilities. Because of his negative self-perceptions, he feared he would not complete the curriculum and would be an embarrassment to his family and friends. A. H. reported that the self-exploration exercise allowed him to overcome the socially imposed self-limiting beliefs about achieving academic success. A. H. eventually realized that success was the result of hard work and the willingness to persevere. Ultimately, A. H. was able to develop a self-representation that validated his accomplishments and transcended his socially and culturally imposed diminished self-identity. After graduation, A. H. plans to develop a mentoring program for adolescents and incorporate some of the concepts from this activity to help adolescents develop a positive self-identity.

In another example, a second student (F. B.) struggled with overcoming her negative self-assessment in regards to the texture of her hair and skin color. F. B. has kinky hair and a black complexion, and she views herself living in a society where her skin complexion and curly hair are viewed as unattractive. Because of this socially imposed definition of beauty—that beauty is measured by Eurocentric ideals of physical attractiveness—F. B. experienced prolonged periods of social isolation beginning in her childhood. Through the process of intense self-exploration, F. B. was able to make a commitment to a redefined self-concept that transcends the purely physical aspects of identity and is instead based on a holistic representation of who she truly is as a person.

# Measuring Progress

The use of vignettes through a process of journal documentation is a critical methodology for assessing progress. This is conducted via a self-report based on information documented in the student clinicians' activity journals. This information documents the initial instructions for completing the exercise, including student clinicians' initial self-representation, peer representation, cultural-identity representation, and identity formation in their social environment. The journal offers students a deeper understanding of events that have shaped their lives. It helps to disentangle thoughts and ideas that have reinforced limiting beliefs. Furthermore, it provides the scope for student clinicians to move toward wholeness and growth, and identify a self-identity based on a positive, life-affirming reality.

# Conclusion

For many participants, the assignment was meaningful because it gave them the opportunity to examine, explore, and ultimately change long-held negative beliefs about their identity that impeded both their personal and professional development. Some student clinicians reported that many of the pejorative identity labels were not externally generated by their peers' evaluations of them, religious teachings, and societal gender-reinforced stereotypes. Others, however, discovered that they were externally generated and found it necessary to establish a new self-concept. By participating in this exercise and undertaking a process of intense self-exploration, many student clinicians were able to abandon some negative beliefs about themselves that were hindering their growth and began to commit instead to a self-defined self. This new self-definition is based on a more holistic and life-affirming view of self.

This activity is especially applicable to clinicians who work with children and adolescents, because they need a strong sense of self both to undertake this challenging work and to serve as a role model for their clients. The fundamental role of mental health providers dealing with children with diminished self-concepts is to be a "sanctioner of capabilities" (Erikson, 1968, p. 87). This involves more than just affirming clients' self-worth; it involves identifying and perhaps even guiding them in identifying what they do very well. Moreover, clinicians and other professionals who work with children should foster an environment where adolescents can explore dimensions of their identity. This process of identity exploration involves showing tolerance, allowing them to take risks, engaging them in a proactive exploration of self-representation, and creating an environment in which adolescents can develop and realize their full potential. In addition, this process can also be applied in settings such as mentoring programs, suicide-prevention programs, and eating-disorder programs (Billig, 2004; Erikson, 1968).

# Additional Resources

Conchas, G. Q. (2006). *The color of success: Race and high-achieving urban youth.* New York, NY: Teachers College Press.

Hamman, D. G., & Hendricks, C. B. (2005). The role of generations in identity formation: Erickson speaks to teachers of adolescents. *Clearing House, 79*(20), 72–75.

Healy, F. J. (2012). *Race, ethnicity, gender, and class: The sociology of group conflict and change.* Thousand Oaks, CA: Sage.

Noguera, P. (2008). *The trouble with black boys and other influences on race, equity, and the future of public education.* San Francisco, CA: Jossey-Bass.

# References

Arnd-Caddigan, M., & Pozzuto, R. (2008). Use of self in relational clinical social work. *Clinical Social Work Journal, 36*, 235–243.

Billig, S. H. (2004). *Impacts of service-learning on youth, schools and communities: Research on K–12 school-based service-learning, 1990–1999*. Retrieved from Education Commission of the States website: www.ecs.org/ecsmain.asp?page=/html/issuesK12.ASP

Chestang, L.W. (1996). Social services and the ethnic community. *Social Service Review, 70*(3), 493.

Dewane, C. J. (2006). Use of self: Primer revisited. *Clinical Social Work Journal, 34*(4), 543–555.

Erikson, E. H. (1968). *Identity: Youth in crisis*. New York, NY: W. W. Norton.

Francis, B., & Skelton, C. (2008). Self-made self: Analyzing the potential contribution to the field of gender and education of theories that dissembled selfhood. *Discourse Studies in Cultural Politics of Education, 29*(3), 311–323.

Ganzer, C. (2007). The use of self from a rational perspective. *Clinical Social Work Journal, 35*, 117–123.

Grotevant, H. D. (1997). Identity processes: Integrating social psychological and developmental processes. *Journal of Adolescent Research, 12*, 354–357.

Harter, S. (1999). *The construction of the self*. New York, NY: Guilford Press.

Karger, H. J., & Stoesz, D. (2014). *American social welfare policy: A pluralist approach*. New York, NY: Pearson.

Marcia, J. E. (1980). Identity in adolescence. In J. Adelson (Ed.), *Handbook of adolescent psychology* (pp. 159–187). New York, NY: John Wiley.

Mikami, Y. A., Gregory, A., Pianta, R. C., & Lun, J. (2011). Effects of a teacher professional development on peer relationships in secondary classrooms. *Psychology Review, 40*(3), 367–385.

Nyarko, K. (2012). The influence of peer and parent relationships on adolescents' self-esteem. *Ife Psychologia, 20*, 161–167.

Reid, D. (2007). Passing that pass in America: Crossing over and coming back to tell about it. *The History Teacher, 40*, 453–470.

Rew, L. (2005). *Adolescent development: A multidisciplinary approach to theory, research, and intervention*. Newbury Park, CA: Sage.

Sadi, O., & Uyar, M. (2013). The relationship between self-efficacy, self-regulated learning strategies and achievement: Path model. *Journal of Baltic Science Education, 12*(1), 21–33.

Sloan, M. M. (2007). The "real self" and inauthenticity: The importance of self-concept anchorage for emotional experiences in the workplace. *Social Psychology Quarterly, 70*(3), 305–318.

Unal, S. (2012). Evaluating the effect of self-awareness and communication techniques on nurses' effectiveness. *Contemporary Nurse, 43*(1), 90–98.

Ying, Y. (2011). The effect of educational disequilibrium in field work on graduate social work students' self-concept and mental health. *Journal of Teaching in Social Work, 31*, 278–294.

# CHAPTER 16

# CREATING A SAFE LEARNING ENVIRONMENT FOR CLINICIANS THROUGH GROUP DISCUSSION AND SUPERVISION

J. Christopher Hall

# Introduction

By all measures, counseling is complex work, and teaching the processes of counseling as they relate to sensitive topics adds a new level of relational complexity, particularly in group settings like courses or group supervision. This chapter describes an experiential exercise that builds on the group work and research of Irving Yalom (Yalom & Leszcz, 2005) and John Sharry (2007). It is designed to develop a safe foundation in a clinical practice course or supervision group that will facilitate the open discussion of sensitive and difficult topics that clinicians often face with clients. Early establishment of safety among group members is of vital importance in order for group members to feel comfortable and open enough to explore these sensitive issues both regarding self-work and in attending to diversity issues among clients (Yalom & Leszcz, 2005). This is especially true in clinical groups with clinicians who are newer to the field.

# Rationale

In order to grow as professionals, clinical supervisees and student clinicians need a safe space where they can process their thoughts and feelings about their clinical work and how it affects them personally (National Association of Social Workers [NASW], 2012). One of the most prevalent findings in the past 50 years of research on group therapy is that a supportive relationship among group members is critical for group development and to achieve positive training outcomes for individual group members (Hogg, 1992; Sharry, 2007; Wampold, 2001). If group members do not feel that they can safely share, be heard, and receive open feedback from the supervisor/teacher and other group members, then group discussions may become truncated and superficial, difficult topics may be avoided, and the group may lack the development that allows its members to trust each other enough to share experiences, provide mutual feedback, and grow (Sharry, 2007). This applies to both clinical supervision groups and to introductory clinical classes.

The exercise described in this chapter was designed to achieve the following three goals: (1) to create group cohesion and investment in the class; (2) to create safety early in the process to facilitate the discussion of sensitive topics; and (3) to experientially help student clinicians and supervisees better recognize what relational qualities clients may desire from them during clinical encounters. Since its development in 2001, this exercise has been used 36 times in both supervisory group settings and in clinical classes and has been refined using feedback from group members. In its 12 years of use, no adverse or negative responses to the exercise have been reported by student clinicians or by supervisees.

# Activity Instructions

This exercise has most commonly been used in master's-level clinical counseling classes with second-year trainees. It is designed to be used on the first day of class or group supervision after general rapport building and introductions have been made. This exercise takes between 40 and 60 minutes and can be completed in a class or during a supervision group of at least three members (the exercise has been used with as many as 25 group members). Materials needed include a whiteboard and dry-erase markers.

The exercise includes five steps. Each step is designed to gradually promote deeper discussion among group members and to encourage meaningful interactions between group members and the supervisor/teacher. The conversation is slowly expanded through each step of the exercise to eventually culminate in a conversation with the entire group.

## Step 1: Raising the Question

The supervisor/teacher should begin the exercise with a simple statement that invites group participation, such as:

*In the counseling profession, clients will come to us with experiences and topics that are sometimes uncomfortable to discuss or even avoided in day-to-day conversation by most people. Part of our service to them is to provide a safe place for these topics to be shared and explored. To that end, the first thing I would like us to talk about is how we can create a safe space in our group where everyone feels comfortable to respectfully and confidentially share our cases with each other and to discuss sometimes uncomfortable topics. Would you like to participate in a short exercise to explore how we can interact with each other to create safety around sensitive topics to make them easier to discuss?*

The primary purpose of this statement is to introduce student clinicians to *how* discussions about sensitive topics will occur. It is important to point out that this is different from *having* conversations *about* difficult topics. The main point of the exercise is to collaboratively discuss what guidelines and values will assist in the discussion of these sensitive topics.

## Step 2: Listing the Topics in Two Categories

The supervisor/teacher then explains to the group that they will name topics that will be listed on the board under two main categories: (a) sensitive topics with clients and (b) sensitive topics within the supervisor–supervisee or teacher–student clinician context (depending on whether the exercise is being implemented in a class or supervision group). The first category includes such topics as child abuse, neglect, rape, and so on. The second category includes sensitive topics about the supervisor–supervisee or teacher–student clinician context, such as grades, reviews, feedback, freedom of opinion, and conflict. These important contextual issues contribute to how safe supervisees/student clinicians feel in the group, which in turn can affect how much or how little group members will share. I wish to emphasize again that the point of listing these topics is not to discuss them but to begin the conversation of *how* safety can be created in order to discuss sensitive issues in the group.

According to White (2007), the act of saying something aloud can be very powerful. Naming these difficult topics provides members with a sense of control. The purpose of displaying the topics on the board is to destigmatize these topics, to begin to take away their power, and to show that they will be handled in a sensitive and safe way.

## Step 3: Determining Group Members' Needs

After the topics have been listed on the board, the supervisor/teacher should ask the group two specific questions:

1. *What do you need from each other, as group members, to feel safe and to be able to discuss sensitive issues in the group, such as the ones listed on the board?*

2. *What do you need from me to feel safe and to be able to discuss sensitive issues in the group, such as the ones listed on the board?*

The supervisor/teacher should write the two questions clearly on the board next to the topics listed under the two categories and then explain the following:

*Take some time to discuss what you need from each other and what you need from me in order to feel safe in class/supervision. It is important that you do this together and come up with a list of things that are of value to you as a group because every group is unique. Your voice matters. I want each of you to see us as a group. I, the supervisor/teacher, am not a class; we are a class together. It is our interactions with each other that create this class. Because I represent power as the facilitator, I'm going to step outside into the hallway to avoid influencing the conversation with my presence. I will be available if you need my assistance. When you have discussed these questions and made a list of things you need from each other and from me, please invite me back and share your responses with me.*

The supervisor/teacher does not need to specify the exact amount of time for this process. In my personal experience, group members typically need 10 to 20 minutes to complete it. The supervisor/teacher's absence allows group members to take ownership of the group, develop cohesion, and discuss their needs without the distracting influence of the supervisor/teacher.

Over the 12 years of using this training exercise, the conversations led by student clinicians have proven to be incredibly powerful for them, for the supervisor/teacher, and for the group as a whole. Throughout this process, student clinicians and supervisees transform from what Foucault (1984) calls docile bodies into active, invested collaborators in the group process. In my own experience as a group facilitator, during my absence from the classroom, group members more readily transform from passive students to active and invested learners. They appreciate the trust and respect given to them and are ready to safely and constructively engage with each other.

**Step 4: Sharing and Discussing Group Members' Needs**

The fourth step involves an open discussion among group members and the supervisor/teacher about what the group has decided they need from each other and from the facilitator to create a safe environment that will facilitate the discussion of sensitive issues. It is important for the supervisor/teacher to write these responses on the board and to explore them with the group. The issue of respect, for example, can be followed up with questions such as "What does respect mean? What does it look like in action? What kinds of things would you be doing or not doing if you were showing respect?" Other common needs suggested by group members include being open, considering all opinions, avoiding judgment, trying to understand others before you speak, and so forth. The resulting list becomes the rules and expectations for interaction and values for the group.

**Step 5: Expanding the Conversation to Clients' Needs**

The final step of the exercise involves reflecting on the list of what the group needs to feel safe and applying it to what clients need in therapy. The supervisor/teacher should ask the following question: "Would your clients want the same or similar things to feel safe when speaking with you?"

The impact of this question cannot be underestimated. The question connects the group members' experiences with the exercise to the experiences of their clients in therapy. It opens the door for group members to consider their own actions in the therapy room and the ways in which they can respect their clients, create a safe environment for them, appreciate their views, make attempts to understand them before speaking, and avoid making judgments, remembering that they also need those things to feel safe. This question provides the bridge from experiential learning to applied learning.

# Examples

Student feedback comes from recent graduates interviewed for this chapter. Over the years that this exercise has been implemented, all groups have shared that the need for respect is paramount and that the discussion of what respect means and how it is operationalized in relationships has been beneficial. Concerning respectful interactions, one class recorded:

*We will be respectful with one another, with respect being defined as trying to understand another's perspective before sharing one's own perspective, allowing others time to talk without interrupting, not putting others down because of their beliefs either directly to them or talking about them, and not pushing others to tell more information than they wish to share at the time.*

Another class incorporated narrative ideas (White, 2007) into how they operationalized respect. While this conversation was very complex, the group of 18 students was able to develop a powerful definition of respect on their first day of class:

*We agree to separate someone's perspective from who they are. We believe it is possible to both like and respect a person but disagree with a belief the person may hold. By separating the belief from the person, we feel that we can respect someone but also respectfully disagree on an idea at the same time.*

Commonly shared themes across classes involving the teacher–student clinician context include:

*Respectful communication, constructive feedback, an organized focus to the class, assignments that are important and teach us, practical advice, real-life examples, consistency, the development of a healthy relationship, and transparency.*

The tone this exercise sets in class leads to more sharing of ideas across the semester that directly contributes to both student learning and satisfaction. When asked about the influence of this exercise, student clinicians universally shared positive comments and vividly recalled the impact it made on them. One student clinician reported:

*After the exercise, I felt like I was respected. I really liked that. I felt like I was really heard and that my voice does matter. This helped me talk about things more, I think, later on in class.*

Another student clinician responded:

*The teacher established a tone of openness. By seeing how the instructor was, it helped me to open up, too. I went from being nervous about class to talking about what we needed as a class to feeling like I was a valued part of the class. It was a great way to set the tone for what we did.*

Student clinicians reported that they were most affected by Step 5 of the group exercise, in which group members discussed how client needs for safety may be directly related to student clinicians' own needs for safety. The empathy they developed as a result of this process was perhaps most influential in their clinical practices. One student clinician stated:

*Of the entire program, this exercise is what I remember most. It is in the back of my mind each time I meet a client for the first time.*

Finally, another student clinician described the effects of the connection between personal needs and client needs:

*I think about this exercise every time I sit down with a client. It helps me get in the mindset of hearing someone else and really respecting that person. I remember being nervous that first day of class—and thinking this was pretty weird—and how the discussion calmed me down. I remember that feeling. I know that my clients are in a similar space, so I do those things we talked about. When it comes down to it, that is what clients want, all those things that we want: nonjudgment, respect, and all of that.*

# Measuring Progress

The effectiveness of this exercise can be evaluated by tracking the following: (a) whether safety and rapport is continuing to develop in the group; (b) whether group members adhere to the guidelines of interaction they established; and (c) whether sensitive topics are brought up in conversation and, if so, whether they are explored in a manner congruent with the rules established by the group. Regular group meetings (or classes) allow the supervisor/teacher to monitor progress regarding goals and to explore with the group how this progress is being made.

In addition to increasing group cohesion, which leads to more investment and interaction, the exercise also allows group members to set relational expectations and monitor themselves. When issues arise, members work together to determine how they can be accountable to each other. This process transforms class learning into experiential learning. It should also be noted that the interaction rules established by the group are not set in stone. If issues emerge, the supervisor/teacher can stop the group and begin to again discuss the needs of group members. This creates an ongoing collaborative relationship of safety and respect, continuing the experiential learning process and modeling the ideal client–clinician relationship, one of continued feedback and adjustment to client needs (Duncan, Miller, Wampold, & Hubble, 2009; Hall, 2012). This monitored feedback loop continually reinforces student clinicians' self-awareness and accountability within the group.

# Conclusion

This group exercise is based on 50 years of group-therapy research supporting the need to create safety in groups to facilitate open interaction among group members (Hogg, 1992; Sharry, 2007; Wampold, 2001; Yalom & Leszcz, 2005). Group safety and cohesion create a context in which open dialogue can occur around sensitive issues. These qualities are paramount in clinical supervision and education because of the complexities of practice and the need to effectively deal with personal and sensitive issues. Without attention to creating safe dynamics in supervision and classes, thin discussions (i.e., discussion that are superficial or do not lead to generative thinking) may arise and important topics may be avoided, resulting in a lack of personal and professional growth. During the 12 years of using this exercise, successful outcomes have been achieved in clinical classes and supervision as evidenced by student feedback, reciprocal monitoring of safety in the group, student clinician and supervisee evaluations, and the safe discussion of sensitive issues in the classroom that have led to complex conversations and clinical case applications.

# Additional Resources

Hall, J. C. (2008). A practitioner's application and deconstruction of evidence-based practice. *Families in Society, 89*(3), 385–393.

Hall, J. C. (2011). A narrative approach to group work with male batterers. *Social Work with Groups, 34*(2), 175–189.

# References

Duncan, B. L., Miller, S. D., Wampold, B. E., & Hubble, M. A. (Eds.). (2009). *The heart and soul of change: Delivering "what works"* (2nd ed.). Washington, DC: APA Press.

Foucault, M. (1984). *The Foucault reader*. New York, NY: Vintage.

Hall, J. C. (2012). Honoring client perspectives through collaborative practice: Shifting from assessment to collaborative exploration. In S. Witkin (Ed.), *Social constructionist informed practice*. New York, NY: Columbia Press.

Hogg, M. A. (1992). *The social psychology of group cohesiveness*. New York, NY: University Press.

National Association of Social Workers (NASW). (2012). *Best practice standards in social work supervision*. Retrieved from http://www.socialworkers.org/practice/naswstandards/social worksupervision/SUPERVISION%20STANDARDS2%20Public%20Comment%20Draft %20August%2016.pdf

Sharry, J. (2007). *Solution-focused groupwork*. Thousand Oaks, CA: Sage.

Wampold, B. E. (2001). *The great psychotherapy debate: Models, methods, and findings*. Mahwah, NJ: Erlbaum.

White, M. (2007). *Maps of narrative practice*. New York, NY: W. W. Norton.

Yalom, I., & Leszcz, M. (2005). *The theory and practice of group psychotherapy* (5th ed.). New York, NY: Basic Books.

# CHAPTER 17

# Increasing Competence for Working With International and National Disasters[1]

Noah Hass-Cohen, Thomas Veeman,
Karina A. Chandler-Ziegler, and Andrew Brimhall

# Introduction

There is an increasing recognition of the need for mental health professionals to respond to the impact of national and international disasters on a multisystemic level (McDowell, Goessling, & Melendez, 2012). These disasters and their aftermath can be caused by natural events, such as Hurricane Katrina in 2005, or by humans, as in the case of the bombing of Hiroshima in 1945. In order to raise self-awareness of the long- and short-term effects of disasters, clinicians should receive trainings to facilitate an increased understanding of large-scale events and their impact on individuals, couples, and families. The Disaster Experiential Activity and Reflection (DEAR) described in this chapter includes a didactic written review, a creative reflection exercise dedicated to the disaster survivors, and a cycle of self-reflexive and interpersonal sharing. The DEAR also fosters the development of intercultural empathy as well as other person-of-the-therapist skills, such as awareness of personal biases, which are vital for treating clients in the disaster context (Dyche & Zayas, 2001).

# Rationale

Training programs have not often prepared clinicians to treat those affected by large-scale traumatic disasters (Fox, 2003; Salston & Figley, 2003). In order to effectively treat these vulnerable clients, clinicians' education must focus on heightening trainees' consciousness of the specific challenges of treating this group while focusing on internationalism and cultural diversity (Bronfenbrenner, 1977; Duran, Firehammer, & Gonzalez, 2008; Fox, 2003). The multiple layers of disaster-based trauma may result in an accumulation of individual traumas caused by experiences such as losing loved ones, witnessing death or suffering, and experiencing racism and historical and social inequalities (Duran et al., 2008). The potential long-term effects and intergenerational effects of these types of disaster-related losses require clinical attention (Fox, 2003; Leong & Leach, 2007). Experiential activities are an effective component of training that can help address these complexities (Kim & Lyons, 2003; McDowell et al., 2012).

Internationalism training prepares clinicians to work with diverse populations in the United States, including immigrants and worldwide refugees (Brown & Brown, 2009; Leong & Leach,

---

1. Dedicated to our editor, Mara Forsythe-Crane, who died tragically shortly after this manuscript was completed.

2007; Leung, 2003; McDowell et al., 2012). Although multicultural therapy training focuses on the diversity of racial and cultural identities, internationalism training focuses on how nationality mediates relationships, attitudes, values, and behaviors (McDowell et al., 2012). This kind of training is designed to increase the critical consciousness of the macro dynamics of power and privilege and how these inform clients' experiences of disaster, crisis, and trauma. In contrast, clinically focusing on the micro levels of interaction of individuals, couples, and families can limit the effectiveness of an intervention and can perpetuate social and systemic injustices (Bronfenbrenner, 1977; Freire, 1970).

Two premises inform the understanding of how macro systems affect individuals and families: (a) Growth and self-awareness can be fostered in an environment free from personal challenges, and (b) the amount of support for individuals, couples, and families influences an environment in which theory or intellectual knowledge about larger systems is separated from emotional impact (Brown & Brown, 2009; Freire, 1970). Similarly, clinicians may perceive macro-level disasters as remote and abstract events that are inaccessible and beyond their ability to intervene.

To date, there has also been a shortage of clinician self-awareness training in international, microspherical, and disaster-related contexts (Brown & Brown, 2009; Leong & Leach, 2007; Leung, 2003; McDowell et al., 2012). Traditional self-of-the-therapist development training in the United States includes self-awareness and empathy development appropriate to the contexts of personal therapy, family-of-origin investigation, and American-based multicultural training (e.g., D'Andrea & Heckman, 2008; Malot, 2010). Yet, treating those impacted by disasters often poses unique challenges for the clinician, involving confrontations with the new information provided by the literature and by clients (Brown & Brown, 2009). The possibility of a larger perspective may present as a personal crisis or culture-shock experience in which the clinician's established rules for making sense of therapy no longer apply.

In order for intercultural/international empathic responses to occur, clinicians must become more familiar with the experiential world and the emotional landscape of others (Dyche & Zayas, 2001), recognizing both similarities and differences between themselves and their clients and reducing the likelihood of staying trapped in closed-minded countertransference-based stereotypes (Yalom, 2009). In a similar vein, countertransference reactions to macro-level phenomena such as disasters are less frequently addressed (Fox, 2003; Salston & Figley, 2003). Experiential activities, which involve both emotional and intellectual clinical training, can be effective in meeting these needs (Dyche & Zayas, 2001; Kim & Lyons, 2003; McDowell et al., 2012). Training activities provide an opportunity for clinicians to explore countertransference-based emotions, protect themselves from becoming overwhelmed by large-scale suffering, and help determine areas in need of personal growth (Fox, 2003; Salston & Figley, 2003).

McDowell et al. (2012) note that the more frequently students experience "social inequalities, the better they [understand] their own privilege, leading to greater commitment to making a social difference" (p. 377). While it may not be possible to fully prepare training clinicians for large-scale events, experiential learning can help clinicians develop empathy for clients suffering from large-scale disasters and related macro-level phenomena that affect recovery, such as privilege and social injustice (Freire, 1970). Experiential training exercises, like DEAR, are designed to train clinicians to become aware of explicit and hidden trauma issues, widening their focus from the family to a larger ecological perspective (Bronfenbrenner, 1977).

# Activity Instructions

Activity facilitators (academic or clinical supervisors) are encouraged to assist clinicians (beginning-level or more experienced) to integrate cognitive and emotive learning by participating in this multistep activity. The activity is best conducted in a group setting and, although the didactic component is self-directed, the sharing and processing of experiential reflections is best facilitated with the guidance of a supervisor or mentor.

Example                                                                                                    105

The purpose of the first step of the activity is for the student clinicians to be exposed to the history of disasters that they may have little to no awareness of and that may have affected their fellow student clinicians. This first step has the potential of bringing the group of students together as they informally discuss the reasons for choosing a particular disaster to review. Use the following steps:

1. Choose a disaster (natural or human-made) to review.
2. Provide a brief historical review of the disaster, describing it factually, identifying its natural or human precursors, and outlining its impact.
3. Describe the immediate and long-term direct and indirect psychological effects of this kind of disaster. Cite pertinent peer-reviewed research and lay/Internet/news information.
4. Describe the post-disaster aid and resources that were provided, including first-response and ongoing aid and dedicated local and/or governmental resources.
5. Perform a literature review on community interventions, family therapy, and individual and couple counseling, including a discussion of cultural and diversity considerations.
6. Write a personal statement explaining why you chose to focus on this particular disaster.

**Step 1: Macro and Micro Context of a Disaster Write-up**

In this section of the activity, student clinicians are asked to use narrative and/or visual expressive means to imagine what is often unspeakable and unaccessible. They prepare for this by reading an article about Ground Zero by Mills (2002). This reading allows students to experience a fuller spectrum of issues experienced by disaster survivors, including the difficulties of finding food, clothes, and shelter. Use the following steps:

1. Narrate a story, write a letter or a poem, create an art piece, write a musical composition, choreograph a dance expression, perform a drama enactment, or take a photograph that is either directed to a survivor or that describes what might have happened to a survivor from his or her own perspective.
2. Provide the disaster sufferers a "voice" within the class. Share and discuss the physical and emotional reactions you experienced while creating your piece.

**Step 2: Walk a Mile in the Survivor's Shoes Expressive Reflection**

Sharing the emotive, clinical, and didactic framework helps consolidate the learning. Ask students the following questions:

1. What did you learn about survivors from your disaster reflective activity?
2. Why is it important to share your efforts from the reflective activity with the group? What did you learn from others' sharing? How will you apply this knowledge clinically?
3. How will you incorporate this knowledge into your future work with clients?
4. Why is it important for clinicians to learn about disasters?

**Step 3: Post-Sharing Questions**

# Example

DEAR was originally completed in a graduate-level course on crisis and trauma; student clinicians first collaborated online and then met in person in Mexico City for an eight-day intensive course. Most participants were student clinicians from the United States who were enrolled in a two-year master's program in counseling immersion. Others were local residents of Mexico or were visiting student clinicians from Southern California. The student body had a diverse international background, with family roots in countries such as Israel, Italy, Kazakhstan, Mexico, the Philippines, Russia, Switzerland, and the United States. The diversity of their backgrounds was a tremendous learning resource, and their personal backgrounds enriched class interactions. In the intimate format of the Mexico City class, student clinicians' emotional responses could be heard and validated—both as individuals and as members of a macrosystem. Many had a history of personal or familial national or international trauma.

One course participant (A.B., coauthor) focused on the Hiroshima nuclear disaster. His grandfather fought in the Pacific region during World War II, and his review focused on the survivors (the Hibakusha) of the Hiroshima nuclear bomb. Long-term effects of mass radiation on the Hibakusha include inherited cell mutations that often lead to cancer, social and employment discrimination, and a mental condition in which sufferers report feeling as if they do not have ownership of their lives (Lifton, 1991). He describes the paper crane story of a child victim who died nearly a decade after the attack from radiation poisoning:

*Sadako Sasaki was just twelve years old when she was diagnosed with leukemia caused by radiation exposure due to the nuclear bomb that was dropped on Hiroshima. While she was in the hospital, her friend brought her a square of golden paper to be folded into a paper crane. A Japanese legend tells that folding 1,000 cranes will bring a miracle by the gods. For three months Sadako folded 644 paper cranes before she died. Her friends completed the 356 cranes, and all 1,000 were buried with her. Sadako's story is a poignant example of the long-reaching effects of a national disaster. A monument in her memory was erected at the Hiroshima peace memorial. My reflective activity is a Photoshopped image—one half of the image displays a black-and-white photo of Hiroshima shortly after its destruction, a stark contrast with the other half, which presents the present-day, newly reconstructed Hiroshima in vibrant colors. In the sky I placed 1,000 paper cranes to symbolize the healing impact of the legend and the real-life young girl who became a symbol of peace (see Figure 17.1).*

*Later in the class I shared that in my youth I had experienced the loss of a close friend of a similar age to the young Japanese girl. Perhaps both the story choice and my reactions were a countertransference; I connected with the subject of my reflection on a level of personal loss that*

**Figure 17.1/This is our cry, this is our prayer, peace in the world. (Brimhall, 2012)**

*I had experienced as a child. Although I am far removed from Japanese events and culture, this work brought up grief in a poignant and personal way. The impact of the child-centric counter-transference no doubt informs my practicum work with children in Mexico and Cambodia and brings a heavy perspective to my life as a father to my own young son.*

In response to these reflections, another student trainee (T.V., coauthor) wrote:

*When Andrew shared his "Cranes Over Hiroshima" reflection, silence spread over the class. I had seen his beautiful rendering of the Hiroshima disaster online, but it didn't come alive for me until he spoke of it. His art and the emotion with which he shared it helped transform statistics and abstract history into personal tragedy and hope. For me, and I think for many others, the history of Hiroshima had been experienced as a sterile collection of facts and numbers: 1945, one bomb, 100,000 dead, another bomb, war over. Andrew's art and his moving discussion of it in class made the disaster personal and human for me. I recall his artwork well—the destroyed view of Hiroshima, the view of the new city built from those ruins, and the cranes over everything. I remember the cranes—a perfect tragic-hopeful symbol. I imagined the little girl folding cranes for a better future, her death before reaching her goal, and the way that others completed the task for her. More than anything else, I take the message from Andrew's reflection that our pain and our hope live longer than we do. We know that trauma outlives individuals and generations to become codified into national and cultural histories; the "Cranes Over Hiroshima" remind us that our messages of hope and purpose can outlive us just as well.*

# Measuring Progress

We conducted a thematic analysis of student clinicians' responses to the question "Why is it important for clinicians to learn about disasters?". Four themes emerged: (a) increased knowledge of a specific disaster, other disasters, and their occurrence; (b) increased empathy and increased personal capacity to relate to people's experience in a deep and meaningful way; (c) growth of the student clinician self—the clinician's ability to recognize the emotional and psychological impact on the self while applying the necessary measures for preventing negative effects of client trauma on clinicians; and (d) recognition of the need for social activism and immediate social support in the wake of disaster. Although there were fewer responses for the last theme, the classroom discussion also reflected student clinicians' increased understanding of immediate crisis intervention, the importance of remembrance, and their desire to prevent such actions in the future.

The most common response to the activity was that participation in DEAR helped student clinicians to develop more empathy and to control personal bias. Irvin Yalom (2009) likens therapeutic empathy to "looking out the patient's window" (p. 18). Clinicians must find the courage to leave their own comfortable windows and practice looking out of windows with very different views (Yalom, 2009). The development of intercultural empathy and viewpoints can assist in cases where clinicians' worldviews contradict their clients' worldviews. Research shows that even though clinicians may exhibit low levels of *explicit* bias, *implicit* bias levels often remain quite high (Boysen, 2009). Following completion of DEAR, another student clinician commented:

*I could see the reactions of sorrow, pain, and hurt while seeing how people come together at times of disaster. In some ways, writing my own reflection allows me to have my own experience of the disaster. Through this activity, I felt I was giving voice to those who no longer have a voice. It was helpful to connect my own personal pain to the pain of my disaster. Sharing this in a supportive environment was healing. Sharing connects us as humans to universal suffering.*

# Conclusion

*I didn't experience the internment of Japanese-Americans firsthand, I wasn't alive when the internment happened, and I am not Japanese-American. But reading the first-person, written accounts, seeing the pictures, and reading and rereading the poetry helped transport me to these*

*WWII camps, which I had written about. I now felt a connection to the people taken from their communities and families. I felt a connection to the way that fear, silence, and the dust of forgetting enveloped the physical locations of the camps. I felt connected to the way that internees returning half a century later to the prison of their childhood met only razed foundations, sagebrush, and lonely wind—a part of who they are forgotten (T.V.).*

As presented in this statement, participating in DEAR can assist student clinicians in developing the kind of self-capacities needed in order to develop macro-level crisis and trauma competencies (McDowell et al., 2012). Through the DEAR assignment, student clinicians attained in-depth learning of the shared experience of disaster victims, as well as the immediate and intergenerational effects such disasters have on victimized groups. The sequence of DEAR's didactic and experiential learning steps can help student clinicians develop several critical person-of-the-therapist attributes, interests, and empathy, while supporting self-confidence. Engaging in experiential activities helps reduce unnecessary pathologizing, lessens the potential negative effects of countertransference, and increases clinicians' capacity for intercultural and international empathy. Overall, an in-depth understanding of how larger systems and global events affect individuals, couples, and families also promotes the growth of the clinician's self and broadens his or her worldview.

# Additional Resources

American Counseling Association. (n.d.). *Disaster mental health.* Retrieved December 9, 2012, from www.counseling.org/knowledge-center/trauma-disaster

Carroll, R. (2005, June). Finding the words to say it: The healing power of poetry. *Evidence-Based Complementary Alternative Medicine, 2*(2), 161–172. doi: 10.1093/ecam/neh096

Hass-Cohen, N. (2012). *Disaster list guide handout: Crisis and trauma syllabi.* Alhambra, CA: California School of Professional Psychology, Alliant International University. Available from nhass-cohen@alliant.edu.

International Art Therapy Organization. (n.d.). International art therapists disaster relief database. Retrieved December 9, 2012, from www.internationalarttherapy.org/disasterrelief .html

Shields, K. (2012, December 19). *Sandy Hook Elementary thousand cranes peace project.* [Video file]. Retrieved December 20, 2012, from http://youtu.be/4JCJp3RPf_o

# References

Boysen, G. A. (2009). A review of experimental studies of explicit and implicit bias among counselors. *Journal of Multicultural Counseling and Development, 37*(4), 240–249. doi: 10.1002/j.2161-1912.2009.tb00106.x

Bronfenbrenner, U. (1977). Toward an experimental ecology of human development. *American Psychologist, 32*(7), 513–531. doi:10.1037//0003-066X.32.7.513

Brown, L., & Brown, J. (2009). Out of chaos, into a new identity: The transformative power of the international sojourn. *Journal of the Society for Existential Analysis, 20*(2), 341–361.

D'Andrea, M., & Heckman, E. F. (2008). A 40-year review of multicultural counseling outcome research: Outlining a future research agenda for the multicultural counseling movement. *Journal of Counseling & Development, 86*(3), 356–363. doi:10.1002/j.1556-6678.2008.tb00520.x

Duran, E., Firehammer, J., & Gonzalez, J. (2008). Liberation psychology as the path toward healing cultural soul wounds. *Journal of Counseling & Development, 86*(3), 288–295. doi: 10.1002/j.1556-6678.2008.tb00511.x

Dyche, L., & Zayas, L. H. (2001). Cross-cultural empathy and training the contemporary psychotherapist. *Clinical Social Work Journal, 29*(3), 245–258. doi: 10.1023/A:1010407728614

Fox, R. (2003). Traumaphobia: Confronting personal and professional anxiety. *Psychoanalytic Social Work*, *10*(1), 43–55. doi: 10.1300/J032v10n01_05

Freire, P. (1970). *Pedagogy of the oppressed*. New York, NY: Continuum.

Kim, B., & Lyons, H. (2003). Experiential activities and multicultural counseling competence training. *Journal of Counseling & Development*, *81*(4), 400–408. doi: 10.1002/j.1556-6678 .2003.tb00266.x

Leong, F. T. L., & Leach, M. M. (2007). Internationalising counseling psychology in the United States: A SWOT analysis. *Applied Psychology: An International Review*, *56*(1), 165–181. doi: 10.1111/j.1464-0597.2007.00283.x

Leung, A. (2003). A journey worth traveling: Globalization of counseling psychology. *The Counseling Psychologist*, *31*(4), 412–419. doi: 10.1177/0011000003031004004

Lifton, R. J. (1991). *Death in life: Survivors of Hiroshima*. Chapel Hill: University of North Carolina Press.

Malot, K. M. (2010). Multicultural counselor training in a single course: Review of research. *Multicultural Counseling and Development*, *38*(1), 51–63. doi: 10.1002/j.2161-1912.2010 .tb00113.x

McDowell, T., Goessling, K., & Melendez, T. (2012). Transformative learning through international immersion: Building multicultural competence in family therapy and counseling. *Journal of Marital and Family Therapy*, *38*(2), 365–379. doi: 10.1111/j.1752-0606.2010 .00209.x

Mills, L. (2002). What he knew before it all changed: A narrative from Ground Zero. *Brief Treatment and Crisis Intervention*, *2*(1), 23–31. doi: 10.1093/brief-treatment/2.1.23

Salston, M. D., & Figley, C. R. (2003). Secondary traumatic stress effects of working with survivors of criminal victimization. *Journal of Traumatic Stress*, *16*(2), 167–174. doi: 10.1023/A:1022899207206

Yalom, I. D. (2009). *The gift of therapy: An open letter to a new generation of therapists and their patients*. New York, NY: Harper Perennial.

# CHAPTER 18

# Developing Supervision Skills for Resiliency and Decreased Vicarious Trauma[1]

Noah Hass-Cohen and Karina A. Chandler-Ziegler

## Introduction

Clinicians treating traumatized populations are likely to experience secondary traumatic stress (STS) in the form of vicarious traumatization (VT). Clinicians' STS and burnout reactions mimic clients' posttraumatic stress disorder symptoms (Figley, 1995), whereas VT affects clinicians' views of themselves, others, and the world (Baird & Kracen, 2006; Figley, 1995). These negative changes usually result from exposure to clients' traumatic narratives (McCann & Pearlman, 1990).

Figley (1995) coined the term *burnout* for clinicians who have not practiced self-care, whereas STS and VT describe the negative effects of clinicians' exposure to trauma therapy work. Although self-care is a necessary part of clinical practice, it may not sufficiently mitigate the impact of increased exposure to the traumatized (Baird & Kracen, 2006). In these situations, clinicians need to actively engage in vicarious resiliency and growth (VRG) practices. Clinicians' VRG responses may not only mirror but also contribute to clients' posttrauma resiliency (Hernández, Engstrom, & Gangsei, 2010; Satkunanayagam, Tunariu, & Tribe, 2010). VRG processing is "characterized by a unique and positive effect that transforms clinicians in response to client trauma survivors' own resiliency" (Hernández et al., 2010, p. 72). Developing positive beliefs about client- and self-resiliency, deepened appreciation of interpersonal relationships, positive beliefs in the future, personal strength-based characteristics, and increased valuing of therapeutic endeavors contributes to VRG. VRG also contributes to a global recognition of the human capacity to survive (Hernández et al., 2010; Satkunanayagam et al., 2010).

This chapter presents a trauma-focused simulated supervision that is enhanced by expressive writing. It can assist in mitigating the effects of STS and VT, while contributing to clinicians' self-growth and to positive vicarious resiliency. Because novice clinicians may often be even less prepared than experienced clinicians for working with trauma, this activity aims to increase graduate-level mental health student clinicians' traumatology proficiencies.

## Rationale

Research suggests that clinicians who are new to working with traumatized populations are more likely to experience personal difficulties in their work (e.g., Adams & Riggs, 2008). Furthermore, as mental health funding declines, inexperienced student clinicians will find they are called to provide direct traumatology services where they may be more likely to experience VT (Knox, Burkard, Jackson, Schaack, & Hess, 2006; McAdams & Foster, 2000). Following the suicide of a client, most trainees report lingering feelings of anger and sadness and a sense of clinical inadequacy. Consequently, the provider may withdraw from traumatized clients (Etherington, 2000).

---

1.  Dedicated to our editor, Mara Forsythe-Crane, who died tragically shortly after this manuscript was completed.

Clinicians may also develop traumatic symptoms by indirect exposure; for example, by observing a training video (Smith, Kleijn, Trijsburg, & Hutschemaekers, 2007). Following exposure to unexpected trauma, student clinicians may experience specific reactions, such as shock, anxiety, and intense sadness (Smith et al., 2007). Clinicians-in-training who have a history of trauma are also more vulnerable to VT (Linley & Joseph, 2007) and more likely to develop maladaptive coping, such as isolation, acting out, and dissociation, which supervisors address (Adams & Riggs, 2008; Knox et al., 2006; Sommer & Cox, 2005). However, significant gaps exist in the supervision literature on the development of VRG for clinicians-in-training (Etherington, 2000). Although some research exists on VRG for traumatology clinicians (Hernández et al., 2010; Satkunanayagam et al., 2010), little research was found regarding student clinicians providing services to trauma-affected clients (Chandler-Ziegler & Padilla, 2011).

Participation in class role-plays and supervision allows student clinicians and instructors to deviate from traditional roles and focus on personal and professional development. Processing and confronting traumatic events through talking and writing contributes to supportive meaning-making and assists in long-term stress reduction (Pennebaker, Kiecolt-Glaser, & Glaser, 1988). In fact, Pennebaker et al. (1988) found that when healthy graduate students were asked to write about actual or imagined traumatic events over a period of four consecutive days, they exhibited better physical health than they did before beginning trauma writing (measured through cellular immune system functioning). This suggests that, when trauma is processed in writing, long-term negative responses may be prevented. When supervising clinicians-in-training who work with survivors of sexual violence and with trauma, supervisors should (a) provide them with the opportunity to talk about their personal feelings; (b) explicitly address VT in supervision; (c) maintain a collaborative and respectful interpersonal relationship with student clinicians; (d) be calming and collaborative in promoting self-care; (e) consider issues such as power differentials and/or inadequate time or priorities; and (f) have a strong understanding of the treatment of trauma (Sommer & Cox, 2005).

# Activity Instructions

In the course of the activity, student clinicians experience how supervision and expressive writing contribute to developing VRG skills and support self-of-the-therapist growth. Much of new clinicians' growth comes from interacting with a seasoned clinician in a safe and caring environment. Therefore, the instructions for this activity are written specifically for the supervisors.

In preparation, participants review information on trauma types, posttraumatic stress disorders (PTSD) criteria (American Psychiatric Association, 2000), complex PTSD, developmental trauma disorders, and treatment (Courtois & Ford, 2013). It is beneficial if they understand that personal traits such as creativity, bravery, kindness, perseverance, and optimism bridge across cultures and protect trauma workers from negative mental health implications (Kobau et al., 2011). Trainees are also asked to make a trauma-based self-genogram so that they consider their personal reactions within the context of their family's history of disaster, trauma, and crisis. In doing so, the supervisor seeks to inspire student clinicians to search for self-growth in the face of adversity.

For the simulated supervision activity, student clinicians view an excerpt from the movie *For Colored Girls* (Perry et al., 2010), which is based on Shange's (1980) book and play *For Colored Girls Who've Considered Suicide When the Rainbow Is Enuf*. Showcasing the characters' incredible resilience, the excerpt exposes the struggles and obstacles that African American women have faced and continue to face as a result of social injustice and personal circumstances. While watching the movie clip, the students-in-training are exposed to a domestic violence scene. Following the clip, they identify and analyze and reflect on their reactions orally and in a creative writing exercise.

This simulated supervision provides a supportive environment for participants to continue to explore possible trauma work influences. Instructors and supervisors teach how to process vicarious trauma and vicarious resiliency reactions, and engaging in reflective writing aims to support hope and resiliency. Before viewing the movie clip, the instructor cautions about its traumatic nature and encourages using stress reduction and grounding skills. He or she may also need to adjust the timing, duration, and balancing of didactic preparatory versus experiential activities.

In the first movie clip, the main character, Crystal, loses her two young children. In the scene, her inebriated boyfriend, a veteran, pleads with Crystal to marry him. She refuses; he hits her and subsequently drops their two children from the apartment window, resulting in their death (we recommend stopping the video before the children are dropped from the window). In an effort to escape her feelings of grief and self-blame, Crystal attempts suicide. Unsuccessful, she returns to her apartment where Gilda, her property owner, confronts her by suggesting that Crystal may help other women save their babies (Perry et al., 2010). Post-observation the student clinicians first complete the VT checklist (see Table 18.1) to identify and quantify the frequency of any symptoms that they may have experienced during and immediately after viewing the clip.

They then share their reactions. Some may follow Gilda's example and talk about Crystal's options for the future, others may grieve for her, and some may express judgment.

The supervisor highlights the differences between the STS and VT symptoms. The STS symptoms are similar to those of PTSD and include: reexperiencing Crystal's trauma, flashbacks, somatic symptoms, avoidance, anxiety, and sadness. VT-type symptoms are associated with disturbances in clinicians' self-schemas. They include inferred negative thoughts and feelings about relationships, and difficulties with trust, intimacy, and personal and professional confidence. It is the VT that consolidates professional burnout and STS. In discussing the checklist and Crystal's experience, the group learns that a client's grief and complicated bereavement can greatly increase the client's risk for suicide (Bonanno, Brewin, Kaniasty, & La Greca, 2010), whereas familial, communal, and medical support serve as protective factors (Taylor, Asmundson, & Carleton, 2006). Student clinicians are encouraged to discuss how they might react to client suicide and to understand that self-doubt about one's clinical abilities is to be expected (McAdams & Foster, 2000).

To begin the expressive writing component, a VRG-oriented scene from *For Colored Girls* (Perry, 2010) is projected. Standing among friends, Crystal recites a poem from Shange (1980) and speaks about surviving her children:

> *I sat up one night walking my apartment floors screaming, crying. The ghost of another woman who was missing what I was missing. I wanted to jump outta my bones and be done with myself. Leave me alone and go on in the wind. It was too much. I fell into a numbness 'til the only tree I could see took me up in her branches held me in the breeze. Made me dawn dew that chill at daybreak, the sun wrapped me up, swingin' rose light everywhere, the sky laid over me like a million men. I was cold. I was burnin' up. A child and endlessly weaving garments for the moon with my tears. I found God in myself, and I loved her, I loved her fiercely.* (Shange, 1980, p. 63)

Following this survival monologue, the student clinicians are to write a letter or poem to themselves or to Crystal. Writing a poem to Crystal allows some of the students to feel closer to experiences of adversity. Others who may have experienced self-adversity may prefer writing to themselves. Reflective writing allows processing at a self-pace, without worrying about immediate opinions or reactions of the supervision group or supervisor. It is a protected and confidential means of communicating experienced feelings (Pennebaker et al., 1988). Letters or poems and the VRG checklist (Table 18.2) are subsequently shared with the group.

# Examples

As the examples demonstrate, the reflection writing experience allows student clinicians to simultaneously recognize their resiliency and/or the resilience of persons who have experienced trauma. Zerina's poetic lines demonstrate personal identification with Crystal, feelings of grief, as well as perseverance and resilience:

> *I want to help you remember. What you feel that you have lost. What you have lost or don't remember you ever had. Like you, I was a flower once. So bright, radiant, glittering. Full of possibilities and hope. Now, I am full and far from bloom, I have forgotten the beauty, I have forgotten myself, My Sun. Helping you remember your brilliance. Only then, I may see that I am, you are, we are the light.*

David's letter, written from the perspective of a clinician who had been working with Crystal following the death of her children, embraces her survival monologue. He praises Crystal

**Table 18.1 Vicarious Trauma Checklist**

Instructions: Identify and rate the frequency of the items that you have experienced while and immediately after watching the movie clip.

### REEXPERIENCING

*I reexperienced the traumatic interactions between the characters*:

**0** not at all     **1** once     **2** some of the time     **3** most of the time     **4** all the time

*I had flashbacks of the traumatic events*:

**0** not at all     **1** once     **2** some of the time     **3** most of the time     **4** all the time

### AVOIDANCE

*I felt numb*:

**0** not at all     **1** once     **2** some of the time     **3** most of the time     **4** all the time

*I wanted to avoid recalling what happened in the movie*:

**0** not at all     **1** once     **2** some of the time     **3** most of the time     **4** all the time

*I could not believe what happened*:

**0** not at all     **1** once     **2** some of the time     **3** most of the time     **4** all the time

### AROUSAL

*I wanted to leave*:

**0** not at all     **1** once     **2** some of the time     **3** most of the time     **4** all the time

*I felt anxious*:

**0** not at all     **1** once     **2** some of the time     **3** most of the time     **4** all the time

*I did not feel safe*:

**0** not at all     **1** once     **2** some of the time     **3** most of the time     **4** all the time

### MOOD

*I experienced depressive symptoms such as sadness*:

**0** not at all     **1** once     **2** some of the time     **3** most of the time     **4** all the time

*I felt anger*:

**0** not at all     **1** once     **2** some of the time     **3** most of the time     **4** all the time

### PHYSIOLOGICAL

*I experienced at least one somatic symptom (e.g., cold hands, sweat, upset stomach, nausea)*:

**0** not at all     **1** once     **2** some of the time     **3** most of the time     **4** all the time

### RELATIONSHIPS

*I felt or thought negatively about interpersonal relationships*:

**0** not at all     **1** once     **2** some of the time     **3** most of the time     **4** all the time

*I felt or thought negatively about interpersonal trust or intimacy*:

**0** not at all     **1** once     **2** some of the time     **3** most of the time     **4** all the time

### PERSONAL CONTROL

*I felt or thought about a restriction in freedom and autonomy*:

**0** not at all     **1** once     **2** some of the time     **3** most of the time     **4** all the time

*I experienced a sense of personal vulnerability*:

**0** not at all     **1** once     **2** some of the time     **3** most of the time     **4** all the time

Table 18.1 (continued)

| *I experienced feeling or thinking about hopelessness*: | | | | |
|---|---|---|---|---|
| **0** not at all | **1** once | **2** some of the time | **3** most of the time | **4** all the time |

| *I experienced feeling or thinking about powerlessness*: | | | | |
|---|---|---|---|---|
| **0** not at all | **1** once | **2** some of the time | **3** most of the time | **4** all the time |

### PROFESSIONAL CONFIDENCE

| *I doubted my ability to work with people*: | | | | |
|---|---|---|---|---|
| **0** not at all | **1** once | **2** some of the time | **3** most of the time | **4** all the time |

| *I felt a decreased sense of self-worth and esteem*: | | | | |
|---|---|---|---|---|
| **0** not at all | **1** once | **2** some of the time | **3** most of the time | **4** all the time |

Adapted from: Chandler-Ziegler, K. A., & Padilla, I. (2011).

Table 18.2 Vicarious Resilience Growth Checklist

Instructions: Identify and rate the frequency of the items that you have experienced after participating in the discussion and creating the reflective writing.

| *I experienced positive feelings about the character's resilience*: | | | | |
|---|---|---|---|---|
| **0** not at all | **1** once | **2** some of the time | **3** most of the time | **4** all the time |

| *I experienced an increased positive outlook on life*: | | | | |
|---|---|---|---|---|
| **0** not at all | **1** once | **2** some of the time | **3** most of the time | **4** all the time |

| *I was able to recognize the importance of social relationships*: | | | | |
|---|---|---|---|---|
| **0** not at all | **1** once | **2** some of the time | **3** most of the time | **4** all the time |

| *I experienced an enhanced understanding of what personal strength means*: | | | | |
|---|---|---|---|---|
| **0** not at all | **1** once | **2** some of the time | **3** most of the time | **4** all the time |

| *I experienced an enhanced recognition of the human capacity to survive*: | | | | |
|---|---|---|---|---|
| **0** not at all | **1** once | **2** some of the time | **3** most of the time | **4** all the time |

| *I experienced an increased sense of spirituality*: | | | | |
|---|---|---|---|---|
| **0** not at all | **1** once | **2** some of the time | **3** most of the time | **4** all the time |

| *I experienced an enhanced value of my work as a clinician*: | | | | |
|---|---|---|---|---|
| **0** not at all | **1** once | **2** some of the time | **3** most of the time | **4** all the time |

Did you experience or observe in Crystal or in your reactions any of the following personal strengths: open-mindedness, creativity, bravery, perseverance, honesty, love, collaboration/teamwork, forgiveness, bravery, self-regulation, hope, trust, spirituality, or respect? If so, please comment on three such strengths:

**1**.

**2**.

**3**.

Adapted from: Chandler-Ziegler, K. A., & Padilla, I. (2011).

for her resilience as he touches on the difficulty and importance of simply providing space for grieving:

> *Crystal, Thank you! The expression you have given me these weeks and months is a gift unique in its meaning for me. To recall the beaten shell that has transformed into a woman engulfed with the fire's power within that I see in you today inspires me. You have taught me once again that sometimes the most I, as a therapist, can do is simply be present with another person to bear witness to her journey. In the story of that truth, you have indeed helped me along in mine. As you move forward in your life, when that inner goddess seems distant or gone, remember you formed her inside and she is there. Those times of doubt and confusion that might come cannot crush you. May your spirit burn with a fire, passion, wherever you go.*

John, who works with cases of complex trauma in Mexico City, vocalized a reminder that he is making a difference and that things can change:

> *In order to alleviate my feelings of helplessness in situations like the one Crystal went through (i.e., have more resources on choices, especially here in Mexico), I love to fight for a change in the mindset that nothing can be done. Things can change and we can make a difference. One of the most fundamental parts of this is the belief that it is possible and that the cycle of violence doesn't have to continue.*

# Measuring Progress

When working with people with a diversity of adverse life circumstances, STS and VT threaten the therapeutic alliance. Developing awareness of traumatic therapist reactions and learning how to transform those to posttraumatic growth are therefore critical skills. For the purposes of this activity, the VRG checklist can be used as a measure of such progress (Table 18.2).

# Conclusion

Clinicians-in-training are increasingly asked to provide traumatology services. It is therefore imperative that they receive quality STS and VT training. Our supervision and expressive writing activity is designed to help student clinicians learn to (a) explain STS and VT long-term impacts, (b) recognize self-symptoms of STS and VT, (c) acknowledge posttrauma recovery and resiliency, and (d) use supervision, peer group support, and expressive writing in order to self-regulate, and access hope and VRG. This activity is well-suited for courses such as crisis and trauma, psychopathology, and practicum. Similarly, experienced clinicians can benefit from this activity, particularly when they are asked to provide trauma-based work.

# Additional Resources

Baranowsky, A. B., Gentry, E. J., & Schultz, F. D. (2010). *Trauma practice: Tools for stabilization and recovery*. Cambridge, United Kingdom: Hogrefe.

Skovholt, T. M. (2001). *The resilient practitioner: Burnout prevention and self-care strategies for counselors, therapists, teachers, and health professionals*. Boston, MA: Allyn & Bacon.

# References

Adams, S. A., & Riggs, S. A. (2008). An exploratory study of vicarious trauma among therapist trainees. *Training and Education in Professional Psychology, 2*(1), 26–34. doi: 10.1037/1931-3918.2.1.26

American Psychiatric Association. (2000). *Diagnostic and statistical manual of mental disorders* (4th ed., text rev.). Washington, DC: Author.

Baird, K., & Kracen, A. C. (2006). Vicarious traumatization and secondary traumatic stress: A research synthesis. *Counseling Psychology Quarterly, 19*(2), 181–188. doi: 10.1080/0951507060081189

Bonanno, G. A., Brewin, C. R., Kaniasty, K., & La Greca, A. M. (2010). Weighing the costs of disaster: Consequences, risks, and resilience in individuals, families, and communities. *Psychological Science in the Public Interest, 11*(1), 1–49. doi: 10.1177/1529100610387086

Chandler-Ziegler, K. A., & Padilla, I. (2011). *The effects of trauma exposure on novice therapists and implications for supervision*. Unpublished manuscript, Alliant International University, Alhambra, CA.

Courtois, C. A., & Ford, J. D. (2013). *Treatment of complex trauma: A sequenced relationship-based approach*. New York, NY: Guilford Press.

Etherington, K. (2000). Supervising counselors who work with survivors of childhood sexual abuse. *Counselling Psychology Quarterly, 13*, 377–389. doi: 10.1080/713658497

Figley, C. R. (1995). *Compassion fatigue: Coping with secondary traumatic stress disorder in those who treat the traumatized*. New York, NY: Bruner/Mazel.

Hernández, P., Engstrom, D., & Gangsei, D. (2010). Exploring the impact of trauma on therapists: Vicarious resilience and related concepts in training. *Journal of Systemic Therapies, 29*(1), 67–83. doi: 10.1521/jsyt.2010.29.1.67

Knox, S., Burkard, A. W., Jackson, J. A., Schaack, A. M., & Hess, S. A. (2006). Therapists-in-training who experience a client suicide: Implications for supervision. *Professional Psychology, Research & Practice, 37*(5), 547–557. doi: 10.1037/0735-7028.37.5.547

Kobau, R., Seligman, M. P., Peterson, C., Diener, E., Zack, M. M., Chapman, D., & Thompson, W. (2011). Mental health promotion in public health: Perspectives and strategies from positive psychology. *American Journal of Public Health, 101*(8), e1–e9. doi: 10.2105/AJPH.2010.300083

Linley, P. A., & Joseph, S. (2007). Therapy work and therapists' positive and negative well-being. *Journal of Social and Clinical Psychology, 26*, 385–403.

McAdams, C., & Foster, V. A. (2000). Client suicide: Its frequency and impact on counselors. *Journal of Mental Health Counseling, 22*(2), 107–121.

McCann, I. L., & Pearlman, L. A. (1990). Vicarious traumatization: A framework for understanding the psychological effects of working with victims. *Journal of Traumatic Stress, 3*, 131–149.

Pennebaker, J. W., Kiecolt-Glaser, J., & Glaser, R. (1988). Disclosure of traumas and immune function: Health implications for psychotherapy. *Journal of Consulting and Clinical Psychology, 56*(2), 239–245.

Perry, T. (2010). *For colored girls*. [Movie script]. (p. 87A). Available from: http://moviecultists .com/wp-content/uploads/screenplays/for-colored-girls.pdf

Perry, T., Shange, N., Hall, P., Bobb, R. M., Areu, O., Genier, J. P., … Passornex, M., (Producers), & Perry, T. (Director). (2010). For colored girls *[Motion picture]*. United States: Lionsgate.

Satkunanayagam, K., Tunariu, A., & Tribe, R. (2010). A qualitative exploration of mental health professionals' experience of working with survivors of trauma in Sri Lanka. *International Journal of Culture and Mental Health, 3*(1), 43–51. doi: 10.1080/17542861003593336

Shange, N. (1980). *For colored girls who've considered suicide when the rainbow is enuf*. New York, NY: Scribner Poetry.

Smith, A. J., Kleijn, W. C., Trijsburg, R. W., & Hutschemaekers, G. J. (2007). How therapists cope with clients' traumatic experiences. *Torture, 17*(3), 203–215.

Sommer, C. A., & Cox, J. A. (2005). Elements of supervision in sexual violence counselors' narratives: A qualitative analysis. *Counselor Education and Supervision, 45*(2), 119–134.

Taylor, S., Asmundson, G. G., & Carleton, R. (2006). Simple versus complex PTSD: A cluster analytic investigation. *Journal of Anxiety Disorders, 20*(4), 459–472. doi: 10.1016/ j.janxdis.2005.04.003

# CHAPTER 19

# DEALING WITH TRAUMA USING SELF-AWARENESS AND SELF-CARE

Kami L. Schwerdtfeger

## Introduction

The wide prevalence of trauma experiences in clinical populations and the advancement of trauma-informed services require that clinicians are well-trained in dealing with trauma issues. This chapter demonstrates the use of four specific activities to assist clinicians' self-awareness of trauma-related experiences and self-care needs. Increasing awareness of personal trauma triggers and the necessity for self-care serves to protect clinicians against compassion fatigue and professional burnout.

## Rationale

The term *trauma* refers to an event resulting in severe psychological shock and emotional distress. The psychological stress related to the traumatic incidents often can be so disabling and distressing that a person's ability to cope with the situation is overwhelmed. Traumatic events that can trigger mental health problems include violent personal assaults such as rape or mugging, natural or human-caused disasters, military combat, and interpersonal traumas. It is estimated that 74.2% of women and 81.3% of men in the general population have experienced at least one traumatic event (Stein, Walker, Hazen, & Forde, 1997), while the rate may be as high as 94% among clients receiving mental health services (Switzer et al., 1999).

The trauma experienced by many clients seeking mental health services often is not associated with single-blow traumatic events (Terr, 1991) but rather prolonged and repeated interpersonal traumas that may extend over many years. These experiences include sexual abuse or incest, physical abuse, severe neglect, and serious emotional and psychological abuse. These traumas can have wide-ranging impacts on the trauma survivor, affecting identity, relationships, emotional regulation, and worldview (McCann & Pearlman, 1990). Although the majority of clients seeking clinical services are trauma survivors (Najavits, Weiss, & Shaw, 1997; Polusny & Follette, 1995), initial research has shown that trauma and posttraumatic stress disorder (PTSD; American Psychiatric Association, 2000) often went unrecognized (Mueser et al., 1998; Saunders, Kilpatrick, Resnick, & Tidwell, 1989) and that related clinical services were frequently inadequate (Amaya-Jackson et al., 1999). These findings led many state and national mental health agencies and organizations, including the National Association of State Mental Health Program Directors and the Substance Abuse and Mental Health Services Administration, to call for the implementation of trauma-informed services that effectively attend to the needs of trauma survivors.

Trauma-informed clinical services are those in which service delivery is influenced by both knowledge of past and/or current abuse in the client's life and an understanding of the impact of interpersonal violence and victimization on an individual's life and development (Harris & Fallot, 2001). Over the past 10 years, specific trauma-informed models have been designed to address traumatic stress and other concerns that are common in the lives of clients seeking mental health services (such as PTSD, borderline personality disorder, anxiety disorders, eating disorders, addictions, depression, and other affective disorders) in a manner that acknowledges the unique vulnerabilities of trauma survivors and allows services to be delivered in a way that facilitates ongoing participation in treatment (e.g., Ford, Courtois, Steele, van der Hart, & Nijenhuis, 2005; Mueser, Rosenberg, Goodman, & Trumbetta, 2002).

Recognizing the wide prevalence of trauma experiences in clinical populations and the advancement of trauma-informed services, it is imperative that clinicians be well-trained in dealing with trauma issues. In addition to being familiar with current literature on trauma and effective trauma-informed treatment models, clinicians must be prepared for the unique challenges present when working with individuals, couples, and families in trauma and crisis situations. This challenging and complex work requires trauma-informed clinicians who are self-aware of their own trauma history and are equipped to actively and consistently implement self-care strategies within their work. Activities aimed at helping clinicians to explore their own experiences and relationship with trauma and to sort out the strong feelings that can be elicited when working with trauma survivors are imperative steps in developing competent, trauma-informed clinicians.

# Activity Instructions

The following trauma-informed self-awareness activities are utilized as part of a clinical training module on family stress, trauma, and resilience. The training module is designed to introduce student clinicians to traumatic stress and trauma-informed treatment from both individual and systemic theoretical perspectives. As a part of the four-week module, student clinicians are introduced to and review the theoretical and historical beginnings of the concept of trauma, which includes the acceptance of PTSD as a diagnosis in the *DSM-III* (American Psychiatric Association, 1980). This training module discusses various trauma reactions and the effects of stressful events, as well as the treatment of trauma, stress, and crises. Resilience and transcendence of trauma are also outlined, with an emphasis on the importance of self-care for clinicians and other helping professionals working with traumatized clients.

Most central to the development of the clinicians' trauma-informed self-awareness is the completion of weekly self-awareness activities. These weekly activities are best conducted when assigned by a supervisor as part of a class requirement, training exercise, or workshop. Because these activities are designed to elicit strong emotions and insights, they are meant to be conducted in a supervised environment with ongoing follow-up and discussion. Although individuals could answer the questions while working on a self-assigned basis, they would miss out on the significant growth opportunities that come from discussion with a trusted mentor or supervisor. Therefore, the instructions are directed mainly to supervisors.

Each journal activity is specifically aimed at assisting the student clinician to perform a thorough self-assessment of the personal role, impact, and response to stress and trauma. Student clinicians are instructed that they will be required to keep a weekly journal of their thoughts and feelings about the training content and current events related to trauma and crisis, as well as their implications for clinical, family, and community practice. Weekly journal entries provide the supervisor a method to assess and monitor student clinicians' responses to the often emotionally difficult activities and topics discussed as part of student clinicians' training and clinical work (e.g., suicide, domestic violence, physical and sexual abuse).

Journal entries are to be handwritten essays of one to three pages in which student clinicians explore a real-life situation and apply training materials, concepts, and/or discussion. Supervisors should provide specific questions or thinking points to direct each entry, but student clinicians are encouraged to be self-reflective by considering their own values, beliefs, and attitudes. Student clinicians are expected to dedicate the time necessary each week to thoroughly complete the journal activity and entry prior to weekly supervision. Journal activities 1 and 2 are specifically designed to increase clinicians' awareness of their own personal trauma history, as well as their posttrauma experiences of healing and growth. Journal activities 3 and 4 are designed to assist clinicians in understanding the challenge of balancing personal and professional roles and providing self-care.

As a note to supervisors, the highly personal nature of this assignment does require specific precautions. As an example, student clinicians have been instructed to complete the journal assignment in two parts: a personal entry and a graded portion. In the personal portion, clinicians are instructed to complete the journal entries knowing that they are the only ones who will ever see the entries. This personal entry is then folded and stapled together and is not read or graded by the supervisor. In the graded portion, clinicians are encouraged to write down their thoughts and feelings but are not forced to divulge any information that they are uncomfortable sharing.

As the first step in self-assessment, each clinician is instructed to complete a lifeline. The lifeline exercise is adapted from a therapeutic technique outlined in KIDNET, a child-friendly exposure treatment for children and adolescents with PTSD that can also be used with adults (Schauer, Neuner, Schauer, & Elbert, 2003). In this technique, a small rope is used to represent the individual's lifeline. Flowers are used to mark positive experiences along the lifeline, while stones are used to mark negative and traumatic experiences. For the activity, each student clinician is given a lifeline (length of rope) and a selection of stones of varying characteristics and sizes, as well as flowers of varying sizes and colors. Each student clinician is instructed to take 20 to 30 minutes constructing their lifeline, outlining the major life events using flowers for positive events and stones for negative events in a chronological order. Student clinicians are instructed to include as much or as little as they feel comfortable sharing about each event marked. After completing the lifeline, student clinicians are instructed to take a photo or make a sketch of the completed lifeline to include in their personal journal as they begin to explore the role or themes of stress, crisis, and trauma in their lives. Student clinicians are then instructed to complete a three- to four-page journal response to the following questions about their experience and relationship with trauma:

1. As you look back over your lifeline, what themes do you notice across your life?
2. What roles have stress and trauma played in your life?
3. How has trauma affected your growth and your identity?

**Journal Activity 1: Personal Trauma Self-Assessment**

Despite the strong focus on the negative implications of trauma within research and literature, positive adaptation and changes following trauma have also been noted (Linley & Joseph, 2004). Terms including "stress-related growth" (Park, Cohen, & Murch, 1996), "thriving" (O'Leary & Ickovics, 1995), "adversarial growth" (Linley & Joseph, 2004), and "posttraumatic growth" (Tedeschi & Calhoun, 1995) have all been used to refer to the phenomenon in which individuals overcome trauma with improved psychological, cognitive, and emotional functioning. The term "posttraumatic growth" (Tedeschi & Calhoun, 1995) clearly expresses the concept within the literature, referring to those trauma survivors who not only bounce back but go on to excel beyond what would be expected because of past traumatic experiences. Calhoun, Cann, Tedeschi, and McMillan (2000) define *posttraumatic growth* as "the experience of significant positive change arising from the struggle with a major life crisis" (p. 521).

Posttraumatic growth is characterized by significant positive changes in the survivor's perception of self, approach to interpersonal relationships, and philosophy of life (Tedeschi & Calhoun, 1995; Tedeschi, Park, & Calhoun, 1998). Examples of specific domains of positive growth and change possible after trauma include the identification of new possibilities for one's life, more intimate and meaningful relationships with others, a general sense of increased personal strength, positive spiritual change, and increased appreciation of life (Tedeschi et al., 1998). Within their model of posttraumatic growth, Tedeschi and Calhoun (2004) conceptualize that positive growth occurs as a result of a trauma experience that challenges an individual's personal goals, beliefs, and ability to manage emotional distress. Tedeschi and Calhoun (2004) also suggest that individual characteristics, social support, and disclosure play an important role in the ongoing growth process.

To assist student clinicians in understanding the resilience and growth that are possible as a result of trauma and stress, student clinicians are instructed to examine their own process of healing, growth, and resilience. Student clinicians are instructed to begin the activity by envisioning themselves sitting in the therapy chair. Thinking back on their own lifeline, they are directed to explore the strengths and resources they relied on to survive times of stress, crisis, or trauma, and develop a metaphor, song, phrase, or other medium that meaningfully describes their own posttraumatic growth or healing. Student clinicians are then directed to include the lyrics of

**Journal Activity 2: Posttraumatic Growth and Healing**

the song, drawing, metaphor, or other medium illustrating their personal process of growth and resilience in their personal journal and complete a three- to four-page written journal response to the following items:

1. Describe your journey in healing and/or growing from trauma, crisis, or stress in your own life.
2. How did you cope/are you coping with or recovering from the stones placed along your lifeline?
3. What role, if any, have the flowers along your lifeline played in your healing journey?
4. What signs of posttraumatic healing or growth have you seen or noted in your life?

**Journal Activity 3: Personal Trauma-Informed Mission Statement**

Compassion fatigue (Figley, 1995) is a natural occupational hazard for helping professionals and clinicians. Compassion fatigue is the natural consequence of being human, of connecting to and caring about clients as clinicians hear about and see the effects of trauma in clients' lives. It is important that student clinicians understand that the intensity of clinical work will affect them and that it is important for them to develop a plan to balance caring for their clients and caring for themselves. In an effort to protect against compassion fatigue, it is important to begin assisting clinicians in developing an awareness of their own personal needs and a plan for balancing their personal and professional roles. Student clinicians are instructed to complete a three- to four-page journal response to the following questions:

1. What led you toward helping others?
2. What values will you never compromise in your work with clients/participants/agencies?
3. What are you committed to offer clients/participants/agencies?
4. What are you committed to offer yourself?
5. What do you believe about your clients/participants/agencies?
6. What do you believe about your own strengths?
7. If you were to become your ideal caregiver, how would life look to you?
8. How would you maintain the balance between caring for others and caring for yourself?

**Journal Activity 4: Letter From the "Great Supervisor"**

This exercise is frequently utilized with military combat chaplains in an effort to ease the stress and fatigue of caregiving in the stressful combat environment. Student clinicians are instructed to write a letter from the "Great Supervisor" using the following instructions:

1. This letter should be written to yourself from an omniscient (all-knowing) and omnibenevolent (all-good) source.
2. This letter should reflect the nurturance, support, and validation that you have wanted and needed to hear from someone in authority.
3. It should focus on your strengths, assets, and goodness. The more honest and sincere that you make this letter, the more benefit you will receive.

# Example

These trauma-informed self-assessment journal activities have been used in a four-week master's-level graduate course on family stress, trauma, and resilience. In course evaluations, student clinicians have frequently reported that the journal assignments were the "most challenging, yet fruitful" exercises of the course. Overall, student clinicians report that they enjoyed the experiential activities that personalized the often "intense" training topics and materials, allowing them to "recognize their own emotions and how their response could impact their work with clients." Student clinicians frequently mention that they appreciated the prompts provided by the supervisor. While guided, student clinicians appreciated that they were allowed freedom to utilize their personal journal in a manner that was most effective for their personal growth and development. Additionally, student clinicians have frequently commented that they appreciate having the journal entries to go back to and read even after the module is over.

# Measuring Progress

Journals are formally evaluated using three criteria: (1) the seriousness and sincerity of the student clinician's work, indicated by the degree to which course content (e.g., readings, discussions) has been incorporated; (2) the student clinician's capacity to express her- or himself clearly; and (3) the extent to which the student clinician has carried out the task. Because of the personal nature of the activities, successful and thorough completion of each exercise is the first sign of student clinician progress and increased self-awareness. It should be noted that the student clinician's level of self-awareness is best illustrated not by the level of detail of events but by the personal insights into the themes and the role of stress, crisis, and trauma in the student clinician's life. Furthermore, the student clinician's development of a thorough and insightful plan for self-care to avoid compassion fatigue or burnout provides additional criteria for measuring progress.

The degree to which the journal entries promote ongoing processing and discussion is perhaps the greatest measure of progression of self-awareness. As they complete the journal activities, student clinicians are encouraged to consult family members or friends who were part of their social support network during or following various lifeline experiences to gain insight on the impact of the event and the process of healing and growth. It is important to note that all student clinicians in the training module are engaged in weekly individual and group supervision. Student clinicians are encouraged to discuss their journal entries and personal insights in individual supervision as they relate to their current caseload or their personal theory of change in individual supervision. Student clinicians are also encouraged by the supervisor to share, as they are comfortable, any personal insights with cohort members/classmates in group supervision contexts.

Additionally, these activities must be completed as part of a formal supervision, training module, or course that allows for ongoing follow-up and discussion of the strong emotions or insight that the activities are designed to elicit. In cases in which the student clinician has unresolved personal trauma or is experiencing avoidance or intolerance for the strong emotions that accompany trauma-focused work, supervisors may need to refer student clinicians for more focused individual counseling to process their personal experiences.

# Conclusion

These activities and accompanying journal entries can be beneficial for all clinicians who will come face-to-face with clients' stress, crisis, and trauma experiences, and the strong emotions that often accompany such experiences, as part of their daily work. As student clinicians complete the journal activities, they not only explore their own relationship with trauma but also learn potential trauma triggers they must be aware of in their work with clients. Additionally, student clinicians begin to challenge their own assumptions about trauma survivors as victims as they begin to acknowledge their own personal strengths and resources that promote healing and growth. As a result, student clinicians begin to redefine their roles as helpers and adjust their behaviors to promote their clients' own coping capacity—ultimately learning how to attend to clients' stress, crisis, or trauma while still balancing their own self-care.

# Additional Resources

Baird, K., & Kracen, A. C. (2006). Vicarious traumatization and secondary traumatic stress: A research synthesis. *Counselling Psychology Quarterly, 19*(2), 181–188. doi: 10.1080/09515070600811899

Rothschild, B. (2006). *Help for the helper: The psychophysiology of compassion fatigue and vicarious trauma*. New York, NY: W. W. Norton.

Stamm, B. H. (1999). *Secondary traumatic stress: Self-care issues for clinicians, researchers and educators*. Baltimore, MD: Sidran.

# References

Amaya-Jackson, L., Davidson, J. R., Hughes, D. C., Swartz, M., Reynolds, V., George, L. K., & Blazer, D. G. (1999). Functional impairment and utilization of services associated with posttraumatic stress in the community. *Journal of Traumatic Stress, 12*, 709–724. doi: 10.1023/A:1024781504756

American Psychiatric Association. (1980). *Diagnostic and statistical manual of mental disorders* (3rd ed.). Washington, DC: Author.

American Psychiatric Association. (2000). *Diagnostic and statistical manual of mental disorders* (4th ed., text revision). Washington, DC: Author.

Calhoun, L. G., Cann, A., Tedeschi, R. G., & McMillan, J. (2000). A correlation test of the relationship between posttraumatic growth, religion, and cognitive processing. *Journal of Traumatic Stress, 13*, 521–527. doi: 10.1023/A:1007745627077

Figley, C. R. (Ed.). (1995). *Compassion fatigue: Secondary traumatic stress disorders from treating the traumatized*. New York, NY: Brunner/Mazel.

Ford, J., Courtois, C. A., Steele, K., van der Hart, O., & Nijenhuis, E. R. S. (2005). Treatment of complex posttraumatic self-dysregulation. *Journal of Traumatic Stress, 18*, 437–449. doi: 10.1002/jts.20051

Harris, M., & Fallot, R. D. (2001). *Using trauma theory to design service systems*. San Francisco, CA: Jossey-Bass.

Herman, J. (1997). *Trauma and recovery*. New York, NY: Basic Books.

Linley, P. A., & Joseph, S. (2004). Positive change following trauma and adversity: A review. *Journal of Traumatic Stress, 17*, 11–21. doi: 10.1023/B:JOTS.0000014671.27856.7e

McCann, I. L., & Pearlman, L. A. (1990). *Psychological trauma and the adult survivor*. New York, NY: Brunner Mazel.

Mueser, K., Goodman, L. A., Trumbetta, S. L., Rosenberg, S. D., Osher, F. C., Vidaver, R., … Foy, E. W. (1998). Trauma and posttraumatic stress disorder in severe mental illness. *Journal of Consulting and Clinical Psychology, 66*, 493–499. doi: 10.1037//0022-006X.66.3.493

Mueser, K. T., Rosenberg, S. D., Goodman, L. A., & Trumbetta, S. L. (2002). Trauma, PTSD, and the course of schizophrenia: An interactive model. *Schizophrenia Research, 53*, 123–143. doi: 10.1016/S0920-9964(01)00173-6

Najavits, L. M., Weiss, R. D., & Shaw, S. R. (1997). The link between substance abuse and posttraumatic stress disorder in women: A research review. *The American Journal on Addictions, 6*, 273–283. doi: 10.3109/10550499709005058

O'Leary, V., & Ickovics, J. R. (1995). Resilience and thriving in response to challenge: An opportunity for a paradigm shift in women's health. *Women's Health: Research on Gender, Behavior, and Policy, 1*, 121–142.

Park, C. L., Cohen, L. H., & Murch, R. (1996). Assessment and prediction of stress related growth. *Journal of Personality, 64*, 71–105. doi: 10.1111/j.1467-6494.1996.tb00815.x

Polusny, M. A., & Follette, V. M. (1995). Long-term correlates of child sexual abuse: Theory and review of the empirical literature. *Preventive Psychology, 4*, 143–166. doi: 10.1016/S0962-1849(05)80055-1

Saunders, B. E., Kilpatrick, D. G., Resnick, H. S., & Tidwell, R. P. (1989). Brief screening for lifetime history of criminal victimization at mental health intake: A preliminary study. *Journal of Interpersonal Violence, 4*, 267–277. doi: 10.1177/088626089004003001

Schauer, M., Neuner, F., Schauer, E., & Elbert, T. (2003). *Training manual for Narrative Exposure Therapy (NET)—A short term intervention for the treatment of traumatic stress disorders in children & adults*. Cupramontana, Italy: Vivo.

Stein, M. B., Walker, J. R., Hazen, A. L., & Forde, D. R. (1997). Full and partial posttraumatic stress disorder: Findings from a community survey. *American Journal of Psychiatry*, *154*, 1114–1119. Retrieved from http://ajp.psychiatryonline.org

Switzer, G. E., Dew, M. A., Thompson, K., Govcoolea, J. M., Derricott, T., & Mullins, S. D. (1999). Posttraumatic stress disorder and service utilization among urban mental health center clients. *Journal of Traumatic Stress*, *12*, 25–39. doi: 10.1023/A:1024738114428

Tedeschi, R. G., & Calhoun, L. G. (1995). *Trauma and transformation: Growing in the aftermath of suffering*. Thousand Oaks, CA: Sage.

Tedeschi, R. G., & Calhoun, L. G. (2004). Posttraumatic growth: Conceptual foundations and empirical evidence. *Psychological Inquiry*, *15*, 1–18. doi: 10.1207/s15327965pli1501_01

Tedeschi, R. G., Park, C. L., & Calhoun, L. G. (1998). Posttraumatic growth: Conceptual issues. In R. G. Tedeschi & L. G. Calhoun (Eds.), *Posttraumatic growth: Positive changes in the aftermath of crisis* (pp. 1–22). Mahwah, NJ: Lawrence Erlbaum.

Terr, L. (1991). Childhood traumas: An outline and overview. *American Journal of Psychiatry*, *148*, 10–20.

# CHAPTER 20

# ALIGNING ORGANIZATIONAL AND INDIVIDUAL CULTURE AND VALUES

Sue Steiner and Kathy Cox

## Introduction

All organizations have cultures. Although these cultures often go unnoticed by providers, they do affect the experiences of all staff members, volunteers, and clients within an organization. As Deal and Kennedy (1983) noted, an organization's distinct culture often evolves "through trial and error" and "includes shared values, heroes that embody these values, rituals and ceremonies, and cultural networks" (p. 498). Others have noted that organizational culture can be referred to as "the way we do things around here" (Martin, 2006). Culture is evident throughout an organization, from the way employees dress to how management communicates to the organization's mission statement. In order to work more effectively, clinical providers should understand the organization's culture and learn how to navigate within it.

Whether or not there is a good fit between an organization's culture and the needs, values, and expectations of individual staff members can shape employees' experiences with their jobs. Mismatches between individuals and the organizational culture can occur in several domains. For the purposes of this chapter, we will focus on the following three areas, which are particularly relevant in clinical and social service arenas: (a) degree of hierarchy, (b) information processing and sharing, and (c) importance of tasks versus relationships. The following activity was designed to help clinicians analyze themselves in relation to their respective organizations in order to better understand the level of match or mismatch with some important aspects of an organization's culture. This activity was developed to help clinicians first learn to assess the match and mismatch and then to receive suggestions for addressing areas of mismatch that seem most problematic to improve their clinical effectiveness and satisfaction at work.

## Rationale

Individual employees' values and expectations can clash with an organization's culture. When a mismatch is significant, it can negatively impact employees' enjoyment at work, level of stress, and job performance and effectiveness. Extreme mismatches can result in lower individual and organizational effectiveness and can lead to burnout. As Maslach and Leiter (2005) noted, "Burnout reflects an uneasy relationship between people and their work. Like relationship problems between two people, those between people and their work usually indicate a bad fit between the two, rather than *just* individual weaknesses, or *just* evil workplaces" (p. 44). The fit that individuals have with their work's organizational culture can affect their commitment to and satisfaction with the job as well as turnover rates (Adkins & Caldwell, 2004). Additionally, mismatches can increase levels of stress (Edwards & Shipp, 2007), resulting in a variety of well-documented stress-related challenges, such as diabetes, hypertension, obesity, and heart attacks (Pandy, Campbell Quick, Rossi, Nelson, & Martin, 2010).

Increasing the understanding of personal preferences and needs at work and recognizing mismatches with the organizational culture can benefit clinicians in several ways. Developing a greater awareness of their preferences at work, as contrasted with the expectations embedded within the workplace, can contribute to more effective clinical practice. Practice may be enhanced when clinicians are less preoccupied with the tensions inherent in employee–agency mismatches and are more focused on learning about their clients' needs and providing competent clinical services. Job satisfaction can be significantly improved when employees are assisted either in increasing their fit within the organizational work culture or in minimizing the stress or conflict that occurs for them in relationship to others at work. Prior research suggests a link between job satisfaction and job performance (Judge, Thoresen, Bono, & Patton, 2001; Wright & Cropanzano, 2000). Thus, both job satisfaction and performance may be increased when creative solutions for mismatches are developed that allow clinicians to articulate their needs, increase their tolerance toward others, and ultimately feel more connected and committed to organizational goals.

# Activity Instructions

This activity helps clinicians explore their preferences at work, their organization's culture, and the fit between the two. Clinicians from a variety of experience levels can benefit from this activity. Ideally, it should be completed by practicing clinicians as part of their ongoing training, as well as by graduate students who have begun working in an organizational setting. This activity includes individual observation of organizational culture followed by a written exploration and group discussions. It can either be self-assigned or assigned by a supervisor as part of a training exercise, class requirement, or a workshop. However, we believe that this activity works best when conducted in a class or group supervision setting; therefore, the following instructions are directed primarily to course instructors and clinical supervisors.

## Activity Preparation

This activity focuses on exploring individual preferences at work, organizational culture, and the fit between the two in the three areas of potential conflict: (a) degree of hierarchy, (b) information processing and sharing, and (c) importance of relationships. Prior to completing this activity, clinicians should become familiar with each of the three areas of potential conflict or mismatch, which are briefly described here, and should be instructed to pay particular attention to these aspects of their organization's culture for a week or two and reflect on their own thoughts and feelings about these areas.

It should also be noted that individuals' perspectives and comfort levels toward each of these three areas are likely affected by many factors, including individual social identities such as gender, race, and ethnicity. Our own cultural backgrounds and the relationship between our subculture and the dominant culture shape our values and behaviors as clinical providers. For example, some cultures are more collectivistic, whereas others are more individualistic (Triandis, 2001). Clinicians from more collectivistic cultures may be particularly challenged in traditional or mainstream organizations that are more individualistic in nature.

Gender may also play a role in one's preferences at work and the mismatches that can arise. A large body of research has examined gender differences in communication, management style, and leadership approach. Some research suggests that women tend to be less direct communicators (Sheridan, 2007) and that they have a preference for less hierarchy and more participation in decision making (Meier, O'Toole, and Goerdel, 2006; Van Oudenhoven, 2001). All of this may be particularly important to understand in social service organizations, where the staff is primarily composed of women and people of color and white men tend to be the administrators. If the culture of an organization is influenced from the top, many organizations will have cultures that may not be comfortable for women and people of color.

**Degree of hierarchy.** The degree of hierarchy refers to the importance placed on hierarchical structures and status in an organization. It also describes how firmly those in the organization adhere to an established chain of command. An organization is very hierarchical when most decisions come from the top and staff is expected to be very deferential to those who have more power, authority, and status in the organization. An organization's degree of hierarchy can be assessed by the following characteristics:

- The importance placed on formal titles and rank
- The amount of interaction among people in different levels of the organization
- The degree to which superiors tell staff members what to do without consulting them
- The amount of questioning of superiors by clinicians that is welcomed or tolerated

**Processing and sharing.** Some clinicians tend to be external processors, working through challenges by openly discussing them with friends and colleagues. Others tend to be internal processors, tending to first understand and solve problems on their own. Organizations may have a culture that supports one or the other of these approaches to processing information. Clinicians in some organizations are encouraged or even required to go to supervisors or to their colleagues to discuss challenging situations they are having with clients. In other organizations, they are discouraged or criticized for spending too much time receiving help or support and openly processing issues of concern. Differences in how people process and share information are manifest in organizations in the following ways:

- Whether supervision is more focused on productivity and billing or on processing feelings and solving problems about cases
- Whether clinicians are discouraged from obtaining outside assistance and taking time to process or are encouraged to seek out supervision and assistance
- Whether there is an open-door policy in the organization where clinicians know others are available and open to discuss difficult cases or there is rarely someone available when processing seems warranted
- Whether time is built into the workweek for process-oriented supervision

**Importance of relationships versus tasks.** Differences can be seen in an organization's culture based on how the organization balances creating relationships with accomplishing tasks. This aspect is evident by examining the common interactions among staff members. In a more task-oriented environment, clinicians tend to begin work quickly without much socializing; while socializing may occur, it is generally short in duration or done after tasks are completed. In relationship-oriented cultures, clinicians tend to see building strong relationships as an important precursor to accomplishing tasks. Mismatch in this area can be particularly challenging in clinical environments where the focus of therapy is on building and repairing relationships, but financial pressures force the organization to focus on productivity and billing. Variations in task-oriented versus relationship-oriented cultures can be seen in the following areas:

- How much time is spent discussing nonwork topics during meetings and other work activities
- Whether praise and rewards tend to be given for achieving goals or for building relationships
- How frequently the organization employs relationship- and team-building activities
- How often and to what degree colleagues socialize inside and outside of work

Once the clinicians have achieved familiarity with the four potential areas for conflict and have had time to consider their organizations' cultures, they are ready to begin the activity. After a brief introduction, the supervisor will distribute the Organizational Culture Evaluation Form for the clinicians to complete (see Table 20.1). Supervisors should note that some clinicians are reluctant to engage in the activity because they worry that finding areas of mismatch might compel them to engage in a conflictive process in order to change their situation. It can be helpful to remind clinicians that it is not necessary for them to change their environment whenever they find mismatches; just knowing that a mismatch exists can help them think about their work

**Table 20.1 Organizational Culture Evaluation Form**

Each of the three sections below contains four rating questions followed by a consideration question. In each section, please write your rating in the box provided at the right and answer any follow-up questions.

**Degree of Hierarchy**

1. How would you rate the culture in your organization in terms of hierarchy on a scale of 1 to 10, with 1 being nonhierarchical and 10 being very hierarchical? What specific things have you noticed about your organization that support this rating?

2. How would you rate your preference in terms of hierarchy on a scale of 1 to 10, with 1 being a strong preference for a nonhierarchical environment and 10 being a strong preference for a very hierarchical environment? What specific things have you noticed about yourself that support this rating?

3. How well-matched are your preferences with the reality in your organization, rated on a scale of 1 to 10, with 1 being not at all matched and 10 being very well matched?

4. How much does any mismatch in this area result in a negative experience at work, rated on a scale of 1 to 10, with 1 being not at all and 10 being a great deal? What are the specific negative effects?

5. What do you think are the values held by people who want more hierarchy and what are the values held by people who prefer less hierarchy?

**Information Processing and Sharing**

6. How would you rate the culture in your organization in terms of information processing and sharing on a scale of 1 to 10, with 1 being a strong focus on external processing and 10 being a strong focus on internal processing? What specific things have you noticed about your organization that support this rating?

7. How would you rate your preference in terms of information sharing and processing on a scale of 1 to 10, with 1 being a strong preference for an external processing environment and 10 being a strong preference for an internal processing environment? What specific things have you noticed about yourself that support this rating?

8. How well-matched are your preferences with the reality in your organization, rated on a scale of 1 to 10, with 1 being not at all matched and 10 being very well matched?

9. How much does any mismatch in this area result in a negative experience at work, rated on a scale of 1 to 10, with 1 being not at all and 10 being a great deal? What are the specific negative effects?

10. What do you think are the values held by people who are external processors and what are the values held by people who are internal processors?

**Importance of Tasks Versus Relationships**

11. How would you rate the culture in your organization in terms of a task versus relationship focus on a scale of 1 to 10, with 1 being a strong focus on tasks and 10 being a strong focus on relationships? What specific things have you noticed about your organization that support this rating?

12. How would you rate your preference in terms of a task or relationship focus on a scale of 1 to 10, with 1 being a strong preference for a task focus and 10 being a strong preference for a relationship focus? What specific things have you noticed about yourself that support this rating?

13. How well-matched are your preferences with the reality in the organization, rated on a scale of 1 to 10, with 1 being not at all matched and 10 being very well matched?

14. How much does any mismatch here result in a negative experience at work, rated on a scale of 1 to 10, with 1 being not at all and 10 being a great deal? What are the specific negative effects?

15. What do you think are the values held by people who want a task focus and what are the values held by people who prefer a relationship focus?

situations differently, which can help to reduce the discomfort on its own. It is also possible for clinicians to make small adjustments in their expectations and behaviors that are enough to reduce the mismatch and conflict.

After completing the evaluation form, the supervisor will divide participants into groups of four to six clinicians to discuss their experiences and their responses. Clinicians are encouraged to talk about how specific areas of mismatch may be affecting them clinically and their levels of satisfaction and stress at work. Clinicians are asked to share their assessments of conflicts that seem most problematic and to openly discuss how to address these situations.

| Cultural Orientation | Sample Core Values |
|---|---|
| More hierarchy | Clarity in roles, efficiency, respect, order |
| Less hierarchy | Autonomy, flexibility, creativity, openness |
| Relationship | Trust through knowing others |
| Task | Trust through merit |
| Internal processing | Self-sufficiency, individual efforts |
| External processing | Increased input, group support |

**Table 20.2 Values and Beliefs Underlying Various Cultural Dimensions**

Following the small-group discussions, the supervisor will bring the groups together to share their findings with the large group. As appropriate, the supervisor should supplement the discussion by presenting the solutions described as follows:

- **Highlight the values underlying people's positions in each of the areas discussed.** Understanding the underlying values might reveal that situations or behaviors that are challenging to some clinicians may come from the good intentions of others.

  - What do you think are the values held by people who want more hierarchy, and what do you think are the values held by people who prefer less hierarchy?

  - What do you think are the values held by people who are external processors, and what do you think are the values held by people who are internal processors?

  - What do you think are the values held by people who are task oriented, and what do you think are the values held by people who are relationship oriented?

- *Imagine you are in the position of the person or people in your organization with whom you differ strongly on any of these organizational cultural dimensions.* Write a few sentences about the values you might have as someone on the other side of the cultural dimension. For example, you might write, "As a task-oriented person, I need to see people follow through and complete their work before I can trust them enough to build a productive working relationship with them." This process might make it easier to understand where others are coming from.

- *Now that you are aware of the challenges caused by mismatch, consider the possibility that a relatively small behavior change on your part might reduce some of the tension you are feeling at work.* Is it possible for you to make that small change, knowing a better work environment may be the result?

- *Discuss your concerns with colleagues on the other side of the cultural dimension.* Once they understand your struggle, they might be willing to shift their behaviors to reduce the difficulty. A compromise may also be possible where you each change your behaviors some so that friction is reduced or eliminated.

# Examples

Many clinicians are not aware of the organizational culture that surrounds them in the workplace, even though its effect is significant. They may also be unaware of their own preferences and needs that might be clashing with the organizational work culture, resulting in increased levels of stress and reduced productivity. Increasing self-awareness by paying closer attention to their environment and to their reactions can reduce stress and improve clinicians' satisfaction with and effectiveness in their job. Participants in this exercise sometimes express surprise regarding how much experience in their agencies has been shaped by an organizational culture that they previously did not consciously acknowledge or consider. As one clinician noted:

*I never realized how important it is to me that organizations I work in have an open-door policy. I need to process out loud, and I work so much more effectively when that is welcomed and modeled.*

Some clinicians are able to move beyond understanding and acknowledging areas of mismatch to considering change or actually attempting to change their situation. One clinician noted:

*The exercise made me aware how difficult it has been for me to be in a very hierarchical environment where I always feel micromanaged. I knew I was struggling with some things about the administration, but I wasn't aware of the specifics of why I was so unhappy. I've been thinking about ways I might address this and have been considering whether this might not be the place for me.*

# Measuring Progress

Progress can be measured in the following two ways. First, participants are asked to respond in writing to the following questions (after completing the activity), and their responses are discussed in group or individual supervision settings:

- What insights did you have as a result of completing the Organizational Culture Evaluation Form? Which questions, if any, did you have difficulty answering?

- Did the group discussion help you better understand areas of match or mismatch between you and others in the organization? If so, how? If not, why?

- Are you considering any behavior change as a result of this activity? Please describe.

- How can others in the organization support you in minimizing stress related to areas of mismatch?

Second, a pre-posttest may be used to assess changing levels of job satisfaction in activity participants. A time-efficient tool that is recommended for this purpose is The Brief Index of Affective Job Satisfaction (Thompson & Phua, 2012). We suggest that the post-administration of this instrument be conducted one to two months following the clinicians' participation in the activity. This will allow the posttest to capture the benefits of behavior change that typically occur over time.

# Conclusion

Clinicians will likely experience challenges fitting in with particular organizational cultures at some point in their careers. Obtaining knowledge about personal preferences and needs in the workplace, as well as a better understanding of some components of organizational culture, can help them better understand what may be causing problems at work. This increased awareness may allow clinicians to assess the situation more effectively and to then develop an appropriate response to reduce their levels of work-related stress. Resolution of mismatch dynamics can allow for a greater focus on clients' needs and effective clinical services.

# Additional Resources

Abigail, R. A., & Cahn, D. D. (2010). *Managing conflict through communication* (4th ed.). Boston, MA: Pearson.

House, R. J., Hanges, P. J., Javidan, M., Dorfman, P. W., & Gupta, V. (2004). *Culture, leadership, and organizations: The GLOBE study of 62 cultures*. Thousand Oaks, CA: Sage.

Kirsh, B. (2000). Organizational culture, climate and person-environment fit: Relationships with employment outcomes for mental health consumers. *Work: A Journal of Prevention, Assessment and Rehabilitation, 14*(2), 109–122.

Schmitz, J. (2006). *Cultural orientations guide* (5th ed.). Princeton, NJ: Princeton Training Press.

Stone, D., Patton, B., & Heen, S. (2000). *How to discuss what matters most*. New York, NY: Penguin.

# References

Adkins, B., & Caldwell, D. (2004). Firm or subgroup culture: Where does fitting in matter most? *Journal of Organizational Behavior*, *25*(8), 969–978.

Deal, T. E., & Kennedy, A. A. (1983). Culture: A new look through old lenses. *Journal of Applied Behavioral Science*, *19*(4), 498–505.

Edwards, J. R., & Shipp, A. J. (2007). The relationship between person-environment fit and outcomes: An integrative theoretical framework. In C. Ostroff & T. A. Judge (Eds.), *Perspectives on Organizational Fit* (pp. 209–258). Mahwah, NJ: Lawrence Erlbaum.

Judge, T. A., Thoresen, C. J., Bono, J. E., & Patton, G. K. (2001). The job satisfaction-job performance relationship: A qualitative and quantitative review. *Psychological Bulletin*, *127*(3), 376–407.

Martin, M. J. (2006). That's the way we do things around here: An overview of organizational culture. *Electronic Journal of Academic and Special Librarianship*, *7*(1).

Maslach, C., & Leiter, M. P. (2005). Reversing burnout: How to rekindle your passion for your work. *Stanford Social Innovation Review*, *3*(4), 43–49.

Meier, K. J., O'Toole, L. J., & Goerdel. H. T. (2006). Management activity and program performance: Gender as management capital. *Public Administration Review*, *66*, 24–36.

Pandy, A., Campbell Quick, J., Rossi, A. M., Nelson, D. L., & Martin, W. (2010). Stress and the workplace: 10 years of science, 1997–2007. In R. Contrada & A. Baum (Eds.), *The handbook of stress science: Biology, psychology, and health* (pp. 137–149). New York, NY: Springer.

Sheridan, F. (2007). Gender, language and the workplace: An exploratory study. *Women in Management Review*, *22*(4), 319–336.

Thompson, E. R., & Phua, F. T. T. (2012). A brief index of affective job satisfaction. *Group & Organization Management*, *37*(3), 275–307.

Triandis, H. C. (2001). Individualism-collectivism and personality. *Journal of Personality*, *69*(6), 907–924.

Van Oudenhoven, J. P. (2001). Do organizations reflect national cultures? A 10-nation study. *International Journal of Intercultural Relations*, *25*(1), 89–107.

Wright, T. A., & Cropanzano, R. (2000). Psychological well-being and job satisfaction as predictors of job performance. *Journal of Occupational Health Psychology*, *5*(1), 84–94.

# CHAPTER 21

# COLLABORATIVE REFLECTIVE TRAINING FOR MENTAL HEALTH CLINICIANS IN MEDICAL SETTINGS

Barbara Couden Hernandez and Lana Kim

## Introduction

Nonmedical mental health clinician trainees (NMHCs) often express uncertainty when their work calls on them to interact with physicians. This is largely because of stereotypes and anecdotal stories regarding the social power of physicians, as well as past experiences with and biases against physicians. The use of collaborative reflective trainings (CRTs) for residents and physicians can assist NMHC trainees to examine their own biases toward and internal responses to physicians, to raise awareness regarding the work of physicians, and to help position themselves as clinicians within medical culture.

## Rationale

Clinical supervisors of NMHCs frequently encounter trainees who feel intimidated by the idea of working with physicians. Medical family therapists, medical social workers, and psychology interns often seek training in medical settings in order to learn how to specialize in issues that arise around illness. Typically, student clinicians participate in courses that explain medical culture and settings, address medical language and hospital culture, and explain physician socialization. However, many nonmedical practitioners hold the idea that a physician is a larger-than-life icon of power and that interactions with doctors will be different than they are with other professionals (Seaburn, Lorenz, Gunn, Gawinski, & Mauksch, 1996). Physicians can be seen as skeptical about behavioral health integration (O'Donohue, Cummings, Cucciare, Runyan, & Cummings, 2006) or unable to be convinced of the value of the clinicians' interventions without "a lot of hard work" (Stout & Grand, 2005, p. 182). It is, therefore, important for NMHC trainees to examine their assumptions and projections regarding physicians in order to ensure that they can address arising issues and needs of patients with physicians in a collegial manner. As with any relationship, unresolved past issues or unexamined attitudes pertaining to physicians can result in a trainee taking a defensive stance, avoiding contact, being unduly deferent, or even being passive-aggressive. Failure to establish an attitude of cooperation with physicians interferes with the fundamental function of NMHCs, whose role is to promote a spirit of collaboration among themselves, patients, and doctors (Rolland, 1994).

The use of reflection in clinician education is not a new concept in either family therapy (Andersen, 1987; Tomm, 1984; Young et al., 1989) or medicine (Bacal, 1972; Rüth, 2009). This technique was designed to promote change in family therapy by offering feedback about client process without arousing resistance or defensiveness and by fostering a curiosity about the presenting problem(s) under discussion (Friedman, 1995). We have adapted this approach to the medical education setting because learning in this field tends to be skill based and focused solely on the physiological issues of patients. We have discovered that hearing the reflections of others promotes a reflexive frame of mind (Roberts, 2002) that allows for the consideration of many possibilities and perspectives, thus expanding trainees' experiential and behavioral repertoire (Kjellberg, Edwardsson, Niemela, & Oberg, 1995). Conducting CRTs for physicians, residents, and medical students provides an opportunity for immediate feedback as they learn to give bad news to simulated patient families, known as *confederates*. A simulation is a role-play in which physicians give bad news or discuss a poor prognosis with NMHCs who play the part of patients and their family members. NMHC trainees who are not involved in the role-play participate by observing and reflecting on their impressions.

The emotional vulnerability and apparent eagerness of the physicians to hear the perspectives of the NMHC trainees in ensuing conversations allow the student NMHCs to observe and interact with physicians in a setting where the usual power differential is reversed. This experience encourages trainees to value their own expertise more highly as they see physicians receive their comments with enthusiasm and press them for further articulation of their perspectives. The mutual respect and increased understanding that occurs with this activity leads to the exploration of biases that NMHC trainees may have toward physicians. Contact with medical simulation that involves shock, outrage, loss, or sudden death can assist trainees in identifying personal unresolved issues related to health care while developing a new appreciation for the role of medical care in their lives—two critical elements that must be resolved to successfully work with individuals with life-threatening illnesses (Griffith & Griffith, 1994).

# Activity Instructions

This activity is a CRT simulation designed to assist NMHC trainees to examine their own biases and responses to physicians and increase their awareness of the work of physicians. This activity is best conducted when led by a seasoned clinician who is deeply familiar with working with others in the medical field; therefore, these instructions are directed specifically to supervisors. Prior to the simulation, NMHC training programs may collaborate with medical schools or house staff offices of hospitals to network and subsequently engage physicians, residents, or medical students for this training. Offering continuing medical education credit for the training increases the likelihood of physician attendance. Also, note that residents and medical students are often more forthcoming if their attending physician is absent, as they are less concerned about evaluation.

In addition, NMHC interns who will participate in this CRT must be trained in Tom Andersen's (1991) reflecting team methodology, either in a class or in a clinical site placement that uses reflecting teams in mental health settings (see Friedman, 1995). Trainees must be actively engaged in clinical work in a medical setting with ongoing weekly supervision by a licensed professional. NMHC trainees must also participate in a brief explanatory meeting in which the goals and processes of the CRT takes place. This process is most successful when mental health clinicians are included whose professional development allows them to identify as a clinician already. Openness to personal growth and their ability to contribute to the professional development of physicians are underscored.

For the simulation, a training clinic room with a one-way mirror is an ideal setting, but placing the simulation at one side of a large room and the reflecting team on the other side can also be effective. Prior to the simulation a supervising physician is asked to write a medical scenario sheet that places a fictitious patient in dire circumstances that correspond to the specialty area of the medical learners. Typical scenarios include delivering bad news such as traumatic brain injury, the need for a heart transplant, or a request to discontinue life support; giving death notices in the emergency department; or notifying a pregnant mother that her fetus is not viable. It is imperative that the scenario accurately reflect a typical patient in the physicians' specialty area. A corollary scenario is written for the confederates by the NMHC supervisor. The scenario should provide a brief overview in layman's language regarding the patient's medical situation and prompt a particular type of response to the exchange with physicians.

A reflecting team (composed of other physicians, medical students, and NMHC trainees) is asked to observe the simulation and to reflect on their impressions. Instead of giving evaluative or performance-based comments to physicians, the reflecting team speculates about the experience of participants, affirms strengths observed, and expresses curiosity about what they see and hear

(Andersen, 1991; Tomm, 1984). Sample comments from these basic reflection categories are provided as follows:

- **Speculation of experience:** "I could see myself becoming really angry hearing such horrible news about my middle-aged parent. I almost think I would have started to yell or something, having to face what I was being told."

- **Affirmation of strengths:** "When Dr. Gomez was telling the mother that her baby would live on a ventilator for the rest of his short life, I saw his eyes mist over. If I were the mother, I would have felt comforted that he feels terrible about the dilemma that I was facing by discontinuing life support."

- **Expression of curiosity**: "I wondered how Dr. White felt while she was trying to get the patient's brother to hear her explanation of this complication, because I was feeling really tense just seeing how hard it was to get through to him."

Care should be taken to avoid making direct comments to the physicians and confederates who have taken part in the simulation by voicing reflections to other team members only. Doing so diminishes defensiveness and encourages a greater ability to process personal issues that may arise during simulation and reflection.

A sample schedule for the reflective training simulation is detailed as follows. Flexibility is needed in cases in which personal issues arise or the vulnerability of a physician or trainee invites longer discussion.

- **Introductions of all team members and facilitators** (10 minutes): Physicians are identified for participation in the simulation and are given the opportunity to review the medical scenario information. Confederates are given their overview of the case with time to review (this often works best if the case can be given to the confederates the day before, with the instruction not to discuss it with others).

- **Overview of the purpose/structure of reflecting teams** (10 minutes): Discussion of the value of reflection in bridging cognitive, behavioral, and experiential components of learning; reference to medical literature that normalizes the need for physicians-in-training to learn these skills (Groopman, 2003); review of learning objectives; orientation to the process; instructions for reflecting team

- **Simulation** (10 minutes): The physician(s) give bad news to confederate family members.

- **Reflecting team interaction** (10 minutes): NMHC trainees and other physicians from the reflecting team raise questions, affirm strengths observed, and muse aloud to one another about what they have witnessed in the simulation scenario. The following prompts may be used to elicit comment:

  - "Can you share your emotional response to what you saw and heard here?"

  - "Did you see any change in demeanor that was interesting to you?"

  - "Is there anything that you wondered about as you observed this exchange?"

- *Medical team session* (10 minutes): Physician learners in the simulation are then asked, "Did you hear anything from the reflecting team that caught your interest or that you would like to discuss further?" and "How did you experience giving bad news to these individuals?" The physician(s) are asked if they have any questions for the confederates regarding their experience in receiving bad news from them. The confederates are then encouraged to explain the impact of hearing bad news from the physician(s) and discuss the reflecting team's comments further.

- *Group debriefing* (10 minutes): The entire group is reconvened in a circle to continue the conversation about what was learned, address the challenges for the physician(s) in the simulation, and clarify reflections/feedback from the NMHCs. Participants are asked, "What will you take home from this experience today that might impact the way you practice medicine or medical family therapy?" or "Is there anything in the way you interact with patients that you think you might change as a result of today's simulation?"

# Example

A recent simulation centered on the death of a 16-year-old male in a downtown explosion and included two nurses, an orderly, two resident physicians, and two confederates. The emergency department physician and orderly delivered the death notice to the young man's mother and younger brother, who expressed shock, grief, and outrage at the death of their loved one. As the mother cried out, hugged her son, and asked the doctor incoherent questions, the reflecting team behind the one-way mirror recorded their thoughts, observations, and questions. After five minutes, the physician was paged to return to the emergency department to assist other casualties from the explosion and left the confederates in the company of a nurse and an orderly. The nurse asked if they would object to having a chaplain called, and the scenario ended.

The reflecting team consisted of five NMHC trainees, an attending physician, and the NMHC supervisor (first author). The resident physician's warmth, attunement to the mother, and calmness were affirmed. That the physician did not become impatient or stressed with the mother's expressions of grief and requests to help her son were noted with admiration.

A sample of comments from the reflection team follows:

- "I wonder if anyone was actually with the son when he died and if anyone thought to make a mental note of what he looked like or did, so they could tell the mother that he didn't die alone."

- "I was reminded of some of the patients that I work with who are close to hysterical, and my heart went out to the medical team."

- "I wonder what was happening for the orderly because he was really, really quiet during all of this."

- "I was wondering if the mother and son even heard anything else the doctor said after they heard the words 'Your son is dead.'"

- "I was feeling really shaky and tearful watching this. I don't know how the staff could sit there with the family expressing such intense emotions and not fall apart!"

The facilitator (second author) then invited the medical team and confederates to discuss comments from the reflecting team that offered points of curiosity or resonation and received the following comments:

- "I've had the unfortunate experience of someone telling me that my father had died. So I consider it a sacred privilege to be with families who go through something similar."

- "I have to be careful what I say to the family at times like this, because whenever they think of their son dying, I will be part of that story. So even though I didn't know what to do, I wanted to be very sincere in what I said."

- "I felt really calmed when the doctor put her hand on my arm."

- "People think that medical professionals know exactly what to do at times like this, but I don't ever remember getting told how to manage these kinds of things. And I think we were all gulping back our own sadness."

- "He didn't die alone. That is something I can't get out of my head, because that is something that would be really reassuring for many of us to hear if we were in that situation."

Later, when the entire group reconvened for the group debriefing, the trainees commented:

- "I had no idea how hard it would be to be a doctor! My respect and admiration for [physicians] is much greater after this."

- "I think I have held a deficit model of doctors—you know, the ones with the bad bedside manner who say awkward things to the patients that we [NMHCs] are then called to see. But I think that we are all really the same at heart, and seeing the struggle in this kind of situation, I realize that I need to rethink some of the attitudes that I have. Thank you for this."

- "I think I have some processing to do about an experience with my own loss after seeing this simulation."

- "It is quite easy to understand and explore the concerns of patients who are upset with their doctor but not as easy to understand and explain where the doctor is coming from or why he has said what he did or how he has responded to the patient. I think I can do that better now."

- "I am struck by the fact that this was such a powerful event and that doctors go through things like this every week at least. Thank you for being there for us."

- "I'm so glad that you said you didn't know what to do [at one point in the simulation]. That is just not consistent with what I think about doctors ... but I thought doctors knew everything. There are times when I don't know what to say in therapy, but I just didn't realize that it happens to you, too."

Physicians received the comments with gratitude and one physician tearfully commented, "This is so valuable! We almost never get validation for this painful part of our jobs. Thank you!" Evaluations of the training were then collected from both the NMHC trainees and the physicians. NHMC trainees met together following the activity for further discussion of how the experience impacted them personally and professionally. Identification of unresolved grief, stories of interacting with an arrogant doctor as a patient, and decreased intimidation by physicians were common themes in this conversation.

# Measuring Progress

The progress of the NMHC trainees is largely measured through observation and informal conversations during supervision. It has been our experience that trainees often refer back to these CRT experiences as pivotal to their understanding of medical culture, giving them a clearer idea about the value and role of their skills and helping them form relationships with physicians as people, not icons. Some helpful questions to facilitate continued awareness are as follows:

- "What did you learn about your ability to track process by participating in the reflection team?"

- "How will this experience influence your future interactions with medical staff?"

- "Does this experience help you identify ways that you can offer support to physicians as well as to patients in your care?"

These questions are offered during ensuing supervision sessions as a way to incorporate the learning experience into clinical practice. By assisting trainees in identifying their biases about physicians and medical care, we help them draw on their strengths as mental health providers in creating appropriate roles for themselves in medical settings.

# Conclusion

NMHC trainees are often intimidated by the thought of working in medical settings with physicians. In order to collaborate successfully as part of a medical team, trainees must examine their biases and attitudes toward physicians in order to meet the emerging issues and needs of patients in their care. CRT benefits both physicians and NMHC trainees by exposing stereotypes, interrupting typical power hierarchies, and introducing each discipline to experiential issues that influence their respective clinical practices. It is anticipated that this cross-disciplinary experience will encourage trainees to examine their own attitudes and experiences with physicians, thus laying the groundwork for successful role identification in future collaboration.

# Additional Resources

Dankowski, M. E., Pais, S., Zoppi, K. A., & Kramer, J. S. (2003). Popcorn moments: Feminist principles in family medicine education. *Journal of Feminist Family Therapy, 15*(2–3), 55–73.

Frake, C., & Dogra, N. (2006). The use of reflecting teams in educational contexts. *Reflective Practice, 7*(2), 143–149.

Friedman, S. (Ed.). (1995). *The reflecting team in action: Collaborative practice in family therapy.* New York, NY: Guilford Press.

Prest, L. A., Darden, E. C., & Keller, J. F. (1990). "The fly on the wall" reflecting team supervision. *Journal of Marital and Family Therapy, 16*(3), 265–273.

# References

Andersen, T. (1987). The reflecting team: Dialogue and meta-dialogue in clinical work. *Family Process, 26*(4), 415–428.

Andersen, T. (1991). *The reflecting team: Dialogues and dialogues about dialogues.* New York, NY: W. W. Norton.

Bacal, H. A. (1972). Balint groups: Training or treatment? *Psychiatry in Medicine, 3*(4), 373–377.

Friedman, S. (Ed.). (1995). *The reflecting team in action: Collaborative practice in family therapy.* New York, NY: Guilford Press.

Griffith, J. L., & Griffith, M. E. (1994). *The body speaks: Therapeutic dialogues for mind-body problems.* New York, NY: Basic Books.

Groopman, J. (2003). *The anatomy of hope: How people prevail in the face of illness.* New York, NY: Random House.

Kjellberg, E., Edwardsson, M., Niemela, B. J., & Oberg, T. (1995). Using the reflecting process with families stuck in violence and child abuse. In S. Friedman (Ed.), *The reflecting team in action* (pp. 38–61). New York, NY: Guilford Press.

O'Donohue, W. T., Cummings, N. A., Cucciare, M. A., Runyan, C. N., & Cummings, J. L. (2006). *Integrated behavioral health care: A guide to effective intervention.* New York, NY: Humanity Books.

Roberts, J. (2002). Reflecting processes and "supervision": Looking at ourselves as we look at others. In T. C. Todd & C. L. Storm (Eds.), *The complete systemic supervisor: Context, philosophy, & pragmatics* (pp. 334–347). Lincoln, NE: Author's Choice.

Rolland, J. S. (1994). *Families, illness, and disability: An integrative treatment model.* New York, NY: Basic Books.

Rüth, U. (2009). Classic Balint group work and the thinking of W. R. Bion: How Balint work increases the ability to think one's own thoughts. *Group Analysis, 42*(4), 380–391.

Seaburn, D. B., Lorenz, A. D., Gunn, W. B., Gawinski, B. A., & Mauksch, L. B. (1996). *Models of collaboration: A guide for mental health professionals working with health care practitioners.* New York, NY: Basic Books.

Stout, C. E., & Grand, L. C. (2005). *Getting started in private practice: The complete guide to building your mental health practice.* Hoboken, NJ: Wiley.

Tomm, K. (1984). One perspective on the Milan systemic approach, Part II: Description of session format, interviewing style and interventions. *Journal of Marital and Family Therapy, 19*(3), 253–271.

Young, J., Perlesz, A., Paterson, R., O'Hanlon, B., Newbold, A., Chaplain, R., & Bridge, S. (1989). The reflecting team process in training. *Australian and New Zealand Journal of Family Therapy, 10*(2), 69–74.

# CHAPTER 22

# USING MEDICAL GENOGRAMS IN CLINICAL SUPERVISION

Tai Justin Mendenhall and Stephanie Trudeau-Hern

## Introduction

Mental health care that is provided within medical contexts is, in many ways, different than care that is provided within conventional private practices or academic training sites (Gawinski, Edwards, & Speice, 1999). A Medical Clinician (MedC)—whether he or she is a health psychologist, medical family therapist, hospital chaplain, or any other provider type—works with patients and families who are struggling with circumstances outside of the typical scope(s) of what is taught about in baseline clinical programs (Hodgson, Lamson, Mendenhall, & Crane, 2012). Bearing witness to devastating diagnoses, serious accidents and injuries, acute trauma, long-term suffering, and death is commonplace (Edwards & Patterson, 2006; Mendenhall, 2007). As clinicians-in-training learn to do this, they must also learn how to enhance self-awareness regarding their own experiences with health-related foci.

The medical genogram is a useful and effective tool for MedC trainees to identify and gain awareness about their own personal experiences and family illness narratives. Processing how these stories connect to trainees' clinical practice can identify—and rectify—a variety of countertransference and "blind spots" that could otherwise sabotage or immobilize care. Medical genograms are also helpful in identifying areas of personal work for burgeoning therapists in their own self-care and growth.

## Rationale

Student clinicians have long been encouraged to use genograms to explore their own families-of-origin for interpersonal patterns and content that could influence their clinical work (e.g., Guldner, 1978; McDaniel & Landau-Stanton, 1991). In a similar fashion, medical genograms can uncover bidirectional effects between a patient's illness and personal narratives maintained by a trainee (McDaniel, Hepworth, & Doherty, 1997; McDaniel & Landau-Stanton, 1991). Just as a trainee working with a couple who is on the brink of a divorce can experience personal reactivity triggered by his or her own parents' divorce, a MedC working with a family who is about to lose a beloved member to cancer can experience personal reactivity triggered by his or her own parent's cancer (Gawinski et al., 1999).

In comparison to their counterparts who are training in more conventional mental health settings, MedCs are often less able to work through the complications associated with their personal experiences interacting with the clinical issues that they are treating (Trudeau-Hern, Mendenhall, & Wong, in press). Many struggle with a strong sense of professional isolation vis-à-vis their colleagues and standard professional support systems. As mental health providers, they often face a "less than" status in relation to biomedical providers in a world where the designation of "MD" is the mark of a "real doctor" and "PhD" is frequently described as "only a PhD" or mental health doctor. At their home-base departments, MedC trainees often struggle with neglect from other trainees because—within the contexts of required group supervision—conventional students are commonly uncomfortable talking about cases that involve acute violence and physical injury, sexual abuse, tragic accidents, or long and drawn-out family struggles with a patient who is slowly dying via physical shutdown or psychological dementia (Edwards & Patterson, 2006; Trudeau-Hern et al., in press). Without readily fitting in with either group (i.e., biomedical or conventional mental health), MedCs repeatedly sense that they must go it alone.

Not talking about these issues, however, positions MedC trainees at significant potential risks for compassion fatigue and/or vicarious traumatization. *Compassion fatigue* is defined as a physical, emotional, and spiritual exhaustion that overcomes a person and causes concomitant declines in his or her ability to experience joy or empathize and compassionately care for others (Figley, 2002, 2013). Common physical indicators of this condition include chronic tiredness, insomnia, headaches, gastrointestinal distress, and frequent illnesses. Psychological indicators include depression, anxiety, irritability, and feeling overwhelmed by one's caseload. Over time, clinicians can lose their baseline capacity for empathy and can experience a decline in personal responsiveness and warmth toward patients and families. They may feel numb to, cynical about, or even annoyed with patients' stories.

*Vicarious traumatization* is defined as a manifestation of trauma-related reactions in an individual as a function of his or her exposure to another's trauma experience (Neumann & Gamble, 1995). Indicators echo many of those evidenced in compassion fatigue, including difficulty making decisions, interpersonal conflict with loved ones, feeling disconnected from what is going on around one's self, and struggling with the management of good personal and professional boundaries.

Any supervisor who is familiar with symptoms of compassion fatigue and vicarious traumatization can use a medical genogram when a trainee's self-awareness seems low. After all, the more aware clinicians are about their own personal issues, the more they can effectively focus on their patients' issues (Bowen, 1978; Napier & Whitaker, 1978). This activity can be carried out in both individual and group supervision settings.

# Activity Instructions

The primary purpose of a genogram is to offer a visual depiction of complex family patterns through the use of standardized symbols and formats (McGoldrick, Gerson, & Petry, 2008). First discussed by McDaniel, Hepworth, and Doherty (1992) and later expanded on by Rolland (1994) and Wright, Watson, and Bell (1996), the medical genogram is similar to a basic genogram in its structure, but different because it explicitly focuses on health-related issues. Concentrating on their own families-of-origin, clinicians work to identify, process, and reflect on personal experiences and family narratives about illness and disease, grief and loss, and death and dying. New awareness regarding potential triggers, roadblocks, or reactivity in clinical practice is gained, together with new cognizance about unique sensitivities and strengths that clinicians bring to their work as corollaries of their personal and/or family experiences with a particular health issue.

All MedC clinicians, whether novices or more experienced, can benefit from this activity; however, it is recommended that trainees engage in this type of training exercise earlier in their clinical programs. Of course, genograms can be re-created and revisited anytime there are indicators of low self-awareness or personal struggles with particular cases (Wright et al., 1996). It is also recommended that facilitators provide clinicians with standard genogram guidelines (e.g., McGoldrick et al., 2008) before presenting the following exercise using a medically oriented version.

To create a medical genogram, trainees are instructed to construct a three-generation personal family map focusing on illness, trauma, and medical conditions. This activity facilitates a deeper awareness about the interconnectedness of major life events—such as a medical diagnosis—and family functioning. The foundation of the genogram will include history of medical diagnoses, accidents or hospitalizations, acute or chronic illnesses, deaths and causes of deaths, and unexplained or undiagnosed medical symptoms in family members. If specific events or diagnoses need further exploration, the supervisor can suggest a timeline to gain a better understanding of the events' or diagnoses' evolution and course within the family.

Next, the trainee is asked to fill in information about relationships to illness. This includes how the trainee's family members related to illnesses, to the medical system, and to each other

Example                                                                                     143

from the time of diagnosis through the course of a medical condition. Possible questions include:

- Who were the caregivers in your family?
- How did your family reorganize around the illness?
- How did your family talk about (or not talk about) the diagnosis?
- How was the illness communicated (or not communicated) to others?
- What were your family's beliefs about the illness, either implicit or explicit?
- What were your family's traditions around illness or death?

This sets the stage for the trainee to consider how his or her own experiences influence—and/or are influenced by—his or her clinical work.

A MedC trainee then presents—or revisits—a clinical case in much the same way that he or she would in any standard individual or group supervision meeting. The supervisor asks starter questions to help the trainee consider the explicit role(s) of medical issues and their impact(s) on the patient and family. Examples of initial questions include:

- What is the patient's medical diagnosis?
- What is the context around the diagnosis?
- Who is in the patient's family configuration?
- What is the medical history of the family?
- What is the family's history of interacting with illness?
- What are the observed interactions between the family and the patient?
- What are the observed interactions between the family and the illness?
- What is the family's view of the issue?
- How is the patient coping with the illness?
- How is the family coping with the illness?
- How is the illness affecting relationships within the family?

Further questioning can then be linked to the trainee's personal experiences to the patient's—or family's—experiences with whom he or she is working. This can also bring about a resource-based discussion between the supervisor and the trainee. Examples of such queries include:

- How does observing death from illness in your family impact your "match" with this family as their provider?
- What understandings do you have about illness and loss that another clinician may not have?
- As you were experiencing this loss in your own family, what do you wish would have been different?
- What coping patterns have you witnessed in your own family that you would like to keep and build upon?
- What coping patterns have you witnessed in your own family that you would like to let go?
- How can you use your personal experiences to intervene with this family?

# Example

The following is an illustration of a MedC trainee's experience in constructing and using a personal medical genogram (identifying characteristics have been changed to maintain confidentiality). Mary was a first-year doctoral student and intern at an oncology clinic. After working for a couple of months at this clinical site, she presented the following case during clinical supervision:

Mr. C was a 45-year-old married white male with stage IV lung cancer whom Dr. L referred to Mary for therapy. Mr. C was struggling with depression and had demonstrated a long-standing pattern of noncompliance with the treatment protocol. He had chosen to continue smoking during his care and was not consistent in keeping his radiation and chemotherapy infusion appointments. Dr. L made it clear to Mr. C and his family that if he chose to continue smoking and missing his oncology appointments, he would likely die within one month.

When Mary met with Mr. C, he appeared to be withdrawn and demonstrated a very flat affect. When asked about his family, he stated plainly that he had a wife and two kids in high school. When asked what brought him to therapy, he responded that he attended the appointment because one of his nurses had scheduled it for him. Although Mary did not feel like much was accomplished during this initial visit, she was able to secure Mr. C's agreement to return with his wife at a follow-up session.

During the second session, Mr. C brought in his wife and two teenage children. There was minimal verbal communication among them, and their nonverbal communication suggested some distance and hostility. Spatially, nobody sat together. Mr. C's wife of 25 years had taken on the caregiving role with her husband and was currently over functioning; she spoke for all members of her family. She hoped that if Mr. C would stop smoking and comply with his chemotherapy regimen, he would have more time to spend with the family. The two sons appeared angry with their father but also expressed sadness and grief for his impending loss.

Mary was reluctant to address the sons' feelings about their father because of her own anxiety and countertransference with him. In the process of attempting to join with the family and develop more trust, Mary felt both apprehension and somatic symptoms (e.g., headache, stomachache). When the family scheduled a session for the following week, Mary was already feeling hesitant and frustrated about how to structure and prepare for the visit.

While presenting all of this information to her clinical supervisor, Mary maintained that she really had no idea what to do with Mr. C and his family. She explained how their interpersonal distance and blunted communication made her feel apprehensive. She also noted that she could not help but feel angry with Mr. C for—in her view—choosing to smoke and refusing to comply with treatment. She described feeling outraged that he was actively defying his oncologist's recommendations and creating such emotional turmoil within his family.

Mary's supervisor asked her several reflective questions about her expectations for this family. He proposed completing a medical genogram to elicit further awareness into Mary's own interactions with illness, explaining how doing so could potentially help her work with Mr. C and his family. The supervisor suggested this activity based on his—albeit minimal—awareness that Mary had a family history that included some losses secondary to cancer. She agreed to do the exercise.

Mary's supervisor instructed her to develop a genogram going back three generations. Its focus would be on illness and the communication sequences, learned coping patterns, and management of anxieties related to it. As Mary did this, she discussed her own family-of-origin's connections to lung cancer. She described how she had observed the deaths of three family members, along with watching many other members struggle with smoking and alcohol abuse. Mary explained how the members of her family who had died from lung cancer were all young, and how they continued to smoke right up until the time of their deaths.

Principal themes in Mary's family-of-origin revealed patterns of framing illness as a "secret," wherein communicating about emotions was not allowed. Mary's supervisor asked about her anger with her own family members for not stopping smoking once their respective cancer diagnoses were discovered. He also asked Mary about her coping at that time and what strengths she was able to elicit. He asked about how she would have changed the situation in her own family if she could go back and do it again. What would she have done differently? And finally, were there experiences or insights where self-of-the-therapist could be integrated into the therapy room in a manner of clinical transparency?

Mary met with Mr. C and his family the following week and was able to use a more open, curious clinical approach rather than the anxious, closed presence she may have brought if a deeper self-awareness had not been elicited. She was able to recognize when she was feeling uneasy by monitoring her body and noted when she was pulling in her own experiences rather than listening to the unique experiences of the family in front of her. By having Mary more deeply reflect upon her own family-of-origin, she and her supervisor were able to watch for possible countertransference sequences or times when she may have been trying to "fix" Mr. C and his family so that she could rewrite her own family's story. In turn, they were able to watch for the clinical strengths Mary had gained through her own unique experiences that could enhance her clinical conduct.

# Measuring Progress

Measuring progress after using a medical genogram is as important as any other endeavor used to assess and track increases in a trainee's competence. There are many early indicators of improved self-awareness related to health foci. Examples include a MedC's demonstrated ability to better articulate: (a) personal family patterns in relationships and roles vis-à-vis illness; (b) family functioning in response to critical diagnoses and other life events, long-term adjustment processes, and anniversary reactions; (c) common couple and intergenerational triangles, interpersonal boundaries, communication styles, and narratives about the meaning(s) of illness; and (d) tracking resilience and coping patterns (healthy or unhealthy).

Later—more developed, mature—indicators of self-awareness are evident within the unique clinical course(s) of a trainee's work with patients and families. Examples here are also myriad; the following is an illustration from a MedC trainee:

*I remember feeling so stuck and angry with a patient of mine who was struggling with alcoholism. He had everything: a great education and job, a beautiful wife and kids, lived in a nice neighborhood … and yet time and again, he would come to treatment, get sober, leave, relapse, and come back. Eventually he lost his job. His wife left him and took him for almost everything he had. He moved back in with his parents, and then ultimately came back for another round of treatment. I knew that I wasn't offering him good care, because—honestly—he disgusted me. My supervisor asked me to work through a medical genogram. I knew about the struggles that my grandparents and father had with alcohol, but as we explored it further I came to understand how much they (i.e., my own family) were really "with" me in terms of this. My own want to never follow that path is what was getting in the way with my patient; I almost felt like I would "catch" his addiction because I was (am) already "at risk" in the sense that this stuff can run in families. Ultimately I was able to put these anxieties in their place and harness some of my own motivation not to abuse alcohol to energizing sessions rallying around this patient's genuine want to do the same—to stay sober. He's a couple of years strong and counting now; so far, so good.*

The following is another example of increased self-awareness in a trainee, this time through the eyes of a supervisor:

*"Jim" began his clinical placement in our hospital last semester. Having never worked in a medical setting before, this was uncharted territory for him. During his first week, Jim was connected to a family with a seriously ill teenager. She had cystic fibrosis. He presented the case to me in distress, asking what he could do in light of knowing that she would die soon. Jim had obviously joined very well with the patient and her family, and was tearful because he was feeling some of the same kinds of impending loss and pain that they were. When we constructed his medical genogram, Jim talked with me about how one of his cousins had died in a car crash when she was sixteen, and about how the older sister he had never met passed away before he was born due to a heart defect. He processed how his family's baseline stoicism was such that nobody ever talked about either child. He shared how he still had more questions than answers about them, but that he "knew better" than to ask.*

*It took some time, but eventually Jim was able to use these insights about his discomfort with talking about death to do something different—to talk about it. And this is what the family he was seeing wanted his help to do! As they began to do this, a beautiful sharing of love and support followed. They talked about their memories (fond and otherwise). They shared each other's sadness about the things that they will not have because of the disease. Shortly before she died a few months later, the young woman talked with her family and Jim about how she was thankful for all they had been through and how she was ready to go. After she died, Jim further worked with the family to celebrate her life and to mourn her passing. He did an extraordinary job, and he has grown a great deal as a clinician.*

In both of these examples, trainees and supervisors worked closely together to construct and process medical genograms with relevant connections to clinical struggles and impasses. These began as events in time (i.e., initiating the exercise) but were revisited in subsequent conversations along the trainee's journey in personal insights and professional growth. After first developing self-awareness about their own health and illness experiences and narratives, these trainees were able to purposefully integrate these into their work and improved clinical practice.

# Conclusion

Clinical work in medical settings can expose trainees to some of the most heartwarming, heart-breaking, inspiring, and painful cases they will ever encounter. Although functioning within these contexts can be immensely rewarding, MedCs must understand that their choice to work in healthcare will also put them at risk of professional isolation, compassion fatigue, and vicarious traumatization. Continuous reflection about how one's family-of-origin influences work with clients and patients is essential, given that families that we see present us with varying challenges both professional and personal. Constructing a medical genogram, and revisiting it with supervisors and colleagues along the way as often as needed, is an excellent way to equip and maintain us for the work that we do.

# Additional Resources

Kottler, J. (2010). *On being a therapist* (4th ed.). San Francisco, CA: Jossey-Bass.

McGoldrick, M. (2011). *The genogram journey: Reconnecting with your family*. New York, NY: W. W. Norton.

Mendenhall, T. (2012). Practicing what we preach: Answering the call for responder self-care and resilience. *The Dialogue*, *8*(3), 2–4. Retrieved from www.samhsa.gov/dtac/dialogue/Dialogue _vol8_issue3_Final.pdf

# References

Bowen, M. (1978). *Family therapy in clinical practice*. New York, NY: Aronson.

Edwards, T., & Patterson, J. (2006). Supervising family therapy trainees in primary care medical settings: Context matters. *Journal of Marital and Family Therapy*, *32*, 33–43. doi: 10.1111/ j.1752-0606.2006.tb01586.x

Figley, C. (2002). Compassion fatigue: Psychotherapists' chronic lack of self-care. *Journal of Clinical Psychology*, *58*, 1433–1441. doi: 10.1002/jclp.10090

Figley, C. (2013). *Treating compassion fatigue*. New York, NY: Brunner-Routledge.

Gawinski, B., Edwards, T., & Speice, J. (1999). A family therapy internship in a multidisciplinary healthcare setting: Trainees' and supervisor's reflections. *Journal of Marital and Family Therapy*, *25*, 469–484. doi: 10.1111/j.1752-0606.1999.tb00263.x

Guldner, C. (1978). Family therapy for the trainee in family therapy. *Journal of Marriage and Family Counseling*, *4*, 127–132. doi: 10.1111/j.1752-0606.1978.tb00503.x

Hodgson, J., Lamson, A., Mendenhall, T., & Crane, R. (2012). Medical family therapy: Opportunity for workplace development in healthcare. *Contemporary Family Therapy*, *34*, 143–146. doi: 10.1007/s10591-012-9199-1

McDaniel, S., Hepworth, J., & Doherty, B. (1992). *Medical family therapy: A biosocial approach to families with health problems*. New York, NY: Basic Books.

McDaniel, S., Hepworth, J., & Doherty, B. (1997). *The shared experience of illness*. New York, NY: Basic Books.

McDaniel, S., & Landau-Stanton, J. (1991). Family-of-origin work and family therapy skills training: Both-and. *Family Process, 30*, 459–471. doi: 10.1111/j.1545-5300.1991.00459.x

McGoldrick, M., Gerson, R., & Petry, S. (2008). Genograms assessment and intervention. New York, NY: W. W. Norton.

Mendenhall, T. (2007). Crisis land: A view from inside a behavioral health team. *Psychotherapy Networker, 31*(3), 32–39. Retrieved from www.psychotherapynetworker.org/component/content/article/82-2007-mayjune/212-crisis-land

Napier, A., & Whitaker, C. (1978). *The family crucible*. New York, NY: Harper & Row.

Neumann, D., & Gamble, S. (1995). Issues in the professional development of psychotherapists: Countertransference and vicarious traumatization in the new trauma therapist. *Psychotherapy, 32*, 341–347. doi: 10.1037/0033-3204.32.2.341

Rolland, J. (1994). *Families, illness, & disability*. New York, NY: Basic Books.

Trudeau-Hern, S., Mendenhall, T., & Wong, A. (in press). Self of the medical family therapist: Functioning as a clinician across the multiple worlds of healthcare. In J. Hodgson, A. Lamson, T. Mendenhall, & R. Crane (Eds.), *Medical family therapy: Advanced applications*. New York, NY: Springer.

Wright, L., Watson, W., & Bell, J. (1996). *Beliefs: The heart and healing in families and illness*. New York, NY: Basic Books.

# PART II

# DIVERSITY-FOCUSED COMPETENCE AND SELF-AWARENESS

# CHAPTER 23

# Increasing Awareness of Multicultural Issues in Therapy and Supervision

Karen L. Caldwell and Shari Galiardi

## Introduction

Multicultural competency includes awareness of one's own assumptions, values, and biases as foundational to understanding the worldviews of culturally diverse clients and clinicians. Developing this awareness can be a process filled with emotionally challenging moments as one continually examines one's own sense of self. This chapter describes the use of a cultural card activity designed to stimulate thoughts about oppression and privilege in relation to a range of multicultural issues, such as gender, age, body size, ethnic/racial background, family constellation, sexual orientation, ability/disability, educational background, religion, and socioeconomic status.

## Rationale

Changes in the United States' demographics and cultural complexion are compelling clinicians to develop competency in working with culturally diverse clients. As a result, cross-cultural competency training is prevalent in the mental health and medical health fields. Empirical studies demonstrate that multicultural education for clinicians increases clinicians' self-perceived competence in treating culturally diverse populations (Smith, Constantine, Dunn, Dinehart, & Montoya, 2006). Studies of clinical supervisory relationships also have identified relationships between supervisor multicultural competence and the processes and outcomes of supervision (Constantine, 1997; Inman, 2006). Unfortunately, only a limited amount of research has examined the association between cultural competency training and improved client or patient outcomes, and this research is of low-to-moderate quality (Langer, 1999; Lie, Lee-Rey, Gomez, Bereknyei, & Braddock, 2010). The current evidence appears to be neither robust nor consistent enough to develop clear guidelines from cross-cultural training to generate the greatest patient or client impact. An integrative position is proposed by Whaley and Davis (2007), who advocate for the idea that evidence-based practice and cultural competence are complementary perspectives.

The process of developing multicultural competency can be filled with emotional upheavals, because it involves addressing questions of identity that challenge clinicians' deeply held beliefs about themselves and others. Multicultural competencies include the following: (a) awareness of one's own assumptions, values, and biases; (b) understanding the worldview of culturally diverse clients; and (c) developing appropriate interventions, strategies, and techniques (Sue, Arrendondo, & McDavis, 1992).

Experiential learning has been widely recommended as an important method for engaging clinicians in considering their own cultural backgrounds and the impact of these on the therapeutic process (Achenbach & Arthur, 2002). Kolb (1984) described the experiential learning process as one in which experience in the present is the basis for reflective observation. Out of this reflective observation emerges a conceptual analysis that can be tested in an active fashion. This active experimentation then continues the cycle as the basis for further reflective observation.

Clinicians' cultural worldviews affect the therapeutic alliance, the negotiation of treatment goals, the model of communication, and the definition of what is normal and healthy (Langer, 1999; Sue et al., 1992; Sue & Sue, 2008; Whaley & Davis, 2007). If the focus of training remains within the domains of clinical knowledge and skills, it is easy to maintain distance from cultural issues by focusing on the lives of others (e.g., the clients) without personal self-reflection (Sue & Sue, 2008). Although an external focus can be valuable for gaining knowledge about culturally diverse clients, increasing self-awareness is vital for developing competencies in other domains and translating learning into cultural empathy and effective professional practice (Ladany, Walker, Pate-Carolan, & Evans, 2008; Ridley & Lingle, 1996).

# Activity Instructions

The cultural card activity involves taking on the identity of another and considering the influence of a combination of sociocultural factors, in addition to the issues of social privilege, power, and oppression. This activity is not intended to duplicate another person's exact experience but is expected to develop an appreciation for the viewpoints of others and to move beyond culturally encapsulated worldviews (Pedersen & Ivey, 1993). Through this process, individuals are given an opportunity to empathize with the experience of the "other" and gain awareness of existing personal assumptions and biases. Because this process of developing self-awareness involves lifelong learning, the cultural card activity has been used with clinicians at a wide range of developmental stages, from undergraduate student clinicians to seasoned clinicians and supervisors. This activity has also been used with English-speaking international visitors to the United States.

It can be overwhelming to consider so many different elements of identity in this activity; however, the reality of clinical practice is one of working with complex individuals having many facets of identity. In fact, considering only one aspect of identity can lead clinicians to apply stereotypes in the mistaken notion that all individuals of a particular group are the same (Grayson & Marini, 1996).

Background reading in cultural identity development may be helpful in a classroom setting to prepare participants for the range of possible responses that they and others in the group may experience (see Atkinson, Morten, & Sue, 1998; Lee, Blando, Mizelle, & Orozco, 2007). A variety of multicultural identity models have been developed for aspects of identity, including racial identity (e.g., Sue & Sue, 2008), ethnic identity (e.g., Sodowsky, Kwan, & Pannu, 1995), gender identity (e.g., Downing & Roush, 1985), sexual orientation (e.g., McCarn & Fassinger, 1996), and spiritual/religious identity (e.g., Fowler, 1991). Ladany and colleagues (2008) have observed common themes across these identity models as people progress from a less developed to a more advanced stage. This development often includes movement from a stage of limited awareness or complacency, through a stage of cognitive conflict into a stage of exploration, and then to integration.

## Materials Needed

Because a discussion leader is a necessary component of this activity, the activity instructions are directed specifically to the leaders. The cultural card activity is a group activity that has been used with groups as small as 6 and as large as 50, although the ideal-sized group is between 12 and 15 participants. The activity is appropriate for single workshop settings, classroom settings, and, with modifications, small supervision groups. Prior to the session, the leader of the session will need to prepare a set of 10 cards for each participant, indicating a range of possibilities for 10 cultural factors:

1. Race and Ethnicity (White, Irish; Black, African-American; etc.)
2. Socioeconomic Status (High, Middle, or Low)
3. Age (Teenager, ages 13–17; Young adult, ages 18–22; etc.)
4. Educational Background (High school drop-out, High school graduate, etc.)
5. Body Size (Underweight, Normal weight, Overweight, or Obese)
6. Ability (Visible physical disability, Learning disability, etc.)

7. Sexual Identity (Heterosexual, Homosexual, or Bisexual)

8. Religion (Devout Catholic, Atheist, etc.)

9. Family Background (Raised by a single parent, One parent is in the military, etc.)

10. Gender (Male or Female)

For ease of use, the cards should be approximately 2 to 3 inches by 3 to 4 inches and may be color-coded for ease of identification. Each set of 10 cards should be arranged so that the Race and Ethnicity card will be the first card to be viewed by the individual receiving his or her new identity and the Gender card will be the last. Some individuals can be given two different Race and Ethnicity cards to be considered biracial.

## The Process

- **Individual Reflection** (10 minutes): To begin the activity, ask the participants to prepare to imagine taking on a new identity. Give each person a set of cards, and ask them to do some individual reflection. Tell participants to slowly review their cards, in order, and to take a close look at their newly assigned identity. Instruct them to pay attention to the storyline they develop about their new identities as they view each card. After they have viewed all of the cards, ask them to reflect on the following questions:

  - Which aspects of your new identity do you connect with personally?

  - Which aspects are foreign to you?

  - What assumptions did you make about each aspect and your new identity as a whole?

  - Why did you make these assumptions?

- *Small Group Discussion* (20 minutes): To create small groups, tell the participants to find others within the large group who are similar to them, based solely on the racial/ethnic identity listed on the top card. Have those assigned to similar racial/ethnic groups sit together and share their new identities and initial assumptions with their new racial/ethnic group, then respond to the following questions:

  - What are your similarities and differences within your racial/ethnic group?

  - What social privileges does your new identity give you? What aspects of your new identity have you been oppressed for?

  - Has anyone ever made an incorrect assumption about your real identity, not the new identity you have just experienced?

  - What social privileges do you possess as part of your real identity? What aspects of your real identity have you been oppressed for?

  - How do you feel about the contrast between your assigned new identity and your real identity?

- *Large Group Processing* (30+ minutes): If the group is large enough to have been able to create several small groups, allow additional time for large group processing. After participants have processed all of the questions in the small groups, bring them back together as a large group and discuss the following questions (note that if the group is large, choose about five to seven people to share their answers to each question):

  - What was your initial reaction to your new identity? What assumptions did you make about each aspect of your new identity? How did your experience with a new identity affect how you view your real identity?

  - What is social privilege? In what ways are you privileged in your real identity?

  - How are assumptions and stereotypes related to social privilege?

  - How do assumptions and stereotypes perpetuate oppression? Why do humans make assumptions?

  - How can you use your privileges to combat oppression? What will you commit to do?

- What are the implications for treatment of clients, students, and supervisees? How will you engage people in discussions about race and oppression? In what arenas would this be useful?

## Considerations for the Leader of the Exercise

Experiential learning is different from the traditional lecture method, and Woolfe (1992) notes that this difference has several implications for leaders of experiential training. First, control of the exact nature and content of learning is shifted from the leader to the participants, a shift that requires a degree of risk and uncertainty on the part of the leader. In addition, the leader has to allow participants to make mistakes. The leader must be aware that people learn in different ways and need different types of opportunities, so it is important that participants choose the extent of their involvement in the experience. Next, the leader will need to be prepared to feel not needed or wanted if an effective group process develops. Finally, Woolfe notes that groups sometimes develop an identity by coalescing against a person perceived as an "outsider." This outsider is often the group leader, who will need to be self-aware enough to know that this rejection is more about the needs of the group than the personal qualities of the leader.

Other considerations for the leader of this experiential activity are offered by Achenbach and Arthur (2002). Educators in traditional classroom settings are encouraged to protect students by making it clear that participation is voluntary and not a condition of a course grade or evaluation, and educators should seek informed consent from their students. To the extent possible, a safe context must be fostered, which can include limiting the amount of student self-disclosure in reaction to the process.

Debriefing is an essential component of experiential learning and can include discussions with participants at several points throughout the activity about the learning objectives of the activity. The activity can be introduced as a means of assisting participants in making connections to previously assigned multicultural reading material. The small-group and large-group process questions offered as part of the cultural card activity can be used as part of debriefing the activity to encourage reflection on the personal and professional implications of the cultural assumptions participants have discovered during the activity. Achenbach and Arthur (2002) stress that the leader should not allow the debriefing process to be an open-ended flow of reactions and personal disclosures but rather a guided exploration of personal experiences that then links the experience to the development of multicultural competencies.

# Example

Because a wide range of combinations of sociocultural factors can be considered in this activity, participants are able to explore many different assumptions during the activity. In past activities, assumptions related to single factors, such as sexual orientation or religion, have been expressed in statements such as "I never thought about what it would be like to not be able to talk with anybody about my sexual orientation" or "I'm from the military, and people of Middle Eastern backgrounds are viewed with a great deal of suspicion." Others have found they know very little about a particular religious preference or sexual orientation. Participants have also examined assumptions related to a combination of factors and reflected on questions such as "How could I be Buddhist and Middle Eastern? This isn't a combination I expected." Another participant commented, "I didn't know you could be Black and Catholic."

Depending on the degree of racial identity development among participants (Atkinson, Morten, & Sue, 1998) and the degree of safety experienced in the group, the depth of the group discussion regarding social privilege, assumptions, stereotypes, and oppression can vary from superficial to very personal. At the low end of the spectrum of group acceptance, in processing assumptions related to educational privilege, one white woman who was a university student commented, "I can't get a scholarship. All these minority students are given priority for scholarships." This prompted an emotional exchange between the white woman and an Asian woman who also could not get a scholarship, despite her hard work and good grades. The white woman could not seem to understand how the Asian woman could find her comment to be hurtful. Even though the white woman maintained her defensive posture, the Asian woman was able to accept the group support in expanding her repertoire of skills in coping with racist comments.

On the other end of the spectrum, a Latina woman participating in a group who had developed a desirable degree of safety expressed her frustration with people assuming she is White because of her fair skin, an assumption that was offensive to her because she was proud of her Latina heritage. Members of the group respectfully inquired about her heritage, and a rich discussion ensued. In another group, a female supervisor talked about her experiences working with a male supervisee who initially refused to take her seriously because she was not a man. The group then discussed issues of male privilege and power and the effects this can have on supervisory and therapeutic relationships.

As these examples illustrate, group facilitators of this activity must be skilled at supporting individual reactions that may be triggered and must also be prepared to manage the emotionally laden group dynamics that often emerge during experiential exercises. There is potential for adverse reactions, and participants who have strong emotional reactions may require additional time and resources to manage new levels of self-awareness (Achenbach & Arthur, 2002). A thorough debriefing at the end of the activity offers participants the opportunity to reflect on their experience and understand the professional and personal implications of what they have learned. Facilitators are encouraged to structure the debriefing so that it is linked to the development of multicultural competencies such as those identified by Sue et al. (1992), including multicultural attitudes/beliefs, knowledge, and skills.

# Measuring Progress

Developing self-awareness of one's cultural assumptions, values, and biases is a lifelong process, and the progress individuals make through this activity can vary widely. If the group is meeting for a single session, signs of progress often become evident in the process of completing the activity. Participants may spontaneously remark on learning something new or having never considered a particular point of view. If the group is meeting on an ongoing basis, signs of progress can be assessed through a writing assignment based on the question "What aspects of yourself or your assumed identity were most surprising or most compelling for you and why?" If participants are seeing clients, ratings of satisfaction with service can also measure changes in clinicians' multicultural competence.

# Conclusion

Multiculturally competent clinicians are aware of their own assumptions, values, and biases, and are able to understand the worldview of culturally diverse clients. However, developing multicultural competency is a lifelong process that can be filled with emotional upheavals for clinicians from challenging deeply held beliefs about themselves and others. The cultural card activity described in this chapter gives clinicians an opportunity to practice empathy with the "other" and to gain awareness of the clinicians' existing personal assumptions and biases. This activity has been successfully implemented with clinicians at all stages of experience level, from beginning training to experienced supervisors.

# Additional Resources

Day-Vines, N. L., Wood, S. M., Grotaus, T., Craigen, L., Holman, A., Dotson-Blake, K., & Douglas, M. J. (2007). Broaching the subjects of race, ethnicity, and culture during the counseling process. *Journal of Counseling & Development, 85*, 401–409.

Kim, B. S. K., & Lyons, H. Z. (2003). Experiential activities and multicultural counseling competence training. *Journal of Counseling & Development, 18*(4), 400–408.

# References

Achenbach, K., & Arthur, N. (2002). Developing multicultural counseling competencies through experiential learning. *Counselor Education and Supervision, 42*(1), 2–14.

Atkinson, D. R., Morten, G., & Sue, D. W. (1998). *Counseling American minorities: A cross-cultural perspective* (5th ed.). Dubuque, IA: Brown.

Constantine, M. (1997). Facilitating multicultural competency in counseling supervision: Operationalizing a practical framework. In D. B. Pope-Davis & H. L. Coleman (Eds.), *Multicultural counseling competencies: Assessment, education and training, and supervision* (Vol. 7, pp. 310–324). Thousand Oaks, CA: Sage.

Downing, N. E., & Roush, K. L. (1985). From passive acceptance to active commitment: A model of feminist identity development for women. *Counseling Psychologist, 13*, 695–709.

Fowler, J. (1991). Stages in faith consciousness. *New Directions for Child Development, 52*, 27–45.

Grayson, E., & Marini, I. (1996). Simulated disability exercises and their impact on attitudes toward persons with disabilities. *International Journal of Rehabilitation Research, 19*, 123–131.

Inman, A. (2006). Supervisor multicultural competence and its relation to supervisory process and outcome. *Journal of Marital and Family Therapy, 32*(1), 73–87.

Kolb, D. A. (1984). *Experiential learning: Experience as the source of learning and development.* Englewood Cliffs, NJ: Prentice-Hall.

Ladany, N., Walker, J. A., Pate-Carolan, L. M., & Evans, L. G. (2008). Understanding your self as a therapist. In *Practicing counseling and psychotherapy: Insights from trainees, supervisors, and clients* (pp. 35–55). New York, NY: Taylor & Francis.

Langer, N. (1999). Culturally competent professionals in therapeutic alliance enhance patient compliance. *Journal of Health Care for the Poor and Underserved, 10*, 19–26.

Lee, W. M. L., Blando, J. A., Mizelle, N. D., & Orozco, G. L. (2007). *Introduction to multicultural counseling for helping professionals* (2nd ed.). New York, NY: Routledge.

Lie, D. A., Lee-Rey, E., Gomez, A., Bereknyei, S., & Braddock, C. H. (2010). Does cultural competency training of health professionals improve patient outcomes? A systematic review and proposed algorithm for future research. *Journal of General Internal Medicine, 26*, 317–325.

McCarn, S. R., & Fassinger, R. E. (1996). Revisioning sexual minority identity formation: A new model of lesbian identity and its implications for counseling and research. *The Counseling Psychologist, 24*(3), 508–534.

Pedersen, P., & Ivey, A. (1993). *Culture-centered counseling and interviewing skills: A practical guide.* Westport, CT: Praeger.

Ridley, C. R., & Lingle, D. W. (1996). Cultural empathy in multicultural counseling: A multidimensional process model. In P. Pedersen, W. Lonner, & J. Draguns (Eds.), *Counseling across cultures* (pp. 21–45). Thousand Oaks, CA: Sage.

Smith, T. B., Constantine, M. G., Dunn, T. W., Dinehart, J. M., & Montoya, J. A. (2006). Multicultural education in the mental health professions: A meta-analytic review. *Journal of Counseling Psychology, 53*(1), 132–145.

Sodowsky, G. R., Kwan, K. L., & Pannu, R. (1995). Ethnic identity of Asians in the United States. In J. G. Ponterotto, J. M. Cases, L. A. Suzuki, & C. M. Alexander (Eds.), *Handbook of multicultural counseling* (pp. 123–154). Thousand Oaks, CA: Sage.

Sue, D. W., Arrendondo, P., & McDavis, R. J. (1992). Multicultural competencies/standards: A call to the profession. *Journal of Counseling and Development, 70*(4), 477–486.

Sue, D. W., & Sue, D. (2008). *Counseling the culturally different: Theory and practice* (5th ed.). Hoboken, NJ: Wiley.

Whaley, A. L., & Davis, K. E. (2007). Cultural competence and evidence-based practice in mental health services: A complementary perspective. *American Psychologist, 62*(6), 563–574.

Woolfe, R. (1992). Experiential learning in workshops. In T. Hobbs (Ed.), *Experiential training: Practical guidelines* (pp. 1–13). London, UK: Routledge.

# CHAPTER 24

# EXPLORING OTHER PERSPECTIVES OF GENDER AND ETHNICITY

Roy A. Bean, Alexander L. Hsieh, and Adam M. Clark

## Introduction

The purpose of this activity is to have clinicians explore a change in one key element of their identities (e.g., gender, sexual orientation, ethnicity/race) within the unchanged context of their life circumstances (e.g., family-of-origin characteristics, individual personality). This allows clinicians to focus on and process elements from their own histories within the context of a different perspective through an imagined switch in a salient socio-demographic factor. This activity is designed to help clinicians develop greater perspective-taking abilities and improve their awareness of some of the factors that have heavily influenced, and perhaps even defined, their own life experience.

## Rationale

Prior research suggests that clinicians who can develop strong therapeutic relationships tend to have more positive experiences with their clients in session (e. g., Spinhoven, Giesen-Bloo, van Dyck, Kooiman, & Arntz, 2007; Zuroff & Blatt, 2006). Key elements in the development of a strong therapeutic relationship include both therapist empathy and perspective-taking ability. Empathizing with clients is a basic ability that is essential for all therapy models and interventions. Without empathy, clinicians and client systems may disconnect, and clients may miss out on the acceptance and comfort they often need to feel before change can occur. In relation to perspective taking, not only is it an essential tool in developing a relationship with clients, but it also affects how psychotherapists react and respond to clients' situations and struggles (Galinsky & Moskowitz, 2000; Johnson, 1975; Todd, Bodenhausen, Richeson, & Galinsky, 2011). Because clinicians have their own personal experiences and formulated preferences, natural biases do develop that could conflict with their clients' worldviews. Therefore, clinicians must work to make room for clients' perspectives in therapy while limiting the impact and interference of their personal and often very specific contextual biases (Todd et al., 2011).

Clinicians, at all experience levels, inevitably encounter client systems that differ from their own in terms of gender, culture, sexual orientation, or other salient sociodemographic characteristics. This activity provides an opportunity for clinicians to examine their own social locations regarding challenges and privileges while interpreting these experiences through the eyes of an imagined self. Depending on the identity factor selected for this assignment, participating clinicians will learn how to challenge levels of societal prejudice, mean-spirited stereotypes, and/or unearned privileges. This self-awareness activity is designed to help both new and experienced clinicians improve their ability to empathize with clinical populations that are different from themselves, allowing clinicians to walk, for a minute, in their clients' shoes. Almost all clinicians can benefit from completing this exercise, because it is designed to push them to consider how their lives would be different (in terms of opportunities and successes) with a shift in their gender, race, or another key sociodemographic category. Consequently, no intrapersonal or interpersonal characteristics would preclude a clinician from participating in this exercise.

# Activity Instructions

For this activity, clinicians need to identify a single socio-demographic factor they would like to better understand (e.g., gender, sexual orientation, ethnicity/race), gain a deeper understanding of how this factor affects individuals, and then write about what their lives would have been like if they had been born and raised as a member of this different socio-demographic group. This activity consists of two preparatory exercises followed by an exploratory essay and can be either self-assigned and carried out by a clinician or assigned by a supervisor as part of a training exercise, class requirement, or workshop training. Therefore, the instructions are directed mainly to clinicians.

## Identification Exercise

For the purpose of the identification exercise, clinicians will select a single socio-demographic factor they would like to better understand. Clinicians will then need to review their lives in light of many socio-demographic factors, retaining as much as possible about their own life history (e.g., social class, family structure, birth order), so that their primary focus can remain on what would happen if just one salient socio-demographic characteristic were changed. In other words, clinicians should try to understand what aspects of their lives would change if they were born male instead of female or Latino instead of African American.

## Insider's Perspective Exercise

Before beginning the writing process, clinicians need to get an "insider's perspective," seeking to better understand this socio-demographic group by watching relevant movies, browsing applicable Internet content, and talking to members of this particular group. These interactions will help clinicians consider the reality beyond their own experiences as they collect more information about the formative years of another person within that group. It may also be helpful for clinicians to review other family-of-origin assignments so they are aware of how they have presented their lives in the past.

## "What If" Paper

Clinicians should write a paper seven to eight pages in length that addresses the following questions:

1. What would have been different about your life growing up? Share detailed moments from your new, imagined life, reporting on what would have happened differently, how it would have felt, and so forth.
2. What types of oppressive experiences do you imagine you would have experienced? What privileges would you have had?
3. Which of your personality traits or skills would be different, having less/more reinforcement or fewer/more opportunities? Which would be the same?
4. What expectations for your future would be different? Would you still be a mental health provider/student?
5. What realizations did you have while completing this assignment?

We strongly recommend that this paper focus on changing just *one* main socio-demographic factor. We have tried this exercise allowing clinicians to vary more than one key identity characteristic in their papers (e.g., writing it as if they are both of another gender group *and* another ethnic group); however, this usually results in a more cursory exploration of the characteristic and its effects on their lives. We recommend that clinicians focus on the depth, rather than the breadth, of the experience so they can see more clearly how a single crucial difference may affect their lives, giving them an entirely different set of opportunities and barriers.

# Example

This "what if" exercise has been used in master's-level and doctoral-level clinical courses over the past 15 years. The following excerpts are taken from student papers, with identity and other

Example 161

characteristics changed to preserve students' confidentiality. Although students have discussed many socio-demographic factors over the years, for the purposes of this section we will focus on gender and race/ethnicity.

The gender-based insights that clinicians discover during this assignment can help them become more self-aware as clinicians and more empathic as they interact with clients who are strongly influenced by societally based gender roles. In one paper, a female student (28 years old, European American) writes about what would have been different in her family if she were born a boy:

*As a boy, I would have been able to develop talents and confidence in systems outside of the home; I would have been able to see how [I], as a person, contributed to many different systems. This sense of self could have made the difference when adjusting to my parents' divorce. Instead of wondering where and how I will fit into this new world, I could have held onto the one thing I knew to be constant in my life: sports.*

Through the paper, this female student imagines a different life experience, as informed by gender, regarding how she could have responded to her parents' divorce and the type of meaning that she made about herself. In addition, this student examines both advantages and disadvantages of societal gender roles, writing:

*The future seems a little scarier as a male. No more only worrying about providing for me, suddenly the pressure is a bit more overwhelming. I will have a wife and kids to think about. I think I would feel more in control though …. Maybe that is a power thing. If I were a male it would seem that I would have more control over getting what I want instead of taking what I get.*

On the same topic, another female student (25 years old, European American) shared the following:

*I imagine I'd be like [my brother] and like my dad, feeling a lot inside but not knowing how to appropriately express it. Eventually I would just shut it off and function on autopilot. I don't want to imagine how hollow I might come to feel one day …. I might have felt oppressed as my emotions would have had to take a backseat to my sister's and as I would have been expected to be strong at all times to take care of the women in my life.*

This student takes into account how she might have been socialized differently in handling emotions and conflict if she had been born a male.

One male student (33 years old, European American) expresses how his relationship with his parents could have differed based on a change in his gender:

*If I were a girl in my family, my activities, fun, and discipline received from parents would've been similar to what my sisters experienced. They [my sisters] express having regrets about the lack of opportunities to connect to my dad. It makes me sad to imagine myself without the experiences I had with him and my mom, as they have been important in my formation over the years. I think there was a theme throughout our upbringings that relates to our experiences scholastically and athletically: It was okay for a male to take on seemingly feminine traits but not okay for a female to take on masculine traits.*

Another male student (30 years old, European American) reacts to how his education might have taken a different path if he were born a female.

*Obviously, my future would be very different if I were female in my family, as I probably would have been encouraged to be a stay-at-home mom. My continued education might have been marginalized and put off because it doesn't serve a direct purpose in the economic well-being of my family.*

Similar to the insights gained from a focus on gender, clinicians can develop more personal awareness of certain privileges and specific challenges they would have faced if they were born of a different race or ethnicity. One male student (28 years old, European American) interviewed a man from Rwanda and described the man's experience during tribal wars, feeling so unsafe that he could not go outside without fearing for his life because his neighbors were of other tribes. In response to this information, the student reported:

*This is really hard for me to comprehend emotionally, being that my current privilege has not led me to have to consider such a state of living. I realize as I write this paper that [this memory from his formative years] probably explains why it is hard for him to remain connected to his family-of-origin back home and complicates the process of developing a safe home for his own family here.*

Another male student (28 years old, European American) examined his life through the lens of being Mexican American. From his understanding of Mexican American culture, he reflects on how his family interactions and dynamics could have been different.

*Despite this necessity of living, I probably would have had a closer, more involved family than the one I grew up with. I may have had extended family living nearby that had come to join us from our home country. Even if we had to drive far to get there, we would have gotten together often to celebrate birthdays, holidays, and other special events…. Being together often with extended family would have been a high priority, and I would have had close relationships with my cousins.*

Continuing, he shares a realization that many other clinicians may share: That we approach those who are different from us through a set of faulty preformed beliefs and stereotypes.

*In writing this paper I realized that I have maintained a number of stereotypes and assumptions about Latinos that are negative and possibly even hurtful…. I have also found that it is very difficult and uncomfortable to face one's own biases and the stereotypes one uses. It is something that we do unconsciously and without intention. I certainly meant no harm by the things that I thought and believed about immigrant families and I harbor no animosity toward Latinos as a group…. However, any stereotype, no matter how benign, limits individuals, and hiding from the stereotypes and biases that pervade our society will not make them go away. Only by becoming aware of them and talking about them will we be able to move beyond them to a more equal society.*

# Measuring Progress

Increasing one's self-awareness is an ongoing and often difficult journey. During the "what if" activity, clinicians can chart their progress by measuring their connection to clients, by becoming more consciously aware of their own reactions to clients' problems, and by expressing their experiences of awareness achieved by completing this assignment. Through ongoing conversations with colleagues and in the context of supervision groups, various perspectives and insights can be shared, adding to this self-awareness experience. The viewpoints from colleagues can offer a broader perspective for the clinician's own personal experience.

As applicable, supervisors should take an opportunity to facilitate open discussions with clinicians about insights gained and any difficulties experienced while completing this activity. Topics for discussion or supervision can include clinicians' experiences while interviewing a member of the "other" group, privileges clinicians have previously taken for granted, oppressive experiences or life challenges that have served a purpose in the clinician's development, how forced reliance on rigid stereotypes about group members may illustrate differences between actual experiences and their "what if" experiences, and the power of societal expectations and accompanying opportunities.

As an additional training note, when clinicians struggle with this assignment, several domains should be explored by supervisors, including therapist cognitive rigidity, emotional immaturity, or past trauma experiences or conflict in relation to members of the other group. One additional difficulty that comes up regularly is where a clinician struggles to separate from family loyalties and the way that they have been taught to think about those of a different ethnicity, gender, or sexual orientation. For instance, if a clinician grows up in circumstances where she is taught to not trust men because they just leave the family, it will be challenging for her to fully explore the oppression and disadvantages of being male. Similarly, if a clinician is brought up in a family that regularly uses ethnic slurs and devalues members of a particular ethnic group (e.g., African Americans), then he will be more restricted in his ability to switch perspectives from that of a white man to that of a black man. For clinicians who are struggling with this activity to a minor degree, supervisors may need to just be patient and continue to engage them in conversation. In more extreme cases, supervisors may need to refer clinicians for focused counseling to help them deal with the topic. The most extreme cases may even warrant a discussion on the prospects of a job change or a shift in career goals.

# Conclusion

By trying to imagine the perspectives of members of other marginalized groups, clinicians can more closely evaluate their personal biases, which can improve the likelihood that they will create space for differences and help them to better empathize with diverse clients. It is expected that this activity will help beginning clinicians to identify their limits in perspective taking and understanding others. It is also expected that this exercise will help clinicians at all experience levels to have more to discuss and share with colleagues and supervisors on this important topic.

# Additional Resources

Epley, N., & Caruso, E. M. (2009). Perspective taking: Misstepping into others' shoes. In K. D. Markman, W. P. Klein, J. A. Suhr, K. D. Markman, W. P. Klein, & J. A. Suhr (Eds.), *Handbook of imagination and mental simulation* (pp. 295–309). New York, NY: Psychology Press.

Quintana, S. M. (2008). Racial perspective taking ability: Developmental, theoretical, and empirical trends. In S. M. Quintana & C. McKown (Eds.), *Handbook of race, racism, and the developing child* (pp. 16–36). Hoboken, NJ: Wiley.

# References

Galinsky, A. D., & Moskowitz, G. B. (2000). Perspective-taking: Decreasing stereotype expression, stereotype accessibility, and in-group favoritism. *Journal of Personality and Social Psychology, 78*(4), 708–724.

Johnson, D. W. (1975). Cooperative and social perspective taking. *Journal of Personality and Social Psychology, 31*(2), 241–244

Spinhoven, P., Giesen-Bloo, J., van Dyck, R., Kooiman, K., & Arntz, A. (2007). The therapeutic alliance in schema-focused therapy and transference-focused psychotherapy for borderline personality disorder. *Journal of Consulting and Clinical Psychology, 75*(1), 104–115.

Todd, A. R., Bodenhausen, G. V., Richeson, J. A., & Galinsky, A. D. (2011). Perspective taking combats automatic expressions of racial bias. *Journal of Personality and Social Psychology, 100*(6), 1027–1042.

Zuroff, D. C., & Blatt, S. J. (2006). The therapeutic relationship in the brief treatment of depression: Contributions to clinical improvement and enhanced adaptive capacities. *Journal of Consulting and Clinical Psychology, 74*(1), 130–140.

# CHAPTER 25

# UNDERSTANDING POWER IMBALANCES IN THE CLINICAL ENCOUNTER

Kimberly A. E. Carter, Jayme R. Swanke, and Venessa A. Brown

## Introduction

Clinicians engage in both conscious and unconscious actions and interpret the actions of their clients through varying cultural viewpoints. One such dimension of culture that deserves attention is the concept of *power*. The activity outlined in this chapter will help clinicians increase their awareness of how culturally informed power dynamics and imbalances have the potential to inform the clinician–client relationship and impact the clinical encounter.

## Rationale

*Power* is defined by Merriam-Webster's (n.d.) as "the possession of control, authority, or influence over others." According to the feminist approach to therapy, power is seen as a central component of the therapeutic engagement process (Brown, 2008). According to this framework, power is an act of undue influence that can potentially happen between the clinician and client (Zur, 2009). This power differential inadvertently happens because of the dominant social status (i.e., privileged state) of the clinician. The resulting product is a therapeutic encounter where the privileged group (i.e., therapists) exercises cultural domination over the less privileged or vulnerable group (i.e., the clients). To circumvent this power imbalance, Marecek and Kravetz (1998) argue that clinicians must reconsider the prolific assumption that a client is capable of objective choice and self-determination void of undue influence. Clinicians must recognize their influence in the therapy process, seek a position of value neutrality, engage in work that values an egalitarian, cooperative relationship, and favor less judgment in treatment choices (Marecek & Kravetz, 1998; Zur, 2009).

This chapter will help clinicians gain this level of consciousness using two clinical vignettes and an associated set of discussion questions. Two key attributes of power expression will be examined: intrapersonal (i.e., client-based) and interpersonal (i.e., relational-based). Client-based attributes include individual sociodemographic and sociocultural characteristics, such as age, race, ethnicity, marital status, sexual orientation, gender, ability, physical and mental health, religion, family structure, class, and education (Korin, 1994). Relational-based attributes include interactions between individuals that demonstrate how individuals relate to each other, assert power, or succumb to power based on presumed social status or social role.

For each of the vignettes, special attention will be paid to key intrapersonal and interpersonal attributes that are worthy of mention. In each vignette, several client-based attributes that reflect contemporary issues in counseling today are highlighted. The first vignette highlights ethnic status and age. These were specifically chosen because increasing trends in ethnic and racial minority subgroups are driving clinicians to pay closer attention to these populations. It is projected that, by 2050, ethnic and racial minority subgroups will outnumber white populations in the United States (Passel & Cohn, 2008). Moreover, the older adult population is also large, with census data indicating that approximately 40 million Americans (13%) are ages 65 or older (U.S. Census Bureau, 2011) and that life expectancy is increasing. This means that clinicians are likely to have more therapeutic encounters with older adults as well.

In the second vignette, military status and physical disability are highlighted. There are a reported 22.7 million veterans ages 17 years or older in the United States (U.S. Department of Veterans Affairs, 2010). Upon returning from deployment, there is evidence that these individuals have many psychosocial and/or physical disability issues requiring clinical care (Henry J. Kaiser Family Foundation, 2010). Clinicians are expected to work with veterans and their myriad needs in a way that demonstrates sensitivity and professional competence.

In the activities, participants will be asked to examine each vignette and identify relational-based attributes that are prominent in the clinical encounter. In particular, three key areas of interpersonal therapeutic power imbalances will be highlighted. The first is *Assumptions of Client Control*. This is based on the idea that individuals often seek therapeutic assistance because they feel helpless or lack control in some aspect of their lives. The client is thus seen as less powerful, and their expert knowledge (i.e., expertise gained through experience) is not always recognized (Zur, 2009). The second area is *Behavioral Practices and Language*. This area looks at how clinicians use language and labels to inadvertently exercise power. Dichotomous terms like clinician/client, professional/patient, provider/consumer and pronouns that denote ownership such as "my client," "our agency's consumer," or terms that denote control such as "compliance," "mandated," "directives," and "adherence" are all examples of behavioral practices that exercise power (Zur, 2009). Finally, the third area is *Professional Role Assumptions*. This area of power imbalance considers how professionals have the capacity to use their privileged titles (e.g., care provider, service broker, case manager) and roles to exercise undue influence (Winslade, Crocket, & Monk, 1997; Zur, 2009). All of these areas impact consent to therapeutic actions, treatment outcomes, and biased evaluations of success (Largo & Thompson, 1996).

# Activity Instructions

After reviewing the following vignettes, participants will engage in a facilitated dialogue to explore how power and privilege shape the client. It is important to note key parameters that must be met in order for this activity to be implemented successfully. The preferred audiences for this activity are trained clinicians seeking to improve their skills and clinicians-in-training. It is best implemented with small work groups of three to five persons. The activity should last 90 minutes. Facilitators should have demonstrated skill at encouraging participant input and transparency.

Prior to the activity, the facilitator will need to obtain a flipchart, sticky notes (in three different colors), masking tape (to create a continuum line on the wall), poster-size signs (reading High and Low), and paper, pens, and markers. Additional materials that are needed include:

- Printed copies of the vignettes
- Pre- and Post- Knowledge Assessment [two copies per participant] (see Table 25.1)
- Facilitator Lesson Plan (see Table 25.2)

The facilitator should prepare the classroom for the activity by using the tape to make a continuum on the wall or on the floor with the *High* sign on one end of the continuum and the *Low* sign on the other. This continuum represents the sense of power that is experienced by the clients in the vignettes. To begin the activity, the facilitator should distribute the first copy of the Knowledge Assessment (see Table 25.1) and instruct participants to complete only the sections designated as PRE-. These assessments should be immediately collected by the facilitator. Next, each participant should be given one vignette to read silently.

Vignette 1    *Carlos is a 70-year-old Latino male who has recently lost his wife to breast cancer. His primary health-care provider has referred Carlos to you. Additionally, Carlos' adult children have noticed that his health has been declining. He cries frequently and is no longer interested in spending time with the family or going to religious services or the coffee shop.*

Table 25.1 Pre- and
Post-Knowledge
Assessment

**Knowledge Assessment**

*Items 1 through 5 should be completed by indicating how much you agree with the following statements.*

| | Self-Awareness Outcomes | Strongly Agree | Agree | Neither | Disagree | Strongly Disagree |
|---|---|---|---|---|---|---|
| **PRE & POST** | 1. I have a clear understanding of the definition of power. | 1 | 2 | 3 | 4 | 5 |
| | 2. I feel challenged by understanding power in context of serving different groups. | 1 | 2 | 3 | 4 | 5 |
| | 3. I understand how cultural factors are related to power. | 1 | 2 | 3 | 4 | 5 |
| | 4. I am able to identify the influence of my power in a therapeutic situation. | 1 | 2 | 3 | 4 | 5 |
| **POST** | 5. This activity was beneficial as a reflection exercise on my professional life | 1 | 2 | 3 | 4 | 5 |

Understanding Outcomes *[For items 6 through 9, please repond by writing a brief statement.]*

|  |  |
|---|---|
| **PRE & POST** | 6. How is the dimension of power related to cultural competence? |
| | 7. What is your understanding of <u>intrapersonal & interpersonal characteristics that contribute to power</u>? |
| |    a. PRE-TEST: What is your current understanding ? |
| |    b. POST-TEST: How has your understanding changed? |
| | 8. How do you address <u>power imbalances in your therapeutic work</u>? |
| |    a. PRE-TEST: What is your current understanding ? |
| |    b. POST-TEST: With this training in mind, how might you address this in the future? |
| **POST** | 9. Every person has a motivation for change or improvement. Based on this activity, what is yours? |

From Carter, K. (2008). Cultural Competence and Awareness: Human Resource Training Curriculum. C-E Consulting Inc. Reprinted with permission.

*At his first appointment, Carlos seems very guarded. He lets you know immediately that he can handle his own problems. He is only there to appease the concerns of his adult children. He reveals that his wife passed away six months ago. For 40 years, he was the sole provider for the family, his wife, and four children. After retiring from a management position at an industrial facility, he continued to pick up odd jobs to stay busy. When Marta became ill, Carlos spent his time at home providing intimate care for her and taking care of the house. He states that he has always been able to stand on his own, and he has often been the "go-to" person in his family and local community. However, lately he has not felt up to the task of helping others.*

*Josephine (Jo) served as a member of the Marine Reserves until she graduated from college and was then commissioned as a Second Lieutenant and became an active-duty officer. Although Josephine has been a commissioned officer for 10 years, she had to work hard to prove her worth to the rest of her company because of her female status. During a 22-month deployment to Iraq, Jo increased her rank from Second to First lieutenant. Recently, Jo received a combat injury that caused her to lose her right leg and left her vision impaired. She was honorably discharged.*

*Jo has been referred to you, for vocational rehabilitation and psychosocial support. At the first meeting, she is unable to fit her wheelchair through your office door, and the session has to be relocated to the staff conference room. Jo promptly shares her anger about the lack of accessibility in your building. Jo tells you about her military career and her difficulty transitioning to a civilian career. It is imperative for her to find a job, because she is the sole provider for her younger sister, a college student who lives with her. Another issue for Jo is adjusting to civilian life with a disability. She is proud to have served her country.*

**Vignette 2**

Once the participants have finished reading the vignette, the facilitator should explain that the continuum represents a measurement of an individual's sense of power. The *High* and

*Low* indicate levels of personal power. The facilitator should then ask the following series of questions. Participants will answer each question by writing their name on a sticky note and placing it at the preferred point on the continuum. A different-colored sticky note should be used for each question so that the differences in responses to each question can be better appreciated visually.

1. The facilitator should start by asking: "Now that you are done reading the case, put yourself in the shoes of this individual (Carlos or Jo) and think about how much power you would have felt in your life, *prior* to coming for therapy."

2. Next, the facilitator should inquire about the client's sense of power given the clinical situation: "Now, consider how much power you would feel if you were [describe vignette character using key demographic characteristics], who was seeking help for [fill in the appropriate blank using the vignette]." For example, for Vignette 1, the facilitator might say: "Now, consider how much power you would feel if you were an older adult Hispanic male seeking help for depression."

3. Finally, the facilitator should ask about the perceptions of client power now that they have to meet with the clinician for the first time: "Now, consider how much power you would feel when you meet with the clinician if you were Carlos (or Jo)."

Once all of the sticky notes have been placed, the facilitator should ask participants to look at the continuum and quietly reflect on the varying perceptions of power demonstrated by the sticky notes. Small work groups (three to five individuals) should be organized. They should spend 15 to 20 minutes on this portion of the activity. The facilitator should visit each group to provide guidance and support. To ensure critical consideration of key concepts, the following questions should be asked of the participants:

1. Why are there differences in the sticky note placements?

2. What does this say about how you (the participant) and your colleagues perceive power?

3. Where did you place your sticky notes, and what justification can you give for your choices?

4. What client-based attributes of power do you think a clinician needs to consider?

5. How do client personal attributes inform the clinician–client dyad?

After the completion of the small-group activity, participants should reconvene as a large group. The facilitator should open the floor to discuss small-group responses, examine the participants' reactions to the exercise, and examine the group members' general knowledge of power. Responses should be recorded on the flipchart. After recording responses, the facilitator should provide a brief lesson on power (recommended lesson plan, see Table 25.2). This lesson will focus on intrapersonal and interpersonal power as it exists within a clinical encounter. Following the lesson, participants should complete the Knowledge Assessment again (see Table 25.1). They should be instructed to complete all questions (PRE and POST). A final group discussion should ensue to recap the overall impact of the exercise.

# Example

This self-awareness activity has been implemented on multiple occasions. The most recent implementation was with a participant audience (n = 13) of seasoned licensed clinical social workers. These practitioners represented a variety of service sectors, including mental health, immigrant and international services, child and family welfare, and substance abuse. The activity was offered as professional development training, attendance was voluntary, and continuing education units were offered. Analysis of the knowledge assessment results revealed that participants had an increased understanding of the therapeutic dynamic of power and how cultural factors are related to power. Participants demonstrated their knowledge in narrative comments such as, "Power plays a role in our lives, understanding power within one's culture brings competence." Moreover, post-assessment revealed that more participants (92% post versus 69% pre) felt more confident in their ability to identify the influence of power in clinical encounters. In particular,

**Table 25.2  Facilitator
Lesson Plan**

1.  Define *Power*

    - "The possession of control, authority, or influence over others" (Merriam-Webster, n.d.)

    - An act of undue influence that can potentially happen between the clinician and client (Zur, 2009)

    - A dimension of cultural competence; a social and cultural construct of human existence

2.  Two Primary Attributes of Power

    - Client-based (intrapersonal): Sociodemographic and sociocultural characteristics such as age, race, ethnicity, marital status, sexual orientation, gender, ability, physical and mental health, religion, family structure, class, and education

    - Relational (interpersonal): Interactions between individuals that demonstrate how individuals relate to each other, assert power, or succumb to power based on presumed social status and roles

3.  Power Imbalances Exist in Therapeutic Relationships and Are Related to:

    - Assumptions of Client Control: Related to competing interest. Individual perceptions of power; the nature of help seeking (people seek help when they feel powerless); lack of recognition of client's personal sense of power

    - Behavioral Practices and Language: Use of language and labels that inadvertently exercise power. Dichotomous terms such as clinician/client, professional/patient, provider/consumer; pronouns that denote ownership such as "my client," "our consumers"; control terminology such as "compliance," "mandated," "directives," "adherence"

    - Professional Role Assumptions: How privileged titles and roles (e.g., care provider, service broker, case manager) are unintentionally used to exercise undue influence

4.  Power Imbalances Influence Treatment Goal-Setting and Outcomes

    - Clinician recognition of the person and presenting problem

    - Clinician choice of treatment protocol and implementation of said treatment

    - Clinician comfort minimizing personal power and working toward empowerment

From Carter, K., & Swanke, J. (2012). Facilitator Lesson Plan: Power Imbalances in Therapeutic Work. Reprinted with permission.

they commented on their increased awareness of the impact of language, unconscious authority, and clients' personal sense of powerlessness. This awareness was clearly stated by one participant: "You have to recognize your level of power in a relationship in order to work effectively with a client."

# Measuring Progress

Self-reflection and self-awareness are critical to the therapeutic process. Clinicians should develop an ongoing way to evaluate themselves in the context of their practice in order to check in about their biases and challenges. Learning to *walk in the client's shoes* reminds the clinician of the value of individual assessment and treating clients the way in which they wish to be treated. Although much of the clinician's progress will be qualitative, the pre- and post-activity assessments will measure the participant's understanding of the key activity concepts (see Table 25.1). Comparing these assessments will help facilitators gauge knowledge gains and assist them in improving the activity for future implementation.

# Conclusion

The concept of power is an essential element of culture that requires attention. Either based on subjective perception or objective reality, the notion of power reveals how individuals see themselves in the social dimension. This is particularly true in emerging populations such as older adults, military, persons with disabilities, and minorities. Moreover, in clinical situations where people seek help to feel empowered, power dynamics and privileged status shape treatment appraisal and goals. Thus, it is expedient for clinicians to explore their own power status and imbalances that might occur within the clinical encounter. In the words of Raheim and colleagues (2007) in their address on the influence of privilege and dominance in therapy, "If we do not proactively look at how relations of power operate to create advantages for some and deny these advantages to others, it hinders our work as therapists." This activity provides a safe environment for clinicians to do just that.

# Additional Resources

*Cultural Safety: Module 2, Peoples' Experience of Oppression.* Online educational module that examines the dynamics of power with international populations. Retrieved from http://web2.uvcs.uvic.ca/courses/csafety/mod2/las.htm

Flaskas, C., & Humphreys, C. (1993). Theorizing about power: Intersecting the ideas of Foucault with the "problem" of power in family therapy. *Family Process 32*(1), 35–47.

Larner, G. (2005). The real as illusion: Deconstructing power in family therapy. *Journal of Family Therapy, 17*(2), 191–217.

Sleeter, C. E. (2001). *Culture, difference, & power: Instructor's manual and interactive video.* New York, NY: Teacher's College Press.

West, C. (2011). When the doctor is a "Lady": Power, status, and gender in physician-patient encounters. *Symbolic Interaction, 7*(1) 87–106.

# References

Brown, L. S. (2008). Feminist therapy. In J. L. Lebow (Ed.), *Twenty-first century psychotherapies: Contemporary approaches to theory and practice* (pp. 277–306). Hoboken, NJ: Wiley.

Carter, K. (2008). Cultural competence and awareness: Human resource training curriculum. C-E Consulting Inc.

Carter, K., & Swanke, J. (2012). Facilitator lesson plan: Power imbalances in therapeutic work.

Henry J. Kaiser Family Foundation. (2010). Distributions of U.S. population by race/ethnicity, 2010 and 2050. Kaiser Fast Facts: Kaiser Slides. Retrieved from http://facts.kff.org/chart .aspx?ch=364

Korin, E. C. (1994). Social inequalities and therapeutic relationships. *Journal of Feminist Family Therapy, 5*(3–4), 75–98.

Largo, C., & Thompson, J. (1996). *Race, culture and counseling*. Ann Arbor, MI: Open University Press.

Marecek, J., & Kravetz, D. (1998). Power and agency in feminist therapy. In I. B. Seu & M. C. Heenan (Eds.), *Feminism and psychotherapy: Reflections on contemporary theories and practices* (pp. 13–29). Perspectives on Psychotherapy Series. London, United Kingdom: Sage.

Merriam-Webster's Online Dictionary (11th ed.). (n.d.). Power. Retrieved from www.merriam-webster.com/dictionary/power

Raheim, S., White, C., Denborough, D., Waldegrave, C., Tamasese, K., Tuhaka, F., ... & Carey, M. (2007). An invitation to narrative practitioners to address privilege and dominance. Dulwich Centre Foundation Inc. Retrieved from www.dulwichcentre.com.au/ privilege.html#invitation

Passel, J., & Cohn, D. (2008). Population projections: 2005–2050. Retrieved from www.pewsocialtrends.org/2008/02/11/us-population-projections-2005-2050/

U.S. Census Bureau. (2011). The older population in the United States 2011. Retrieved from www.census.gov/population/age/data/2011.htm

U.S. Department of Veterans Affairs. (2010, December). Veteran population projections: FY2000 to FY2036. Retrieved from www.va.gov/vetdata/docs/quickfacts/Population-slide show.pdf

Winslade, J., Crocket, K., & Monk, G. (1997). *Narrative therapy in practice: The archaeology of hope*. San Francisco, CA: Jossey-Bass.

Zur, O. (2009). Power in psychotherapy and counseling: Exploring the "inherent power differential" and related myths about therapists' omnipotence and clients' vulnerability. *Independent Practitioner*, *29*(3), 160–164.

# CHAPTER 26

# INVITING A BETTER UNDERSTANDING OF PRIVILEGE AND DISADVANTAGE

Peggy McIntosh

## Introduction

This activity was designed to help participants recognize their own privileges and disadvantages, which is an important element of self-awareness. This activity and its accompanying directed reading have been used by more than 40,000 individuals from various disciplines and professions. It has been found to be especially useful in raising awareness and encouraging self-reflection in those practitioners working in clinical professions. In most professional, human-service training programs, practitioners are encouraged to acquire specific knowledge and understanding about the groups that they serve clinically. Unfortunately, many clinical programs do not help practitioners examine their own locations in the social structure or system and the associated privileges and disadvantages afforded to them by their respective social locations.

The exercise described in this chapter provides a systemic and an individual framework for better understanding privilege and power in society and the role that it plays in each clinician's life. The exercise also encourages an examination of the link between the inner and outer operations of power. The primary aim of this exercise is to help clinicians become more aware of how power has worked in their own lives and to increase their ability to imagine how social forces may have affected others. It draws attention to one's experiences of both privilege and oppression, and posits that we all experience both in our lives.

For some participants, this exercise may be a very early experience (perhaps the first occasion) wherein they become aware of unearned advantages and disadvantages. As such, this may be some participants' first experience in seeing that their life (with all its associated successes and failures) is significantly related to arbitrary membership in groups whose status has been favored or disfavored within societal hierarchies (e.g., gender-based or race-based hierarchies). Engagement in this activity allows participants to consider that their own arbitrarily assigned social locations (as a function of gender, race, social class, ability-level, and so forth) have as much to do (or more to do) with their accomplishments and struggles as do their individual efforts. It has been my experience that participants often go through a period of self-reflection following this activity and develop a clearer understanding of how their ascribed societal status (as a function of group memberships) has affected and shaped their life experiences.

This exercise, although intensely personal and "political," was constructed to avoid eliciting any feelings of blame, shame, and guilt. It was designed to reduce the fear of talking about how power relations affect one's daily experience and to increase the clinician's ability to talk about privilege and oppression. It is believed that through participation in this exercise and focused supervision, clinicians will gain new insights and empowerment.

## Rationale

At this time, most people in the United States are unaware of how societal power (and its associated privileges) strongly influences life outcomes. The U.S. educational system generally rests on the myth of meritocracy—that people get what they individually want, work for, earn, and deserve. Therefore, those in positions of power (including many clinicians) tend to think of themselves as truly superior rather than as having been favored by hierarchical social systems that empower people differentially. Individuals who are in the helping professions may unintentionally be condescending toward clients or colleagues who have less access to financial resources, education, security, confidence, and well-being. For example, Caucasian practitioners may be quite unaware of the dominance of the white majority culture in shaping their paradigms, workplaces, and their sense of themselves. This brief exercise serves as an introduction to seeing societal forces that many clinicians have been taught not to notice.

# Activity Instructions

The facilitator should prepare for the group activity by reading my previous publications on the topic (i.e., *White Privilege and Male Privilege: A Personal Account of Coming to See Correspondences Through Work in Women's Studies* [McIntosh, 1988] and *White Privilege: Unpacking the Invisible Knapsack* [McIntosh, 1989]). Additional resources for the facilitator and for participants can be found at The National SEED Project on Inclusive Curriculum (Seeking Educational Equity and Diversity, http://www.nationalseedproject.org). It is especially important that the facilitator be thoughtful and open, because this groundbreaking work in race relations requires such honesty and candor. In addition, it is important to remember that the facilitator is not an expert but is a co-learner and participant.

This self-awareness exercise usually takes about an hour to complete and is best done in a group setting (two to fifty members). The facilitator distributes *White Privilege: Unpacking the Invisible Knapsack* (1989) so that every participant has a copy (see Appendix 26.1 below). Facilitators should be mindful of varying reading levels and speeds when assigning this reading, but in most cases, a 15-minute time period will suffice.

After all participants have had a chance to read the paper, participants should be divided into dyads. This self-awareness exercise does not work as well with three people in a group, because group members will not all be able to speak within the tightly allotted time, which is usually one minute each. If the group is larger, the facilitator is encouraged to ask anyone who does not have a partner to stand and find another person who is not yet matched. The facilitator should volunteer to be the partner of anyone who is still unpaired.

The facilitator should announce, "Don't begin to discuss this topic yet. First you need to find out which of you is speaker #1." The facilitator waits until the room or auditorium is quiet and then asks, "In your pair, which of you has the earliest birthday in the year?" The first speaker can then be designated by which of the dyad's members has the *latest* birthday in the year. After everyone has quieted down again, the facilitator gives the instructions to the first speaker and starts timing the exercise. He or she should firmly and quickly cut the speaker off as the minute ends, and then give the instructions for the second speaker to begin. The facilitator must not be informal, even if the group is only one pair. The method is very intentionally structured and is not effective for awareness-raising when it is not firmly followed. The purpose of the strict structure is to not unwittingly afford one participant more advantage or disadvantage than another in terms of time spent talking.

The facilitator's instructions to the first speaker should go as follows:

*Speaker #1, please tell your talking partner for one minute, uninterrupted, about one or more ways in which you have had unearned disadvantage in your life. You did not ask for it. It was circumstantial. But in some ways it has made your life harder. It is not a matter for blame, shame, and guilt. You didn't invent the systems you were born into. You did not invent your disadvantages. They are not your fault, but in some ways they have given you difficulty. Your disadvantage may have to do with your place in the birth order in your family, or whether you were the sex of child your parents wanted. Your disadvantage may come from your parents' relation to money or to education; what language you spoke at home; your neighborhood; your gender, ethnicity, race, religion, sexual orientation, physical appearance, stereotypes about your family; your physical coordination; your handedness—were you left-handed? What else gave you some unearned disadvantage? Please tell your partner about one or more of these things that have arbitrarily set you back and made your life harder, through no fault of your own. Whatever you say is for your partner alone, not to be repeated to anyone else.*

Although this is a lengthy introduction for the first speaker in this exercise, it has the advantage of giving both partners some time to think through what they might want to say. Additionally, some participants need a little more time to consider all of the factors that can be discussed in relation to privilege, because the article can make some worry that the *only* topic they will be asked to talk about is race. Realizing that privilege comes in a variety of forms can come as a relief to some, especially those who have strong reactions to the topics of race and gender.

At the end of the minute, stop the first speaker and transition to the second speaker. Instructions for the second speaker are as follows:

*Speaker #2, your role is extremely weird. Normally, if you had listened to someone telling for a full minute about things that have made their life difficult, you would show that you have been listening. But do not do that. This is not a social event. Start fresh. Pretend you are the first speaker and that nothing has been said. Do not empathize, echo, piggyback, or show that you have heard anything that the first person has said. This is your minute. Please tell your talking partner about one or more of your experiences of having unearned disadvantage in the world. You did not ask for it and it is not your fault. It is not a matter for blame, shame, or guilt, but it has made life harder for you in some ways. It could include many things that I have already mentioned, or others like hair, or body type, or being short or tall or having a certain kind of voice, or your gender, race, ethnicity, religion, sexual orientation, class, your parents' reputation, your neighbors, your siblings and relatives, and so on.*

The facilitator once again monitors the talk time for the speaker and cuts off the speaker at one minute. Next, the facilitator shares the following instructions and provides examples of unearned advantages if necessary:

*Now we go to the second part of this exercise. As you may have guessed, this second part is an opportunity to share some of your experiences of unearned advantage. Unearned advantage is privilege that was given to you arbitrarily. It is not a matter of blame, shame, or guilt, but it has helped you out and made life easier for you in some ways. It can have to do with any of the things that are disadvantages to some people, but in this case you were on the lucky side. You are talking about circumstances that helped you. Speaker #1, please tell your talking partner about one or more ways that you have had unearned advantage in your life as a function of your race, class, gender, or anything else that represents something that has helped you through no virtue of your own.*

Speaker #1 is given one minute to talk on this subject, and then speaker #2 is given the following instructions:

*Even if you were about to say what you partner has said, start fresh and speak from your own experience. Please tell your partner about your unearned advantage. To highlight the subtlety and the complexity of privilege, here I usually give several new and different examples of unearned advantage related to living in the United States. These include coming to expect hot and cold running water, which is not available to most people on the face of the earth; having a currency that buys a lot of goods from other places in the world; or having your nation's language spoken in virtually all airports in the world.*

After these exchanges, it is advisable for the facilitator to communicate the following: "I know it can feel brutal to be cut off after 60 seconds, especially when you are talking about difficult things, but the author of this activity (Peggy McIntosh) refers to this aspect of the exercise as 'the Autocratic Administration of Time in the Service of Democratic Distribution of Time' for a reason. Abrupt though it may feel, the reality is that time *is not* democratically distributed in our personal lives or professional duties." The facilitator should explain that with this method, "Talkers must talk less and listen more. People who usually do not talk get to talk, if they like. And because each person is speaking about their own experience, they cannot be questioned. This is their experience and something on which they are the sole authority." Furthermore, the topic being presented is one's own experience of what I call the *politics of unearned circumstance*, and it is something that no other person can question or second-guess. What each person has experienced is what that person has experienced.

This process of taking turns speaking about one's own experience and listening to another person's experience is something that I have named Serial Testimony. In brief, it is a mode of timed discourse that requires participants to take turns speaking about personal *experience* as opposed to opinions, in a setting without being cross-examined, questioned, agreed with, or disagreed with. I have found it to be more useful than traditional forms of professional discourse, instruction, and counseling, many of which reflect hierarchies of power and privilege. I attribute part of the success of the National SEED Project on Inclusive Curriculum, now in its 27th year, to this kind of lateral pedagogy. This kind of speaking and listening process respects the experience of all participants. Serial Testimony allows people to make sense of their own experience while hearing about others' lives. It allows for what I call "deeply personal group work."

If a person wishes not to talk about their unearned privilege and disadvantage, they should let their partner know before the exercise begins. Infrequently, individuals decline to participate in the activity and leave the room before it begins. An effective facilitator, when orienting the group to the activity, should inform them that they will have an opportunity to talk about their experiences of disadvantage and privilege, which can make them feel vulnerable and challenged, but probably also rewarded. This type of statement allows participants the chance to decide whether they want to participate fully in the activity or not.

As additional guidance to the facilitator, debriefing after this exercise is not recommended, because debriefing can be seen as a filtering mechanism that leaves out some of what has been said and tends to overgeneralize. Debriefing can also turn into a popularity contest, wherein some comments are spotlighted while others are ignored. In my experience, a debrief can destroy (in just a few seconds) the rare and precious honesty of testimony produced in the whole group when each person knows they may speak for one minute and no one will interrupt, question, or even mention what they have said. I feel that the tendency to debrief is an enculturated and mostly unconscious reflex on the part of a facilitator or teacher to regain control, to be in charge, to indicate to people what they should have heard, or what was most significant.

However, shared conversation following the exercise can be beneficial. Victor Lee Lewis sometimes asks participants whether they have any "new learnings" from this exercise. He requests that those who choose to participate at this stage only speak to what they have learned from doing the exercise, avoiding what their partner said. The testimony should emphasize the "new learning" acquired and not knowledge or insight that they had when they walked into the room. Listeners often find that other people's comments illuminate or resonate with their own experience of doing the exercise. The "new learnings" comments should follow the Serial Testimony format, and remarks should be short and to the point (no more than 30 seconds in duration). This timing helps prevent participants from trying to outdo each other in their observations and allows the facilitator to remain as a participant rather than being reinstalled as the authority or authorizer.

# Examples

The Invisible Knapsack paper and the exercise described here have had a powerful effect on both people of color and white people. It has helped many people of color feel relief after years of experiencing subtle (and overt) resistance by white people to their pursuit of advancement and well-being. This resistance sometimes takes the form of direct interference from white individuals, but it also appears more indirect in nature, such as the hindering assistance sometimes offered by organizations run by the white majority. The resistance and lack of support felt by people of color today may not include outright racist incidents; most often the resistance comes from a pervasive and intractable lack of trust by white society regarding the worth, abilities, and deservedness of people who are not white. I feel that all disadvantaged people suffer under privilege systems that advance those around them while neglecting them, but most have not been able to name what they are suffering from. After all, in the United States, societal and educational structures have not taught them to see or name systems of privilege, for such teaching would blow away the myth of meritocracy—that everyone gets what they deserve.

Despite the incredible variety of settings, professional grouping, and diverse circumstances of my presentations, when I have talked about how I came to see I have white skin privilege, there has been a very singular response from participants. In fact, regardless of whether they are people of color, poor people, gay and lesbian people, biracial people, and/or immigrants, participants often thank me profusely. They report that they now feel validated and "less crazy." I have given them some names for the power dynamics they have experienced at the hands of more-privileged people or institutions. Furthermore, the reading on privilege and the activity inevitably help many white people realize they have been born into a favored and dominant group in the United States, whose social and financial power benefited them without their having earned all of their prominence. Most report that they did not know they had racial experiences and often thought of themselves as "just normal," whereas "others" had a race. Most white readers can relate to the examples I described regarding my own unearned freedom of choice and comparative ease of mind and action, within societal frameworks and institutions that support "me and my kind." Participants in this exercise are also helped to see and testify to the phenomena of systemic privilege and disadvantage in their own lives, seeing more clearly how they are embedded in cultural frameworks like language, manners, assumptions, education, medicine, and law enforcement. Many find this hour-long exercise to be transformative, and I have heard repeatedly from people in all stations of life that "Your work changed my life."

# Measuring Progress

I believe that working in the helping professions tends to encourage one to feel superior, or on a vertical axis, to those being helped. The exercise on privilege and disadvantage encourages providers to think twice about whether they have really earned their positions or how their circumstances of birth may have propelled them upward or downward arbitrarily. They may develop more empathy for others after they have realized how much society has worked for or against them without their knowing it. Helpers may realize that they have developed traits of arrogance or feelings of virtue because they have benefited from a society that favors their groups. They may come to question whether the strengths that their social groups reward are in fact broadly useful to humans' well-being.

# Conclusion

As I see it, there is a hypothetical line of social justice running parallel to the ground. Below it people or groups are pushed down in a variety of ways. Above it, people and groups are pushed upward in a variety of ways. I believe that all of us have a combination of experiences that place us both above and below the hypothetical line of social justice. An hour spent doing this exercise can be fascinating, shocking, illuminating, disconcerting, or enlightening. Those who refer to this paper and activity as "transformative" have sometimes said that they feel they have been relocated and reoriented in the world, or even the universe. This is a testament to the power of seeing systemically rather than only in terms of individuals, and to the power of understanding that there is an unjust "upside" in addition to the unjust "downside" in circumstances to which we were born.

# Additional Resources

Butler, S. (Producer), & Butler, S. (Director). (2006). *Mirrors of privilege: Making whiteness visible*. Oakland, CA: World Trust Educational Services.

Case, K. (2013). *Deconstructing privilege: Teaching and learning as allies in the classroom*. New York, NY: Routledge.

Dill, B. T., & Zambrana, R. E. (Eds.). (2009). *Emerging intersections: Race, class and gender in theory, policy and practice*. New Brunswick, NJ: Rutgers University Press.

Ferber, A. L. (1998). *White man falling: Race, gender, and white supremacy*. Lanham, MD: Rowman & Littlefield.

Ferber, A. L., with Kimmel, M. S. (Eds.). (2010). *Privilege: A reader* (2nd ed.). Boulder, CO: Westview Press.

Kendall, F. E. (2006). *Understanding white privilege: Creating pathways to authentic relationships across race*. New York, NY: Routledge.

McIntosh, P. (2012). Reflections and future directions for privilege studies. *Journal of Social Issues*, *68*(1), 194–206. doi: 10.1111/j.1540-4560.2011.01744.x

McIntosh, P. (2013). Teaching about privilege: Transforming learned ignorance into usable knowledge. In K. Case, *Deconstructing privilege: Teaching and learning as allies in the classroom*. New York, NY: Routledge.

Rich, A. (1984). Notes toward a politics of location. In *Blood, bread, and poetry: Selected essays, 1979–1985*. New York, NY: W. W. Norton.

Wildman, S. M., Armstrong, M. J., Davis, A. D., & Grillo, T. (1996). *Privilege revealed: How invisible preference undermines America*. New York, NY: New York University Press.

# References

McIntosh, P. (1988). *White privilege and male privilege: A personal account of coming to see correspondences through work in women's studies* (working paper no. 189). Wellesley, MA: Wellesley Centers for Women.

McIntosh, P. (1989). White privilege: Unpacking the invisible knapsack. *Peace and Freedom*, July/August, 10–12. Philadelphia, PA: Women's International League for Peace and Freedom.

## Appendix 26.1
## WHITE PRIVILEGE: UNPACKING THE INVISIBLE KNAPSACK[1]

Through work to bring materials from Women's Studies into the rest of the curriculum, I have often noticed men's unwillingness to grant that they are over-privileged, even though they may grant that women are disadvantaged. They may say they will work to improve women's status, in the society, the university, or the curriculum, but they can't or won't support the idea of lessening men's. Denials which amount to taboos surround the subject of advantages which men gain from women's disadvantages. These denials protect male privilege from being fully acknowledged, lessened or ended.

Thinking through unacknowledged male privilege as a phenomenon, I realized that, since hierarchies in our society are interlocking, there was most likely a phenomenon of white privilege that was similarly denied and protected. As a white person, I realized I had been taught about racism as something that puts others at a disadvantage, but had been taught not to see one of its corollary aspects, white privilege, which puts me at an advantage.

I think whites are carefully taught not to recognize white privilege, as males are taught not to recognize male privilege. So I have begun in an untutored way to ask what it is like to have white privilege. I have come to see white privilege as an invisible package of unearned assets that I can count on cashing in each day, but about which I was "meant" to remain oblivious. White privilege is like an invisible weightless knapsack of special provisions, maps, passports, codebooks, visas, clothes, tools and blank checks.

Describing white privilege makes one newly accountable. As we in Women's Studies work to reveal male privilege and ask men to give up some of their power, so one who writes about white privilege must ask, "Having described it, what will I do to lessen or end it?"

After I realized the extent to which men work from a base of unacknowledged privilege, I understood that much of their oppressiveness was unconscious. Then I remembered the frequent charges from women of color that white women whom they encounter are oppressive.

---

I began to understand why we are justly seen as oppressive, even when we don't see ourselves that way. I began to count the ways in which I enjoy unearned skin privilege and have been conditioned into oblivion about its existence.

My schooling gave me no training in seeing myself as an oppressor, as an unfairly advantaged person, or as a participant in a damaged culture. I was taught to see myself as an individual whose moral state depended on her individual moral will. My schooling followed the pattern my colleague Elizabeth Minnich has pointed out: Whites are taught to think of their lives as morally neutral, normative, and average, and also ideal, so that when we work to benefit others, this is seen as work which will allow "them" to be more like "us."

I decided to try to work on myself at least by identifying some of the daily effects of white privilege in my life. I have chosen those conditions which I think in my case *attach somewhat more to skin-color privilege* than to class, religion, ethnic status, or geographic location, though of course all these other factors are intricately intertwined. As far as I can see, my African American co-workers, friends, and acquaintances with whom I come into daily or frequent contact in this particular time, place and line of work cannot count on most of these conditions.

1. I can if I wish arrange to be in the company of people of my race most of the time.

2. If I should need to move, I can be pretty sure of renting or purchasing housing in an area which I can afford and in which I would want to live.

3. I can be pretty sure that my neighbors in such a location will be neutral or pleasant to me.

4. I can go shopping alone most of the time, pretty well assured that I will not be followed or harassed.

5. I can turn on the television or open to the front page of the paper and see people of my race widely represented.

6. When I am told about our national heritage or about "civilization," I am shown that people of my color made it what it is.

7. I can be sure that my children will be given curricular materials that testify to the existence of their race.

8. If I want to, I can be pretty sure of finding a publisher for this piece on white privilege.

9. I can go into a music shop and count on finding the music of my race represented, into a supermarket and find the staple foods that fit with my cultural traditions, into a hairdresser's shop and find someone who can cut my hair.

10. Whether I use checks, credit cards or cash, I can count on my skin color not to work against the appearance of financial reliability.

11. I can arrange to protect my children most of the time from people who might not like them.

12. I can swear, or dress in second-hand clothes, or not answer letters, without having people attribute these choices to the bad morals, the poverty, or the illiteracy of my race.

13. I can speak in public to a powerful male group without putting my race on trial.

14. I can do well in a challenging situation without being called a credit to my race.

15. I am never asked to speak for all the people of my racial group.

16. I can remain oblivious of the language and customs of persons of color who constitute the world's majority without feeling in my culture any penalty for such oblivion.

17. I can criticize our government and talk about how much I fear its policies and behavior without being seen as a cultural outsider.

18. I can be pretty sure that if I ask to talk to "the person in charge," I will be facing a person of my race.

19. If a traffic cop pulls me over or if the IRS audits my tax return, I can be sure I haven't been singled out because of my race.

20. I can easily buy posters, postcards, picture books, greeting cards, dolls, toys, and children's magazines featuring people of my race.

21. I can go home from most meetings of organizations I belong to feeling somewhat tied in, rather than isolated, out-of-place, outnumbered, unheard, held at a distance, or feared.

22. I can take a job with an affirmative action employer without having co-workers on the job suspect that I got it because of race.

23. I can choose public accommodations without fearing that people of my race cannot get in or will be mistreated in the places I have chosen.

24. I can be sure that if I need legal or medical help, my race will not work against me.

25. If my day, week, or year is going badly, I need not ask of each negative episode or situation whether it has racial overtones.

26. I can choose blemish cover or bandages in "flesh" color and have them more or less match my skin.

I repeatedly forgot each of the realizations on this list until I wrote it down. For me, white privilege has turned out to be an elusive and fugitive subject. The pressure to avoid it is great, for in facing it I must give up the myth of meritocracy. If these things are true, this is not such a free country; one's life is not what one makes it; many doors open for certain people through no virtues of their own.

In unpacking this invisible knapsack of white privilege, I have listed conditions of daily experience that I once took for granted. Nor did I think of any of these prerequisites as bad for the holder. I now think that we need a more finely differentiated taxonomy of privilege, for some of these varieties are only what one would want for everyone in a just society, and others give license to be ignorant, oblivious, arrogant and destructive.

I see a pattern running through the matrix of white privilege, a pattern of assumptions that were passed on to me as a white person. There was one main piece of cultural turf; it was my own turf, and I was among those who could control the turf. *My skin color was an asset for any move I was educated to want to make.* I could think of myself as belonging in major ways and of making social systems work for me. I could freely disparage, fear, neglect, or be oblivious to anything outside of the dominant cultural forms. Being of the main culture, I could also criticize it fairly freely.

In proportion as my racial group was being made confident, comfortable, and oblivious, other groups were likely being made inconfident, uncomfortable, and alienated. Whiteness protected me from many kinds of hostility, distress and violence, which I was being subtly trained to visit, in turn, upon people of color.

For this reason, the word "privilege" now seems to me misleading. We usually think of privilege as being a favored state, whether earned or conferred by birth or luck. Yet some of the conditions I have described here work systematically to overempower certain groups. Such privilege simply *confers dominance* because of one's race or sex.

I want, then, to distinguish between earned strength and unearned power conferred systemically. Power from unearned privilege can look like strength when it is in fact permission to escape or to dominate. But not all of the privileges on my list are inevitably damaging. Some, like the expectation that neighbors will be decent to you, or that your race will not count against you in court, should be the norm in a just society. Others, like the privilege to ignore less powerful people, distort the humanity of the holders as well as the ignored groups.

We might at least start by distinguishing between positive advantages, which we can work to spread, and negative types of advantage, which unless rejected will always reinforce our present hierarchies. For example, the feeling that one belongs within the human circle, as Native Americans say, should not be seen as privilege for a few. Ideally it is an *unearned entitlement.* At present, since only a few have it, it is an *unearned advantage* for them. This paper results from a process of coming to see that some of the power that I originally saw as attendant on being a human being in the United States consisted in unearned advantage and conferred dominance.

I have met very few men who are truly distressed about systemic, unearned male advantage and conferred dominance. And so one question for me and others like me is whether we will be like them, or whether we will get truly distressed, even outraged, about unearned race advantage and conferred dominance, and, if so, what will we do to lessen them. In any case, we need to do more work in identifying how they actually affect our daily lives. Many, perhaps most, of our white students in the U.S. think that racism doesn't affect them because they are not people of color, they do not see "whiteness" as a racial identity. In addition, since race and sex are not the only advantaging systems at work, we need similarly to examine the daily experience of having age advantage, or ethnic advantage, or physical ability, or advantage related to nationality, religion, or sexual orientation.

Difficulties and dangers surrounding the task of finding parallels are many. Since racism, sexism, and heterosexism are not the same, the advantages associated with them should not be seen as the same. In addition, it is hard to disentangle aspects of unearned advantage which rest more on social class, economic class, race, religion, sex, and ethnic identity than on other factors. Still, all of the oppressions are interlocking, as the Combahee River Collective Statement of 1977 continues to remind us eloquently.

One factor seems clear about all of the interlocking oppressions. They take both active forms, which we can see, and embedded forms, which as a member of the dominant group one is taught not to see. In my class and place, I did not see myself as a racist because I was taught to recognize racism only in individual acts of meanness by members of my group, never in invisible systems conferring unsought racial dominance on my group from birth.

Disapproving of the systems won't be enough to change them. I was taught to think that racism could end if white individuals changed their attitudes. But a "white" skin in the United States opens many doors for whites whether or not we approve of the way dominance has been conferred on us. Individual acts can palliate, but cannot end, these problems.

To redesign social systems, we need first to acknowledge their colossal unseen dimensions. The silences and denials surrounding privilege are the key political tool here. They keep the thinking about equality or equity incomplete, protecting unearned advantage and conferred dominance by making these taboo subjects. Most talk by whites about equal opportunity seems to me now to be about equal opportunity to try to get into a position of dominance while denying that *systems* of dominance exist.

It seems to me that obliviousness about white advantage, like obliviousness about male advantage, is kept strongly inculturated in the United States so as to maintain the myth of meritocracy, the myth that democratic choice is equally available to all. Keeping most people unaware that freedom of confident action is there for just a small number of people props up those in power and serves to keep power in the hands of the same groups that have most of it already.

Although systemic change takes many decades, there are pressing questions for me and I imagine for some others like me if we raise our daily consciousness on the perquisites of being light-skinned. What will we do with such knowledge? As we know from watching men, it is an open question whether we will choose to use unearned advantage to weaken hidden systems of advantage, and whether we will use any of our arbitrarily awarded power to try to reconstruct power systems on a broader base.

---

*This is an authorized excerpt of McIntosh's original white privilege article, "White Privilege and Male Privilege: A Personal Account of Coming to See Correspondences through Work in Women's Studies," Working Paper 189 (1988), Wellesley Centers for Women, Wellesley College, MA, 02481. **Anyone who wishes to reproduce this article must apply to the author, Dr. Peggy McIntosh, at mmcintosh@wellesley.edu. This article may not be electronically posted.**

# CHAPTER 27

# REEXAMINING SOCIAL CLASS, ETHNICITY, AND AVAILABLE RESOURCES

Kerri E. Newman, Haley V. Pettigrew, Cecily R. Trujillo, and Sara A. Smock Jordan

## Introduction

White privilege can occur when people from a White, Caucasian, or European American background view their social, cultural, and economic standards as the norm rather than as an advantage. Because most clinicians in the United States come from White or Caucasian backgrounds, it is particularly important for clinicians to increase their awareness of racial and socioeconomic bias, as well as their understanding of how White privilege may influence their work with diverse client populations. Ultimately, there is a significant risk that any differences between providers and clients that carry a legacy of power imbalance and oppression—such as class, race, gender, disability, or sexual orientation—may be carried into the treatment room in a negative way (Balmforth, 2009). Clients of all backgrounds are benefited when self-awareness in this area increases, because clinicians become more mindful of the biases that clients experience as a function of their ethnicity, culture, social class, and so forth.

## Rationale

Training and educational materials for psychotherapists on ethnic and socioeconomic group membership are important to both new and experienced clinicians; however, these materials are lacking (Ancis & Szymanski, 2001; Hays & Chang, 2007). The need for increased training is even more pressing when one considers that most therapy educators are White with Eurocentric viewpoints (Hanna, Talley, & Guindon, 2000) and that relatively few clinicians recognize the power structures and privileges responsible for racial and ethnic oppression.

Toward that end, Hays and Chang (2003) define White privilege as:

*the belief that only one's own standards and opinions are accurate (to the exclusion of all other standards and opinions) and that these standards and opinions are defined and supported by Whites in a way to continually reinforce social distance between groups, thereby allowing Whites to dominate, control access to, and escape challenges from racial and ethnic minorities. (p. 135)*

Battling against the limitations imposed by White privilege and fostering a therapeutic alliance in multicultural counseling requires a specific level of therapeutic dedication, as well as specialized attention to accurate assessments (Burkard & Knox, 2004; Constantine, 2007). Chao, Wei, Good, and Flores (2011, p. 80) suggested that, with more training and practice, clinicians-in-training may have a greater sensitivity about "each racial/ethnic group's culture, racial identity bias, and differences among cultural groups," which, in turn, could improve multicultural counseling and the therapeutic alliance.

Like race, class can be communicated in many different ways, often unconsciously (e.g., on the phone, directions to a particular part of town, possessions on display in the provider's office), and can have a similar negative effect on the therapeutic alliance (Balmforth, 2009).

Although critical contexts like gender, race, and sexuality are often included in training courses for providers, differences in power based on class are usually not included. It is important for providers to explore their own class backgrounds and acknowledge this frame of reference as they treat clients, because differences in class can have direct implications for development of the early therapeutic relationship with clients (Smith, Perkins, & Ampuero, 2011).

The purpose of these exercises is twofold: (1) to encourage participants to better understand the pervasiveness of White privilege, the majority's resistance to change, and the effects of privilege on minority groups; and (2) to move participants to initiate action by challenging others' racism and classism. Participants' racial distortions or lack of awareness will be challenged during this activity, encouraging student clinicians to assist clients to find their own personal resources and strengths, regardless of race and ethnicity.

# Activity Instructions

These exercises are appropriate for graduate-level student clinicians and are easily adapted to accommodate more-experienced clinicians. Although it is possible for clinicians to carry out parts of this exercise on a self-assigned basis, these activities work best when assigned by a supervisor as part of a graduate-level clinical program. Therefore, the following instructions are written only for the supervisors.

The activity series comprises assessment questions, a guided imagery exercise, and group discussions. The group activities work best within a classroom or supervision session and require at least four people, excluding the facilitator. It is particularly important that supervisors familiarize themselves with the material in this activity prior to administering it to the participants; this is especially true for the guided imagery exercise, because tone, voice inflection, and dramatic pauses will enhance the guided imagery experience.

The supervisor may begin the activity by briefly introducing the topic of race, ethnicity, and socioeconomic status. The supervisor should establish an atmosphere of safety for the group so the participants feel comfortable disclosing personal opinions. Following the introduction, the supervisor should distribute the preactivity questionnaire, which was developed to provide participants with key words that prepare them for the content of the activity. Participants will then be asked to complete the Issues of White Privilege and Social Class assessment (Table 27.1), which helps to reveal participants' socioeconomic status, race, and privilege. The results of the assessment will help both the supervisor and the participants gauge the amount of relevant experiences that group members have encountered regarding racial and/or socioeconomic discrimination in their own lives. These results may be kept private in the brief group discussion that follows, in which participants who desire to share may process their responses to the assessment aloud.

## Activity 1: Issues of White Privilege and Social Class

After the initial introduction, the supervisor should begin this portion of the exercise by distributing the preactivity questionnaire. Participants should complete this preactivity assessment without discussing their answers with one another. Questionnaire items include the following:

1.  What is race? What messages have you heard growing up about your race?

2.  What is racism? Do you believe yourself to be a racist? Describe your thoughts.

3.  What is White privilege? Give examples.

4.  Can people with privilege affect society more than people without privilege? If so, how?

5.  How can racism affect the therapeutic relationship?

When all participants have completed the questionnaire, the facilitator should distribute the Issues of White Privilege and Social Class assessment (see Table 27.1) and instruct participants to respond to the items, reflecting back to when they were children.

While the scoring of this assessment is not intended to be diagnostic, more false statements can indicate prevalent experiences of racial and socioeconomic discrimination. The supervisor should be aware of possible negative reactions by students who have experienced discrimination

| | | | |
|---|---|---|---|
| We lived in a good neighborhood where I was able to go outside and play with my friends. | □ True | □ False | **Table 27.1 Issues of White Privilege and Social Class Assessment** |
| Our electricity and water were never turned off, and we were never evicted. | □ True | □ False | |
| At the grocery store, we never had to worry about keeping a running total, putting items back, or getting only the generic brands of food. | □ True | □ False | |
| I always had clothes that fit me and were fairly new. | □ True | □ False | |
| I went to a good school and was able to get a good education. | □ True | □ False | |
| My parents were available to help me with my homework if I needed it. | □ True | □ False | |
| I was able to do sports or other extracurricular activities. | □ True | □ False | |
| My parents did the parenting, and the kids were able to be just kids. | □ True | □ False | |
| We always had plenty of food to eat. | □ True | □ False | |
| At least one of my parents was home in the evening. | □ True | □ False | |
| I was able to sleep at night and did not worry about break-ins or drive-bys. | □ True | □ False | |
| My parents took me on vacations. | □ True | □ False | |
| My parents attended every parent-teacher conference. | □ True | □ False | |
| I was able to go to play with my friends and have sleepovers. | □ True | □ False | |
| I felt safe, loved, and secure. | □ True | □ False | |
| I knew I would go to college and that I would have a way to pay for it. | □ True | □ False | |
| Money was never a worry in my family. | □ True | □ False | |
| I never had to have a job in high school. | □ True | □ False | |
| We never had to be on food stamps. | □ True | □ False | |
| All of my siblings have the same two parents. | □ True | □ False | |
| Whether I use checks, credit cards, or cash, I can count on my skin color not to work against me in others' perceptions of my financial reliability. | □ True | □ False | |
| I can be pretty sure that if I ask to talk to the "person in charge," I will be facing a person of my own race or ethnicity. | □ True | □ False | |
| If a traffic cop pulls me over, or if the IRS audits my taxes, I can be sure I have not been singled out because of my race. | □ True | □ False | |
| I can take a job with an affirmative action employer without having coworkers suspect that I got the job because of my race. | □ True | □ False | |

based on race or class. If any of the participants are willing, the supervisor may ask them to process their reactions aloud with the class during a brief group discussion.

Following a brief discussion of their reactions to the assessment items, participants will listen to a guided imagery activity that focuses on an individual and the socioeconomic and racial issues that she has encountered in a single day. This activity is designed to highlight participants' conscious and unconscious assumptions of race and class, as they initially receive no identifying demographic information about this individual. Participants will be given the opportunity to write a detailed mental picture of the individual behind the story. Following this, the supervisor

**Activity 2: Racial and Social Class Assumptions**

will divide the group in half, and each half will be given different demographic information that reveals the individual's race as either White or Minority, with the specific minority chosen in advance to reflect the geographic area in which participants live. Each group will then discuss among themselves any initial assumptions they had about the individual's race, ethnicity, strengths, and resources based solely on the experiences detailed in the vignette.

While reading the vignette aloud, it is important that the supervisor's tone is soft, inviting the students to experience the struggles described in the vignette. Nonverbal cues like sighs and dramatic pauses are indicated by brackets and ellipses, and words requiring emphasis are underlined. Introductory instructions for the imagery activity are as follows:

> *Close your eyes as I begin reading a description of a client's experience. This client is suffering from clinical depression. While I am reading this experience, I would like you to create a detailed mental picture of the individual behind the story.*

Then the supervisor should read aloud the vignette below, being mindful of how his or her tone, voice inflection, and dramatic pauses may affect the participants' experience.

> *It's four-thirty in the morning. I am awake and gathering all of my clothes in a bag. A friend of mine is letting me use her shower. My water was turned off yesterday, and I need to go have it turned back on, but it is a sixty dollar reconnection fee, and I don't have that kind of money right now. [Pause.] I need to be ready and at work by six o'clock. I work at a dry cleaner's during the day. I don't particularly like it, but it's a paying job. My kids catch the bus to school in the morning and are there for most of the day. [Pause.]*
>
> *It's lunch time. I didn't bring anything today. I usually never bring anything. Sometimes the boss will bring donuts or buy us lunch. That's the only time I really eat at work, and I often feel guilty. Like, "How dare I eat and enjoy this food when my kids could be enjoying it?" Sometimes I sneak food into my purse when people aren't looking. I feel ashamed when I'm doing it ... but I know the kids will like a little treat. If there are leftovers, my boss always lets me have them.*
>
> *It's close to three o'clock when I get off of work. I have to go and renew our food stamps application today. I take a fifteen-minute bus ride across town to the office. I wait for an hour. The woman comes out and tells us that they will no longer be seeing people today and we will have to come back another day. Great ... a bus ride and two hours wasted. I take the bus back to my part of town and walk to the grocery store. Our food stamps have run out, so I am paying for this food out of pocket. I'd love to go to the store and buy whatever my kids wanted to eat. I'd pile the basket as high as I could, walk up to the cashier, place everything on the conveyor belt, and wait as she rang it up. I wouldn't monitor the total, second-guess any purchases, or take anything out. [Pause.] "Oh, two hundred ten dollars? All right, here's my card." But I only have a twenty-dollar bill, so I have to stretch it as far as I possibly can. I stand at the checkout line, watching my final total slowly creep up to twenty dollars and seventy-six cents. [Pause.] I have to put something back. The woman behind me is staring. She sees the twenty-dollar bill in my hand. I know she's thinking "How can this woman not have seventy-six cents?" The cashier is thinking it too. I look over the items ... quickly ranking them by their price and how much food they will yield. [Pause.] I put back the jar of jelly ... peanut butter sandwiches will have to do without the jelly. I can only imagine what everyone is thinking of me right now. [Pause.] You'd think I'd get used to it ... but I don't. [Pause.] No one ever gets used to it.*
>
> *By the time I walk from the store to our apartment, my kids are already there. I tell them to do their homework, but I have no way of knowing if they did it right. They are learning stuff now I never learned. I rely on my oldest child to help the younger ones. [Pause.] But there is no one to help him. I leave him in charge when I'm not here ... I wish that he could just be a kid—go to the mall, go to his friends' houses, play sports. But I need him here. I need him to help me. Most nights I get to spend an hour with my kids, then I have to go to my second job. I clean offices at night for extra money. I use our neighbor's kitchen to make dinner for the kids tonight—rice with beans. [Pause.] They hate it, I know, but it is cheap and fills their bellies. [Pause.] I don't eat.*
>
> *It's nearly seven o'clock when I start to get my things together. My youngest is pleading for me not to go tonight. [Sigh.] It breaks my heart every day to have to leave them alone. [Pause.] I wish I could stay with them, but the money I make from this night job pays for the extra things, like field trips, and other stuff that gives my kids a chance to still feel normal. So every night, I go clean the offices of people who are at home with their children. I dust their family portraits, throw away*

*their half-eaten food that's in the fridge … and wonder what my life could be like if only I had better opportunities.*

*It's quarter to ten and time to leave. The buses do not run as often at night, so if I get to the stop even one minute past ten o'clock, I have to wait a whole hour before the next bus comes. I get home and all my children are asleep. I kiss them all goodnight and get ready for bed. [Pause.] Tomorrow will be here before I know it.*

After the guided imagery activity, the facilitator should distribute the Small-Group Assumptions Discussion Guide to every student, with one group receiving Guide A and the other group receiving Guide B. Please note that Guides A and B are the same except that question #1 is modified to emphasize the minority group selected in advance by the supervisor (e.g., Would it surprise you to know that the client is Hispanic?).

**Activity 3: Small and Large Group Discussions**

**Table 27.2  Small-Group Assumptions Discussion Guides (A and B)**

---

**Small-Group Assumptions Discussion Guide A**

1. Would it surprise you to know that the client is White? Why or why not?

---

2. What resources do you assume this woman has for coping with her depression?

---

3. Do you think it is likely she would seek help from a counselor/therapist? What would she have to do to gain access to a counselor/therapist?

---

4. What do you think about the stability of her financial situation?

---

5. How close do you think her family is to one another?

---

6. Based on the information you have received, what do you hypothesize about the cause of her depression?

---

**Small-Group Assumptions Discussion Guide B**

1. Would it surprise you to know that the client is [Minority]*? Why or why not?

---

Questions 2–6 are the same as those from Guide A.

---

The small groups should be given enough time to read and discuss their assigned discussion guides. When the discussion is finished, the supervisor should bring both groups back together and inform them that each group was given different demographics for the client. Then the supervisor should invite participants from both groups to share aloud their answers with the larger group, encouraging open discussion about the differences and similarities in their answers. The supervisor should also listen for and highlight racial or economic assumptions that arise based on the information they received about the vignette. Then the supervisor should distribute the Large Group Discussion Guide.

**Table 27.3 Large Group Discussion Guide**

| Large Group Discussion Guide |
| --- |
| 1. How might clinicians look at clients differently based on their race or ethnicity? |
| 2. Do you think that we associate race with economic stability/reliability, even on a subconscious level? |
| 3. Would you feel more relatable to a client who shared your same ethnicity or social background? |
| 4. If someone is White, do they have more access to resources than their minority counterparts? |
| 5. Do you think clinicians may conceptualize symptoms or presented problems differently based on ethnicity, race, or social class? |
| 6. Would treatment look different for two women struggling with the same problem but who are of a different ethnicity/race or social class? |
| 7. What can clinicians do to prevent making assumptions about their clients based on race/ethnicity or socioeconomic status? |

These questions are intended to link the activity back to clinical work and to the assumptions clinicians bring to their work with minorities and racially underprivileged clients. When the supervisor feels that the group has had sufficient time to process the activity and subsequent discussion questions, students will be asked to reevaluate their responses to the Issues of White Privilege and Social Class assessment (items inspired and adapted from list of white privileges; McIntosh, 1998). The supervisor may discuss changes between the initial and final tests to gauge the progress.

# Examples

In past use of these exercises, students reported not being aware of the actual definition of White privilege and how their answers in the true/false assessment affected their biases. One student noted how difficult it was to define if he was a racist because of the messages he received from his parents about different ethnicities. He said that "While I didn't believe myself to be racist, I fear that some of those messages may affect my future therapeutic relationship with that population." Another student added that she answered false to several of the true/false statements. She elaborated by saying, "My background and non-White ethnicity will hopefully allow me to connect with other clients in a different way and see their strengths."

During the guided imagery activity, the low-income mother is described in the vignette without specifying her ethnicity. In reaction to this, students have the opportunity to assess their own racial and ethnic power they bring to the therapy room. One student stated, "As I was listening to the vignette, I kept thinking 'This is actually how some people live.' The struggles were very foreign to me. This activity made me realize that I am very different from some of my clients (and potential clients) and what kind of power I bring into the room with me without even really realizing it."

Participants have described the exercise as being helpful by opening their eyes to their own personal biases. One student stated, "It is easy for those of us in this world, that are privileged enough to have white skin and little racial discrimination, to sit back and not worry about others struggling just like this woman in the story." One student noted how she often automatically thought of the woman in the vignette as being a particular ethnic group, because where she grew up, most of the low-socioeconomic status citizens in her neighborhood were that particular ethnicity. Another student commented on the importance of seeking resources and discovering a client's own unique resources.

# Measuring Progress

Privilege, whether racial or socioeconomic, can be difficult to recognize in oneself. Progress can be measured by how students reevaluate their responses to the Issues of White Privilege and Social Class assessment after completing the remaining portions of the exercise. This positions the participants to more easily see and challenge their preexisting stereotypes and biases and start the process of further reflection and personal growth on this topic. After completing this activity, clinicians should be more aware of the misperceptions and stereotypes they have that may have been previously unknown to them. Once participants have a deeper awareness of their own privilege and how it has influenced their lives, they are able to take further action and address these issues through appropriate discussions or during clinical supervision.

# Conclusion

Challenging the established assumptions of White privilege helps to increase self-awareness and encourages a deeper understanding of racism and oppression. Ancis and Szymanski (2001) support the use of activities that promote an exploration of the limits of White counselors' own biased and privileged positions. Through these exercises, participants can begin to recognize the privileges and resources they have received and can address the perpetuation of racism, classism, sexism, and so forth, in professional and personal settings.

# Additional Resources

Carter, B., McGoldrick, M., & Garcia-Preto, N. (2012). *The expanded family life cycle: Individual, family, & social perspectives* (4th ed). New York, NY: Pearson.

Doane, A. W., & Boniall-Silva, E. (2003). *White out: The continuing significance of racism.* New York, NY: Routledge.

Kendall, F. E. (2006). *Understanding White privilege: Creating pathways to authentic relationships across race.* New York, NY: Taylor & Francis.

McGoldrick, M., & Hardy, K. V. (2008). *Re-visioning family therapy: Race, culture, and gender in clinical practice* (2nd ed.). New York, NY: Guilford Press.

Walsh, F. (Ed.). (2012). *Normal family processes: Growing diversity and complexity* (4th ed.). New York, NY: Guilford Press.

# References

Ancis, J. R., & Szymanski, D. M. (2001). Awareness of White privilege among White counseling trainees. *The Counseling Psychologist*, *29*, 584–569.

Balmforth, J. (2009). 'The weight of class': Clients' experiences of how perceived differences in social class between counselor and client affect the therapeutic relationship. *British Journal of Guidance and Counselling*, *37*, 375–386.

Burkard, A. W., & Knox, S. (2004). Effect of color-blindness on empathy and attributions in cross-cultural counseling. *Journal of Counseling Psychology*, *51*, 387–397.

Chao, R. C., Wei, M., Good, G. E., & Flores, L. Y. (2011). Race/Ethnicity, color-blind racial attitudes, and multicultural counseling competence: The moderating effects of multicultural counseling training. *Journal of Counseling Psychology*, *58*, 72–82.

Constantine, M. G. (2007). Racial microaggressions against African American clients in cross-racial counseling relationships. *Journal of Counseling Psychology*, *54*, 1–16.

Hanna, F. J., Talley, W. B., & Guindon, M. H. (2000). The power of perception: Toward a model of cultural oppression and liberation. *Journal of Counseling and Development*, *78*, 430–441.

Hays, D. G., & Chang, C. Y. (2003). White privilege, oppression, and racial identity development: Implications for supervision. *Counselor Education and Supervision*, *43*, 134–145.

McIntosh, P. (1998). White privilege: Unpacking the invisible knapsack. In M. McGoldrick (Ed.), *Revisioning family therapy: Race, culture, and gender in clinical practice* (pp. 147–152). New York: Guilford Press.

Smith, L., Mao, S., Perkins, S., & Ampuero, M. (2011). The relationship of clients' social class to early therapeutic impressions. *Counselling Psychology Quarter*, *24*, 15NN27.

# CHAPTER 28

# EXPERIENCING POVERTY THROUGH A LARGE-GROUP ROLE-PLAY

Andrae Banks and Larry D. Williams

## Introduction

Poverty is a major issue facing many people in the United States. In 2012, the U.S. Census Bureau reported poverty rates of 15%, or 46.2 million people. This troubling economic trend has slightly increased since 2011 and must be addressed in order to create a healthier society (2012b). The first step in addressing this issue is increasing awareness of poverty for all people living in the United States. With education and interventions centered on poverty, we can strive for a positive change. Conducting poverty role-plays is a viable way to begin this process on multiple levels for clinicians and for student clinicians.

This chapter focuses on poverty and introduces role-play activities to simulate the experience of poverty in order to positively impact client–clinician relationships. This activity enables clinicians to experience poverty through a more realistic replication of everyday situations that impoverished individuals often encounter. Clinicians and trainees will be able to recognize their own personal biases about the socioeconomically disadvantaged and develop more empathy for individuals who must take extraordinary measures to achieve even the most basic life necessities and accomplish everyday tasks. This increased awareness will lead to improved treatment, improved programming, and knowledge that can be taught to others.

## Rationale

It is critical that clinicians and student clinicians become more aware of poverty and its ramifications, because many of the individuals who need mental health and substance abuse services are impoverished. Pasic, Russo, and Roy-Byrne (2005) studied what populations were the highest utilizers of psychiatric emergency services. They reported that the highest utilizers had greater odds of being homeless, having developmental delays, possessing a mental health plan, having a history of hospitalizations, having personality disorders, lacking social support, being jailed, and abusing substances. Each of these alone, and surely combined, would impact an individual's financial health and increase the likelihood of poverty. Examining the relationship between healthcare expenses and mental health services, researchers reported that patients who presented with mental health issues incurred greater expenses compared to those who did not have mental health issues (Cawthorpe, Wilkes, Guyn, Li, & Lu, 2011). This suggests that paying more for health services could be a factor that leads to or maintains impoverishment.

The U.S. Census Bureau (2012a) released statistics that concluded certain populations may be at greater risk of increased poverty. Specifically, the largest income group of uninsured individuals made less than $25,000 annually. Unfortunately, this group of Americans not only received the smallest amount of income but also had to face the expensive possibilities that come with not having health insurance. Additionally the highest-earning Americans were the smallest group of uninsured people. Because many clinicians and student clinicians may never have been exposed to poverty, let alone the day-to-day experiences of living in poverty, it is imperative that they better understand the life experiences that affect impoverished individuals and develop insight that can guide treatment and policies of programs for these individuals.

Balmforth (2009) studied the experience of working-class individuals receiving counseling from middle-class clinicians. Findings suggested a class difference and a deficit in the clinicians' understanding of the impoverished life experience, including differential access to opportunities and the tangible ways that poverty impacts the choices that can be made. The class differences made the counseling relationship ineffective, as the social dynamics that existed in the client's daily life manifested in the therapeutic relationship as well. In order to improve services to clients who are in a different economic class, awareness about poverty and how it can be manifested must be attended to in clinical training programs.

The effectiveness of using poverty simulations to facilitate learning and to improve client outcomes has been demonstrated in a variety of clinical settings worldwide. Davidson, Du Preez, Gibb, and Nel (2009) presented the results of a poverty role-play that was conducted in South Africa. They noted that poverty role-plays were interactive, required minimal input, produced high output, and forced clinicians and student clinicians to take part in the activity and make decisions. More importantly, the lessons learned could be more easily transferred to the real world.

It should be noted, however, that this activity could potentially have an uncomfortable mental or emotional impact on participants. This varies depending on the personal level of connection to and understanding of poverty; disparities in wealth, health, and resources among various socioeconomic groups; and the clinician's professional role. Ultimately, with proper supervision and support, any experiences of discomfort can lead to professional growth and improved treatment for impoverished clients.

# Activity Instructions

This activity was designed to expose clinicians to the realities of poverty through a reproduction of the responsibilities and hardships that impoverished clients often face. Clinicians from a variety of experience levels and personal circumstances can benefit from this activity. It works best when conducted in a class or group setting; therefore, the instructions are directed primarily to clinical supervisors and instructors. There are no required readings for clinicians prior to completing this activity. Although there is a great deal of literature on poverty and its ramifications, reading about poverty and its challenges cannot adequately prepare clinicians for participation in this activity or give them the direct experience this simulation provides. The supervisor should administer the preactivity surveys to individuals in order to assess their baseline awareness of poverty (see Table 28.1). This self-report survey can be given on site before the start of the actual activity or can be given ahead of time to participants to bring to the activity. With that taken care of, the activity is outlined in the following steps.

## Step 1: Arranging the Role-Play Room

Before the activity begins, the supervisor should arrange the tables and chairs around the perimeter of the room to replicate the different community institutions impoverished people tend to interact with on a daily basis. Please include the following institutions: a pawn shop; a bank or loan trustee; a currency exchange; a food pantry; a welfare office complete with waiting room, receptionist, and two caseworkers; a school with a teacher's desk and student chairs; a rent collector; a utility collector; a grocery store; a welfare-rights office; a legal-assistance office; a jail; and an employment office. The supervisor will also need a podium and a microphone.

The interior of the room should include the living areas for families, which represent homes. The living areas should include chairs in numbers equal to the family members of each individual household. The chairs should be facing each other in order to facilitate more family interaction. The borders of these homes and the neighborhood(s) can be imagined during this activity since the concept of physical borders is not extremely important here. Volunteers will be needed to serve in a variety of roles, including shopkeepers, caseworkers, and more. A police officer is also needed to patrol the community. Clinicians, supervisors, or other volunteers can serve in these roles, and approximately 15 to 20 helpers are needed in order to accomplish the purposes of the role-play.

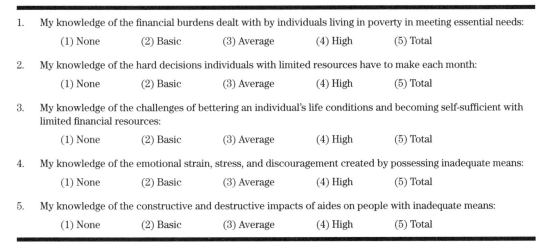

1. My knowledge of the financial burdens dealt with by individuals living in poverty in meeting essential needs:

   (1) None          (2) Basic          (3) Average          (4) High          (5) Total

2. My knowledge of the hard decisions individuals with limited resources have to make each month:

   (1) None          (2) Basic          (3) Average          (4) High          (5) Total

3. My knowledge of the challenges of bettering an individual's life conditions and becoming self-sufficient with limited financial resources:

   (1) None          (2) Basic          (3) Average          (4) High          (5) Total

4. My knowledge of the emotional strain, stress, and discouragement created by possessing inadequate means:

   (1) None          (2) Basic          (3) Average          (4) High          (5) Total

5. My knowledge of the constructive and destructive impacts of aides on people with inadequate means:

   (1) None          (2) Basic          (3) Average          (4) High          (5) Total

**Table 28.1 Poverty Role-Play Survey (administered preactivity and postactivity)**

## Step 2: Assigning Family Roles

The families will be arranged using the participants and other volunteers. Families should include at least one adult and no more than two children. The supervisor will assign the roles, such as father, mother, grandparent, or children of various ages, to clinicians and student clinicians and provide scenarios that include different resources and life challenges. For example, a male may be assigned to be a single father who has two kids, a minimum-wage job, no personal transportation, and no assets. He has appointments at an employment office, a welfare office, and his child's school. The father will have to ensure that the children make it to school each day, the bills are paid, there is food in the home, and so on. Real-life case studies from the supervisor's experience can be used to model families and situations to make this activity even more applicable to the real world.

## Step 3: Determining the Time Frame

In addition to assigning the roles and scenarios, the supervisor will oversee the activity, keep time, and distribute materials, including bus passes, various amounts of money, and potential resources. The time frame for the simulation is flexible. Therefore, the training could potentially take place in a three-hour block of time consisting of 15 minutes for preactivity survey completion, four "15-minute weeks" for the role-play, 15 minutes for postactivity survey completion, a 45-minute debriefing, 15 minutes for evaluation form completion, and 15 minutes to collect materials. The additional 15 minutes can serve as buffer time between segments or as additional time for segments that take longer than expected. This format for time can be increased as desired to amplify the experience. Regardless of the actual training time, the clinicians' obligations in the roles they play may encompass from several days' to weeks' worth of activities and experiences during the actual simulation.

## Step 4: Implementing the Role-Play

During the actual role-play, participants will decide how to manage the duties within their respective roles. The experience will be full of decisions, as is the reality for most people. Participants may experience deciding between two or more obligatory options repetitively. For example, a mother may have to choose between getting to work on time, feeding her children, and taking the kids to school at virtually the same time with only public transportation or walking as travel options. The supervisor's job will be to keep time, ensure consistency of the activity, answer questions for participants, and keep everyone on task in general by making announcements of pertinent information. For example, the supervisor will announce the beginning and end of the allotted time for each simulated week.

Supervisors may also announce information such as the start of the business day, end of the business day, or events in the community, like food being given out at a food pantry. Information like this will also impact the decision-making process and is likely to increase the stress of the participants within their roles. If participants are off task or mismanage their roles in some respects, they will potentially receive appropriate simulated consequences, such as visits from social workers, eviction notices, repossession of items not paid for, or even arrest. These actions will then lead to more decisions that must be made with limited time and resources available.

These consequences will become an important part of the experience and discussion during the debriefing.

**Step 5: Debriefing and Evaluating the Role-Play**

After the role-play has been completed, the supervisor should conduct a debriefing about the activity with all participants. The supervisor determines the length of time allotted for this step. The debriefing will be an open discussion in which individuals can freely share their experiences. The supervisor should set the ground rules, including showing respect for all and speaking one person at a time. The facilitator will be responsible for prompting dialogue, acknowledging each participant's contribution, and keeping the discussion moving. This may result in sharing what participants learned, what they did not learn, and any thoughts or feelings that they may have encountered. Hopefully, the experience will leave individuals with more questions about poverty and a desire to seek knowledge, understanding, and solutions for poverty. In addition to the debriefing, the supervisor should administer post-activity self-report surveys to gather data from participants regarding their experiences and understanding of living in poverty.

Focus groups can also prove valuable for gaining additional information after the participants have had a chance to reflect over the long term (e.g., three to six months later). The facilitator should use the following questions to prompt discussion and manage the focus group by clarifying statements, summarizing, and ensuring even participation from all group members. The focus group should begin by having people introduce themselves and share the roles they played in the role-play. Among the important question to discuss are the following:

1. What was your general impression of the poverty role-play experience? (Prompts: What did you like about it? What did you not like about it?)

2. Please share with us how you think your experience was similar to or different from the real-life experiences of impoverished families.

3. Did the role-play experience change your understanding of the condition of individuals in poverty in any way? If so, how? (Prompt for specifics, such as difficulty meeting basic needs, time frustrations, worries about having enough food, and so on.)

4. Describe any differences you made in the way you relate to impoverished people, based on your participation in the role-play.

5. Based on the role-play experience, did your organization make any changes to its programs or policies to better meet the needs of clients and families? (If "Yes," what kind of changes? Are the changes helping? How do you know? If "No," do you see a need for changes to programs or policies? What are the barriers preventing change to programs and policies?)

6. Did the role-play experience increase your understanding of the barriers faced by those experiencing poverty in achieving food security, managing their households, seeking employment, and so on?

7. Has this experience altered the way you will interact professionally and personally with individuals living in poverty? Why or why not?

8. What do you see as the next step for yourself and your organization or community in order to improve the situation for those in poverty?

9. Are there any additional comments on the experience or outcomes?

10. Would you be interested in any additional follow-up about this experience? What type of follow-up would be suitable for you? Who would participate? What would be the goals? Who would plan and facilitate?

# Examples

This activity is administered as described. Another specific example is a scenario in which the clinician or student clinician role-plays a single mother who has two school-aged children, no car, and no job and who relies on public assistance to survive. She is responsible for attending all appointments with her service providers at the times they set for her and ensuring her children are fed, are able to get to and from school, and are supervised at home while she is out taking care of her business, even though she has limited resources for food, travel, and miscellaneous things, such as a babysitter. In her four weeks of poverty, this mother will potentially interact with service professionals, school professionals, the police officer, potential employers, and so on, depending on her choices.

Participants will find they are unable to complete the role-play without major issues. For example, children left unattended may be taken into custody because the mother has no options for childcare. She had a job interview and two appointments with service providers and had to secure groceries using the only bus ticket she had for that day. This forced her to make the decision to leave her children unattended after school, and a neighbor reported her to the police for child abuse and neglect. Clinicians who have participated in this activity have reported that they gained knowledge and awareness about poverty and the challenges the impoverished deal with on a daily basis.

# Measuring Progress

Signs that clinician awareness of poverty is increasing may include more positive thoughts and feelings toward impoverished clients, improved understanding of clients' decision making, more willingness to empathize with clients, increased positive attitudes and energy, and improved treatment of clients. Clinicians may also start to think more critically—and begin to express their thoughts—about policies and macro-level issues that impact individuals on the micro-level. In supervision, supervisors can discuss the findings from the pre- and post-activity surveys and discuss the experience freely to gauge the impact the activity had on clinicians. Supervisors can also ask clinicians to present a past or current case, using the new insights they have gained. Supervisors can identify changes in thought patterns or feelings based on differences in the clinicians' understanding and delivery of the case presentation. Supervisors can also request that clinicians create sample policies or program changes that would positively impact work with the impoverished.

# Conclusion

Poverty is a troubling issue facing millions of U.S. citizens, including clinicians in the helping professions. There is a need for increased awareness of poverty, education on poverty, more focused supervision for clinicians dealing with impoverished clients, and interventions that address the issue on multiple systemic levels. Exposing clinicians to poverty role-plays as an intervention, supervision tool, and growth activity can help to start addressing this societal problem. With benefits for clinicians, supervisors, clients, and communities as a whole, this relatively simple, efficient, and wide-reaching activity has unlimited potential to effect positive change.

# Additional Resource

Ware, N. C., Tugenberg, T., & Dickey, B. (2004). Practitioner relationships and quality of care for low-income persons with serious mental illness. *Psychiatric Services*, *55*, 555–559.

# References

Balmforth, J. (2009). 'The weight of class': Clients' experiences of how perceived differences in social class between counsellor and client affect the therapeutic relationship. *British Journal of Guidance & Counselling*, *37*, 375–386.

Cawthorpe, D., Wilkes, T. C. R., Guyn, L., Li, B., & Lu, M. (2011). Association of mental health with care use and cost: A population study. *La Revue Canadienne de Psychiatrie*, *56*, 490–494.

Davidson, J. H., Du Preez, L., Gibb, M. W., & Nel, E. L. (2009). It's in the bag! Using simulation as a participatory learning method to understand poverty. *Journal of Geography in Higher Education*, *33*, 149–168.

Pasic, J., Russo, J., & Roy-Byrne, P. (2005). High utilizers of psychiatric emergency services. *Psychiatric Services*, *56*, 678–684.

United States Census Bureau. (2012a). *Income, poverty, and health insurance in the United States: 2011, highlights*. Retrieved from www.census.gov/hhes/www/poverty/data/incpovhlth/2011/highlights.html

United States Census Bureau. (2012b). *Current Population Survey, 2011 and 2012 Annual Social and Economic (ASEC) Supplements*.

# CHAPTER 29

# FOSTERING AWARENESS OF ABILITY AND DISABILITY THROUGH GROUP INCLUSION AND EXCLUSION

Kathleen Nash

## Introduction

Providing culturally sensitive therapy is an ongoing learning process for all mental health clinicians. The abilities of clients and their family members, which are often overlooked, also need to be taken into consideration during therapy sessions. Clinicians' personal perceptions and experiences with individuals coping with disabilities need to be examined. Ability-awareness training can promote fair relating and more mutual trust and understanding between clinicians and clients.

The Americans with Disabilities Act (ADA) was passed in 1990 in order to increase access to community services for individuals coping with disabilities. The U.S. Department of Justice (2009) stated that "public accommodations must comply with basic nondiscrimination requirements that prohibit exclusion, segregation, and unequal treatment" (ADA Title III: Public Accommodations, 2009, para. 2). The U.S. Department of Justice went on to explain that all organizations need to offer "reasonable modifications to policies, practices, and procedures; effective communication with people with hearing, vision, or speech disabilities; and other access requirements" (ADA Title III: Public Accommodations, 2009, para. 2). Yet, the ADA cannot guarantee or mandate that administrators and staff in these organizations understand the culture of disability.

Mental health professionals provide therapeutic services to diverse client populations. Yet, individuals with disabilities who are seeking therapy to address psychological, family, and emotional issues continue to have difficulty accessing mental health services because of inadequate physical access to buildings or because clinicians discount a disability that is part of a client's identity (Smart & Smart, 2006). Although understanding specific disabilities is needed to effectively work with clients, it is more important for clinicians to understand, to value, and to see each person as an individual. This stance helps to promote fair relating among clinicians, clients, and their communities. As stated by Boszormenyi-Nagy and Krasner (1986), "Individual freedom is most effectively won through a consideration of balance of fairness between the self and all the significant others with whom the self is in relationship" (p. 16). As clinicians begin to understand the experiences of clients living with diverse abilities, they will create opportunities for fairness and trust within the therapeutic relationship.

## Rationale

Increasing clinicians' understanding of the culture of disability can provide clinicians with new insights and allow them to address potential biases and misconceptions to better help their clients address emotional, relational, and psychological concerns. According to Smart and Smart (2006), disability is both an everyday and an ordinary part of life because all people, including individuals with disabilities, have diverse characteristics, responsibilities, and backgrounds. Olkin and Pledger (2003) state that each client with a disability is unique and that each characteristic of the disability is diverse with regard to the age of onset, the demographics, and the impact on life-cycle stages and psychosocial development. Therefore, increasing clinicians' understanding of all aspects of clients' lives is crucial—from the initial assessment and joining phase to the treatment planning and the development of effective interventions.

Awareness of the culture of disability provides three mutually beneficial outcomes. First, clinicians can develop a better understanding of their clients' strengths and needs. Some clients view their disability as an important and positive part of their self-identity that they would not eliminate if given the option; in contrast, few clinicians "conceptualize the client's disability as a source of self-actualization" (Smart & Smart, 2006, p. 30). Second, clients who work with more-aware clinicians have an opportunity for an inclusive mental health care experience—something that may have been denied them in the past. Third, clinicians can increase their self-awareness and create new insights about disabilities, which in turn will foster more acceptance and understanding between clinicians and their clients with disabilities.

# Activity Instructions

The following ability-awareness activity has been used with beginning clinicians during individual and group supervision sessions, although this activity could also be adapted for use in classes or seminars. Because an experienced clinician is needed to lead this activity, these instructions are directed specifically to clinical supervisors or trainers. This activity is divided into two components: (1) an individual supervision exercise and (2) a group supervision exercise. The individual supervision exercise provides an opportunity for self-reflection as student clinicians explore their early memories and narratives about individuals living with disabilities. The group supervision exercise offers clinicians-in-training a brief and focused opportunity to personally experience disability stereotypes and to increase their understanding of the prejudices and frustrations of being labeled with a disability. Ultimately, both of these activities work together to increase clinicians' personal awareness about the culture of disability.

## Individual Supervision Exercise

The individual supervision exercise includes answering and reflecting on the ability memories questions (see Table 29.1). This exercise is designed to help student clinicians explore the culture of disability narratives that are embedded within personal experiences involving their own families, friends, schools, and communities. After completing the ability questions, supervisors should initiate a discussion about the clinicians' answers and emotional responses and any new insights gained about the culture of disability. In particular, supervisors should ask how the activity pertains to current or past clients. The amount of time spent discussing student clinicians' responses will be determined by supervisors and will depend on the issues, biases, or insights that emerge during the exercise. This discussion often leads to processing the potential impact and influences that these narratives have on work with specific clients (past and/or present).

## Group Supervision Exercise

Based on a common party game, the group supervision exercise will help clinicians understand what it feels like to be labeled with a disability. The facilitator should use the following steps for conducting the exercise:

1. Divide the group into smaller groups of three to six student clinicians.
2. Give each participant a card with the label facing away from the participant and emphasize that participants should not read what is written on their own cards. Direct the participants to place the cards on their shirts as they would a nametag, with the top folded over to prevent the participants from seeing their own cards (see Figure 29.1).
3. Give each group a blank piece of paper and coloring supplies.
4. Instruct each group to work together to draw a picture of a house or a farm. The group will discuss and decide the type of house or farm that they will collaboratively draw together.

5.  Explain that as the student clinicians work together, they should interact with each other only as described on the cards worn by each participant. In other words, they should disregard everything they know about the other participants and focus only on the labels.

6.  Inform the groups that they will have five minutes to create their collaborative drawings.

Supervisors should remind the groups that they will not answer questions from the participants once the group exercise has begun. If participants ask questions, simply redirect them back to their collaborative work. Participants may also need to be reminded to interact based solely

**Table 29.1  Ability Memories**

Directions: Think back to your early childhood experiences that include family and friends as well as people you knew in your school and your community. Try to think of the earliest experience you remember having with a person with a disability. After reflecting for a few moments, answer the questions below.

Who was this person with a disability, and what was the nature of his or her disability?

_____

What was your relationship to this person, and how old were you when you met this person?

_____

What were some of the feelings you remember about meeting this person for the first time? What questions did you have?

_____

Did you talk with anyone about your questions or concerns? How did he or she respond?

_____

Do you remember how this person's disability was explained to you? If it was not explained to you, what were you thinking about and feeling toward him or her?

_____

Did others use inappropriate names for or narratives about this person?

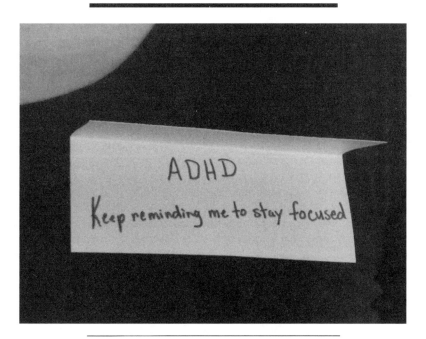

**Figure 29.1**/Correct placement of the label

**Table 29.2  Ability Cards**

| | |
|---|---|
| **ADHD** Keep reminding me to stay focused. | **Emotional Disturbance or Posttraumatic Stress Disorder (PTSD)** Speak slowly and explain everything with kind words. |
| **Aggressive** Be cautious and stay clear; I may hit you. | **Gifted and Talented** Ask me what to do and do everything I say. |
| **Anxious** Remind me not to worry—everything will be fine. | **Hearing Impaired** Speak loudly and slowly to me. |
| **Autistic Spectrum Disorder**—* | **Learning Disability** Explain everything to me several times. |
| **Contagious** Keep away; do not let me touch anything. | **Visually Impaired** Hold everything close to my face. |
| **Depressed** Only say happy things to me; don't make me sad. | |

*(Note that the *autism spectrum disorder* label does not include a description. This omission is intentional and will encourage conversation after the activity about whether student clinicians attempted to learn more about the person wearing this label.)

on the cards that they are wearing. During the five-minute drawing session, supervisors should make observations and write notes describing how participants react to each other. For example, note how the person wearing the *contagious* label reacts to being rejected and how the person with the *hearing impaired* label responds to the group yelling at him or her. Supervisors should also record which participants become their disabilities by starting to behave the way that they are being treated and which participants tend to rebel against their labels and attempt to make the group interact with them differently. These observations are critical to the group discussion that follows the group exercise.

As often as necessary, facilitators should encourage student clinicians to stay on task to complete the group exercise. Before this exercise begins, the supervisor will need to gather several materials, including index cards, paper, coloring supplies (e.g., crayons or markers), and tape or pins with which to affix the cards. Be sure to obtain enough index cards for each member in the group. Supervisors should prepare the index cards by writing labels and stereotype descriptions on the bottom half of individual index cards (as presented in Table 29.2). Once the labels are written on the cards, supervisors should fold each card in half and affix a small piece of tape to the back of each card.

When the group drawing exercise is over, the supervisor will engage the group in postactivity discussions. Clinicians are encouraged to share their personal reactions, emotions, and insights resulting from the exercises and the group interactions. The supervisor will share his or her notes and observations to guide and facilitate the conversation. Clinicians and supervisors will discuss how new insights and understandings will enhance therapeutic relationships and interventions with clients.

# Examples

Second-year clinicians-in-training at an accredited family therapy program engaged in both self-awareness activities. The examples discussed in this section resulted from the group exercise (titled "Beyond Labels"). As the discussion began, clinicians were reminded that they were given a label to live with for a brief period of time, whereas clients with disabilities face ongoing struggles and the challenges of wearing labels for a lifetime. This perspective provides a foundation for clinicians to process their experiences and to encourage fair relating in their clinical work.

The clinicians-in-training were completely engaged in the group task and their labeled roles. Some participants looked for ways to include those who were excluded. For example, one participant gave the person wearing the *PTSD* label (Participant A) her own piece of paper and art supplies. She kindly explained that Participant A could create her own farm, separate from the group. Participant A, with the *PTSD* label, was tenacious! She kept trying to join the group and refused to be excluded. During the postactivity discussion, one student clinician said, "I felt bad that [Participant A] had to wear that label. I know she is working on attachment issues." Participant A said, "That's why I was not going to give up on being part of the group." The exercise triggered her feelings of abandonment, but she did not withdraw and was successful in expressing her emotions, thoughts, and needs. The group discussed and processed this experience of feeling excluded, marginalized, and on the outside.

Participants were able to compare their experiences to how clients desire to be accepted and included with peers in their schools, communities, and workplaces; however, these clients are often kept at arm's length because of misconceptions and lack of knowledge about their disabilities. Clients with differing abilities need the opportunity in therapy to share their experiences of tenacity, acceptance, and fair inclusion. It is important for clinicians to discuss "separate but not equal" experiences with clients.

This group conversation encouraged another clinician to talk about a recent intake with a mother and her son. This clinician (Participant B) presented a different issue that sometimes arises among clients with differing abilities. Instead of focusing solely on a disability, the clinician did not acknowledge or discuss disability at all.

> I had an intake with a teen and mother, and the mother was blind. I felt uncomfortable asking the mom questions about her visual impairment. Her child had to sign paperwork because she could not. They did not return for their next session, and I feel awful! I don't know if they did not return because of my lack of awareness or because of the family problems that led them to seek therapy. How could I have better asked her what she needed?

Participant B offered her own answer to her question. Clinicians need to create their own narrative to elicit clients' answers to the question, "What do you need to feel included in therapy?" Narratives that ask clients about the accommodations they need that will enhance their therapeutic experience do not need to be complicated. As developed by these participants, questions that can be used by clinicians include the following:

1. What accommodations have been helpful to you in the past?

2. How can I make our therapy environment more accessible for you?

3. Are there any barriers here that might obstruct your participation in therapy?

The information and awareness obtained during these conversations can also help clinicians gain new insights regarding the emotional, social, and relational issues that brought the client into session. For example, Participant C, who was wearing the *learning disability* label, was asked specifically about her experiences during the activity because the supervisor observed a change in her behavior. Participant C shared the following during the discussion:

> I started to believe I was doing something wrong and must be confused about how to do the activity. I thought I was doing the right thing, but when the group kept explaining the directions, I asked questions to get it right.

Participant C found herself transforming into the description on her label in an attempt to gain positive affirmation from the group. This discussion was an example of how some individuals with disabilities become their labels. The constant struggle to show others who they really are and what they can do becomes too much, and some clients feel overwhelmed. As clinicians learn to see the person beyond the labels, their roles expand to incorporate self-advocacy as a therapeutic goal, which is not only needed in educational and community settings but may also be needed within the clients' families to increase fair relating.

# Measuring Progress

Measuring progress can begin during the debriefing and group discussion following the activity. As described in the previous examples, each clinician-in-training is asked to share his or her thoughts and feelings after completing the activities and focus on new insights. The supervisor also shares his or her observations of the group interactions and communication patterns. Progress can be assessed in the following three areas of personal and clinical growth:

1. *Supervisors will observe an increased focus on the person and a decreased focus on the disability.* As student clinicians present and discuss cases, they will display more awareness by focusing on client strengths instead of client limitations. For example, they will present narratives similar to the following:

*My client Leslie is making great progress. She is a 12-year-old who has been experiencing issues related to difficulties with peers. Leslie was diagnosed with an autism spectrum disorder four years ago. During family sessions, the focus has been on her strengths in the areas of computers, math, and piano playing as a foundation to help her learn new social skills. The focus on fair relating and communicating encouraged her brother Phil to offer to practice new skills with her at home.*

By focusing on strengths during sessions, the clinician serves as a role model of fair relating that will guide communication and interaction in the family's home. In doing so, therapy centers on healing relationships and encouraging fairness instead of focusing on a disability label and its related challenges.

2. *Clinicians-in-training will begin to use more appropriate nomenclature when presenting cases.* "Positive language empowers. When writing or speaking about people with disabilities, it is important to put the person first" (U.S. Department of Labor, n.d., para 2). When clinicians discuss cases, as described in the previous example, the person comes first, followed by the diagnosis. Using this type of narrative innately personalizes all clients. With this focus on fairness and trustworthiness, clients within the culture of disability will sense the clinicians' desires to get to know more about their unique hopes, dreams, strengths, and successes. Student clinicians will seek to foster and understand clients' capabilities to make life, relationship, and work decisions with increased independence.

3. *Student clinicians will acknowledge and discuss links between their personal experiences, biases, and misconceptions related to current cases.* These discussions will help clinicians-in-training avoid projecting their personal biases or expectations onto their clients. When student clinicians are consistently aware of the impact their experiences have on their clinical work, they will have a clearer view of the pride in identity, the advocacy, the social change, the struggles, and the resilience of their clients with divergent abilities (Olkin & Pledger, 2003).

# Conclusion

After years of segregation and discrimination, civil rights legislation is now in place to increase independence and improve the quality of life for individuals with disabilities. Yet, the laws that prohibit discrimination do not guarantee that the dominant culture will learn and better understand the culture of disability. Communication and self-awareness are the keys to unlocking the door of accommodation for individuals with disabilities who are seeking access to fair therapy services. Supervised self-awareness activities can help clinicians-in-training move away from a focus on deficits toward a focus on strength-based narratives. Joining with clients around these narratives is an enlightening, humbling, and inspiring experience.

This exercise is designed to provide clinicians with "heightened self-awareness at a deep personal level and the consequent assumption of greater responsibility for one's self and one's issues in the therapeutic encounter with clients" (Aponte et al., 2009, p. 384). The increased awareness that student clinicians achieve through participating in this exercise creates a valuable foundation on which to build client relationships based on fairness, trust, communication, advocacy, and acceptance. Student clinicians' increased self-awareness opens the door to clients, ensuring that clinicians include the person beyond the labels in sessions.

# Additional Resources

Meyer, D. (1997). *Views from our shoes: Growing up with a brother or sister who has special needs.* Bethesda, MD: Woodbine House.

National Alliance on Mental Illness (NAMI). (2007). The ADA—Americans with Disabilities Act. Retrieved from www.nami.org/Content/ContentGroups/Helpline1/The_ADA_-_Americans_with_Disabilities_Act.htm

National Dissemination Center for Children with Disabilities. (n.d.). Retrieved from www .nichcy.org

Rosenbaum, S. (2007). The Americans with Disabilities Act in a health care context. In M. J. Field & A. M. Jette (Eds.), *The future of disability in America*. Washington, DC: National Academies Press. Retrieved from www.ncbi.nlm.nih.gov/books/NBK11429/

U.S. Department of Education. (n.d.). The Individuals with Disabilities Education Act (IDEA). Retrieved from http://idea.ed.gov

# References

Aponte, H. J., Powell, F. D., Brooks, S., Watson, M. F., Litzke, C., Lawless, J., & Johnson, E. (2009). Training the person of the therapist in an academic setting. *Journal of Marital & Family Therapy, 35*, 381–394.

Boszormenyi-Nagy, I., & Krasner, B. R. (1986). Between give and take: A clinical guide to contextual therapy. New York, NY: Brunner-Routledge.

Olkin, R., & Pledger, C. (2003). Can disability studies and psychology join hands? *American Psychologist, 58*, 296–304.

Smart, J. F., & Smart, D. W. (2006). Models of disability: Implications for the counseling profession. *Journal of Counseling & Development, 84*, 29–40.

U.S. Department of Justice. (2009). *A Guide to Disability Rights Laws*. Information and technical assistance on the Americans with Disabilities Act. Retrieved from www.ada.gov/cguide.htm

U.S. Department of Labor, Office of Disability Employment Policy. (n.d.). *Communicating with and about people with disabilities*. Retrieved from www.dol.gov/odep/pubs/fact/comucate .htm

# CHAPTER 30

# ENHANCING SELF-AWARENESS FOR WORKING WITH DEAF CLIENTS

Mary C. Hufnell

## Introduction

The Personal Identity Exercise (PIE) and deaf-related identity questions are tools that might be used during group supervision in any number of clinical settings to improve clinical self-awareness. The activity requires that the group members journal and discuss their cultural identity in order to explore how their personal biases or views might affect the developing therapeutic bond and clinical work with deaf clients. Wu and Grant (2013) emphasize that there is a wide spectrum of experiences in this community, ranging from individuals who identify as culturally Deaf[1] and are from a Deaf family to individuals who see deafness as a loss, impairment, or disability and do not identify with Deaf culture at all. Another important part of deaf-related identity is the linguistic dimension, which is determined by individual and family choices, as well as educational, medical, and sociopolitical experiences (Leigh, 2009; Wu & Grant, 2013). Clinicians should integrate the additional dimension of deaf-related identity into their multicultural training when working with deaf clients and their families (Wu & Grant, 2013).

## Rationale

Understanding cultural identity is a critical part of appreciating individual clients and families from a more holistic perspective (Frew & Spiegel, 2013; Sue & Sue, 2013). Sue and Sue (2013) define cultural competence as including three components: (a) self-awareness; (b) knowledge of culturally diverse groups; and (c) specific clinical skills to generate a variety of verbal and nonverbal helping responses, which work together to form a therapeutic alliance, and to intervene at both individual and system levels with culturally diverse groups. Clinicians must be aware that stereotypes, biases, and negative points of view may result in responses that can negatively affect the therapeutic process.

In *A Lens on Deaf Identities*, Leigh (2009) describes the process of developing a deaf identity and how cultural and linguistic dimensions are essential aspects of this identity (see also Oliva & Lytle, in press, and Wu & Grant, 2013). Parents or family members will often determine an individual's linguistic identity, and American Sign Language (ASL) may be the first language for a deaf client. At the other end of the continuum is an oral/aural approach to communication; for example, deaf clients who consider spoken English to be their first language. There are many variations in sign communication and combined sign and speech (Leigh, 2009; Oliva & Lytle, in press; Wu & Grant, 2013). Furthermore, some families and individuals choose a

---

1.  Padden and Humphries (2005) identified that the use of a capitalized *d* highlights a difference between community and condition; *Deaf* refers to members of the Deaf community who adhere to beliefs and practices of Deaf culture—particularly the central role of sign language—whereas *deaf* refers to people who do not identify with Deaf culture but instead with the condition of being audiologically deaf. For ease of reading, the term *deaf* will be used to refer to both groups and *Deaf* will be used in relation to culture.

cochlear implantation, and the interface of this choice with identity has been debated in the Deaf community (Leigh, 2009).

Increasingly, academic departments across the counseling disciplines have incorporated multicultural sensitivity training and awareness; yet, the breadth and depth of this training varies. The activity described in this chapter includes one set of questions that are general to developing multicultural awareness and another set of questions that was developed to guide an exploration of deaf-related identity development among clinicians and deaf clients at Gallaudet. Gallaudet University is dedicated to the education of deaf and hard-of-hearing students, as well as hearing students who plan to serve deaf and hard-of-hearing clients. Relevant content and experience have been infused into the curriculum of the graduate programs in clinical psychology, counseling, and social work to prepare student clinicians to competently work with deaf and hard-of-hearing individuals (in addition to working with hearing clients).

This activity uses the multidimensional identity model described by Jones and McEwen (2000), which considers the multiple identities and associated oppressions that an individual experiences. In order of progression from earliest developmental stage to latest and most complex, the four stages are (a) identifying with only one aspect of self in a *passive* manner by accepting an identity as assigned by others, such as society, peers, or family members (e.g., identifying as African American as assigned by others); (b) identifying with only one aspect of self as determined or named by the individual (e.g., identifying only as a lesbian or only as an Asian Pacific American, without acknowledging other identities); (c) identifying with multiple aspects of self but choosing to do so in a *segmented* manner, frequently one at a time (e.g., identifying in one instance as African American and in another instance as Deaf); and (d) identifying with multiple aspects of self, especially multiple oppressions, and both *consciously choosing* them and *integrating* them. Clinicians ideally will appreciate the multiple oppressions involved and how the process of identity development would optimally result in conscious choosing and integrating of the identities (Jones & McEwen, 2000; Reynolds & Pope, 1991).

Frew and Spiegel (2013) similarly emphasize that, in order to become culturally sensitive, clinicians must become aware of their own worldviews—assumptions, values, and biases—as well as their clients' worldviews and the worldviews embedded in the theoretical approach they are using. Vasquez (2013) also noted that both the APA and ACA codes of ethics recognize the importance of diversity and the need to support the dignity of clients in the context of the relevant social and political environments. Clinicians are encouraged in the ethics codes to eliminate the effects of bias based on factors of age, gender, gender identity, race, ethnicity, culture, national origin, religion, sexual orientation, physical and mental ability, language, and socioeconomic status (Vasquez, 2013); this is the ideal to which all mental health practitioners should always be striving to achieve. The Personal Identity Exercise (PIE) and deaf-related identity questions are tools that might be used during group supervision in any number of clinical settings to improve this clinical self-awareness to aid in eliminating bias.

# Activity Instructions

The goal of the Personal Identity Exercise (PIE) and the deaf-related identity questions described as follows is to provide an opportunity for clinicians-in-training to become more aware of the multiple identities in their lives—based on salient aspects such as their race, religion, culture (including Deaf culture), socioeconomic status, and sexual orientation—and to consider how these identities impact their sense of self in their collegial relationships and clinical work.

The PIE can be self-directed but was originally developed for group supervision by Forrest (2004). The deaf-related identity questions are based on what has been discussed in group supervision experiences at Gallaudet's Mental Health Center and relevant Deaf culture literature (Leigh, 2009; Wu & Grant, 2013). It may also be adapted to coursework that addresses multicultural sensitivity or counseling with deaf people. Ideally, clinicians in the supervision group are already working with deaf clients and have had some training or coursework in cultural sensitivity. Group supervision should be conducted weekly, and the length of time for each session should be approximately an hour and a half. Allowing time for the group to become comfortable and familiar with each other and with one another's current clinical cases (which could possibly take five or six sessions) is recommended before proceeding with the activity; however, the amount of time needed will vary depending on the composition of the group and their previous experiences or relationships with each other. If the group includes clinicians completing their training experiences, group supervision may be conducted for the length of the training experience. If the exercise is conducted in a clinic or agency, it would be best to conduct it over the course of four to six months at a minimum.

The group supervisor follows the protocol for the clinical setting and for running a supervision group and establishes expectations and guidelines for the group at the start. A group supervision contract is recommended. Required reading for clinicians includes Reynolds and Pope's (1991) multidimensional identity model and Chapter 2 in Leigh's (2009) *A Lens on Deaf Identities*, which provides an overview of deaf-related identity used in theory and research. Additionally, it is recommended that clinicians read Kiselica, Clark, and Sue's (2013) personal narratives about their journeys to become more culturally self-aware. The group supervisor assigns the readings and requests that the clinicians read prior to journaling. In the first or second group supervision session, the supervisor introduces the activity to allow the clinicians time to begin to journal.

For the journaling process, clinicians respond to questions about the role of the identities of race, religion, culture (may include some about Deaf culture here as well as other cultures), socioeconomic status, and sexual orientation (see Table 30.1). Responding to the questions for each identity requires approximately two to three pages of journaling. Additional questions focused on the deaf-related identity or Deaf cultural identity are included in Table 30.2. Clinicians are informed that they are not required to share the journal with their supervisor or other group

**Table 30.1 Personal Identity Exercise (PIE)**

Answer the following questions for each of the following identities: (1) race, (2) religion, (3) culture, (4) socioeconomic status, and (5) sexual orientation.

1. Describe your earliest memory of an experience with a person or people of a cultural group different from your own.

2. Who or what has had the most influence in the formation of your attitudes and opinions about people of different cultural groups? In what way(s)?

3. What influences in your experience have led to the development of positive feelings about your own cultural heritage or background?

4. What influences in your experience have led to the development of negative feelings about your own cultural heritage or background?

5. What changes, if any, would you like to make in your attitudes or experiences in relation to people of other ethnic or cultural groups?

6. Describe an experience in your life when you felt you were discriminated against for any reason, not necessarily because of your culture.

7. How do you feel you should deal with (or not deal with) issues of cultural diversity in American society?

Adapted from Forrest (2004). Reprinted with permission.

**Table 30.2 Deaf Culture and Deaf-Related Identity Questions**

Outline your journey in regard to deaf-related identity:

1. How do you identify yourself regarding this dimension? Describe.

2. How do you identify in different contexts? Describe and provide some examples.

3. What is your family constellation around deaf-related identity? Do you have family members who are deaf or hard of hearing?

4. Do you identify with Deaf culture and, if so, for how long have you identified with Deaf culture? What influenced this for you? What are some of the challenges in your journey regarding this culture?

5. What is the history of your linguistic identification? What is your first language? Other languages? Sign communication systems? What are some of your experiences of oppression or privilege related to communication?

Adapted from group supervision experiences and relevant deaf-related identity literature (Leigh, 2009; Oliva & Lytle, in press; Wu & Grant, 2013) members, although some supervisors may decide to require that clinicians will submit their journals weekly so that their supervisors can provide individual feedback.

The PIE questions and additional deaf-related identity questions are answered individually by journaling and are a starting point for stimulating the discussion in group supervision. Questions may be systematically covered in the order listed in Tables 30.1 and 30.2 or in an order that the group supervisor believes is more suitable for the nature and composition of the group or the clinical setting. If time permits, one full supervision session is dedicated to each identity domain; additionally, for deaf-related identity and Deaf culture, at least two sessions are recommended to cover all of the aspects of deaf-related identity. If clinicians have not been educated or trained in a Deaf-centric environment, additional readings and more time devoted to deaf-related identity are recommended.

All clinicians in the group are given time to share their responses, thoughts, and feelings with others as they feel comfortable. The group supervisor may want to set an agenda. An agenda might specify the order in which clinicians share and the amount of time permitted for each clinician; supervisors should note that the allotted time should be brief enough to allow for more in-depth open discussion in the same session. Clinicians might begin these open discussions by summarizing or sharing their response to the questions. Clinicians are asked to consider at each session if the activity has influenced their case conceptualization or approach in their current clinical work with deaf and hard-of-hearing clients. This is an opportune time for the supervisor to emphasize how diverse the various identity constructions of deaf clients can be (Leigh, 2009; Oliva & Lytle, in press; Wu and Grant, 2013).

Individual supervisors should be made aware of the PIE and deaf-related identity questions. During individual supervision, clinicians may explore further their own responses to the questions and what the group discussion brought up for them. They may discuss the related perceptions of each of their clients' multiple identities and present dilemmas. If group supervision stimulates or triggers more to consider that is directly relevant for their current work or sense of a developing professional self, then the clinicians might also choose to bring that to individual supervision. Again, it is particularly salient for clinicians who work with deaf and hard-of-hearing clients to consider their own journey in regard to deaf-related identity and Deaf culture and how this journey is being integrated with their work.

# Example

Preliminary responses to the PIE and deaf-related identity questions in supervision groups suggested that some of the group may not have had many opportunities to consider multiple identities in other academic discussions. The group began by describing their general thoughts and feelings about the activity and focused first on the categories of race and religion, considering their earliest memories and feelings about their own heritage. They were encouraged to share their responses to other questions in Table 30.1. The group member from Europe expressed that she had not been exposed to the idea of diversity until coming to Gallaudet (and the United States). She said her initial thought was that in her country, "everyone [describes themselves as] White and Catholic and straight—they are not open about their identity." She enthusiastically endorsed the activity as enhancing her self-awareness and anticipated a greater ability to appreciate the significance of cultural identity for her clients. Another deaf clinician said that she often did not "think about race, just think Deaf" despite her own mixed racial heritage. One deaf group member noted, "I was surprised to consider how I identified as a member of a minority (Deaf), but until I start signing, other people are probably more likely to see me as part of the White majority."

In subsequent sessions, we proceeded to consider culture (including Deaf culture), socioeconomic status, sexual orientation, and their responses to the questions in Table 30.1, and we began to address the deaf-related identity questions in Table 30.2. The group considered who and what influenced their attitudes about their own or a differing group, reflecting on discrimination they may have experienced. Thought-provoking and emotion-laden discussions ensued related to how categories intersected. The intersection of religion with sexual orientation and deaf-related identity initiated some intense discussion about the clinicians and their clinical work. They considered their own religious cultural heritage and how this heritage influenced their views in their work with their clients.

For some clinicians, there was considerable concern about how to work with deaf and hard-of-hearing undergraduate clients who were wrestling with their sexual orientation identity, having been raised in strict religious families in which this identity might be seen as morally wrong. A deaf client often may have had little opportunity to talk, because of lack of communication or social isolation, about the conflicts in his or her religious upbringing and his or her developing sexual orientation identity. Clinicians identified challenges regarding how to respectfully engage with a client who was just beginning to establish a sense of self separate from parents or family and to arrive at a questioning stage of sexual orientation identity.

After reflecting on some of their own histories regarding religion and sexual orientation, the clinicians saw a need to carefully explore or monitor their own biases. For instance, they might be prepared to criticize the family or the religion and encourage the clients to accept and integrate an aspect of self prematurely, perhaps not allowing clients to assess the decision for themselves and to process their thoughts and feelings at their own pace. Group members discussed strong reactions they experienced, particularly to the clients' families' responses. In addition to religious values and beliefs that might conflict with sexual orientation identity, the limited communication or lack thereof for some deaf clients in hearing families was also a highly charged topic for the group.

Interviews conducted a few months later with four out of the six clinicians provided additional information. This provided deeper reflection on the activity and has been used in professional presentations (see Hufnell, 2009). Clinicians were interviewed about whether this activity contributed to an improved understanding of their own multiple identities, to group cohesion, and to the ability to engage effectively in group supervision. Clinicians were also asked whether they noted any change in their understanding of their clients' diverse cultural backgrounds, in the development of therapeutic alliances with their clients, or both. The group overwhelmingly stated that they found that the activity improved their understanding of their own cultural identity and enhanced group cohesion. One clinician said, "I had doubts . . . and fear of being judged" in group supervision, but that changed. Another member stated "I saw how we were different but also how we were similar." Finding the commonalities was reassuring and allowed her to be more comfortable proceeding with the activity and later in discussing cases more openly. The activity appeared to increase clinicians' feelings of comfort and safety and allowed them to explore how they were working with their clients regarding diversity issues in their clinical work. They believed themselves to be more open to the breadth and depth of their clients' experiences.

Deaf-related identity is significant for this clinical setting and is most likely a sensitive issue in settings where deaf and hearing clinicians work together. One deaf clinician remembered during the follow-up interviews that she was reticent to bring up deaf-related identity. She said, "I was concerned that I might offend someone." The oppressions that deaf clinicians have experienced and the naming of hearing privilege and audism (e.g., hearing paternalism manifested in numerous ways; Leigh, 2009) were difficult for the group to bring to the discussion. Deaf and hearing clinicians in the group had various identities along the continuum of Deaf culture with differing histories of engagement in the Deaf community. The clinicians clearly expressed willingness and a desire to discuss this dimension, although time constraints only permitted some initial work on how it was affecting the group, their collegial relationships, and their developing sense of professional identity.

# Measuring Progress

Self-awareness and cultural sensitivity with regard to deaf-related identity, as well as other cultural identities, may be assessed in various ways. Clinicians assess themselves through what they describe in journals, how they discuss topics in group supervision, and how they discuss their concerns in individual supervision. In the example, group supervisors and individual supervisors assessed clinicians' self-awareness and the application to clinical work through observation, in addition to the mid-semester and end-of-semester written evaluations. Other clinical staff provided input about the general performance and growth of the clinicians-in-training at the time of these written evaluations. Supervisors should evaluate based on how clinicians are observed to incorporate multicultural awareness in their work during individual supervision sessions and through a review of video-recorded sessions with clients.

Individual supervisors assess and rate the clinicians' progress on a Likert scale. Individual supervisors use these department evaluation forms to rate clinicians-in-training on cross-cultural sensitivity and their ability to respect alternative worldviews, knowledge of self in a diverse world, knowledge about the nature and impact of diversity in clinical work, knowledge and skills related to providing services to deaf and hard-of-hearing clients, and ability to work with diverse others. Supervisors would expect to observe that clinicians demonstrate an ability to appreciate and name how each client's worldview influences his or her own counseling goals and what the client expects in the relationship with the clinician. They would also expect to see clinicians exhibit an ability to respectfully acknowledge thoughts or feelings that are perhaps very different from their own regarding what a client might want to change or how a client might approach a situation, for example. Supervisors would expect to see clinicians begin to recognize when they are making assumptions and judgments based on their own worldview, to question those judgments, and to consider a different perspective.

Clinicians, along with the supervisors, can monitor growth in self-awareness and cultural sensitivity. In other settings, clinicians might observe their own progress by asking themselves questions or by addressing in peer supervision how they are attending to cultural identity and deaf-related identity and how this is affecting their work with each client. They might name the possible diversity concerns that may be overlooked in conceptualizing a case. It is highly recommended that clinicians who are inexperienced with deaf-related identity read more and seek further consultation on the subject.

# Conclusion

Being self-aware with regard to clinicians' own multidimensional identity development facilitates an ability to engage in a culturally sensitive manner with clients who will represent a wide scope of cultural identities. Multicultural considerations at Gallaudet University's Mental Health Center include deaf-related identity. Considering deaf-related identity for clinicians who are deaf, hard of hearing, and hearing is highly relevant to professional self-awareness. The PIE (Forrest, 2004) and deaf-related identity questions can assist clinicians in considering their own history and sense of self as they relate to cultural identity. Observations and assessment by self and supervisors suggest that clinicians can use these questions to develop greater self-awareness. Through a purposeful activity such as the one previously described, it is likely clinicians will better conceptualize the concerns of their deaf and hard-of-hearing clients and engage with them in a more meaningful manner.

# Additional Resources

Glickman, N. S. (Ed.). (2013). *Deaf mental health care*. New York, NY: Routledge.

Padden, C. A., & Humphries, T. L. (2005). *Inside deaf culture*. Cambridge, MA: Harvard University Press.

# References

Forrest, B. J. (2004). *Personal identity exercise in training clinics*. Paper presented at a preconference meeting of the Association of Directors of Psychology Training Clinics at the American Psychological Association Convention, Honolulu, HI.

Frew, J., & Spiegel, M. D. (2013). Introduction to contemporary psychotherapies for a diverse world. In J. Frew & M. D. Spiegel (Eds.), *Contemporary psychotherapies for a diverse world* (pp. 1–18). New York, NY: Routledge.

Hufnell, M. C. (2009, April). Personal identity exercise in team supervision: Impact of multiple identities on clinical work. *Paper presented at the European Society for Mental Health and Deafness*, Rome, Italy.

Jones, S. R., & McEwen, M. K. (2000). A conceptual model of multiple dimensions of identity. *Journal of College Student Development, 41*(4), 405–414.

Kiselica, M. S., Clark, L. O., & Sue, D. W. (2013). The multicultural journey to cultural competence: Personal narratives. In D. W. Sue & D. Sue (Eds.), *Counseling the culturally diverse: Theory and practice* (pp. 5–31). Hoboken, NJ: Wiley.

Leigh, I. W. (2009). *A lens on deaf identities*. New York, NY: Oxford University Press.

Oliva, G., & Lytle, L. (in press). *Turning the tide: Making life better for deaf and hard of hearing school children (tentative title)*. Washington, DC: Gallaudet University Press.

Reynolds, A. L., & Pope, R. L. (1991). The complexities of diversity: Exploring multiple oppressions. *Journal of Counseling and Development, 70*, 171–180.

Sue, D., & Sue, D. W. (2013). Culturally competent assessment. In D. W. Sue & D. Sue (Eds.), *Counseling the culturally diverse: Theory and practice* (pp. 345–361). Hoboken, NJ: Wiley.

Vasquez, M. J. T. (2013). Ethics for a diverse world. In J. Frew and M. D. Spiegel (Eds.), *Contemporary psychotherapies for a diverse world* (pp. 19–38). New York, NY: Routledge.

Wu, C. L., & Grant, N. C. (2013). Multicultural deaf children and their hearing families: Working with a constellation of diversities. In C. C. Lee (Ed.), *Multicultural issues in counseling: New approaches to diversity* (4th ed., pp. 221–257). Alexandria, VA: American Counseling Association.

# CHAPTER 31

# PREPARING CLINICIANS TO WORK WITH CO-OCCURING DISABILITIES AND SUBSTANCE ABUSE

Ally DeGraff, Phillip Sorenson, Alane Atchley, and Sara Smock Jordan

## Introduction

Individuals with a disability co-occurring with substance abuse make up at least half of clients seen in most mental health treatment centers (Ziedonis, 2004). The number of dual-diagnosis cases appears to be growing in populations including vocational rehabilitation cases (Paugh, 2003), high-risk manual labor professionals, and returning war veterans.

The effects of not addressing a co-occurring dual diagnosis include negative psychosocial factors such as unstable housing and homelessness (Brunette, Mueser, & Drake, 2004), higher rates of mental illness relapse (Swofford, Kasckow, Scheller-Gilkey, & Inderbitzin, 1996), hospitalization (Haywood et al., 1995), and incarceration (Abram & Teplin, 1991). The co-occurrence of a mental illness and a physical disability can create additional feelings of powerlessness and lack of control (Alexander, 1996), leaving individuals and families feeling trapped, which, in turn, can increase the severity of symptoms.

## Rationale

It is of vital importance that, in the training of clinicians, we allow room to discover personal biases and assumptions because of the impact these biases can have on therapy (Helmeke & Prouty, 2001). This chapter is designed to assist clinicians in gaining a better understanding of co-occurring diagnoses. As with any special topic area, clinicians must begin their journey through training and by gaining awareness of their own preconceptions of substance abuse and of physical and mental disabilities. Awareness of co-occurring disabilities and the treatment modalities is critical for practicing mental health clinicians (DeLambo, Chandras, Homa, & Chandras, 2008). Unfortunately, most treatment programs have not effectively addressed these individuals' needs, even though strong evidence shows that adequate treatment of the co-occurring disabilities is valuable in individuals' experiences in treatment (Ziedonis, 2004).

## Activity Instructions

This activity is intended for clinicians-in-training, so the instructions are written for supervisors in the mental health field. The ideal group size would be six to sixteen student clinicians, equally divided into two groups. Before this activity is presented, the facilitator should help the group establish rules for safety, confidentiality, and respect. The supervisor should plan for discussion time and should be prepared for more in-depth questions from the students about the listed diagnoses. If personal issues arise for participants during these exercises, it is the facilitator's responsibility to provide support and resources. The facilitator should also establish a safe and validating environment for participants to share their personal biases.

## Activity 1: Discovering Disability Bias

This activity is intended to create awareness of the prevalence of physical and mental disabilities/disorders co-occurring with substance abuse. Because most clinicians are likely to have more experience with disabilities that are psychological in nature, this activity aims to raise clinicians' awareness about the prevalence of substance abuse among both the psychologically and physically disabled. Research shows that individuals with physical disabilities struggle to adjust to life with a disability, and those who fail to adapt to life with a disability are more likely to have substance abuse problems. This becomes a circular relationship, because those who have substance abuse problems are less likely to adapt to living with their disability, and those who don't adapt are much more likely to have substance abuse problems (Elliot, Watson, Goldman, & Greenberg, 2004).

The facilitator begins the activity by handing out the following list of disabilities:

_____ PTSD

_____ Seizures

_____ Traumatic Brain Injury

_____ Mania

_____ Spine Injuries/Disorders

_____ Generalized Anxiety Disorder

_____ Hearing Loss/Deaf

_____ Developmental Disabilities

Participants are asked to rank these disabilities in order from 1 to 8 (with 1 being the most common co-occurring disorder with substance abuse and 8 being the least common co-occurring disorder with substance abuse). Explain that the term "substance abuse" is used to represent only individuals who can be clinically diagnosed with either a substance abuse or dependence problem. This does not include individuals who have some impairment caused by substance abuse but are not as of yet in the clinical range of impairment. After the participants complete their rankings, the facilitator presents the following data:

1.  _____ Traumatic Brain Injury 60% rate of substance abuse
2.  _____ Spine Injuries/Disorders 17% to 62% rate of substance abuse
3.  _____ Mania Rates greater than 35% of substance abuse
4.  _____ PTSD 25% rate of substance abuse
5.  _____ Generalized Anxiety Disorder Rates greater than 22% of substance abuse
6.  _____ Hearing Loss/Deaf Rates greater than 20% of substance abuse
7.  _____ Seizures 14% rate of substance abuse
8.  _____ Developmental Disabilities At least 12% to 14% rates of substance abuse

The facilitator then processes this information with the participants, who are asked to divide into smaller groups of three to five people and answer the following questions:

- What was most shocking about this activity?
- What were some misconceptions you held about substance abuse and disabilities?
- How do you think these misconceptions were developed?
- What was the hardest part about this exercise?
- What are some beliefs you hold about substance abuse and disabilities?
- Have you ever had any experience in this area?

While addressing the answers to these questions with the group, the facilitator should be aware of some potential responses from the trainees and should be prepared to handle situations that may arise. For instance, the smaller groups may have different opinions. In this situation, it is useful for the facilitator to compare differences in their responses and discuss the justifications that the smaller groups used to rank each disability. Questions that the facilitator should be prepared to ask include:

- What were some reasons that you decided [X disability] was more prevalent than [Y disability]?
- [Group A] decided that [X disability] was more common than [Y disability] while [Group B] decided differently. Can each group describe how they came to these decisions and what influenced the differing opinions?

Facilitators should also be prepared for trainees to display a variety of responses; some trainees may not have a strong reaction to this activity, whereas others may feel very reactive. The facilitator should be sensitive to the trainees' reactions and help them explore the meaning behind their responses. This could be done by exploring personal family/social experiences, relevant clinical/professional experiences, and the role of society and media. Sample questions could include:

- When was the first time you experienced substance use or mental illness and in what context?
- How does your opinion on disabilities/substance use show up in your personal life?

Finally, it is expected that biases from the facilitator and trainees will be reflected in their responses. Facilitators should be aware of their own biases about substance use and the specific disabilities noted in order to best process this activity. The facilitator can then help discuss the trainees' biases by exploring where they may have originated from, the purpose these biases serve in their personal lives and in their clinical work, and the potential effects these biases could have on their professional work. Sample responses for this situation include:

- What would a session with someone with a disability and substance use disorder look like if you were the therapist? What would be hard for you?
- Can you give examples of what came to mind when you pictured someone with PTSD and a substance use disorder?

Once the small groups have processed the questions, the facilitator can move on to the second activity.

## Activity 2: Guided Case Perspective Activity

This activity is intended to help clinicians gain perspective on and a better understanding of individuals with disabilities co-occurring with substance abuse. To that end, the facilitator will ask for two volunteers to read aloud the following vignettes:

*Vignette 1*: *Okay, so, my name is Steven—I'm from around here. And I'm here for drugs and alcohol, and my thing is I wanna really leave it alone because I hurt a lot. I live with my mother. I steal from my mother to buy alcohol and drugs. I was drinking when I was 22 in Korea. I used to see the dope fiends—I could see that they was high. But I—in a way—wanted to be like them. I wanted to be in their group. No one takes me seriously—they call me a retard. I ain't like anyone else. They don't know what I been through. They just gonna throw me in the looney bin for no one to deal with.*

*Vignette 2*: *Steven is a 48-year-old male. He has been diagnosed with mild mental retardation but suffered from a severe traumatic brain injury while on a combat tour when he was in the military (the mild mental retardation was diagnosed when he was medically discharged). He was married, but his wife left him while he was on tour overseas. They had a daughter named Isabella, but her mother got custody of her when Steven was medically discharged. Steven began living with his mother when he returned home so he would not have to live in an assisted-living facility. He recently got arrested for public intoxication while he was at the park with his friends at 3 a.m.*

*When they drug-tested him, he tested positive for alcohol and amphetamines. Because this is not his first charge, they are mandating that he spend 90 days in a residential treatment program. You are assigned to be his therapist. (Adapted from ARHC New York City, 2011)*

After reading the vignettes, the facilitator divides the participants into two equal groups. The first group is asked to focus on Steven's mental retardation/traumatic brain injury (MR/TBI) while the second is asked to focus on Steven's substance abuse. Both groups should respond to the following questions:

- What is your therapeutic plan for Steven?

- What special accommodations, if any, will Steven need for therapy?

- How will you alter your therapeutic interventions to fit Steven's needs?

After an appropriate time for discussion and analysis, the facilitator then brings both groups together to discuss their answers and process how their responses are different or similar based on their group's assigned focus. The facilitator can use some of the suggestions from the first activity for processing this activity if he or she feels that it is appropriate. In addition, the facilitator should be looking for key differences in how the group planned therapy for MR/TBI as compared to the group that planned therapy for substance abuse.

After the facilitator helps the trainees highlight differences in the therapeutic plans, the topic of discussion should turn to the benefits and downfalls of focusing only on the MR/TBI diagnosis versus only on the substance use. It is expected that each therapeutic plan will have benefits and downfalls in context of the co-occurring diagnosis. The facilitator should then help the trainees integrate the two therapeutic plans to teach the trainees that integrated therapy approaches are possible for co-occurring disorders and can be helpful. This can be done by taking pieces from each therapy plan or coming up with new ideas as a large group in a discussion setting. The trainees are expected to learn how integration of therapy for co-occurring disorders can be planned.

# Examples

These activities also have helped us understand the differences between physical and mental disabilities. Physical disabilities can occur at birth, through an accident, or from disease; some are temporary, and others are lifelong and irreversible. These limitations can bring up feelings of anger, depression, humiliation, and/or hopelessness in individuals, so substance abuse for physically disabled clients often begins as a coping mechanism to the *physical* pain they suffer. In contrast, those who suffer from mental disabilities may abuse substances to deal with the *psychological* pain that accompanies their ailment. For these individuals, the substance abuse can exacerbate their mental inability to function in society (e.g., keep a job, stay in school). One participant responded by saying:

*Even though I had met people in my life who fit perfectly people mentioned in these activities, such as the severely depressed, an Army vet with PTSD, or homeless and physically handicapped person who had all struggled with substance abuse problems, I had never really considered what was really going on in their lives and what it must be like. Doing these two activities helped me understand their situation so much better.*

Although some comparisons can be made between physical and mental disabilities, a great deal of the time the negative feelings that may accompany a physical disability can also lead to a mental illness. Therefore, it is important to ask each client how his or her physical and/or mental disability influences either substance use or abuse.

In our clinical training, we noticed a lack of training in working with physically and/or mentally disabled clients with co-occurring substance abuse. We decided that a need for creating educational exercises existed. One participant replied by saying:

*As a current Master's student with some clinical experience, I knew I had a little understanding that disabilities co-occurred with substance abuse. Doing these activities helped me realize that there are a great many who have substance abuse problems while having a disability.*

Through our development of these activities, our clinical practice has gained a greater sensitivity to working with clients such as an Army veteran with PTSD and a physically handicapped homeless person who had struggled with substance abuse problems. Our hope is that these activities will positively impact other clinicians.

# Measuring Progress

Progress will be measured by discussing the participants' self-awareness of co-occurring substance abuse disabilities at various points during the exercises. During the discover disability exercise, the facilitator should be aware of participants' reactions and misconceptions. Give participants the opportunity to share stories about their misconceptions. At the end of the guided case perspective, ask participants what they learned from the exercise. Discuss with participants how their new awareness of disabled substance abusers will affect their therapeutic work. One participant reacted by saying, "After I read the vignettes, I went and looked back at the list of disabilities in the discovering our bias activity and thought to myself, 'Wouldn't many of these people also feel alienated, frustrated, different, and alone just like the man I just read about?'" By discussing misconceptions before and after the exercises, the facilitator can gather increased self-awareness. Another response to the activities was: "Understanding that substance abuse has a way of magnifying the difficulties of a disability and vice versa helped me to see that, while these are two different issues, they still have strong ties to each other."

# Conclusion

The discovering our disability bias activity and the guided case perspective activity provide participants with an opportunity to explore their own personal biases regarding the physical and mental disabilities that can co-occur with substance abuse. By exploring personal biases and developing more awareness, clinicians working with substance abusers with disabilities will be more empathic and better serve this underserved population.

# Additional Resources

Bogenschutz, M. P. (2007). 12-step approaches for the dually diagnosed: Mechanisms of change. Alcoholism. *Clinical and Experimental Research*, *31*(3), 64S–66S.

Cloherty, M., & Hill, R. (2011). Working with cognitively impaired substance users. In R. Hill & J. Harris (Eds.), *Principles and practice of group work in addictions* (pp. 165–176). New York, NY: Routledge/Taylor & Francis Group.

Nunes, E. V. (2010). *Substance dependence and co-occurring psychiatric disorders: Best practices for diagnosis and clinical treatment*. Kingston, NJ: Civic Research Institute.

Slayter, E., & Steenrod, S. A. (2009). Addressing alcohol and drug addiction among people with mental retardation in nonaddiction settings: A need for cross-system collaboration. *Journal of Social Work Practice in the Addictions*, *9*(1), 71–90.

# References

Abram, K., & Teplin, L. (1991). Co-occurring disorders among mentally ill jail detainees. *American Psychology*, *46*, 1036–1044.

Alexander, M. J. (1996). Women with co-occurring addictive and mental disorders: An emerging profile of vulnerability. *American Journal of Orthopsychiatry*, *66*(1), 61–70.

Brunette, M. F., Mueser, K. T., & Drake, R. E. (2004). A review of research on residential programs for people with mental illness and co-occurring substance use disorders. *Drug and Alcohol Review*, *23*, 471–481.

DeLambo, D. A., Chandras, K. V., Homa, D., & Chandras, S. V. (2008). Psychiatric disabilities and substance abuse: Applications for rehabilitation professionals. In G. R. Walz, J. C. Bleuer, & R. K. Yep (Eds.), *Compelling counseling interventions: Celebrating VISTAS' fifth anniversary* (pp. 149–160). Alexandria, VA: American Counseling Association.

Elliot, R., Watson, J. C., Goldman, R. N., & Greenberg, L. S. (2004). *Learning emotion-focused therapy: The process experiential approach to change*. Washington, DC: American Psychological Association.

Haywood, T. W., Kravitz, H. M., Grossman, L. S., Cavanaugh, J. L., Davis, J. M., & Lewis, D. A. (1995). Predicting the "revolving door" phenomenon among patients with schizophrenic, schizoaffective, and affective disorders. *The American Journal of Psychiatry, 152*(6), 856–861.

Helmeke, K. B., & Prouty, M. A. (2001). Do we really understand? An experiential exercise for training family therapists. *Journal of Marital and Family Therapy, 27*, 535–544.

Paugh, C. (2003). *Vocational rehabilitation for persons with dual diagnoses: Specific service patterns that enhance earnings at the time of case closure.* (Doctoral dissertation). Retrieved from Dissertation Abstracts International (osu1046216863).

Swofford, C. D., Kasckow, J. W., Scheller-Gilkey, G., & Inderbitzin, L. B. (1996). Substance use: A powerful predictor of relapse in schizophrenia. *Schizophrenia Research, 20*(1–2), 145–151.

Ziedonis, D. M. (2004). Integrated treatment of co-occurring mental illness and addiction. *CNS Spectrums, 12*, 892–904.

CHAPTER 32

# EMPOWERING CLINICIANS TO WORK WITH AFRICAN IMMIGRANTS THROUGH GAME PLAYING

Tohoro Francis Akakpo

# Introduction

Approximately 1.5 million African immigrants were residing in the United States in 2011, up 50% from the 1 million immigrants in the previous decade (Brammer, 2012). With such a large number of African immigrants living in the United States today, mental health professionals must develop clinical approaches tailored for this population using the conceptual framework of person-in-environment. One example of this method is the game Oware, an effective clinical tool that can help U.S. clinicians be more prepared to empower their African-immigrant clients.

Among the many responsibilities facing the mental health fields is addressing the mental health needs of recent African immigrants who continue to embrace the cultural values and beliefs of their native lands. As Brammer (2012) noted (citing Sue, 2006), foreign-born African immigrants do not usually recognize social injustice as experienced by the multigenerational African Americans, who are very much aware of micro-aggressions because of the historical legacy of slavery in the United States. Not only are these new immigrants unaware of racism, they also face difficulties that are compounded by having U.S.-born children who may not have the ability to speak their parents' native language or who do not have an understanding of the traditions and cultural aspects of their African heritage. This bicultural experience can often contribute to parent–child conflict and structural problems in which the children of immigrants are trying to create their own unique identity in the United States.

In addition to coping with the challenges of parenting their children and trying to foster an understanding and appreciation of their African heritage, immigrant parents often wonder whom to consult in times of crisis. The common adage "We do not wash our dirty linens in public" often holds true for recent African immigrants, especially for West Africans. African families prefer to talk to family members about their personal problems or challenges rather than seek the advice of an outside mental health professional. Therefore, it is important for clinicians to understand the socio-cultural values and beliefs of African-immigrant clients in order to best help them in crisis situations. Clinicians should develop a more global perspective when working with this vulnerable population.

With this in mind, the game Oware is an activity that resonates with Africans from across the continent and for those who live in the diaspora. From the Mancala family of socialization and strategic-planning games, this activity can help unify individuals irrespective of ethnicity, race, creed, age, gender, sexual orientation, or national origin. It is a promising method for working with individuals from all walks of life, but especially for recent immigrants from the African continent who will open up when a clinician shows a genuine acceptance of their values and worldviews (Choudhuri, Santiago-Rivera, & Garrett, 2012).

# Rationale

The Oware activity is based on ethnographic studies (de Voogt, 1997) and classroom pedagogy (Mohr, 1997; The Oware Society, n.d.). It is designed to increase self-awareness of clinicians working with African immigrants and the diaspora, allowing them to feel the impact of self-liberating and empowering process through this hands-on method of rapport building. This activity is suitable for clinicians at all experience levels and from a variety of personal circumstances. It can be self-assigned and performed by a clinician or assigned by a supervisor as part of a training exercise, class requirement, or workshop training.

The Oware activity can help clinicians better understand the dynamics of the family, worldviews, cultural values, and life circumstances of their culturally diverse clients (Sue, 2006). As Sue (2006) further suggested, in the United States, white Euro-American culture holds certain values that are reflected in the therapeutic process. In other words, both counseling and therapy have traditionally been conceptualized using Western individualistic terms. It is therefore crucial for clinicians to work outside of the Western values paradigm in order to connect with clients from different backgrounds, especially African-born immigrants who are struggling to practice the culture of their host nation while still parenting their offspring to appreciate the values and culture of their native lands.

The origin of Oware is not clear, but it is a popular board game played across Africa, as well as in Central and Southeast Asia (de Voogt, 1997). With the advent of the computer and the Internet, this game can now be played almost anywhere (Swanson, 1996). Drawing from the extant literature, ample evidence shows that Oware is a helpful tool that clinicians can use to empower their clients, to gain a better understanding of their clients, and to educate themselves about their clients' values and beliefs (de Voogt, 1997; Kloba, 2005). The Oware game is not confined to any one particular group but has both local and regional variations across Africa and the diaspora. For example, among the Ewes of Ghana and Togo, it is called *adi-to*, which literally translates as "seed and hole/hollow." Among the Akan-speaking people, the name of the activity is Oware, which in the Akan language means "he/she marries" and stems from an Asante legend about a man and woman who played the game endlessly to remain married (The Oware Society, n.d.). Even with its ethnic variations, legends, and different names and versions, the concept and rationale of Oware is the same: promoting socialization and teaching social values and norms of society, irrespective of language or ethnic origin.

In addition to its spiritual and socialization components, Oware has also been praised for its focus on experiential learning, which can help participants express their knowledge of mathematical skills and strategic planning (Motune, 2004; Swanson, 1996). These strategies are transferable to social work practice with small groups and family facilitation and counseling that is based on families working together and finding solutions to their challenges (Nichols, 2010). Oware involves decision making wherein clinicians are able to see, feel, sense, and play their roles and experience what it is like to express concerns, challenge past feelings and thoughts, and replace negative thoughts with positive ones (Kennedy & Tang, 2009). Understanding the feelings of others through the Oware activity is a powerful vehicle for helping clinicians become aware of their own feelings. This transfers into empathy toward clients from different cultural backgrounds. It empowers clinicians and promotes self-determination, personal respect, and tolerance by helping them realize they are capable of winning while showing compassion by not denying the opponent the chance to play. (See the rules of the game in the Activity Instructions section for a better understanding of how playing Oware fosters compassion and tolerance.)

# Activity Instructions

The instructions provided were developed based on various manuals on Oware games (Mohr, 1997). The Oware technique is framed as a concrete exercise and action and should be implemented spontaneously after clients have indicated that they are concerned about a conflict. The

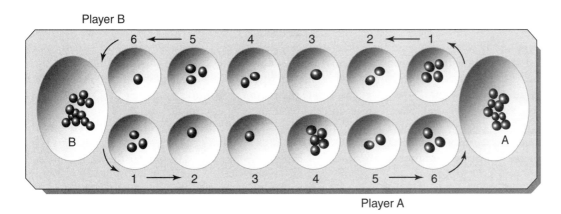

**Figure 32.1**/Sample Oware Board. (From Simonds Mohr, M. (1997). *The new games treasury: More than 500 indoor and outdoor favorites with strategies, rules and traditions.* New York, NY: Houghton Mifflin Company. Reprinted with permission of M. Simonds Mohr.)

following instructions are directed to supervisors, who will assign the game to clinicians to complete during a workshop.

**Number of Players:** Two

**Equipment:** One Oware board (with two rows of six holes and two "storehouse" holes at opposite ends) and 48 small pieces (e.g., nuts, dried beans, seeds, round marbles, pebbles, or any other stone-like objects). The pieces will be referred to as "seeds" in these instructions.

**Objective:** The object of the game is to capture the most seeds by the time all the holes are empty. The winner is the player who obtains more than half of the seeds (25 or more).

**Play:** The players decide who goes first by flipping a coin. The game starts with the 48 seeds equally distributed in the 12 holes, four pieces per hole. The movement of the game is called "sow and reap." The first player scoops the four pieces from one of his or her holes (it does not matter which) and "sows" the seeds one at a time in the holes immediately to the right. (Figure 32.1 shows a sample of the Oware board and the direction of the movement of the seeds.) No seeds are dropped in the storehouse. The two players take turns scooping seeds from one of their holes and distributing. If the last seed is dropped into a hole of the other player that contains only one or two seeds, the player will reap (capture) those seeds. This move is called a "capture by twos or threes." These captured seeds are added to the player's storehouse. A player can only reap or capture seeds on the opposite side of the board.

**The Catch:** According to various manuals, a player cannot capture all the seeds of the other player in a single turn or leave him or her with no seeds to play. If a player does this, he or she automatically loses the game. This rationale is best expressed by a Ghanaian proverb: "If you want to reap, you must sow, and whoever expects to receive must first learn to give." Players, therefore, must plan in advance to avoid this situation.

**End of Play:** Play ends when one player secures 25 or more pieces in his or her storehouse. Play can also end when only a few pieces are left in the holes and neither of the two players can reap or capture any new seeds. By mutual agreement, players can agree to end the game. In this case, each player owns the seeds in his or her storehouse. As always, the one who has garnered the most seeds wins the match.

# Example

In a recent week-long training workshop for clinicians, the Oware activity was used to establish working relationships and to promote self-awareness among clinicians and understanding of mental health issues from African immigrants' perspectives. After making sure that everyone was familiar with the game, the instructor broke the participants into groups of three, with one person receiving a typical "parent" role, another receiving a typical "child" role, and the third person taking on the role of "clinician." Assuming these three respective roles, each subgroup played the game two times per session for the entire week. After the first round of the game, which was led by the "clinician" and took approximately 12 minutes, they began to process the feelings of each person in the group.

Within the conceptual framework of the Oware activity, both parents and children are on a level playing field, because each has an equal number of seeds (48) at the beginning of the game. The context of parent and child in this activity is very important, because in many African societies achievement is respected but age is revered. The individual clinicians were in a position to express the feelings of empowerment and self-liberation using this activity that pits two opponents against each other. Within the activity's framework, the players must be competitive and try to outdo each other. However, the essence of the activity is to socialize and to teach tolerance.

During the activity, the clinician playing the role of the parent hoarded the seeds. The clinician playing the role of clinician stopped the game and declared the person without seeds a winner. The loser felt cheated and demanded to know the grounds on which the child, who did not have the greatest numbers of seeds, was declared the winner. The instructor of the workshop stepped in and pointed out there was a violation of the golden rules of Oware ("the person who wants to reap must first sow" and "one cannot let the other person go hungry"). The opponent did not understand the underlying cultural concept of empowerment or self-liberation that is common among Africans. One African adage states, "I am because you are" (and vice versa). Thus, empowerment or self-liberation from an African perspective does not mean depriving others of an opportunity to partake in any activity based on one's circumstances. The player (the child) who was awarded the winning points surprisingly stated, "I felt stupid and unintelligent when I could not capture any seeds." This feeling resonates as one of the reasons for which individuals from many of the African immigrant groups do not feel comfortable sharing their issues with clinicians. The individual (the parent) who thought he won the game but was declared the loser had to learn how to be compassionate toward others. The self-centered attitude of this player who complained of "taking what he has earned and given to another" stemmed from the traditional practice of individualism that is embedded in White American cultural systems and that excludes other cultures that make a practice of employing communal help.

If the clinician playing the role of the child had refused to engage in the activity, then the instructor would have had the opportunity to address the feelings that occurred when the child refused, particularly those related to shame, a lack of confidence, or inner conflict. It is important for clinicians to address structural functioning issues and to identify the subsystems within a family. In many African cultures, children are not allowed to confront adults. For example, when an individual clinician pays a visit to an African family, it is essential that he or she first recognize the head of the family, which in most cases is the adult male.

# Measuring Progress

In this example, the Oware game was repeated twice during each session of training for one week. After each game, the instructor took notes about the moves, or the sowing of the seeds, as well as any changes, improvements, and/or progress for each player. The clinicians discussed among themselves the level of confidence achieved and how they came to understand what it is like to operate outside of their individual comfort zones. Their struggle to understand and operate within a completely different culture helps them relate to the anxiety their clients experience when meeting them for the first time. Some of the clinicians professed that, as a result of the Oware activity, they became more comfortable with their colleagues and learned to appreciate their collective efforts during the one week they were in training.

Another dimension of cultural competence training discussed was that of peer evaluation provided by their colleagues. The evaluation enabled them to discover another vital point about this particular use of the Oware method; it helped them to realize that individuals can develop their talents and become more proficient in a variety of areas of interest. Also, through these observations, the clinicians were able to assess their own families' functioning and socialization methods, such as boundary making and accommodation (Nichols, 2010). One clinician disclosed with her groups that "As a parent, I am unable to understand the needs of my children because of how little time we spend together to build stronger relationships within our family unit." The importance of the clinician's comment goes to the heart of managing the myriad details of everyday living (Nichols, 2010).

In addition, the exercise helped the clinicians to define comfort zones and to open a channel of effective communication among themselves, which is transferable to client systems. Through the exercise, the clinicians acquired a greater knowledge of cultural competence in decision making and strategic game play among the African immigrant population.

# Conclusion

As a result of this activity, the clinicians became aware that in many African cultures, direct communication and confrontation are considered disrespectful, especially when family members are involved. The implementation of the Oware activity also underscores the original theme of the Asante legend of staying together as a family—in this sense, an extended and nuclear family—which is the cultural norm for African families. Therefore, the Oware activity is a useful tool for increasing clinicians' self-awareness and communication skills for dealing across cultural lines.

# Additional Resources

Lewis, E. A. (2011). Cultural differences and neo-colonialism in social work: Negotiating exchange between Ghana and the United States. *Reflection: Narratives of Professional Helping*, *17*(3), 31–37.

Pressman (n.d.). *Wood mancala: The game of collecting gemstones.* Retrieved from www.dazadi .com/Toys-and-Games/Games-and-Puzzles/Board-Games/Other-Board-Games/Pressman-Toy-Mancala-Board-Game.html

Swigonski, M. E. (1996). Challenging privilege through Africentric social work practice. *Social Work*, *41*(2), 153–161.

Tall, K. (1992). Rules for playing Oware abapa version. Retrieved from www.amazon.com/Rules-Playing-Oware-Abapa-Version/dp/B004V72X1C

# References

Brammer, R. (2012). *Diversity in counseling* (2nd ed.). Belmont, CA: Brooks/Cole.

Choudhuri, D. D., Santiago-Rivera, A. L., & Garrett, M. T. (2012). *Counseling & diversity*. Belmont, CA: Brooks/Cole, Cengage Learning.

de Voogt, A. J. (1997). *Mancala board games*. London, UK: British Museum Press.

Kennedy, K., & Tang, M. (2009). Beyond two chairs: Why Gestalt psychotherapy? *Clinical Psychotherapy Forum*, *194*, 22–25.

Kloba, M. (2005). Sowing the seeds of knowledge in children's literature: Sociocultural values in J.O. de Graft Hanson's *The Golden Oware Counters. Children's Literature Association Quarterly*, *30*(2), 152–163.

Mohr, M. S. (1997). *The new games treasury: More than 500 indoor and outdoor favorites with strategies, rules and traditions*. Boston, MA: Houghton Mifflin Company.

Motune, V. (2004). Oware: Playing the game of kings. *The Voice*. Retrieved from https://ezproxy .uwgb.edu:2443/login?url=http://search.proquest.com/docview/204191596?accountid= 14788

Nichols, M. P. (2010). *Family therapy: Concepts and methods*. Boston, MA: Allyn & Bacon.

Sue, D. W. (2006). *Multicultural social work practice*. Hoboken, NJ: Wiley.

Swanson, C. (1996). [Review of Oware: The national game of Africa.] *Teaching Children Mathematics*, *3*, 156.

The Oware Society. (n.d.). Oware rules. Retrieved from www.oware.org/rules.asp

# CHAPTER 33

# GROUP ROLE-PLAYS AND THE IMMIGRANT EXPERIENCE

Chandra Lasley

# Introduction

In response to scholars' calls for more cultural competence within the field of marriage and family therapy, many clinical programs have been attending to cultural issues using topical courses and more inclusive recruitment efforts (Inman, Meza, Brown, & Hargrove, 2004). However, apart from these initiatives, many clinical programs have not yet systematically addressed cultural topics or advanced clinicians' cultural competence (McDowell, Fang, Brownlee, Young, & Khanna, 2007; Ponterotto, Alexander, & Grieger, 1995). While enhancing cultural awareness by providing clinicians with more cultural content or information about various ethnic groups is important, it is not sufficient for the development of cultural sensitivity (Hardy & Laszloffy, 1995).

*Cultural awareness* is defined as the cognitive and intellectual processing of cultural information, and *cultural sensitivity* is described as an emotional response to this type of information that facilitates more respectful approaches during clinical encounters and interactions (Hardy & Laszloffy, 1995). A combination of cultural awareness *and* cultural sensitivity can help clinicians be better attuned and genuinely empathic to their clients' needs. The following experiential exercise was designed as a classroom and workshop supplement to improve clinicians' cultural awareness and cultural sensitivity toward a unique population—immigrant clients living in the United States. This exercise was designed to help clinicians better understand what it is like to be an immigrant.

# Rationale

The underutilization of mental health services by immigrants in the United States is well documented (e.g., Alegría et al., 2007; Le Meyer, Zane, Cho, & Takeuchi, 2009). Prior studies suggest that this underutilization is the result of many factors, including language and cultural barriers and perceived discrimination (Huang, Appel, & Ai, 2010; Shin, 2002). However, these concerns are rarely addressed during clinical training. As described by Platt and Laszloffy (2012), the concept of diversity within training and education includes gender, sexual orientation, ethnicity, and race but often neglects nationality, suggesting that clinicians' awareness and understanding of clients' presenting issues as they are related to nationality or immigration status should be given more attention in clinical programs.

The greatest challenge for immigrants is *acculturation*, which is defined as "those phenomena which result when groups of individuals having different cultures come into continuous first-hand contact, with changes in the original culture patterns of either or both groups" (Redfield, Linton, & Herskovits, 1936, p. 149). The process of acculturation can be very stressful as immigrants encounter challenges such as identity conflict, culture shock, and language barriers (e.g., Rothe, Pumariega, & Sabagh, 2011). Many scholars have noted that acculturative stress is associated with a higher risk for mental health issues and family or marital relationship difficulties. For example, those who are less acculturated or who experience greater acculturative stress are at higher risk for exhibiting more depressive and anxiety symptoms (Valencia-Garcia, Simoni, Alegría, & Takeuchi, 2012). Furthermore, recent research suggests that acculturative stress may lead to an increase in marital stress and decrease in marital satisfaction (Negy, Hammons, Reig-Ferrer, & Carper, 2010). Families can also be affected by acculturative stress when immigrant parents have to rely on their more-acculturated children as culture and language brokers. Study results, while mixed, suggest that some children of immigrant parents may perceive such roles and responsibilities as a burden and a source of family disagreements (Jones & Trickett, 2005; Morales, Yakushko, & Castro, 2012).

Although immigrants experience personal and relational challenges that may be alleviated through mental health services, language barriers and cultural differences can affect the likelihood that immigrants will seek help. For example, Shin (2002) documented how Korean immigrants are often hesitant to use U.S. mental health services because they feel unable to fully communicate or to describe their emotions in English, especially when their therapists emphasize Western values such as independence and self-control over more traditional Eastern values such as harmony and sensitivity to others. By taking a not-knowing stance and expressing curiosity about how immigrant clients' unique cultures and contexts relate to their presenting problems, clinicians can be more engaging and respectful.

# Activity Instructions

The following experiential exercise was developed to (a) help clinicians explore their own values, prejudices, and beliefs about immigrants; (b) facilitate clinicians' sensitivity toward acculturative stress and their understanding of its impact on individual and relational functioning; and (c) increase clinicians' confidence in helping immigrant populations. The activity's personal nature requires that it be facilitated in a confidential and compassionate environment, but it can be facilitated by any seasoned instructor, clinician, or clinical supervisor. It is especially advantageous if the facilitator is an immigrant, as her or his personal stories can further enrich the exercise.

**Part 1: Reflection and Discussion**

First, participants are asked to explore their personal values and biases regarding immigrants and the topic of immigration. The facilitator should allow approximately 25 minutes to complete this activity and should provide participants with the following instructions: *Please write down your thoughts about the following four statements. Include any personal values that influenced your level of agreement or disagreement with each statement.*

1. Immigrants should (learn to) speak English if they want to come to the United States.
2. Immigrants will have to assimilate if they want to live in the United States.
3. Having their own cultures is fine, but some immigrant behaviors are not acceptable in the United States.
4. It is fine if they want to speak their language at home, but not in front of me because that is rude.

Facilitators should divide participants into groups of three and allow the participants 10 minutes for personal reflection on the statements. Participants should then share their reflections and thoughts with their group members for the remaining 15 minutes. This will allow trainees to compare and contrast their own feelings and personal values.

**Part 2: Role-Play**

Facilitators assign participants, in these same groups, a role-play that simulates one aspect of the immigrant experience (25 minutes allotted). Two of the group members will act in the role of recent immigrants (as a couple), with the third person playing the role of a postal service employee. The husband-wife combination is used here for the sake of simplicity; however, these family roles can be replaced with other family member combinations. The postal employee participant is told to interact with the immigrants in a manner that simulates the difficulties of cross-cultural communication and is provided with the following instructions: *DO NOT SHARE THIS INFORMATION WITH THE HUSBAND AND WIFE. These are the only responses you may give to the couple when they ask you questions about their task.*

- *"I'm sorry; you'll have to go back in line. You have to wait for your turn."*
- *"Follow the instructions on the back of the form."*
- *"Come back tomorrow when your form is filled out."*
- *"I can't understand you."*

Once roles have been assigned, read aloud the activity instructions below and pass out Postal Form 1 (Table 33.1) to each group. This form has been translated into Chinese by the author, modeled after commonly used mailing forms, in order to provide participants with the experience of completing important paperwork in a language in which they are not fluent. The exercise form can be presented in other languages, depending on the languages the clinicians speak. Additionally,

**Table 33.1 Postal Form 1 (Language version that is foreign to role-play participants)**

| Postal Form 1 | | |
|---|---|---|
| 寄件者姓名 (Sender Name) | | |
| 寄件者商業機構 (SB) | | |
| 寄件者地址 (Sender Address) | | |
| 收件者姓名 (AN) | | |
| 收件者商業機構 (AB) | | |
| 收件者地址 (AA) | 路, 巷, 公寓號碼等等 (Road, Street, Apt#, etc.) | |
| 郵遞區號 (PoCo) | 城市 (Ci) | 州, 縣 (St/Pr) |
| 國家 (Co) | | |

| 1. 郵件內容 (Con Dis) | 2. 數量 (Q) | 3. 重量 (克) (W in G) | 4. 價值 (V) |
|---|---|---|---|
| | | | |
| | | | |
| | | | |
| | | | |

請勾選: (Check One)

- ☐ 禮物 (Gift)        ☐ 退換商品 (R Goods)
- ☐ 文件 (D)          ☐ 商業樣本 (C Sample)
- ☐ 商品 (M)          ☐ 其他: (Other)_____

next to each field on the form are English letters that hint what the fields indicate (e.g., (AA) is "Addressee Address"). After 15 minutes, facilitators should hand out Postal Form 2 (English version; Table 33.2) and allow participants to check the accuracy of their work in completing the form.

*The role-play activity you are about to engage in is intended to help you experience what it is like to be an immigrant in the United States where you are unfamiliar with the language and customs. Each group member will play an assigned role (i.e., immigrant wife, immigrant husband, postal employee). In some cases, clarifying information will be on the back of your role card, but please do not share this information with others in your group.*

*Your task, as immigrants, is to fill out an international mailing postal form (Form 1, see Table 33.1) to send a package to your family overseas. You will notice that the form is in another*

**Table 33.2  Postal Form 2 (Language version that is native to role-play participants)**

| Postal Form 2 | | |
|---|---|---|
| Sender Name | | |
| Sender Business | | |
| Sender Address | | |
| Addressee Name | | |
| Addressee Business | | |
| Addressee Address | Road, Street, Apartment #, etc. | |
| Postcode | City | State or Province |
| Country | | |

| 1. Content Description | 2. Quantity | 3. Weight in Grams | 4. Value ($) |
|---|---|---|---|
| | | | |
| | | | |
| | | | |
| | | | |

Check One:

☐ Gift          ☐ Returned Goods

☐ Document      ☐ Commercial Sample

☐ Merchandise   ☐ Other: _____

Example                                                                                                    229

*language to allow you the experience of completing forms in a language in which you are not fluent. Try your best to figure out how to fill out the form in the next 15 minutes. There are small hints in each field to help you guess what information you are to provide. This is to simulate situations in which immigrants may be able to identify certain basic English words but not others. The couple may ask the employee for help. Once 15 minutes are up, we will discuss your experience as a large group.*

The third and final part of the experiential exercise will require at least 40 minutes. Distribute the following questions and allow participants to reflect on them and their role-play experience for 10 minutes. Then guide classroom discussion utilizing the questions.

**Part 3: Reflection and Discussion**

### Husband and wife reflection questions.

1.  Reflect on the difficulty of this task. Was it easy to figure out what each field meant?
2.  Did you feel confident about filling out the form? What are some emotions an immigrant may experience in this situation?
3.  How did the employee's response influence how you felt about your cultural competence as an immigrant (e.g., your ability to cope and thrive in American culture)? How did the employee's response influence how you perceive the employee's cultural competence in understanding your challenges?
4.  Was your partner helpful? How might you feel about your partner? How might you feel about yourself in front of your partner? How might you feel if your children were with you?
5.  How can acculturative stress influence your relationship with your partner? With your children?
6.  How can acculturative stress influence other areas of functioning (e.g., work, health)?
7.  What kind of strengths and resources may an immigrant possess or need to function in such an unfamiliar environment? How about a family?
8.  How can your clinic/agency become more sensitive to communication and cultural barriers?
9.  How might you become more creative with therapy and interventions when working with immigrants? How might you adjust your therapeutic stance or approach?
10. Did you learn something about yourself during this activity? How did the exercise change or influence your view of the immigrant experience?

### Postal service employee reflection questions.

1.  Reflect on your experiences during this task. Why might a postal employee act in such a manner in such a situation? Was it easy or difficult for you to refuse to answer the couple's questions?
2.  How did your actions seem to influence the couple's feelings?
3.  How can your clinic/agency become more sensitive to communication and cultural barriers?
4.  How might you become more creative with therapy and interventions when working with immigrants? How might you adjust your therapeutic stance or approach?
5.  Did you learn something about yourself during this activity? How did the exercise change or influence your view of the immigrant experience?

# Example

This activity has been implemented with a group of first-year trainees in a marriage and family therapy Master's program. The author facilitated the group discussions and activities and noticed that many students shared complex opinions about immigrants and the acculturation experience. As the discussion progressed, the students also shared their personal, or their families', ethnic histories. However, some students reported experiencing great difficulty conceptualizing themselves as immigrants in the United States. For example, one student found it very difficult to imagine how he would feel as an immigrant because his personal experiences as an American living in Europe had informed him that he would not feel terrible about himself or his nationality when he could not fully comprehend the local language and culture. This type of response demonstrated his lack of understanding of how one's nationality and immigrant status can result in disparate social consequences depending on the sociocultural-political context (e.g., American expatriate living in Europe compared to a Mexican immigrant in America).

Some students' responses revealed a lack of cultural sensitivity or self-awareness and presented great opportunities for further discussion. This activity was intended to increase social awareness and to challenge misconceptions, and the students' responses (both positive and negative) demonstrated that the activity had achieved this goal.

# Measuring Progress

As clinicians become more culturally aware and sensitive, their appreciation for the experiences of immigrants will increase. Progress can be first measured by clinicians' increased self-awareness about their own values, biases, limitations, and strengths while clinically working with immigrants. Second, progress is evident when clinicians are able to experience an emotional reaction of respectfulness and compassion when encountering immigrant clients. Third, progress can be measured when clinicians report a greater sense of confidence and competence in working with immigrant clients.

To measure clinicians' increase in cultural competence more quantifiably, instructors or programs can utilize the Cross-Cultural Counseling Inventory—Revised (CCCI-R; LaFromboise, Coleman, & Hernandez, 1991) or the Multicultural Counseling Self-Efficacy Scale—Racial Diversity Form (MCSE-RD; Sheu & Lent, 2007; Sheu, Rigali-Oiler, & Lent, 2012) at baseline and after the activity is completed for comparison. The experiential exercise in this chapter is intended to be an introduction to the immigrant experience, not a representation or summation of the acculturation process. This activity is also not intended as a substitute for more extensive training and education in multicultural counseling competence.

# Conclusion

As clinicians, we value opportunities to expand our appreciation for diverse clients and to improve our clinical skills. By completing this experiential exercise, clinicians at all levels will develop more genuine, empathetic connections with others in and outside of the therapy room.

# Additional Resources

Bulosan, C. (1943). *America is in the heart*. Seattle: University of Washington Press.

Massey, D. S., & Sanchez, M. (2010). *Brokered boundaries: Creating immigrant identity in anti-immigrant times*. New York, NY: Russell Sage Foundation.

Okihiro, G. Y. (1994). *Margins and mainstreams: Asians in American history and culture*. Seattle: University of Washington Press.

# References

Alegría, M., Mulvaney-Day, N., Woo, M., Torres, M., Gao, S., & Oddo, V. (2007). Correlates of past-year mental health service use among Latinos: Results from the National Latino and Asian American Study. *American Journal of Public Health*, *97*(1), 76–83.

Hardy, K. V., & Laszloffy, T. A. (1995). The cultural genogram: Key to training culturally competent family therapists. *Journal of Marital and Family Therapy, 21*(3), 227–237.

Huang, B., Appel, H., & Ai, A. L. (2010). The effects of discrimination and acculturation to service seeking satisfaction for Latina and Asian American women: Implications for mental health professions. *Social Work in Public Health, 26*(1), 46–59.

Inman, A. G., Meza, M. M., Brown, A. L., & Hargrove, B. K. (2004). Student faculty perceptions of multicultural training in accredited marriage and family therapy programs in relation to students' self-reported competence. *Journal of Marital and Family Therapy, 30*(3), 373–388.

Jones, C. J., & Trickett, E. J. (2005). Immigrant adolescents behaving as cultural brokers: A study of families from the former Soviet Union. *Journal of Social Psychology, 145*(4), 405–427.

LaFromboise, T. D., Coleman, H. L., & Hernandez, A. (1991). Development and factor structure of the Cross-Cultural Counseling Inventory—Revised. *Professional Psychology: Research and Practice, 22*(5), 380–388.

Le Meyer, O., Zane, N., Cho, Y., & Takeuchi, D. T. (2009). Use of specialty mental health services by Asian Americans with psychiatric disorders. *Journal of Consulting and Clinical Psychology, 77*(5), 1000–1005.

McDowell, T., Fang, S., Brownlee, K., Young, C. G., & Khanna, A. (2007). Transforming an MFT program: A model for enhancing diversity. *Journal of Marital and Family Therapy, 28*(2), 179–191.

Morales, A., Yakushko, O. F., & Castro, A. J. (2012). Language brokering among Mexican-immigrant families in the Midwest: A multiple case study. *The Counseling Psychologist, 40*(4), 520–553.

Negy, C., Hammons, M. E., Reig-Ferrer, A., & Carper, T. M. (2010). The importance of addressing acculturative stress in marital therapy with Hispanic immigrant women. *International Journal of Clinical and Health Psychology, 10*(1), 5–21.

Platt, J. J., & Laszloffy, T. A (2012). Critical patriotism: Incorporating nationality into MFT education and training. *Journal of Marital and Family Therapy, 38*(4), 1–16.

Ponterotto, J. G., Alexander, C. M., & Grieger, I. (1995). A multicultural competency checklist for counseling training programs. *Journal of Multicultural Counseling & Development, 23*(1), 11–20.

Redfield, R., Linton, R., & Herskovits, M. J. (1936). Memorandum for the study of acculturation. *American Anthropologist, 38*, 149–152.

Rothe, E. M., Pumariega, A. J., & Sabagh, D. (2011). Identity and acculturation in immigrant and second generation adolescents. *Adolescent Psychiatry, 1*(1), 72–81.

Sheu, H. B., & Lent, R. W. (2007). Development and initial validation of the Multicultural Counseling Self-Efficacy Scale—Racial Diversity Form. *Psychotherapy: Theory, Research, Practice, Training, 44*(1), 30–45.

Sheu, H. B., Rigali-Oiler, M., & Lent, R. W. (2012). Multicultural Counseling Self-Efficacy Scale—Racial Diversity Form: Factor structure and test of a social cognitive model. *Psychotherapy Research, 22*(5), 527–542.

Shin, J. K. (2002). Help-seeking behaviors by Korean immigrants for depression. *Issues in Mental Health Nursing, 23*, 461–476.

Valencia-Garcia, D., Simoni, J. M., Alegría, M., & Takeuchi, D. T. (2012). Social capital, acculturation, mental health, and perceived access to services among Mexican American women. *Journal of Consulting and Clinical Psychology, 80*(2), 177–185.

# CHAPTER 34

# SUPERVISING FOREIGN-BORN CLINICIANS IN THE UNITED STATES

Senem Zeytinoglu, Yudum Akyil, and Karni Kissil

## Introduction

Clinicians have been encouraged to increase awareness of their own sociocultural contexts (e.g., race, gender, age) to better connect with their clients and to promote personal and professional growth (Bula, 2000). Although extant literature has addressed many of these contextual dimensions (e.g., Brown, 1994), the influence of being an immigrant on a clinician's clinical work has received very little attention. Foreign-born clinicians lack awareness of how their immigration and acculturation experiences impact their professional lives (Basker & Dominguez, 1984). This chapter provides a clinical guide for foreign-born clinicians and their supervisors for increasing awareness of the ways that immigration and acculturation experiences may impact their professional work.

## Rationale

Immigration and acculturation can have profound effects on multiple domains, such as social status, economic stability, family dynamics, and support systems. Available studies suggest that for foreign-born clinicians, the cultural transition to the United States is experienced as a change to their sense of self and to interactions with their environment (Isaacson, 2002; Mittal & Wieling, 2006). Most studies with immigrant clinicians (usually international counseling trainees) tend to focus on the negative aspects of being a foreigner, such as language difficulties (Morris & Lee, 2004; Nilsson & Dodds, 2006). However, foreign-born clinicians also bring unique positive assets to their clinical work. For example, because of their intimate experiences with at least two cultures and their struggles making sense of and integrating multiple realities, immigrant clinicians are in a privileged position to develop a metaperspective about culture (Kissil, Niño, & Davey, 2013). By *metaperspective*, we refer to the possibility of looking at cultures from the outside and becoming aware of cultures as dynamic human creations. An immigrant clinician can offer American clients an alternative viewpoint (Cheng & Lo, 1991) and might be able to see the culturally bound character of values and social expectations. This might translate into a more flexible, less culturally encapsulated (Cheng & Lo, 1991), and less judgmental approach to therapy.

In addition, foreign-born clinicians can take advantage of their experiences with being an outsider. Immigrant clinicians can use these intense feelings of otherness to better connect with clients who also share experiences of disenfranchisement or marginalization in the United States (Isaacson, 2002; Tosone, 2005). By increasing immigrant clinicians' awareness of these experiences of being the "other," they can learn to harness it to their therapeutic advantage (Kissil et al., 2013).

As foreign-born clinicians become aware of what they bring to the therapy room, including their experiences of immigration and acculturation to the United States, the possibility increases for these clinicians to effectively use all of their multicultural attributes to create optimal therapeutic relationships (Aponte et al., 2009; Bula, 2000). Thus, our clinical guide aims to increase foreign-born clinicians' awareness of their immigration and acculturation experiences, as well as the impact of these experiences on their professional selves. For this purpose, foreign-born clinicians need to develop a comprehensive understanding of the structure, rules, and meanings attached to their own cultures-of-origin, as well as an understanding of their immigration experiences, in order to see the impacts on their therapeutic work.

# Activity Instructions

This activity is designed for clinical supervisors to conduct with their foreign-born supervisees in individual supervision settings; therefore, these instructions are directed specifically to supervisors. As a note, supervisors working with foreign-born clinicians should also work to keep a nonjudgmental attitude, to validate the supervisees' experiences of being an outsider, and to build on the supervisees' strengths. Furthermore, in order to serve supervisees more effectively, supervisors should become more knowledgeable about identity development, acculturation, and the effects of immigration on clinicians' personal and professional identities (Isaacson, 2002). Supervisors can also recommend literature about immigration and the processes involved to their supervisees, which can be validating and normalizing for immigrant clinicians. Examples of such literature can be found in the Additional Resources section of this chapter. If supervisees are going through an especially turbulent time because of the immigration experience, or for any other reason, supervisors should be ready to refer the supervisees to focused counseling.

This activity consists of three steps. The length of time each step takes depends on the frequency of supervision sessions and the depth to which the supervisors and supervisees agree to work on each area. Throughout the supervision process, it is crucial to pay attention to the supervisee's anxieties about working with clients from the dominant culture, which would hinder the supervisee from being emotionally and cognitively present during the session.

## Step 1: Cultural Genogram

The supervisee constructs and presents a personal cultural genogram to gain a better understanding of his or her culture-of-origin and how it impacts personal and professional identity (for specifics on constructing a cultural genogram, see Hardy & Laszloffy, 1995). The cultural genogram process consists of three stages: (1) preparation and construction, (2) presentation and interpretation, and (3) synthesis. While preparing the cultural genogram, the supervisee focuses on the organizing principles as well as pride and shame issues in his or her culture-of-origin. During the presentations, supervisors help supervisees to understand how these issues impact their own family dynamics and to explore any differences between the family-of-origin and culture-of-origin on these issues. Supervisors should attend to the shame issues with care and persistence, because these issues are especially difficult to identify as a result of possible discomfort and pain, which might cause anxiety and reactivity. Lastly, the supervisee explores how the culture-of-origin impacts the clinician. It is strongly recommended that the supervisor construct a cultural genogram beforehand to be aware of what he or she brings to the supervision process.

## Step 2: The Immigration Experience

Supervisors meet one-on-one with supervisees to discuss their immigration experiences. Supervisors can use the Immigration Experience Questionnaire (Table 34.1) as a guide but should focus on the areas that resonate most with the supervisees. If the supervisor is an immigrant, it is crucial to maintain an awareness of the immigration experience and how it has impacted identity development (personal and professional) in order to better connect with supervisees.

## Step 3: Supervision Session

Both supervisor and supervisee should watch a tape that the supervisee has recorded while working with a client family. They then can discuss how the supervisee's immigration and culture-of-origin experiences impact their relationship to the client family. Supervisors and supervisees should also reflect on the therapy process and discuss any areas where the supervisee can adapt, as a foreign-born clinician, to more fully address the needs of clients.

Example                                                                                              235

Table 34.1
Immigration
Experience
Questionnaire

1.  What has been the best thing about your immigrant experience?

2.  What has been the most challenging or difficult aspect of your immigrant experience?

3.  Do you feel that people in American culture appreciate immigrants?

4.  How do you think your culture and/or immigration experience may affect the way you work with families?

5.  What can you bring from your culture that will help the families you work with?

6.  What may be a challenge for you in working with American families?

7.  What was your day-to-day life like in your former country? How does that experience compare to your day-to-day experience now in the United States?

8.  What were the specific circumstances that brought you to the United States? Was it a personal decision to immigrate or one that someone else made for you?

9.  Explain any language barriers that you experience/or currently experience.

10. Did you feel any culture shock? Was it hard to adapt? If so, what challenges did you face? Can you think of a story or experience that will illustrate these challenges?

Adapted from the American Immigration Council. Reprinted with permission.

# Example

The experience of one of the authors (YA), a marriage and family therapy master's student from Istanbul, best shows the impact of the supervision sessions for a foreign-born clinician.

*I (YA) immigrated to the United States at the age of 29 from Istanbul, Turkey, with my husband and 2-year-old son, and enrolled in a marriage and family therapy master's program. As an intern, I worked for a nonprofit agency doing home-based family therapy with African-American, Anglo-American, and Irish-American families. Before I started my internship, I had a lot of anxiety regarding how I would relate to families from a culture that I knew very little about. I had to be cautious with my questions and interventions. What would they think about my accent? What if I said something wrong? Could I really understand their perspective? In the beginning, I felt like I was walking on eggshells. My supervisor/co-therapist was like a cultural guide to me and answered my questions such as "Do we take off our shoes when going in the family's home?"*

*Working with adolescents and parents was challenging at first. I admired their ability to communicate with each other directly and the sense of equality in their interactions. On the other hand, I was stunned with how much independence and responsibility the adolescents had. The future expectation for the adolescent to move out of the home was a frequent topic in the American families, whereas most Turkish adolescents stay with their parents until they get married.*

*I observed that Anglo-American families have extensive means to verbally communicate their affection. They said they loved each other, and they used verbal reinforcements such as "good job," "way to go," or "I'm proud of you." Conversely, Turkish parents show affection nonverbally. Mothers use physical affection (hugs and kisses), even when the children reach adolescence or adulthood, and they cook and clean for their children. Fathers usually are more distant; they express love by providing for their children and by taking them places.*

*All of these experiences and many more taught me a lot about the dominant culture in the United States and about my own culture. I gradually became aware of how my cultural background affected my expectations about how family members should relate to one another—particularly in terms of assigned roles and responsibilities. I tried to explore how my cultural values impacted my relationships with my clients, and how they shaped the questions I asked or didn't ask. At first I really struggled with understanding and responding to the differences, and I even tried to ignore my own values. I tried to learn the best ways to approach my work as a clinician by reading textbooks and by consulting with my supervisors and colleagues. I thought that bringing my values into my work with American families would be inappropriate, unhelpful, or even damaging.*

*However, discussing my immigration experience with my supervisors and preparing my cultural genogram gave me an opportunity to better grasp my experiences, understand the influence of my culture-of-origin, appreciate my background, and see the values and assets that I can bring into my clinical practice with American families. Coming from a collectivistic culture, I had an easier time noting parent–child disconnection (especially between mothers and daughters) than a clinician from an individualistic culture would have. My interventions were also geared more toward repairing broken bonds than restructuring the boundaries or setting rules. Coming from a culture and family that emphasized nonverbal communication of love, I encouraged hugging more than saying that they loved each other.*

*By giving me a voice to talk about my immigration experience, my supervisors helped me to integrate my personal self as an immigrant woman with my professional self as a family clinician. Through this process, I discovered that, if used properly, my values and experiences could provide useful tools for assessment and intervention. With time and experience, I started to see the similarities between the families and myself, which helped lower my anxiety. For example, with some families, we both had an immigration experience, food was an important component of our cultures, and we both had very close ties with our extended families. Feeling less anxious, I started to make jokes about my accent or asked them to repeat a phrase if I did not understand. Today, when I look back, I see that coming from a different culture and feeling some anxiety about misinterpreting my clients may have even helped me become more curious about their realities, be tentative in conceptualizing their problems, and have a less hierarchical relationship with them. These are therapeutic values that I still carry with me after returning to my country of origin.*

# Measuring Progress

The supervisee's comfort level when working with clients from different backgrounds is the most significant indicator of progress. With the help of these activities, the supervisee is expected to be more in tune with personal reactions toward the clients stemming from cultural differences, to have a better understanding of his or her roots, and to be able to use his or her culture-of-origin as a tool for intervention. Supervisors and supervisees can watch the supervisee's session recordings and discuss the key points that indicate growth and areas in need of improvement. The supervisor and supervisee can also use various items from the International Student Supervision Scale (Nilsson & Dodds, 2006) as a guide for discussions about the key issues.

# Conclusion

When the implications of being an immigrant clinician are discussed, they are usually viewed as problematic (Mittal & Wieling, 2006). However, we suggest that the psychotherapy field pay closer attention not only to the challenges but also to the advantages that immigrant clinicians can bring to the therapeutic process. In clinical settings where "otherness" may be perceived as a deficiency, this activity helps foreign-born clinicians learn to see their otherness as a positive asset in their clinical work, where their values and experiences can serve as useful tools in their clinical practice.

# Additional Resources

Killian, K. D., & Hardy, K. V. (1998). Commitment to ethnic minority inclusion: A study of AAMFT conference program content and members' perceptions. *Journal of Marital and Family Therapy, 24*(2), 207–223.

Rastogi, M., & Wieling, E. (2004). *Voices of color: First-person accounts of ethnic minority therapists.* Thousand Oaks, CA: Sage.

# References

American Immigration Council. (n.d.). An immigrant's experience. Retrieved from www.ailf .org/teach/lessonplans/m6_animmigrantsexperience.pdf

Aponte, H. J., Powell, F. D., Brooks, S., Watson, M. F., Litzke, C., Lawless, J., & Johnson, E. (2009). Training the person of the therapist in an academic setting. *Journal of Marital and Family Therapy, 35,* 381–394.

Basker, E., & Dominguez, V. R. (1984). Limits of cultural awareness: The immigrant as therapist. *Human Relations, 37*, 693–719.

Brown, L. S. (1994). *Subversive dialogues: Theory in feminist therapy*. New York, NY: Basic Books.

Bula, J. F. (2000). Use of the multicultural self for effective practice. In M. Baldwin (Ed.), *The use of self in therapy* (pp. 167–189). New York, NY: Hartford Press.

Cheng, L. Y., & Lo, H. (1991). On the advantages of cross-culture psychotherapy: The minority therapists/mainstream patient dyad. *Psychiatry, 54*, 386–396.

Hardy, K., & Laszloffy, T. (1995). The cultural genogram: A key to training culturally competent family therapists. *Journal of Marital and Family Therapy, 21*, 227–237.

Isaacson, E. (2002). The effect of evolving cultural identities on the experience of immigrant therapist [Abstract]. *Dissertation Abstracts International: Section B: The Sciences and Engineering, 63*(5-B), 2586.

Kissil, K., Niño, A., & Davey, M. (2013). Doing therapy in a foreign land: When the therapist is "not from here." *American Journal of Family Therapy, 41*(2), 134–147.

Mittal, M., & Wieling, E. (2006). Training experiences of international doctoral students in marriage and family therapy. *Journal of Marital and Family Therapy, 32*, 369–383.

Morris, J., & Lee, Y. (2004). Issues of language and culture in family therapy training. *Contemporary Family Therapy, 26*, 307–318.

Nilsson, J. E., & Dodds, A. K. (2006). A pilot phase in the development of the international student supervision scale. *Journal of Multicultural Counseling and Development, 34*(1), 50–62.

Tosone, C. (2005). The *guijin* therapist and the nature of therapeutic truth: A relational perspective. *Clinical Social Work Journal, 33*, 9–19.

# CHAPTER 35

# Challenging Heterosexual and Cisgender Privilege in Clinical Supervision

Monique D. Walker and Ana M. Hernandez

## Introduction

This chapter describes a training exercise to help student clinicians develop and maintain cultural humility and self-awareness while working clinically with lesbian, gay, bisexual, trans,*[1] and queer (LGBTQ) clients. Although this exercise was intentionally written for the supervisor–supervisee relationship, it also has implications for clinical training in a broader capacity. Our hope is that this exercise will challenge supervisees to engage in a self-reflexive process—*looking within*—to facilitate the exploration of their own personal beliefs, attitudes, biases, assumptions, and values about sexual orientation and gender identity.

## Rationale

The term *cultural competence* has been overused within the psychotherapy field and has been the subject of much critique. Thus, the term may be losing some of its relevance, as there continues to be a lack of consensus about its definition. Cultural competence is not something that is *obtained* because there is no *endpoint* where one *becomes* 100% culturally competent (Sue, 1998; Tervalon & Murray-Garcia, 1998). Historically, the construct of cultural competence has primarily focused on racial/ethnic minority and cross-cultural populations, and it is only in the last decade that sexual orientation and gender identity have been recognized as critical components for developing cultural competency and awareness (Bidell, 2012). In this chapter, we use the term *cultural humility* to describe the following:

- "The belief that people should not only appreciate and recognize other cultural groups but also be able to effectively work with them" (Sue, 1998, p. 440)

- "Unrelenting curios[ity] not just about the influence of their families of origin on their work but also about the influences of gender, race, religion, class, [sexuality, and gender identity]" … and the "accepted understanding of training that clinical interactions are always cross-cultural interactions between the therapist's self, context, and heritage and those of the client" (Hardy & McGoldrick, 2008, p. 448)

- "Awareness of one's own values, attitudes, and biases, with the goal of understanding and recognizing how these are likely to affect clients who are not of your culture" (Lee & Everett, 2004, p. 88)

---

1.  It is important to make the following caveat to explain the use of *trans* with an asterisk (trans*) and to address a perceived lack of attention to trans* communities. *Trans** is an umbrella term referring to all of the non-cisgender identities within the gender identity spectrum, including transgender, transsexual, transvestite, genderqueer, genderfluid, non-binary, genderless, agender, non-gendered, bigender, third gender, two-spirit, and trans man and trans woman. Some of the ideas and frameworks that are used to shape this chapter are not explicitly inclusive of language identifying trans* individuals and experiences. We have attempted, in the best way possible, to intentionally speak to issues about gender identity and cisgender privilege where applicable but also to respect that gender identity is a construct distinctly different from sexual orientation.

We know that harm can occur when clinicians provide clinical care without an awareness of their own culture and their clients' cultures or without an awareness of how their own personal beliefs, attitudes, biases, assumptions, and values inform their therapeutic practices (Aponte, 1994; Aponte & Carlsen, 2009; Aponte et al., 2009; Cheon & Murphy, 2007; Hardy & Laszloffy, 1995; Hardy & McGoldrick, 2008; Timm & Blow, 1993; Watson, 1993). The same is true of a lack of self-awareness about sexual orientation and gender identity issues. Gender identity and sexual orientation are part of the cultural reality of LGBTQ and heterosexual individuals. Although the nature of gender identity and sexual orientation among heterosexuals is not often discussed, heterosexual individuals' sexual orientation (heterosexual) and gender identity (usually cisgender, meaning one identifies with one's birth-assigned gender, and gender conforming) are informed by society in the same way that nonheterosexual and trans* or gender-nonconforming (those whose gender presentation does not conform with societal expectations or is considered atypical) individuals' identities are informed (Blumer, Green, Knowles, & Williams, 2012).

Supervisees, like their clients, are socialized within the dominant heterosexual discourse of assumed heterosexuality, cisgender identity, and gender conformity until proven otherwise. Additionally, many unquestioned truths have been developed and often applied to individuals even before they are given the opportunity to develop their own truths. For example, some parents believe that having a little girl means that she will like dresses and dolls, develop feminine characteristics, and date boys, among other assumed truths. It is important that supervisees are able to address and understand their own beliefs, attitudes, biases, assumptions, and values related to sexual orientation and gender identity, which can help facilitate a healthier and deeper connection to diverse clients in therapy. Becoming familiar with the following terms can help increase supervisees' understanding of LGBTQ communities and will help challenge some of the myths and assumptions associated with them (see GLAAD, 2010, and Killermann, 2013, for a more comprehensive, but not exhaustive, list of terms):

- *Transgender* (Trans*): Individuals whose inner or psychological self (or gender identity) differs from the social expectations for the biological sex they were born with. Trans* can also be understood as an umbrella term for transsexuals, cross-dressers (transvestites), transgenderists, gender queers, and people who identify as neither female nor male and/or as neither a man or a woman. It is important to note that trans* is not a sexual orientation; trans* individuals vary in their sexual orientations, which are not necessarily based on their gender identities.

- *Gender Nonconforming* (GNC): Individuals who display gender traits that are not normatively associated with their biological sex (e.g., "feminine" behavior or appearance in a male or "masculine" behavior or appearance in a female).

- *Cisgender*: Individuals who, in large part, identify as the gender they were assigned at birth or, in other words, individuals whose biological sex matches their gender identity and expression, which results in others accurately perceiving their gender (the root word *cis* is Latin for "on the near side of," which is the opposite of *trans*).

- *Heterosexual Privilege*: The unearned rights, benefits, and advantages individuals receive solely because of their heterosexual orientation. It refers to individuals who *do not* have to consider their sexuality and have the freedom to publicly express their sexuality without fear or concerns about repercussions.

- *Cisgender Privilege*: The benefits individuals receive from having an assigned identity that matches their perceived gender identity. Cisgender privileges, in large part, are things that most people do not have to think about on a daily basis and that are enjoyed without awareness that they are privileges.

For clinicians and supervisees who are heterosexual and cisgender, understanding these terms and being aware of one's own heterosexual and cisgender privileges are important first steps for effectively and non-judgmentally working with LGBTQ individuals in therapy. Many of these terms and constructs are seldom addressed in family therapy literature or research; however, in the last decade this has begun to change (see Bigner & Wetchler, 2012; Blumer et al., 2012; Carlson, McGeorge, & Toomey, 2013; Hartwell, Serovich, Grafsky, & Kerr, 2012; Henke, Carlson, & McGeorge, 2009; Rock, Carlson, & McGeorge, 2010).

# Activity Instructions

This activity was developed to help supervisees explore their own personal beliefs, attitudes, biases, assumptions, values, and behaviors about sexual orientation and gender identity, as well as to begin a discussion about these topics within the context of clinical supervision. Before starting this activity, supervisors should first discuss the topic with supervisees and introduce some basic information about working with LGBTQ clients, including reviewing key terms and their definitions. In order for this self-awareness activity to be effective, the supervisor must first establish a safe and nonjudgmental training environment. Supervisees should also be willing to challenge themselves and to be challenged by their supervisors (and, if applicable, by fellow supervisees) and be willing to engage in a process of self-reflection.

Although this activity is primarily intended for clinicians who identify as heterosexual and/or cisgender, nonheterosexual and trans* clinicians may also benefit from completing this activity. Ideally, this activity should be completed by graduate student clinicians who are in their second year of coursework, have begun seeing clients, and demonstrate the ability to be introspective, to challenge themselves, and to be challenged by others. Supervisees should also have at least a basic understanding of terms, topics, and issues related to sexual orientation and gender identity. Supervisors can assign readings from the Additional Resources list in order to help supervisees develop a basic understanding of terms, topics, and relevant issues.

The activity includes completing an assessment checklist and then writing a reflection paper, which should be assigned by a supervisor as part of a training exercise, class requirement, or workshop. This activity works best when conducted in a class or group supervision setting; therefore, the instructions are written for supervisors. This activity is best done in a small (four to eight supervisees) class or group supervision setting to help supervisees become self-reflexive and to facilitate constructive dialogue among peers. This environment may be more difficult to achieve as class or group size increases. During the discussion, supervisors should be aware of the atmosphere in the room, and be sure to maintain safety, and respond to comments or actions that may threaten the safety of particular supervisees or the group. It is important that each supervisee feel free to express any thoughts and feelings in a genuine, authentic manner and in a supportive training context as opposed to one of criticism or shaming.

In order to create a safe space for supervisees in both individual and group settings, the supervisor should validate the supervisee's level of openness and identify therapeutic strengths and resiliency factors for each supervisee. The supervisor can respectfully challenge supervisees by maintaining a stance of nonjudgmental curiosity and asking questions like "What does it mean to/to be … ?" and "How does it impact your therapeutic relationship?" In a group setting, the supervisor can model empathy, validation, and respectful challenging to assist the supervisees in having an in-depth discussion on the topics.

## The Assessment Checklist

Supervisees should first complete the assessment checklist (see Table 35.1). The primary purpose of this checklist is (a) to assess for awareness of one's personal beliefs, attitudes, biases, assumptions, and values regarding sexual orientation and gender identity; and (b) to assess for one's heterosexual and cisgender privileges. Completing the checklist should take no more than 10 minutes, so supervisors should give trainees about 5 to 10 minutes to first complete the checklist and instruct supervisees to do so individually and without discussing it with others in the group. After all supervisees have completed their individual checklists, the supervisor can initiate a class discussion about their responses on the checklist, ensuring that group members feel safe. There is no answer key for the checklist, because the purpose is to help supervisees consider their own attitudes based on responses to the checklist. This also means that there are no "correct" or "incorrect" answers for the checklist, and supervisees' responses are meant to invite them to reflect on experiences that they may not have previously considered and to invite an open dialogue about what other people may have experienced in their lives.

If the class or group supervision size is larger than eight student clinicians, it might be helpful to slightly adapt the activity by selecting (either through self-selection or supervisor's selection) four to eight volunteers to share their reflections with the larger class, allowing for ample time for class discussion and for the entire class to still be engaged in the dialogue. Another adaptation

**Table 35.1**
**Heterosexual and Cisgender Privilege Assessment Checklist**

Please consider the statements below and check YES or NO as appropriate. The purpose of this checklist is to conduct a self-assessment of one's own heterosexual and cisgender privilege, thus there are no "correct" or "incorrect" answers or a scoring rubric to accompany the checklist.

| | | | |
|---|---|---|---|
| 1. | It's easy for me to recognize lesbian, gay, bisexual, trans*, or queer people. | ☐ Yes | ☐ No |
| 2. | I have never had to suffer by "holding it" and feel safe using public restrooms without fear of verbal abuse, physical intimidation, or arrest. | ☐ Yes | ☐ No |
| 3. | I tend to use phrases such as "that's so gay" and "no homo" for humor. | ☐ Yes | ☐ No |
| 4. | Strangers do not ask to look at my genitals or wonder how I can have sex. | ☐ Yes | ☐ No |
| 5. | When I first meet people, I assume they identify as heterosexual. | ☐ Yes | ☐ No |
| 6. | My validity as a man/woman/human is not based on how much surgery I've had or how well I "pass"; in fact, I don't think about how well I will "pass" when I get dressed. | ☐ Yes | ☐ No |
| 7. | When I see a lesbian/gay couple, I try to figure out which one is the man/woman in the relationship. | ☐ Yes | ☐ No |
| 8. | Strangers call me by the name I provide and don't ask for my "real, given, or birth name" and then assume they have a right to call me by that name. | ☐ Yes | ☐ No |
| 9. | It's easy for me to express concern, warmth, and affection toward LGBTQ people. | ☐ Yes | ☐ No |
| 10. | I freely and thoughtlessly can go to my doctor, emergency room, or other medical professional without feeling like I'm risking my safety or psychological well-being. | ☐ Yes | ☐ No |
| 11. | I feel comfortable asking someone about his or her sexual orientation. | ☐ Yes | ☐ No |
| 12. | My identity is not considered a mental pathology or a diagnosis (e.g., "gender identity disorder") by major psychological and medical establishments. | ☐ Yes | ☐ No |
| 13. | I can discuss sex with LGBTQ people without feeling uncomfortable. | ☐ Yes | ☐ No |
| 14. | I am not required to undergo an extensive psychological evaluation in order to receive basic medical care. | ☐ Yes | ☐ No |
| 15. | I am concerned with social, legal, and policy issues that affect LGBTQ people even if they don't directly affect me. | ☐ Yes | ☐ No |
| 16. | I do not have to defend my right to be a part of lesbian, gay, or queer communities, and LGBTQ people do not try to exclude me from movements to gain political legitimacy for themselves. | ☐ Yes | ☐ No |
| 17. | I can identify more than three strengths associated with being lesbian, gay, bisexual, trans*, or queer. | ☐ Yes | ☐ No |
| 18. | I don't have to remind people over and over to use proper gender pronouns or my chosen/proper name. | ☐ Yes | ☐ No |
| 19. | When talking with LGBTQ people, I always try to keep communication open and honest. | ☐ Yes | ☐ No |
| 20. | I can and do pretend that anatomy and gender are intertwined when having the "boy parts and girl parts" talk with children and don't have to consider its actual complexity. | ☐ Yes | ☐ No |

Adapted and printed with permission from Sam Killermann (2011, 2012), creator of ItsPronouncedMetrosexual.com that may be useful is to have the larger group divide up into several smaller groups, four or five supervisees per group, to first individually complete the checklist. With this adaptation, the small groups are given approximately 15 to 20 minutes to talk to each other after they fill out their individual checklists before coming back together as a larger group to share themes or similarities that may have emerged from the smaller group discussions.

## The Reflection Paper

After supervisees have completed the individual checklist, the supervisor should then ask them to review their responses and write a three- to five-page reflection paper. This paper provides an open-ended forum for supervisees to develop insight about the origins of their identified beliefs, attitudes, biases, assumptions, values, and behaviors. Papers should be submitted to the supervisor and graded or reviewed on the basis of self-reflection, critical thinking, openness, and adherence to the guidelines described as follows. The self-reflection paper should address the following questions:

1.  What are two or three thoughts and/or feelings you identified regarding your own personal beliefs, attitudes, biases, assumptions, values, and behaviors about LGBTQ clients? What do you understand about the origins of these thoughts and/or feelings?

2.  What behaviors or actions do you think may be impeding the development of a healthy, effective therapeutic relationship with LGBTQ clients?

3.  What are two or three concrete and measurable goals you can set to help you work toward changing, modifying, or understanding your personal beliefs, attitudes, biases, assumptions, values, and behaviors that were identified in the checklist?

Supervisees can use the following headings to organize their self-reflection papers:

*   Identifying and understanding the origins of one's beliefs, attitudes, biases, assumptions, values, and behaviors

*   Identifying behaviors or actions that may impede the development of a healthy, effective therapeutic relationship

*   Setting concrete and measurable goals to work toward changing, modifying, or understanding more about one's identified beliefs, attitudes, biases, assumptions, values, and behaviors

These subheadings are presented as suggestions that the supervisor can modify in order to meet more specific needs within respective supervision groups or classes.

# Case Example

Tonya, a first-year master's student, completed the checklist and her reflection paper. The checklist provided a starting point for assessing Tonya's comfort with clinical issues among LGBTQ individuals, couples, and families. In reflecting about her individual responses to the checklist, Tonya first seemed very comfortable with LGBTQ-related issues. Yet while writing her reflection paper, she discovered some uncomfortable thoughts and feelings, such as how she felt about validating their sexual experiences and feelings of disgust upon hearing details of sexual intimacy that challenged her initial comfort level. In the first section of her paper, Tonya identified these thoughts and feelings and stated, "I believe that I need to work on my attitudes regarding my comfort level working with LGBTQ couples and sexual intimacy." Tonya also identified a second issue during her reflection process that she described as "handling my own homophobia with LGBTQ clients." She elaborated on her "struggles to find compassion and respect for those who identify as homosexual while in session with those who do not."

In the second section of her paper and later during her individual supervision session, Tonya and her supervisor continued to process her feelings. Her supervisor responded from a stance of nonjudgmental curiosity about what *homophobia* meant to her and how she experienced it as a barrier for connecting with LGBTQ clients. Tonya and her supervisor also talked about her biases and assumptions about sexual intimacy among LGBTQ couples and identified some underlying feelings of being "grossed out at the thought" of sexual intimacy between LGBTQ couples and "not understanding how [LGBTQ] couples had sex."

In the third section of her paper, Tonya noted that while working with LGBTQ clients, she may need to work a little harder to build rapport and to find points of connection in order to tap into her empathy and allow for moments of transparency within the therapeutic relationship. Tonya's training goal was to address her homophobia and, if appropriate, share her personal reactions with the couple she was currently working with. Tonya also set a personal goal to educate herself about the experiences of some LGBTQ individuals and couples, including their sexual experiences. In addition to asking her clients to share more about their personal stories, Tonya is planning to attend events in her community to socialize more with LGBTQ individuals outside of therapy and to read more about sexuality and intimacy among LGBTQ individuals so she can be more culturally humble.

# Measuring Progress

It is understood that "cultural [humility] in clinical practice is best [measured] not by a discrete endpoint but as a commitment and active engagement in a lifelong process that individuals enter into on an ongoing basis with [clients, supervisors, colleagues, and themselves]" (Tervalon & Murray-Garcia, 1998, p. 118). For this activity, progress can be measured by supervisees' commitment to increase their own knowledge, awareness, and comfort level while working with LGBTQ clients. Ideally, supervisees would be able to more openly discuss the issues they identified in their reflection papers as possible barriers to developing a therapeutic relationship with an LGBTQ client and develop a plan, along with the supervisor, to address the barriers and work on the identified goals in supervision. Ultimately, their progress can be evaluated through continued engagement in the process of increasing their own knowledge, awareness, and comfort. It is important to understand that the development of cultural sensitivity is not an outcome but a process in which supervisees are intentionally engaged throughout supervision and their continued professional development. Finally, measures to assess clinical competence for working with LGBTQ clients are identified in the Additional Resources section.

# Conclusion

Using an LGBTQ-affirmative therapy framework, we understand that non-heterosexual orientations and non-cisgender identities exist and are fluid and naturally occurring gender identities (Kort, 2008). The activity described in this chapter was designed to help increase supervisees' self-awareness of their own beliefs, attitudes, biases, assumptions, values, and behaviors about sexual orientation and gender identity. Supervisees are additionally encouraged to engage in a self-reflexive process to identify their own heterosexual and cisgender privilege. This activity was developed to improve student clinicians' understanding of themselves and help them develop an increased awareness of how their identities influence therapeutic relationships with LGBTQ clients and their families. As Hardy and McGoldrick (2008) suggested, "Who we are as clinicians, trainers, or researchers shapes how we see the world, and the meanings we attach to the world are powerfully shaped by the nuances of culture" (p. 447). Thus, engaging in a process of understanding one's own culture and cultural beliefs—sexual orientation and gender identity—will help clinicians become more effective, aware, and humble in their clinical work.

# Additional Resources

### Clinical Competency and Affirmative Training Assessment Tools

Bidell, M. P. (2005). The sexual orientation counselor competency scale: Assessing attitudes, skills, and knowledge of counselors working with lesbian, gay, and bisexual clients. *Counselor Education and Supervision, 44*(4), 267–279.

Crisp, C. (2006). The gay affirmative practice scale (GAP): A new measure for assessing cultural competence with gay and lesbian clients. *Social Work*, *51*(2), 115–126.

## Suggested Books

Bieschke, K., Perez, R., & DeBord, K. (Eds.). (2007). *Handbook of counseling and psychotherapy with gay, lesbian, bisexual, and transgender clients* (2nd ed). Washington, DC: APA.

Ritter, K. Y., & Terndrup, A. I. (2002). *Handbook of affirmative psychotherapy with lesbians and gay men*. New York, NY: Guilford.

Stone-Fish, L., & Harvey, R. (2005). *Nurturing queer youth: Family therapy transformed*. New York, NY: W. W. Norton.

Whitman, J. S., & Boyd, C. J. (Eds.). (2003). *The therapist's notebook for lesbian, gay, and bisexual clients: Homework, handouts, and activities for use in psychotherapy*. New York, NY: Haworth Clinical Practice Press.

## Suggested Journal Articles

Butler, C. (2009). Sexual and gender minority theory and systemic practice. *Journal of Family Therapy*, *31*, 338–358.

Green, M. S., Murphy, M. J., Blumer, M., & Palmanteer, D. (2009). Marriage and family therapists' comfort level working with gay and lesbian individuals, couples, and families. *American Journal of Family Therapy*, *37*, 159–168.

# References

Aponte, H.J. (1994). How personal can training get? *Journal of Marital and Family Therapy, 20*, 3–15.

Aponte, H. J., & Carlsen, J. C. (2009). An instrument for person-of-the-therapist supervision. *Journal of Marital and Family Therapy*, *35*(4), 395–405.

Aponte, H. J., Powell, F. D., Brooks, S., Watson, M. F., Litzke, C., Lawless, J., & Johnson, E. (2009). Training the person of the therapist in an academic setting. *Journal of Marital and Family Therapy*, *35*(4), 381–394.

Bidell, M. P. (2012). Examining school counseling students' multicultural and sexual orientation competencies through a cross-specialization comparison. *Journal of Counseling and Development*, *90*, 200–207.

Bigner, J. J., & Wetchler, J. L. (2012). *Handbook of LGBT-affirmative couple and family therapy*. New York, NY: Taylor & Francis.

Blumer, M. L. C., Green, M. S., Knowles, S. J., & Williams, A. (2012). Shedding light on thirteen years of darkness: Content analysis of articles pertaining to transgender issues in marriage/couple and family therapy journals. *Journal of Marital and Family Therapy*, *38*, 244–256.

Cheon, H.S. & Murphy, M. (2007). The self-of-the-therapist awakened: Postmodern approaches to the use of self in marriage and family therapy. *Journal of Feminist Family Therapy*, *19*, 1–16,

Carlson, T. S., McGeorge, C. R., & Toomey, R. B. (2012). Establishing the validity of the affirmative training inventory: Assessing the relationship between lesbian, gay, and bisexual affirmative training and students' clinical competence. *Journal of Marital and Family Therapy*, *39*(2), 209–222.

Gay and Lesbian Alliance Against Defamation (GLAAD). (2010, May). *GLAAD media reference guide* (8th ed.). Retrieved from http://www.glaad.org/files/MediaReferenceGuide2010.pdf

Hardy, K. V., & Laszloffy, T. A. (1995). The cultural genogram: Key to training culturally competent family therapists. *Journal of Marital and Family Therapy*, *21*(3), 227–237.

Hardy, K. V., & McGoldrick, M. (2008). Re-visioning training. In K. V. Hardy & M. McGoldrick (Eds.), *Re-visioning family therapy: Race, culture, and gender in clinical practice* (pp. 442–460). New York, NY: Guilford Press.

Hartwell, E. E., Serovich, J. M., Grafsky, E. L., & Kerr, Z. Y. (2012). Coming out of the dark: Content analysis of articles pertaining to gay, lesbian, and bisexual issues in couple and family therapy journals. *Journal of Marital and Family Therapy, 38*, 227–243.

Henke, T., Carlson, T. S., & McGeorge, C. R. (2009). Homophobia and clinical competency: An exploration of couple and family therapists' beliefs. *Journal of Couple & Relationship Therapy: Innovations in Clinical and Educational Interventions, 8*(4), 325–242.

Killermann, S. (2011, November). 30+ examples of cisgender privilege. [Web log post]. Retrieved from http://itspronouncedmetrosexual.com/2011/11/list-of-cisgender-privileges/

Killermann, S. (2012, January). 30+ examples of heterosexual privilege in the US. [Web log post]. Retrieved from http://itspronouncedmetrosexual.com/2012/01/29-examples-of-heterosexual-privilege/

Killermann, S (2013, January). Comprehensive list of LGBTQ+ term definitions. [Web log post]. Retrieved from http://itspronouncedmetrosexual.com/2013/01/a-comprehensive-list-of-lgbtq-term-definitions/

Kort, J. (2008). *Gay affirmative therapy for the straight clinician: The essential guide*. New York, NY: W. W. Norton & Company.

Lee, R. E., & Everett, C. A. (2004). *The integrative family therapy supervisor: A primer*. New York, NY: Brunner-Routledge.

Rock, M., Carlson, T. S., & McGeorge, C. R. (2010). Does affirmative training matter? Assessing CFT students' beliefs about sexual orientation and their level of affirmative training. *Journal of Marital and Family Therapy, 36*(2), 171–184.

Sue, S. (1998). In search of cultural competence in psychotherapy and counseling. *American Psychologist, 53*(4), 440–448.

Tervalon, M., & Murray-Garcia, J. (1998). Cultural humility versus cultural competence: A critical distinction in defining physician training outcomes in multicultural education. *Journal of Health Care for the Poor and Underserved, 9*(2), 117–125.

Timm, T. M., & Blow, A. J. (1993). Self-of-the-therapist work: A balance between removing restraints and identifying resources. *Contemporary Family Therapy, 21*(3), 331–351.

Watson, M. F. (1993). Supervising the person of the therapist: Issues, challenges and dilemmas. *Contemporary Family Therapy, 15*, 21–31.

# CHAPTER 36

# Exploring Perceptions of LGBTQ Individuals and Couples

Bethany Luna, Cody Heath, Anna Andrews,
Sara A. Smock Jordan, and Monica Higgins

## Introduction

The purpose of this chapter is to help dispel myths about lesbian, gay, bisexual, transgender, and queer (LGBTQ) individuals and their romantic relationships. Clinicians with a greater awareness of same-sex, bisexual, and transgendered relationships will improve the mental health services of this marginalized population by better attending to the unique needs of this community. Through experiential exercises, heterosexist and heteronormative assumptions will be challenged for both new and experienced clinicians alike.

## Rationale

The devastating effects of stereotypes and assumptions about LGBTQ clients have been shown to put this population at a greater risk for mental health concerns (Cochran, Mays, & Sullivan, 2003). Furthermore, studies indicate that providers may approach LGBTQ clients regarding their sexual or reproductive health in disrespectful, heterosexist, and homophobic ways (Platzer & James, 2000). Other studies reveal that sexual orientation microaggressions (e.g., overt heterosexism) have detrimental effects on LGBTQ clients and on the quality of the therapeutic relationship (Shelton & Delgado-Romero, 2011). It is detrimental for LGBTQ individuals who are undergoing therapy to work with a clinician who is unaware of his or her own heterosexist, heteronormative, and/or heterocentric biases (Israel, Gorcheva, Burnes, & Walther, 2008; McGeorge & Carlson, 2011). Israel and colleagues (2008) report that LGBTQ clients most commonly experienced rejection, dissatisfaction, betrayal, hopelessness, and frustration in therapy.

The primary objective of this chapter is to help clinicians examine and address their conscious/unconscious biases toward the LGBTQ population. Accordingly, a better understanding of one's biases should help reduce the detrimental effects of heterosexism, heteronormativity, and/or heterocentric biases on LGBTQ clients, improving the effectiveness of therapy and the therapeutic alliance (Israel et al., 2008).

## Activity Instructions

This three-part activity was developed for graduate-level clinicians but can also be applied to more senior clinical professionals. No prior knowledge of issues specific to LGBTQ communities is required on the part of participants; however, facilitators should be aware of issues facing the LGBTQ population (e.g., the coming-out process, internalized homophobia) and should be self-aware of their own sexual and gender biases. Facilitators should prepare in several other ways before leading the activity, including working with LGBTQ clients, receiving LGBTQ-specific training, and carefully reviewing the available literature (see Additional Resources list).

These exercises are meant to be challenging and thoughtful, not harmful or unbearable for participants. Individuals who are struggling with sexual or gender identity may experience some discomfort in the course of this activity. The facilitator should note at the beginning of the activity that he or she will be available to talk to individuals privately to help them process any concerns. In addition, the facilitator should provide LGBTQ-friendly clinician referrals.

Response Letter

Before beginning the exercise, the facilitator should prepare small strips of paper (one for each participant), each displaying one of the following descriptions of sexual and gender identities: (a) your family member is attracted to both sexes; (b) your family member is attracted to the same sex; (c) your family member feels like a woman trapped in a man's body (for men) or your family member feels like a man trapped in a woman's body (for women); (d) your family member is not sexually attracted to either sex. There should be equal numbers of each statement for the participants (e.g., if there are 20 participants, each of the four statements should appear five times).

When the facilitator is ready to begin the activity, he or she should put the strips of paper into a hat and have each person take one. A 15- to 20-minute time period should be allotted to this part of the activity. Once each person has a strip of paper, the facilitator should read the following instructions:

*First, select a family member who is important to you. It can be anyone in your family. Now imagine that this family member has just told you that he or she has come out about his or her sexual orientation or gender identity. This identity is based on the description on the piece of paper you select; for example, if you choose your father and the paper says "Your family member is attracted to the same sex," imagine that your father has just told you that he is gay. You are now to write a letter to the family member that you selected and share your thoughts and attitudes about this revelation. These attitudes and beliefs may come from your culture, ethnicity, gender bias, family values, and/or religion.*

*Be sure to describe if or how you will include this important family member in your family life, if or how you will accept their partner, and any other questions you might have for them about children, spirituality/religion, gender roles, and so forth. Try to include three to five questions or thoughts in your response letter.*

LGBTQ Quiz

Once the letters are finished, facilitators should introduce the LGBTQ Quiz (Table 36.1), asking participants to mark the answer based on their personal clinical perspectives. The facilitator should encourage participants to answer honestly and openly. Facilitators should also explain that we are often unaware of our thoughts and feelings toward others and that the quiz is designed to assist in identifying conscious and unconscious biases.

Once participants are finished, the facilitator should then go over the following answers (and explanations) to the quiz. During the review of answers, it is important that the facilitator monitor the group closely and strongly encourage participants to be respectful of others' perspectives. Facilitators should note that all answers are considered as LGBTQ-affirming and that participants are likely to differ with one or more of the responses. It is important to support group safety and to allow participants to fully disclose their thoughts, feelings, and unconscious biases. If conducted in this manner, these unconscious biases can be discussed and challenged safely and securely. If the discussion results in escalation, the facilitator should interrupt and model deescalating behavior by using "I" statements and verbally supporting the opposing views.

1. **False.** The term *alternative lifestyle* is a heteronormative assumption and should be discouraged from clinical use. The term *alternative lifestyle* is an example of a microaggression, which is described as "brief and commonplace daily verbal, behavioral, and environmental indignities, whether intentional or unintentional, that communicate hostile, derogatory, or negative slights" (Sue et al., 2007, p. 271).

2. **False.** Same-sex couples generally come to therapy with similar concerns, such as communication, finances, sex, and parenting (Green & Mitchell, 2008).

| | | | |
|---|---|---|---|
| 1. | Homosexuality is an alternative lifestyle. | ☐ True<br>☐ False | **Table 36.1  LGBTQ Quiz** |
| 2. | Homosexual and heterosexual couples do not present to therapy with similar presenting problems. | ☐ True<br>☐ False | |
| 3. | Staying "in the closet" is easier than coming out for LGBTQ individuals and couples. | ☐ True<br>☐ False | |
| 4. | LGBTQ couples should strive to have traditional male/female roles in their partnership. | ☐ True<br>☐ False | |
| 5. | As clinicians, we should utilize inclusive language (e.g. partner, significant other, transgender) and refrain from using exlusive language (e.g., marital status, wife/husband, transvestite) when conducting therapy with same-sex individuals and couples. | ☐ True<br><br>☐ False | |
| 6. | Therapists should avoid discussing spirituality and religion with LGBTQ individuals and couples. | ☐ True<br>☐ False | |
| 7. | Same-sex couples can have long, committed relationships. | ☐ True<br>☐ False | |
| 8. | Coming out to the family is frightening or dangerous because the LGBTQ person expects their news to evoke a negative response. | ☐ True<br>☐ False | |
| 9. | There are certain norms or preestablished steps someone in the LGBTQ community needs to follow when coming out to their family. | ☐ True<br>☐ False | |
| 10. | Most LGBTQ people handle the tumultuous experience of coming out to their family and are able to maintain powerful, lifelong connections. | ☐ True<br>☐ False | |

Quiz created from ideas found in Bigner and Wetchler (2012) and Mitchell (2012).

3. **False.** Although the coming-out process may be difficult and may cause emotional distress resulting in anxiety and depression, research has supported that LGBTQ youths are more resilient in the face of discrimination when they have family support and uplifting role models (LaSala, 2010).

4. **False.** Again, the term *traditional* represents a heteronormative assumption and should be discouraged from clinical use. Furthermore, applying gender conformity without acknowledging the differences in the LGBTQ community can cause an increase in pathologizing views of same-sex and transgendered couples and individuals (Green, Bettinger, & Zacks, 1996). Clinicians should also keep in mind that the roles assumed by LGBTQ couples are as varied as the couples themselves and should be treated on a case-by-case basis.

5. **True.** Cultural sensitivity is influential in fostering a strong therapeutic relationship. Inclusive language such as *partner*, *significant other*, or *transgender* provides a safe environment for LGBTQ individuals and couples; it also aids in normalizing homosexuality (Burckell & Goldfried, 2006). Exclusive language such as *wife/husband, marriage,* or *transvestite* are microaggressions, which are covert ways of continuing to alienate the clients through discrimination (Sue, 2010).

6. **False.** Rostosky, Johnson, and Riggle (2012) suggest utilizing spirituality and spiritual resources through a strengths-based approach to combat minority stress. More specifically, Rostosky and colleagues (2012, p. 324) state that "understanding the social context of same-sex couples' lives, which includes their religious and spiritual backgrounds and values, is important to facilitating their health and well-being."

7. **True.** No statistics suggest that same-sex couples cannot have fulfilling interpersonal relationships. On the contrary, many same-sex couples are resilient and foster healthy, lasting relationships. At times, same-sex couples report higher relationship satisfaction than do heterosexual couples (Gottman et al., 2003; Green et al., 1996).

8. **True.** Research on LGBTQ individuals' preconceptions of coming out to family shows that these individuals often expect the news of their sexuality to be met with disapproval, anger, and a withdrawal of love (Johnston & Jenkins, 2004).

9. **False.** There are no norms associated with such a personal and emotional process. The process of coming out is unique to each individual and couple and should be assessed on a case-by-case basis (Connelly, 2006).

10. **True.** Research suggests that even though the coming-out process is often difficult, familial relationships typically rebound after the coming-out event, (D'Augelli, 1991; Laird, 1996). In the event that individuals or couples do not experience acceptance from their biological families, it is common for LGBTQ individuals to create families of choice and surround themselves with people who provide the support they need to maintain resiliency against minority stress. In these instances, LGBTQ individuals are still able to foster lifelong, lasting interpersonal relationships (Long & Bonomo, 2006).

Once the answers to the quiz have been read, the facilitator should invite participants to discuss their reactions to and thoughts about the quiz. In the course of the discussion, the facilitator should ask these two follow-up discussion questions: (a) What did this activity help you to learn about LGBTQ individuals and relationships? and (b) How will this information affect you as clinicians and how you work with LGBTQ clients?

## Reflection Paper

The facilitator should then assign participants a reflection paper to address any inconsistencies that they might have between their response letter and the information they learned in the quiz. Specifically, in their reflection papers, participants should answer these questions: (a) How might the inconsistencies between my response letter and information provided in the quiz influence my work in the therapy room with a LGBTQ client? and (b) What are some ways I can work to decrease the negative effects of these inconsistencies?

After completing the reflection paper as a take-home assignment, the group should reconvene. The facilitator should lead an open discussion in which participants discuss what they wrote in their reflection papers. Again, the facilitator should encourage honest and open feedback while being respectful of differing opinions.

# Examples

In the response letter to a family member, most respondents made statements toward their family member that were mindful of the societal implications of their family member's sexual orientation, gender identity, or asexuality. These attentive statements included: "I understand if you were to need to move to a more liberal area of the country to avoid possible conservative community backlash … ", and "I understand finding it difficult because the state will not allow our family to give you a proper wedding." Where family members were identified as being asexual, participants acknowledged that it may be very hard for their family member to understand themselves when compared to those who held a clear same-sex or opposite-sex attraction. The majority of these responses also included awareness regarding the level of difficulty experienced by individuals in "coming out" to family members.

Respondents indicated that the quiz was helpful in increasing their respective knowledge and awareness related to the LGBTQ community. Other participants noted that they were holding contradictory belief statements about LGBTQ individuals. For example, several stated that their religious beliefs deem same-sex or transsexual behaviors to be morally wrong but noted that they were working to maintain nonjudgmental attitudes toward LGBTQ individuals in their clinical work. It was explained by a participant that "not practicing judgment towards anyone has been emphasized in my clinical training despite me possessing religious beliefs that disregard LGBTQ behaviors." Identifying conflicting and intolerant beliefs of clinicians is one of the goals of these exercises.

During the final discussion, some participating LGBTQ clinicians reported heterocentric statements such as "I know this (being gay) is wrong, but I am gay" or "I shouldn't feel like a man, but I do" and other similar statements. These statements represented examples of internalized homophobia, displaying a sense of guilt or shame for being an LGBTQ individual. In general, the letters written to homosexual family members were more developed and thoughtful, whereas letters written to transgender family members were less detailed and more abstract. This may indicate a lack of awareness and understanding of transgendered individuals, which may be linked to a higher incidence of microaggressions and heteronormative bias. However, after discussing the quiz, participants showed an increased ability to use concrete examples to discuss transphobia and the stigma that may be encountered.

Participants also reported an increase in awareness of heteroprivilege and heteronormative interactions. Participants commented that many intake packets do not have inclusive language, and they recommended making changes, such as adding the terms *transgender* and *partnership* (instead of marital status). Many of the participants began discussing ways that they could combat their previous transgender bias and reported a desire to experience working with the LGBTQ population in individual and couple constellations.

# Measuring Progress

Progress with this activity is measured by increased self-awareness and by clinicians responding more sensitively to their LGBTQ clients through avoiding microaggressions and utilizing more inclusive language. This understanding should encourage clinicians to begin to challenge their heteronormative, heterocentric, and heterosexist thoughts and beliefs regarding sexual orientation and gender manifestations of LGBTQ clients (Long & Bonomo, 2006). Progress can also be measured in the desire of clinicians to experience the LGBTQ culture by connecting with culturally competent clinicians and establishing relationships with LGBTQ individuals and couples.

If a participant struggles with the activity, the facilitator is encouraged to provide necessary resources, such as additional readings of relevant literature or a referral for mentorship. Participants recommended the LGBTQ quiz and several readings (see Additional Resources section) as being helpful in aiding their development in this area.

# Conclusion

Clinicians should strive to foster healthy, respectful relationships with their LGBTQ clients. In order to achieve this clinical goal, clinicians must be aware of their own prejudices, biases, and expectations regarding LGBTQ issues. Clinicians must also be aware that their clients may be experiencing internalized homophobia. The exercises introduced in this chapter were developed to help clinicians identify their own conscious and unconscious stereotypes of LGBTQ individuals and couples, as well as identifying the areas where they might need further study (e.g., biases or lack of knowledge about transgendered couples).

# Additional Resources

Bernstein, A. C. (2000). Straight therapists working with lesbians and gays in family therapy. *Journal of Marital and Family Therapy, 26*, 443–454.

Gluth, D. R., & Kiselica, M. S. (1994). Coming out quickly: A brief counseling approach to dealing with gay and lesbian adjustment issues. *Journal of Mental Health Counseling, 16*(2), 163–173.

Potoczniak, D., Crosbie-Burnett, M., & Saltzburg, N. (2009). Experiences regarding coming out to parents among African American, Hispanic, and White gay, lesbian, bisexual, transgender, and questioning adolescents. *Journal of Gay & Lesbian Social Services: Issues in Practice, Policy & Research, 21*(2–3), 189–205.

Reynolds, A. L., & Hanjorgiris, W. F. (2000). Coming out: Lesbian, gay, and bisexual identity development. In R. M. Perez, K. A. DeBord, & K. J. Bieschke (Eds.), *Handbook of counseling and psychotherapy with lesbian, gay, and bisexual clients* (pp. 35–55). Washington, DC: American Psychological Association.

# References

Bigner, J., & Wetchler, J. (Eds). (2012). *Handbook of LGBT Affirmative Therapy*. New York, NY: Routledge.

Burckell, L. A., & Goldfried, M. R. (2006). Therapist qualities preferred by sexual-minority individuals. *Psychotherapy: Theory, Research, Practice, Training, 43*, 32–49.

Cochran, S., Mays, V., & Sullivan, J. (2003). Prevalence of mental disorders, psychological distress, and mental health services use among lesbian, gay, and bisexual adults in the United States. *Journal of Consulting and Clinical Psychology, 71*(1), 53–61.

Connelly, C. (2006). A process of change: The intersection of the GLBT individual and his or her family of origin. In J. Bigner (Ed.), *An introduction to GLBT family studies* (pp. 121–147). New York, NY: Haworth Press.

D'Augelli, A. R. (1991). Gay men in college: Identity processes and adaptations. *Journal of College Student Development, 32*, 140–146.

Gottman, J. M., Levenson, R. W., Gross, J., Frederickson, B. L., McCoy, K., Rosenthal, L., … & Yoshimoto, D. (2003). Correlates of gay and lesbian couples' relationship satisfaction and relationship dissolution. *Journal of Homosexuality, 45*(1), 23–43.

Green, R. J., Bettinger, M., & Zacks, E. (1996). Are lesbian couples fused and gay male couples disengaged? Questioning gender straightjackets. In J. Laird & R. J. Green (Eds.), *Lesbians and gays in couples and families: A handbook for therapists* (pp. 185–230). San Francisco, CA: Jossey-Bass.

Green, R. J., & Mitchell, V. (2008). Gay and lesbian couples in therapy: Minority stress, relational ambiguity, and families of choice. In A. S. Gurman (Ed.), *Clinical handbook of couple therapy* (4th ed., pp. 662–680). New York, NY: Guilford Press.

Israel, T., Gorcheva, R., Burnes, T. R., & Walther, W. A. (2008). Helpful and unhelpful therapy experiences of LGBT clients. *Psychotherapy Research, 18*, 294–305.

Johnston, L., & Jenkins, D. (2004). Coming out in mid-adulthood: Building a new identity. *Journal of Gay & Lesbian Social Services, 16*(2), 19–42.

Laird, J. (1996). Invisible ties: Lesbians and their families of origin. In J. Laird & R. J. Green (Eds.), *Lesbians and gays in couples and families* (pp. 89–122). San Francisco, CA: Jossey-Bass.

LaSala, M. C. (2010). *Coming out, coming home: Helping families adjust to a gay or lesbian child*. New York, NY: Columbia University Press.

Long, J. K., & Bonomo, J. (2006). Revisiting the sexual orientation matrix for supervision: Working with GLBTQ families. *Journal of GLBT Family Studies, 2*(3/4), 151–166.

McGeorge, C., & Carlson, T. S. (2011). Deconstructing heterosexism: Becoming an LGB affirmative heterosexual couple and family therapist. *Journal of Marital & Family Therapy, 37*, 14–26.

Mitchell, V. (2012). Coming out to family: Adrift in a sea of potential meanings. In J. J. Bigner & J. L. Wetchler (Eds.), *Handbook of LGBT affirmative therapy* (pp. 131–148). New York, NY: Routledge.

Platzer, H., & James, T. (2000). Lesbians' experiences of healthcare. *Nursing Times Research, 5*, 194–202.

Rostosky, S. S., Johnson, S. D., & Riggle, E. D. B. (2012). Spirituality and religion in same-sex couples' therapy. In J. J. Bigner & J. L. Wetchler (Eds.), *Handbook of LGBT affirmative therapy* (pp. 313–326). New York, NY: Routledge.

Shelton, K., & Delgado-Romero, E. A. (2011). Sexual orientation microaggressions: The experiences of lesbian, bisexual, and queer clients in psychotherapy. *Journal of Counseling Psychology*, *58*, 210–221.

Sue, D.W., Capodilupo, C.M., Christina, M., Torino, G.C., Bucceri, J.M., Holder, A.M., Nadal, K.L., & Esquilin, M. (2007). Racial microaggressions in everyday life: Implications for clinical practice. *American Psychologist*, *62*, 271–286.

Sue, D. W. (2010). *Microaggressions in everyday life: Race, gender, and sexual orientation.* Hoboken, NJ: Wiley.

# CHAPTER 37

# DISCOVERING COMPASSION FOR VICTIMS OF DOMESTIC VIOLENCE

Lisa Vallie Merchant and Jason B. Whiting

## Introduction

The purpose of this chapter is to increase clinicians' awareness of their attitudes regarding victims who are in violent relationships. Using this activity, clinicians gain understanding of victims' experience within violent and controlling relationships. They will also more fully appreciate why victims stay and will see their own reactions and biases more clearly. This information, in turn, may allow clinicians to better help victims to overcome the barriers that keep them trapped in abusive relationships.

## Rationale

An estimated 10 million men and women experience physical violence with an intimate partner every year, and 33% of women and 25% of men are victims of intimate partner violence (IPV) in their lifetime (Black et al., 2011). Because many of these victims present for clinical services, clinicians must be prepared to work with victims of violence. Being prepared includes an examination of personal attitudes and beliefs, because they will shape clinicians' interventions and interactions with victims (Jackson, Witte, & Petretic-Jackson, 2001). Unfortunately, clinicians may espouse attitudes that blame the victim for the violence.

As clinicians, when we have clients who are in abusive relationships, we can become confused and angry. We may lose sympathy and think *it's her*[1] *fault for staying*. We may try to convince her to leave by playing the expert ("It is only going to get worse" or "He's going to kill you"), imposing guilt and shame ("How bad does it have to get before you leave?" or "He's going to start on the kids next"), and threatening isolation ("I can't help you if you aren't going to help yourself"; Jory, 2004). When we see clients being hurt, it is normal to have strong reactions. Unfortunately, these reactions often lead to interventions that are more about unloading the clinician's anxiety than helping the client. Although these approaches may help clinicians feel like they are "doing something," they are all forms of victim blaming—holding the victim responsible for the abuser's actions.

Victim blaming takes many forms, such as exonerating the perpetrator, faulting the victim's behavior or character, deidentifying with the victim, and minimizing the difficulty and dangerousness of leaving. It is not uncommon for both perpetrators and victims to exonerate the perpetrator by attributing violence to drugs, alcohol, stress, psychopathology, or other external factors (Barnett, Miller-Perrin, & Perrin, 2011; Whiting, Oka, & Fife, 2012). Although it is not inappropriate to explore the role of external factors in creating an environment that is conducive to violence, people are ultimately responsible for their own behavior, and attributing violence to external factors relieves that responsibility (Jenkins, 2009). Exonerating the abuser crosses squarely into victim blaming when we think *she should have known not to argue with him*, or worse, *if she had talked to me like that, I would have hit her, too*. Believing *violence*

---

1. We acknowledge that abuse stretches beyond gender lines; however, because the majority of clients in abusive and controlling relationships are women, we have chosen to focus this activity accordingly (Johnson, 2008).

*can be avoided by giving in* and *flirting with someone else is just asking for it* are other common perpetrator-exonerating/victim-blaming attitudes (Peters, 2008). These attitudes hold victims responsible for preventing violence, insinuate that perpetrators are powerless to control themselves, and condone violence as an acceptable response to conflict.

Furthermore, these beliefs blame violence on the victim's behavior and character. Blaming the victim's character is best exemplified by the belief that *victims unconsciously want to be controlled or dominated* (Peters, 2008). Likewise, pathologizing and labeling a victim as co-dependent or borderline suggests that something is inherently wrong with her that is making her a victim (Grigsby & Hartman, 1997). Less obvious is the belief that *it could never happen to me* or *that doesn't happen in my neighborhood*. Like pathologizing, these beliefs assume that something about the victim makes her a victim, and it minimizes the difficulty of leaving. Thinking *if she goes back and gets hit, it's her own fault* or *if she were really afraid, she would leave* ignore the complexity of the leave/stay decision. These beliefs also overlook the dangerousness of leaving, because women are more likely to be killed or severely beaten by their partners when they are leaving or when they have left in the last year (Campbell et al., 2003).

The idea that most victims do not leave is a myth. Researchers have found that most victims eventually leave, although it may be a process with several comings and goings before leaving for good (see Barnett et al., 2011). Leaving is complicated, and victims hesitate to leave for many reasons. According to the Barrier Model (Grigsby & Hartman, 1997), four layers of barriers prevent victims from leaving: (a) environmental, (b) family and societal expectations, (c) psychological consequences of abuse, and (d) history of childhood abuse and neglect. Environmental barriers include practical concerns such as lack of money, housing, childcare, or a means of support, as well as fear that the perpetrator will take the children. Access to funds has been found to be the strongest predictor of leaving, and such economic dependence, low income, and poverty may prohibit many victims from leaving (Barnett et al., 2011). The family and societal barriers include gender expectations (e.g., a woman is not complete without a husband, or mothers must put their children's needs ahead of their own), pressure from family or clergy to stay in abusive relationships, and personal values and identity. Valuing virtues like forgiveness and commitment, wanting an intact family, or having an identity tied to being a strong and dutiful wife may encourage victims to stay. Psychological barriers, such as posttraumatic stress disorder and depression, may also prevent victims from leaving, as may feelings of isolation or hopelessness. Many of these psychological barriers stem from the violence itself. Finally, victims with a history of childhood abuse and neglect might have learned that violence is normal or may equate abusive behavior, like jealousy, with love (Grigsby & Hartman, 1997).

Jackson, Witte, and Petretic-Jackson (2001) suggest that for clinicians to be effective with victims of intimate partner violence, they must identify and diffuse their own victim blaming attitudes. Not doing so may be detrimental to clients. For example, failing to understand why a victim stays or exonerating the abuser may feed a victim's shame and self-blame (Barnett et al., 2011). These attitudes also inhibit empathy, which is essential to a therapeutic relationship (Drisko, 2004; Patterson, Williams, Grauf-Grounds, & Chamow, 1998). Moreover, curiously questioning our own attitudes facilitates the curious questioning of victims' attitudes (Freedman & Combs, 1996). Asking questions from an open, not-knowing stance invites victims to reflect on their own attitudes and experiences, which can lead to therapeutic change (Freedman & Combs, 1996). Finally, theory informs practice. Our explanations of why victims stay will shape our interventions. If we attribute staying to safety concerns, we may recommend a protective order. If we attribute staying to lack of housing, we may refer victims to a shelter. But if we attribute staying to a defect in the victim, then we may do nothing.

# Activity Instructions

These activities provide a venue for raising and exploring clinicians' attitudes toward victims. Because the purpose of this activity is to simply raise awareness and increase understanding, it is not essential that participants have a certain level of experience or maturity. Even clinicians with extensive domestic violence experience have reported discovering new facets of victim blaming and the leave/stay decision through this process. As such, the activity can be used with clinicians at any skill level. Although it is helpful if the facilitator has some knowledge of violence before administering the activity, having specialized expertise is not required. The facilitator's primary role is to guide the conversation and promote curiosity, openness, and reflection. Given the sensitive nature of the topic, it is essential that the facilitator be open and respectful to the attitudes of the participants as they wrestle with these issues. This approach models the respect that is needed when working with people who have been mistreated in violent relationships.

Because the focus of this activity is the clinicians' attitudes and beliefs, no prior knowledge or readings are required. To encourage discussion, these activities work best in groups with no more than 20 to 30 clinicians and no fewer than five. The entire exercise (all four parts) requires approximately two hours. If time is limited, two vignettes and group interviews can be completed in an hour, with the reflection exercise (Part 4) given as a homework assignment. Because violence is a sensitive topic, clinicians should be informed that participation is voluntary and encouraged to be respectful of one another. Facilitators should introduce the topic and state the objectives of the activity (e.g., to increase awareness of attitudes toward victims, to analyze why victims stay with abusive partners, and to increase effectiveness with victims).

## Part 1: Identifying Attitudes

Share common myths and attitudes about domestic violence and have students respond privately to each attitude. Because the purpose is to identify one's own beliefs, clinicians do not need to share their answers. Explain how each belief either exonerates the perpetrator or blames the victim, and then follow with discussion. Also introduce Johnson's (2008) typology of violence and note how not all violence is abuse. Segue into the next exercise by discussing the beliefs about why victims stay in abusive relationships. The following myths and attitudes are from Peters (2008), with the exception of "all violence is the same" and "all violence is abuse":

- If a woman doesn't like it, she can leave.
- Some women unconsciously want their partners to control them.
- Abusive men lose control so much that they don't know what they're doing.
- Getting drunk can lead a man to hit his wife when he otherwise wouldn't.
- Women who make their partners jealous are just asking for it.
- Domestic violence rarely happens in my neighborhood.
- A lot of domestic violence occurs because women keep on arguing about things with their partners.
- If a woman continues living with a man who beats her, then it's her own fault if she is beaten again.
- All violence is the same.
- All violence is abuse.

## Part 2: Vignettes

Provide participants with copies of the vignettes. Have someone read the first vignette out loud, and then pose the discussion questions to the group. As participants answer the questions, allow for reflection and use circular and reflexive questioning to make attitudes overt and to shift thinking to the victim's perspective. Questions may include "Where do you think he learned that violence was okay?" "Where does her hope come from?" "What role does poverty play?" The following vignettes are based on situations with real-life victims of domestic violence. Each of the women presented has different reasons for staying in an abusive relationship. After reading each story, respond to the questions that follow.

**Emily.** *Emily presents at your office for her initial appointment. She is here to fix her marriage. Her husband, Ed, refuses to come. Emily and Ed have been married for three years. Although their arguments have always been loud and volatile, in the last year their fighting has become more intense. Ed took a new high-stress job, Emily went back to school to work on her nursing degree, and they just found out that Emily is three months' pregnant. Ed has started drinking nightly to relax. Ed complains about Emily's cooking and housekeeping since she went back to school, as well as the financial burden of her education and soon-to-be baby. Emily complains that Ed doesn't help around the house and fears that he no longer cares for her.*

*A couple of months ago, after Ed had a couple of beers, Emily began complaining that Ed wasn't helping her out with the housework. Ed rolled his eyes and went into another room. Emily followed him and kept complaining, but Ed continued to ignore her. Emily became angry and yelled at him, calling him lazy and selfish. Ed became enraged, grabbed her arm, and began screaming in her face that she was a bitch and a nag. Emily tried to pull away from Ed, but couldn't break free of his grip, so she slapped him in the face. Ed slapped her back, knocking her to the floor. Although Ed had no lasting injuries, he left bruises on Emily's face and arm. Afterward, Ed was very apologetic, and over the next couple of weeks he was very helpful around the house.*

### Review questions.

- How do you feel about Emily?

- Could this violence have been prevented? How so?

- What factors led to this argument and the ensuing violence?

- Why do you think Emily slapped Ed? Why did Ed hit her back? How is their violence similar? How is it different?

- What hopes do you think Emily has for her family? What do you think stops Emily from leaving?

- What do you think Emily should do? Should she leave or stay?

- How would you work with Emily?

**Mary.** *This is your fourth session with Mary, who has been seeing you because of depression, low self-esteem, and problems in her marriage with Tim. Prior to this session, Mary has canceled several appointments with little notice. Today, Mary has arrived at the appointment wearing a long-sleeved shirt and heavy makeup, despite outside temperatures in the 80s. During the session, Mary unconsciously pulls at one of her sleeves, revealing what you suspect to be fingerprint bruises on her wrist. You ask about the bruises; Mary stammers and begins to cry. Mary discloses something that she has only told one other person: Tim has an anger problem, and sometimes he loses it and will push, grab, and occasionally hit her. Even when Tim is not angry, he is highly critical and demeaning. She walks on eggshells and goes to great lengths to meet his needs to avoid setting him off. Mary has had thoughts of leaving, but Tim has told her that he will kill her if she tries. Mary has told her preacher, who encouraged her to pray and reminded her of her marital commitment and duty to love and honor her husband. Mary has a college diploma, but she married Tim right out of college and has never worked. They have three small children, and Tim earns six figures a year as the CEO of a well-respected and highly visible local corporation.*

### Review questions.

- How do you feel about Mary?

- What do you think Mary should do?

- Who is responsible for this abuse?

- How difficult will it be for Mary to leave?

- If Mary chooses to stay, what does that say about her?

- What values do you think would inform her decision to stay or leave?

- What religious convictions, emotions, or societal expectations might keep Mary in this relationship? What about her depression? How do you think that affects her decision to leave?

- How does her socioeconomic status or other contextual factors impact how you see her?

- How would you work with Mary?

**Meagan.** *While volunteering at the local domestic violence shelter, you begin working with Meagan, who is staying there with her four children. Meagan has been in and out of the shelter for years. Meagan* *dropped out of school in the eighth grade, is illiterate, and works as a stripper. Currently, she is pregnant with her fifth child and is far enough along in the pregnancy that she can't dance. Meagan has left her boyfriend numerous times but goes back each time, saying that she loves him and that he is a good dad. Invariably, a few months after reuniting with her boyfriend, she returns to the shelter sporting new bruises. The beatings often happen when her boyfriend, who occasionally uses meth, becomes paranoid that she is sleeping with her customers. Meagan is pregnant with her fifth child because her boyfriend says only sluts use birth control, and she is dependent on her boyfriend and his family for caring for the other four children. She says that her boyfriend is a good dad and that he has never raised a hand to their children.*

**Review questions.**

- How do you feel about Meagan?
- What do you think keeps Meagan going back to her boyfriend? What do you think their relationship is like between violent episodes?
- What values do you think keep Meagan in the relationship?
- What steps would Meagan need to take to leave for good?
- What do you think about Meagan being a stripper? How do you think she got into stripping? Do you think that if she chose a different occupation the abuse would stop? What if her boyfriend stopped using meth?
- How would you work with Meagan?

**Part 3: Victim Interview**

Select a volunteer and give her these instructions: "Choose one of the vignettes and imagine that you are the victim portrayed in the story. I am going to interview you. Answer the questions as if you were the victim in the vignette." Ask the questions in the order given. You do not need to probe the clinician's responses, as the purpose is simply to get the clinician to put herself in the victim's shoes. After completing the interview, ask the clinician to comment on her experience and the observing clinicians for their thoughts. Then divide the group into partners and have each clinician be both the victim and the interviewer.

- What was it that first attracted you to him?
- What hopes and dreams did you have for this relationship? For your family?
- When did you first notice that something was wrong?
- What did you think was happening?
- How did you try to make things better?
- When did things get worse?
- Was there anything you could do to make things safe?
- What hurt you most of all? What scared you most of all?
- What keeps you from leaving now?
- What continued hopes do you have for your family?
- What would be most helpful for you right now?

**Part 4: Self-Awareness Reflection**

Provide participants with the instructions in the following paragraph and discuss their conclusions as a group. Final points to reiterate in closing include that violence is complex, that leaving is complicated, and that our job as clinicians is to understand the unique situation of the victim before us. End with a call to shift our thinking from "why doesn't she leave?" to "why does he do it?" "how has she survived so long?" and "how can society respond to prevent it?" (Barnett et al., 2011).

*Reflect on your experience in completing Parts 2 and 3. In the time provided by your instructor, write about what you have learned, what new insights you have gained, or how your perspective has (or hasn't) changed as a result of these exercises. You may either free-write your response or use the following process questions as a guide: (a) What was it like to complete this activity? (b) What insights have you had as a result of these discussions? (c) How would you explain to someone why victims stay in abusive relationships? (d) How would you assess or assist a victim as she was making a leave/stay decision?*

# Example

I (L. M.) used the vignettes most recently in a course on the legal aspects of domestic violence. When I asked if the violence could have been prevented in the case of Emily, some student clinicians pointed out that Emily provoked Ed's violence by nagging and following him. To indicate understanding and to clarify their position, I reflected back, "So, if Emily had approached Ed differently, Ed would not have hit her?" I followed this with pointed questions such as "Should Emily have known that Ed would hit her if she followed him?" and "What should she have done instead?" Faced with the bluntness of these questions, many student clinicians became hesitant in their responses. Others exonerated Ed's violence by noting his stress and drinking. They suggested that if he "just got help," he would not be violent. I reflected back, "So, if Ed hadn't been drinking, he would not have hit Emily? The problem is really Ed's drinking?" followed by "Who here, if you had had a couple of beers, would hit someone you love?" I then pointed out how easily the student clinicians fell into the same trap as many victims: They believed the victim could control the violence by changing her behavior or that the violence was caused by external factors such as drinking or stress.

I also used the discussion to explore the many reasons why victims stay in abusive relationships. For example, in the case of Mary, I asked how her religious beliefs could possibly impact her decision to stay. In addition to the more obvious beliefs, like "wives obey your husbands" and "God hates divorce," one student clinician shared how the adage "God will never give you more than you can handle" had kept a church member in an abusive relationship for many years.

With Meagan, we focused on forgiveness, love, and loneliness. I asked, "Has anyone ever gotten back together with an ex-boyfriend or ex-girlfriend because you missed them, even though a part of you knew it was a terrible idea?" Most student clinicians sheepishly raised their hands. We then discussed what Meagan's boyfriend might say to convince her to come home (e.g., "I stopped using," "You know I love you," "We'll get counseling this time") and what her children might say while living at the shelter (e.g., "I miss daddy," "I don't like it here").

Other factors explored across all of the vignettes included economic, educational, and occupational barriers, fear and safety concerns, hopes and values, and gender expectations. As student clinicians named the various reasons why the victims stayed, I wrote them on a whiteboard. At the end of the activity, student clinicians were able to see how varied, unique, and complicated deciding to leave can be.

After the vignettes, we discussed briefly how the different types of violence (see Johnson, 2008), as well as the different theoretical explanations (see Barnett et al., 2011), might affect staying. I concluded by noting how complicated and individualized leaving and staying can be and had student clinicians complete a five-minute self-awareness writing exercise. Participants reported that the activity broadened their understanding of victims and helped them recognize their attitudes. Several student clinicians wrote that the vignettes were "eye opening" and that they came to "understand on a deeper level the plight of victims." Others commented that the activities were helpful in providing insights "about my biases and the biases of others around me" and led to recognition of "how stereotypes shape my attitudes." From a practical standpoint, one student clinician wrote, "I enjoyed listening to the different perspectives. It reminded me that mine is not the only reality and that I need to slow down and think about many angles." Other student clinicians noted that when working with victims, they would seek to understand the victim's reasons for staying, such as "fear, defeated mentality, lack of resources, children, and value systems (religious and cultural)."

# Measuring Progress

Although the measurement of attitudes is difficult, progress can be assessed using written feedback assignments, or through observation in class, supervision, or practicum. In individual supervision, supervisors can follow up with clinicians about particular clients to help them identify the factors influencing their leave/stay decision. Supervisors should also assess the clinician's frustrations for signs of victim blaming. Signs of progress in session include seeking to understand why victims stay, recognizing and exploring barriers to leaving, normalizing and legitimizing victims' conflicted feelings, and reinforcing perpetrators' responsibility for the violence. Progress is apparent when clinicians ask clients questions out of a genuine curiosity that seeks to understand the victim's position (e.g., "How would you know if he had really changed?" "How does loneliness influence your decision to stay?" "When was the first time you felt afraid to fail?").

Crucial to this process of softening attitudes toward victims is the supervisors' extension of acceptance and understanding to supervisees as they struggle with the issue. Exploring clinician attitudes without judgment is especially important if the clinician has attitudes that are affected by experience with violence (e.g., growing up in a violent home or having been in a violent relationship).

# Conclusion

This activity can help clinicians confront their attitudes and explore the many physical, emotional, personal, and societal factors that affect the leave/stay decision for victims of domestic violence. We have used this activity successfully with a wide range of clinicians—from undergraduate student clinicians with very little exposure to domestic violence to doctoral student clinicians with extensive training in violence and compassion. All in all, participants reported an expanded understanding of victims and the complexity of the leave/stay decision.

# Additional Resource

Hunter, J. (2010). *But he'll change: Ending the thinking that keeps you in abusive relationships.* Center City, MN: Hazelden.

# References

Barnett, O. W., Miller-Perrin, C. L., & Perrin, R. D. (2011). *Family violence across the lifespan* (3rd ed.). Thousand Oaks, CA: Sage.

Black, M. C., Basile, K. C., Breiding, M. J., Smith, S. G., Walters, M. L., Merrick, M. T., Chen, J., & Stevens, M. R. (2011). *The National Intimate Partner and Sexual Violence Survey (NISVS): 2010 Summary Report.* Atlanta, GA: National Center for Injury Prevention and Control, Centers for Disease Control and Prevention.

Campbell, J. C., Kozoil-McLain, J., Webster, D., Block, C. R., Campbell, D. W., Curry, M. A., ... & Wilt, S. A. (2003). Assessing risk factors for intimate partner homicide. *National Institute of Justice Journal, 250,* 14–19.

Drisko, J. W. (2004). Common factors in psychotherapy outcome: Meta-analytic findings and their implications for practice and research. *Families in Society, 85,* 81–90.

Freedman, J., & Combs, G. (1996). *Narrative therapy: The social construction of preferred realities.* New York, NY: W. W. Norton.

Grigsby, N., & Hartman, B. (1997). The barriers model: An integrated strategy for intervention with battered women. *Psychotherapy*, *34*, 485–497.

Jackson, T., Witte, T., & Petretic-Jackson, P. (2001). Intimate partner and acquaintance violence and victim blame: Implications for professionals. *Brief Treatment and Crisis Intervention*, *1*, 153–168.

Jenkins, A. (2009). *Becoming ethical: A parallel, political journey with men who have abused*. Dorset, Great Britain: Russell House.

Johnson, M. P. (2008). *A typology of domestic violence*. Boston, MA: Northeastern University Press.

Jory, B. (2004). The intimate justice scale: An instrument to screen for psychological abuse and physical violence in clinical practice. *Journal of Marital and Family Therapy*, *30*, 29–44.

Patterson, J., Williams, L., Grauf-Grounds, C., & Chamow, L. (1998). Essential skills in family therapy: From the first interview to termination. New York: The Guilford Press.

Peters, J. (2008). Measuring myths about domestic violence: Development and initial validation of the domestic violence myth acceptance scale. *Journal of Aggression, Maltreatment & Trauma*, *16*(1), 1–21.

Whiting, J. B., Oka, M., & Fife, S. T. (2012). Appraisal distortions and intimate partner violence: Gender, power and interaction. *Journal of Marital and Family Therapy*, *38*, 133–144.

# CHAPTER 38

# DEVELOPING EMPATHY FOR CO-VICTIMS OF RAPE

Karen Rich

# Introduction

Although estimates vary, approximately one female over age 12 is raped every five minutes in the United States and approximately one in 8 to 12 males has been sexually assaulted by age 18 (Tjaden & Thoennes, 2006). In addition, a large percentage of inpatient and outpatient clients have sexual assault histories (McMahon & Schwartz, 2011). The sequelae of rape may include anxiety, depression, suicidality, eating disorders, sexual dysfunctions, self-injury, and substance abuse disorders (Kaukinen & DeMaris, 2009).

Social support is critical to a victim's recovery from rape (Starzynski, Ullman, Filipas, & Townsend, 2005); victims may decompensate in response to negative reactions from others (Ahrens & Campbell, 2006). As a result, it is recommended that clinicians engage with collaterals to build strong social support networks for victims (McMahon & Schwartz, 2011).

Rape affects not only the immediate victim but closely related individuals (referred to as co-victims) as well. Co-victims can include family members, romantic partners, and close friends who experience secondary trauma, self-blame, grief, fear, embarrassment, doubt, and/or rage (Davis, Taylor, & Bench, 1995) as a result of the crime. This may result in unsupportive behaviors such as overprotectiveness, refusal to discuss the rape, withdrawal, relentless interrogation, or criticizing the victim's pre-rape behavior (Ahrens & Campbell, 2006). Spouses may insist on resuming sexual relations before survivors are ready, or threaten to track down and kill rapists, placing themselves at risk of violence (Smith, 2005). These actions can undermine survivors' therapeutic gains and lead to intensified symptomatology and broken relationships (Starzynski et al., 2005).

Best-practice guidelines recommend psychoeducation, stress reduction, and supportive counseling with co-victims of rape, in order to improve the outcome for primary survivors. However, not all clinicians reach out to co-victims or include them in sessions. They may underestimate co-victims' importance to survivors or experience countertransference toward them. For example, clinicians with sexual assault histories may identify with survivors and view co-victims with suspicion, especially when the latter are the same gender as the perpetrator (Schauben & Frazier, 2006). Rather than framing relationship difficulties as a reaction to the rape, clinicians may assume the rape has brought preexisting interpersonal issues to the surface (Morrison, Quadra, & Boyd, 2007).

Similarly, co-victims who failed to protect the victim from a rapist may try to protect him or her from the clinician instead (Juda, 1995). Clinicians may experience co-victims' typical expectations (e.g., that their loved one quickly get "back to normal") as demanding or narcissistic (Salston & Figley, 2003) and recommend that clients emotionally and/or physically detach from them. Clinicians' lack of empathy for co-victims may stem from reluctance to acknowledge that their own loved ones could be raped (Salston & Figley, 2003). Indicators that a clinician could benefit from training include unexplored anger toward multiple collaterals, reluctance to work with them, and efforts to discourage the identified patient from contact with them.

# Rationale

Empathy is a critical element in building a therapeutic alliance with a co-victim. When clinicians respond empathically, co-victims may display self-empathy, self-awareness, and increased self-disclosure (Smith, 2005). When working with multiple clients simultaneously (e.g., with survivor and co-victim), sustaining empathy can be more challenging, because the clinician may feel a sense of divided loyalties (Schulman, 2013). One way to increase empathy for co-victims is through perspective taking. This involves putting oneself in another's position in order to understand his or her motivations, experiences, and needs either by direct experience or focused visualization (Kuiken, 2004). This can help clinicians overcome empathic blocks and understand clients' experiences on a visceral level, reducing alienation, negative judgment, power struggles, and clinical impasses. Perspective taking is often used with trainees to develop anticipatory empathy for new clients (Schulman, 2013; Turkoski & Lance, 1996).

It is important for clinicians to engage in critical reflection of their work. One pathway involves (a) being exposed to a disorienting experience, (b) experiencing strong emotions, and (c) becoming aware of new psychological truths (Carrol, 2010). Guided imagery exercises, used for this purpose, can be customized and individualized (Kuiken, 2004). Undertaken in the context of a group, insights can be processed collectively (Turkoski & Lance, 1996). In combination with a cognitive component, guided imagery exercises can be a useful supervisory tool.

Although not all student clinicians have clients who have been raped on their caseloads, the principles of working with co-victims can be applied to related cases. For example, student clinicians may interact with co-victims of a bullied child, a mugging victim, or a survivor of kidnapping.

# Activity Instructions

The empathy-building activity uses a series of visualization exercises that accommodate the uniqueness of each participant. Exercises occur sequentially in a single, approximately 90-minute group format—either a clinical supervision group or a master's-level (social work, psychology, or counseling) classroom—where multiple perspectives can be shared simultaneously and follow-up meetings can occur. Groups should be led by a two-person team comprising clinicians, practicum field supervisors, or clinical practice instructors. The ideal group size is 5 to 20 participants; the group should be small enough that each person gets a chance to speak but large enough that multiple perspectives can be accessed. With larger groups, more time should be allotted.

Parallel process is a phenomenon by which relationships (with clients, collaterals, supervisors, and people in the clinician's personal life) influence one another in subtle ways (Morrisey & Tribe, 2010). For example, supervisees learn more about practice from the way their teachers work with them than what those teachers say about practice (Schulman, 2006). In the activity, participants are directed to identify first with co-victims, then with victims, and finally as clinicians working with supervisors—subjectively occupying each role where feelings may originate. It is expected that the supervisor's approach to participants will be re-created in their interactions with co-victims; therefore, supervisors should keep this in mind throughout all stages of the activity. Supervisors should (a) be familiar with issues of countertransference, parallel process, and behavioral responses to trauma; (b) be able to recognize signs of emotional activation and deescalate a participant; and (c) be comfortable discussing issues of victimization, loss, and abandonment.

For participants with normal affect tolerance, the benefits of this exercise will outweigh the risks. However, students in clinical training programs are more likely than others to have experienced childhood trauma (Black, Jeffries & Hartly, 1993; Wells, Trad & Alves, 2003); therefore, a participant could dissociate or become activated during the exercise. Participants should be informed that they can leave at any time they become uncomfortable, but that a group debriefing will take place at the conclusion. In addition, facilitators should follow up with any participant who leaves early. Those exhibiting unusual distress should be referred to professional clinicians (possibly one of the co-leaders). Participants should be encouraged to exercise discretion over what they visualize, how "deep" they go in their process (Turkoski & Lance, 1996), and what they share with peers.

On a flipchart or whiteboard, supervisors should draw columns labeled with the following headings: (1) *Feelings*, (2) *Related Actions*, and (3) *Victim Responses*. These columns are used to structure the exercise. Supervisors should then read the following prompt to participants:

*Think of someone you are close to, someone you care deeply about. You will not be asked to identify the person—only to picture him or her in your mind's eye. Close your eyes and visualize that person smiling at you.* (Wait a minute or so.) *Now, imagine for a moment that you just found out that this person has been raped. Focus on how you feel and the thoughts that are running through your mind. Take your time.* (This directive may result in pained expressions, bowed posture, and extended silence as participants imagine the scenario.)

After providing appropriate time for reflection, ask participants to open their eyes and invite them to share feelings that emerged. The supervisor should acknowledge the difficult nature of the topic, help participants verbalize emotions, and normalize a wide variety of reactions. In the spirit of parallel process, they should model the very behaviors they wish trainees to develop. Each emotion identified should be listed under the Feelings column on the flipchart or whiteboard. Encourage participants to verbalize accompanying thoughts such as "How could he have put himself in that position?" or "Why did I let Jim walk her home?"

This is not an appropriate time to confront any rape myths espoused by participants; instead, the purpose is to air feelings, however irrational, that a co-victim might have. In addition, the goal is to model uncritical acceptance of feelings a co-victim might generate in counseling. Usually, each of the following feelings will emerge: anger (at the rapist, the victim, or themselves), guilt, fear, embarrassment, disappointment, sadness, and confusion. If a variety of emotions are not identified spontaneously, participants can be gently prompted with comments such as "Some people might feel upset with the victim. Would you—even a little bit?" Such normalization reduces the taboo against expressing certain emotions that are common in these situations. When the list is complete, supervisors should be careful to state that each of these feelings is understandable given the circumstances.

The next part of the exercise asks participants to examine each feeling and consider how it might prompt the person to behave toward the victim. For some participants, the accompanying behavior will be expectable—for instance, feelings of anger that result in shouting or blaming. However, other participants will describe idiosyncratic reactions, such as anger resulting in coldness and withdrawal. It is the leader's job to translate, to the best of his or her ability, how emotions may be reflected in body language, posture, vocal intonation, and other nonverbal indicators of emotion. Actions identified by participants should be listed under the *Related Actions* column on the flipchart or whiteboard. Behaviors should be as specific as possible, such as "looking at the floor, raising my voice, and rolling my eyes." All responses should be validated.

For each emotion and attendant behavior, participants are asked to visualize how the victim might respond. Almost invariably, the imagined reactions of the victim are negative or mixed. Participants convey this nonverbally through their tone of voice or facial expressions. If it isn't clear how the victim would respond, group members are asked to describe how they would feel in the situation. To end this part of the exercise on a supportive note, the participants are instructed to visualize hugging the victim and saying, in their own ways, "I'm sorry this happened."

The third part of the exercise asks participants to visualize the aftermath of an actual crisis, either recent or in the past (related or unrelated to sexual trauma). They should also be asked to imagine the sounds, smells, tastes, and sensations that accompanied the incident; however, they are not asked to reveal the content. After a brief period of consideration, participants are asked to identify who they most wanted to be present with them. They are then asked to recall the most supportive response they received. In cases where participants were not supported, instruct them to imagine the response they needed most. Because this can be an emotional activity, facilitators should be prepared to offer grounding and emotional support to any clinicians who need it.

Following this exercise, participants are asked to share the supportive responses with the group as the facilitator lists them in the Victim Responses column. The facilitator reaches for feelings and assists elaboration with questions such as "How was that helpful to you?" It soon becomes apparent that, while each memory is unique, supportive responses contain common components such as attentiveness, availability, validation of feelings, focus on strengths, absence of blaming or shaming, offers of practical assistance, and reflective listening. This exercise encourages participants to reflect on the importance of social support and to identify its most important aspects.

It is important to process experiential exercises by building a bridge between emotional reactions and cognitive understandings; only then can the knowledge be applied to future situations (Yalom, 2005). Therefore, participants are invited to consider the implications of what just occurred, for themselves as clinicians and for their clients. This occurs first within the group setting and, later, in their individual reflection papers. Questions to assist in processing the experience may begin with the most recent visualization and work backward. For example, *As a victim, how important were others' responses to you? Whom did you most want to be there for you?* Questions to underscore the importance of social support from loved ones may include: *What were your immediate needs in the aftermath of your (imagined) crisis, and whom did you want to meet them? How might a clinician be limited in the degree to which he or she might be able to meet those needs (e.g., for 24-hour availability, physical contact, reminder of lifetime acceptance, and loyalty)?* Following this, participants should be asked to recall their "experience" as a co-victim. Questions to elicit empathy might include: *As a co-victim, what were your fears and hopes? How did it feel, despite your best intentions, to discover you'd provided unhelpful reactions to your loved one? Did it mean you didn't care? Did it mean your presence was unnecessary? What did you need in order to be able to help?*

Among the key points to emphasize are that co-victims are important to recovery, that even the most well-meaning co-victims may respond ineffectively, that co-victims need support of their own in order to best assist others, that acceptance is essential when working with co-victims, that one's own experiences can affect perceptions of co-victims, and that supervision is helpful with these cases. Some interpretation is useful, but it is important for participants to struggle, as a group, to generate and articulate their own conclusions. To generalize from this exercise, participants can be asked, *What do you hope to do differently with co-victims?* and *With what other populations can this process (perspective taking) be useful?*

To close this experience, supervisors may ask participants to identify what they will take away from the exercise. This may be something about themselves, their clients, or their agencies. They may be asked to identify something they did well during the exercise, to conclude on a positive note.

In the weeks following the experience, participants may have dreams about victimization, notice more crime stories, or empathize with co-victims they encounter. As a result, opportunities to process additional reactions (in ongoing supervision or classes) should be made available. Participants' reflection papers can be used in these discussions. Reflection papers should explore the following questions: (a) Which exercise was most meaningful and why? (b) How do you think the exercises are related? (c) How is your approach to co-victims different from what you would need in that situation? (d) What did you learn about yourself? (e) What are the implications for your practice?

# Examples

These exercises have been used in a graduate-level social work course on trauma. In the course of the activity, several student clinicians spontaneously disclosed that they were war veterans, domestic violence survivors, or survivors of child abuse. Two were caseworkers with Child Protective Services. The names throughout this example have been changed to protect the participants' identities.

The class topic was rape survivors, and the students had strong feelings about this population. In the discussion leading up to the activity, there were multiple indicators that a perspective-taking exercise would be useful. Sandra commented that, in her experience, family members only make things worse for rape victims. Debra added that husbands are sometimes so unsympathetic that their wives have no choice but to divorce them. Jen, a mandated reporter, added that her adolescent clients usually de-compensated when sexual assaults were reported to their parents. I decided, after seeing nods of agreement, that this would be a good time to introduce the exercise.

When participants were asked to quietly visualize a raped friend or family member, there was a long and painful silence. It was obvious that they were very affected. Although they were eager to share their feelings, most described anger at the perpetrator, sadness, and fear. By making a list on the blackboard, I was able to elicit more sensitive, secondary emotions like guilt and doubt. Marcus admitted he would wonder whether the rape was "real." I wrote "doubt/suspicion" on the board and asked whether others could relate to that feeling. When several women found his comment offensive, I encouraged the group to consider this as one of many contradictory feelings co-victims may have. One of the hardest feelings to admit at first was anger at the victim. "I hate to say it, but I'd feel raped by proxy," said Clarissa, "and that would make me very angry." "It would be an attack on my manhood," Charles said, "if a woman close to me was raped." The discussion was deepening, as taboo feelings were being aired.

When I asked participants how these feelings could make them act toward the victim, some were convinced their spontaneous behaviors were helpful. For example, giving advice, distracting the victim, and expressing one's own grief were initially seen as very supportive (though the literature reports such behaviors to be generally disturbing). I needed to act as a translator, transforming general statements into body language, vocal intonations, and behavioral cues that might accompany their reactions. When I asked the class, "How would it feel to receive this kind of attention after you were raped?" these myths were often dispelled. For example, when Clarissa claimed she would simply keep her feelings to herself, I asked whether the requisite emotional constriction might manifest as aloof body language. This led to a discussion on what they should do to assist a rape victim they knew. "It seems like it's a problem to care," Charles said, "because your feelings, whatever they are, can trip you up." I agreed that this is the co-victim's dilemma—how to respond without making the victim feel worse. After seeing different "positive" behaviors deconstructed, the students moved from black-and-white thinking to an awareness of nuances and subtexts within these difficult transactions. I told them that all suggestions given were correct in that they were honest and well-intentioned.

In the final visualization, students imagined themselves in crisis situations. This was also stressful, as indicated by frowns, hunched posture, and other nonverbal indicators. When asked to describe the most helpful interventions, participants described being held, treated in familiar ways, reassured, offered concrete aid, and told they didn't cause the problem. When asked why these behaviors were helpful, they mentioned returning to the familiar, holding on to their dignity, knowing they had an ally, and feeling safe. Some student clinicians reacted to the sheer simplicity of these responses with perplexity: "Why get a Master's degree if this is all people need?" quipped Marcus. Sandra pointed out that while the behaviors seem simple, they are not always easy to perform under stress.

To facilitate cognitive processing and integration, I pointed to the discrepancy between what they did as imaginary co-victims and what they needed in a real-life crisis. "How can we explain the difference?" I asked. "How does it all add up?" In addition to the class discussion, student clinicians were asked to explore this question in a brief reflection paper. Charles said, "People go into overdrive when they want to help, when all they need to do is be there." Sandra said, "Co-victims let their emotions blind them to the person sitting right in front of them." Troy offered, "The co-victim might be hurting more than the victim, and I can see where you'd be better off giving them help so it would trickle down to the victim." When asked how the exercise affected her, Jen said, "It made me realize that when I have kids I could act just as badly as some of the parents of the girls I work with." Muriel added, "It made me sad to see how much suffering can spring from miscommunication—people wanting to help but not knowing how to go about it." Jennifer interpreted the exercise in terms of her own past: "It made me re-think how my mother reacted when I was raped—I don't think she meant what she said. But nobody was there to help us work it out." When asked how the exercise may affect their work in the future, several students indicated that they would work to help collaterals identify feelings and communicate better with victims. Some stated they would be more understanding when raped clients relayed negative comments about their parents. As Sandra stated, "It's not like I would condone it or anything—words hurt and attitudes need to be changed. But I would reach out and try to understand where those negative comments were coming from and how they [parents] were hurting, too."

# Measuring Progress

Behaviors suggesting increased self-awareness and empathy for co-victims include a reduction in stereotyping or dichotomous thinking about co-victims; increased contact with co-victims, especially through outreach; personal exploration that addresses their own history of victimization and perceived abandonment by co-victims; and developing services tailored to the needs of co-victims (such as support groups within their agency or psycho-educational materials for distribution to co-victims). Students' reflection papers, journaling, and ongoing class discussions of cases in the field are additional ways to observe changes. Journaling can include process recordings that reflect on students' feelings and practices with this population.

Psychodynamic supervision can focus on transference and countertransference among students, sexually assaulted clients, and co-victims. Follow-up questions to the exercises can include: (a) Are there ways in which your client's experience resonates with your own? (b) As a co-victim yourself, do you have any regrets about how you responded to someone? (c) Are there people in your life whom you want to forgive for responding badly to your victimization? (d) How will you know when you are being triggered by a co-victim in the future?

# Conclusions

Co-victims of rape and other crimes can exert powerful effects on the recovery of clients; in addition, they may have counseling needs that go unmet. Clinicians may have victimization histories of their own, resulting in biases against co-victims. However, clinicians can develop empathy for co-victims by participating in guided imagery exercises offered in a group setting. With improved self-awareness, clinicians may be motivated to strengthen the support network of their primary clients.

# Additional Resources

Hall, E., Hall, C., Stradling, P., & Young, D. (2006). *Guided imagery: Creative interventions in counseling and psychotherapy*. London, UK: Sage.

Thomas, R., & Wilson, J. (2004). *Empathy in the treatment of trauma and PTSD*. New York, NY: Brunner-Routledge.

Ullman, S. E. (2010). *Talking about sexual assault: Society's response to survivors*. Washington, DC: American Psychological Association.

# References

Ahrens, C., & Campbell, R. (2006). Being silenced: The impact of negative social reactions on the disclosure of rape. *American Journal of Community Psychology, 38*(3), 263–272.

Black, P., Jeffries, D., & Hartly, D. (1993). Personal history of psychosocial trauma in the early life of social work and business students. *Journal of Social Work Education, 29*(2), 171–180.

Carrol, M. (2010). Development of clinical reflection skills in counselor trainees. *The Clinical Supervisor, 29*(1), 161–173.

Davis, R., Taylor, B., & Bench, S. (1995). Impact of sexual and nonsexual assault on secondary victims. *Violence and Victims, 10*(1), 73–84.

Juda, D. P. (1995). Psychoanalytically oriented crisis intervention and treatment of rape co-victims. *Dynamic Psychotherapy, 27*(3), 68–79.

Kaukinen, C., & DeMaris, A. (2009). Sexual assault and current mental health: The role of help seeking and police response. *Violence Against Women, 15*(11), 1331–1357.

Kuiken, D. V. (2004). A meta-analysis of the effect of guided imagery practice on health and social outcomes. *Journal of Holistic Nursing*, *22*(2), 162–179.

McMahon, S., & Schwartz, R. (2011). A review of rape treatment in the social work literature: A call to action. *Affilia*, *26*(3), 250–263.

Morrisey, J., & Tribe, R. (2010). Parallel process in supervision. *The Clinical Supervisor*, *26*(2), 103–110.

Morrison, Z., Quadra, A., & Boyd, C. (2007). *Ripple effects of sexual assault*. Brisbane: Australian Centre for the Study of Sexual Assault.

Salston, M., & Figley, C. (2003). Secondary traumatic stress: Effects of working with survivors of criminal victimization. *Journal of Traumatic Stress*, *16*(2), 167–174.

Schauben, L., & Frazier, P. (2006). Vicarious trauma: The effects on female counselors of working with sexual violence survivors. *Psychology of Women Quarterly*, *19*(1), 116–129.

Schulman, L. (2006). The clinical supervisor-practitioner working alliance: A parallel process. *The Clinical Supervisor*, *24*(1–2), 23–47.

Schulman, L. (2013). *The skills of helping individuals, families, groups and communities* (6th ed.). Belmont, CA: Brooks/Cole.

Smith, M. (2005). Female sexual assault: The impact on the male significant other. *Issues in Mental Health Nursing*, *26*(2), 149–167.

Starzynski, L. L., Ullman, S. E., Filipas, H. H., & Townsend, S. M. (2005). Correlates of women's sexual assault disclosure to informal and formal support sources. *Violence and Victims*, *20*(4), 417–432.

Tjaden, P. S., & Thoennes, N. (2006). *Extent, nature and consequences of rape victimization: Findings from the national violence against women survey*. Report No. NCJ 210346. Washington, DC: U.S. Department of Justice, National Institute of Justice.

Turkoski, B., & Lance, B. (1996). The use of guided imagery with anticipatory grief. *Home Healthcare Nurse*, *14*(11), 878.

Wells, M., Trad, A., & Alves, M. (2003). Training beginning supervisors working with new trauma therapists: A relational model of supervision. *Journal of College Student Psychotherapy*, *17*(3), 129–137.

Yalom, E. (2005). The therapist: Working in the here and now. In I. Yalom & M. Lezscz (Eds.), *The theory and practice of group psychotherapy* (5th ed., pp. 141–200). New York, NY: Perseus.

# CHAPTER 39

# Increasing Awareness for Working With Overweight Clients

Keeley J. Pratt and Jaclyn D. Cravens

## Introduction

The etiology of obesity is complex, with multiple factors contributing to a person being unhealthy and overweight. Negative stigma attributed to overweight individuals includes labeling them as lazy, unmotivated, lacking in self-discipline, or less competent overall (Puhl & Heuer, 2009). Weight bias includes the negative attitudes, stereotypes, and overt or covert actions and expressions that affect our interpersonal relationships and interactions (Puhl & Brownell, 2007). These biases are harmful yet are rarely called into question (Puhl & Heuer, 2009). It is important for clinicians and clinicians-in-training to discuss their views about body size and weight, allowing them to explore the potentially negative experiences their clients may have had with weight bias and discrimination in society. Even though clients may not be seeking therapy or counseling directly for their weight or weight-related behaviors (e.g., diet or physical activity), this discussion of potential biases regarding weight and body size plays a key role in limiting potentially negative interactions and increasing clinician self-awareness. We suggest five experiential activities to increase awareness about body size and weight and to provide evaluation and discussion questions to monitor change in clinician self-awareness regarding body size and weight.

## Rationale

When talking about oppression, the discussion often centers on groups divided by gender, ethnicity, sexual orientation, or poverty, but body size is often missing from the conversation. For the purposes of this chapter, we will focus on individuals who have a larger body size (i.e., overweight or obese), because this demographic represents a higher proportion of the population and because there are specific considerations to address based on the stigma associated with being overweight or obese. There is an oversimplified perception that weight is within an individual's control and that being overweight reflects an individual's choices, dismissing the moderating effect of a person's physical and social environment and genetic and preexisting health conditions.

Between 1995 and 2006, the incidence of weight discrimination in the United States toward overweight individuals increased by 66 percent, making it comparable to the rates of racial discrimination, particularly for overweight women (Andreyeva, Puhl, & Brownell, 2008; Puhl, Andreyeva, & Brownell, 2008). Currently, more than one-third (35.7%) of adults are categorized as obese (i.e., having a body mass index [BMI] greater than 30; Ogden, Carroll, Kit, & Flegal, 2012). Children are also vulnerable to the effects of weight bias and discrimination from their peers, educators, and parents (Puhl & Latner, 2007). It is evident that children as young as 3 and 4 years of age demonstrate bias toward their overweight peers and attribute the bias to their excess body weight (Cramer & Steinwert, 1998). Research also indicates that both adults and youth with an elevated BMI are also at a higher risk for mood, anxiety, personality, and substance abuse disorders, as well as relational challenges (Petry, Barry, Pietrzak, & Wagner, 2008).

These prevalence rates make it clear that clinicians today, undoubtedly, will be working with individuals, couples, and families of an increased weight and body size.

However, despite the prevalence within the general population, only within the last decade has research been conducted concerning the stigma associated with being a larger body size. Weight bias has been documented among physicians (Campbell, Engel, Timperio, Cooper, & Crawford, 2000), medical students (Wigton & McGaghie, 2001), dieticians (Berryman, Dubale, Manchester, & Mittelstaedt, 2006), and nurses (Hoppe & Ogden, 1997).

Mental health professionals are also not immune to weight bias. In one study of 2,449 women who were overweight or obese, 21% reported experiencing bias from a mental health professional once and 13% reported experiencing bias multiple times (Puhl & Brownell, 2006). Several experimental studies have been conducted in which psychologists are read descriptions of hypothetical patients who are identical in each condition except for their body weight; in these studies, psychologists more frequently assigned negative attributes, more severe psychological symptoms, and more pathology to obese clients than to nonobese clients (Davis-Coelho, Waltz, & Davis-Coelho, 2000; Hassel, Amici, Thurston, & Gorsuch, 2001).

Part of this weight bias may be attributed to pathogen disgust sensitivity, a reaction that is hypothesized to be present when there is a perceived threat of disease (i.e., obesity; Liberman, Tybur, & Latner, 2012). In reaction to this sensitivity, the overweight person is viewed as a danger to one's health and consciously or unconsciously avoided. Furthermore, Latner, Ebneter, and O'Brien (2012) found that when individuals lost a substantial amount of weight, they were still subjected to increased levels of stigma, compared to those who had never been overweight or obese. In other words, even when formerly overweight or obese individuals lost weight, they were still at a higher risk for experiencing weight-related bias. Specifically, in their initial interactions, clinicians' sensitivity with clients assists in building a trusting and respectful relationship, one that is free of pathologizing weight-related language. Client–clinician trust is an essential building block in the early stages of therapy, allowing clients to feel free to disclose and express their feelings associated with possible hardships they have experienced with weight bias and discrimination.

# Activity Instructions

The following self-awareness exercise is broken into several activities, offering a comprehensive exposure to diverse issues that are relevant to working with overweight clients, including privilege and oppression narratives, dominant themes in the media, and the application of biological, psychological, and social (biopsychosocial) considerations to a potential clinical situation (Engel, 1977). Furthermore, these experiential activities are designed to assist clinicians and clinicians-in-training in understanding their own potential biases around weight.

Activities are appropriate for clinicians in all developmental stages, although ideally they would be conducted early on in a clinician's training and before seeing clients. Although it is possible for clinicians to carry out parts of this exercise on a self-assigned basis, these activities work best when assigned by a supervisor as part of a training exercise, class requirement, or workshop. The instructions are therefore directed mainly toward supervisors and facilitators. Furthermore, given the personal and in-depth nature of the content, these activities should be completed in small groups of three to four people or in dyads. Before beginning the activities, supervisors should establish clear ground rules that detail the confidentiality of the content discussed. The supervisor should also establish safety for the group/dyad so clinicians feel they are able to disclose personal opinions as well as conscious and potentially unconscious biases.

As a note to supervisors, it is important not only to pay careful attention to the language used by the clinicians but also to be prepared to model appropriate, bias-free language and be able to direct clinicians to resources as needed. If clients bring up their own weight, clinicians should try to use the clients' language or preferred terms to describe the clients' weight to avoid potentially hurtful terms (Wadden & Didie, 2003). Studies have shown that the words clinicians use are vitally important; 19% of American adults report that they would avoid future healthcare if their physician called them "fat," "obese," or "morbidly obese," and preferred less stigmatizing

Table 39.1 The Weight Bias Questionnaire

For each item, respond by marking how often (0) to rarely/never (4) you experience the following in your clinical work.

1. I do not allow my client's weight to affect my perceptions of my client's personality, intelligence level, therapeutic goals, relationship status, and health behaviors.

| 0 | 1 | 2 | 3 | 4 |
|---|---|---|---|---|
| Often | Usually | Occasionally | Seldom | Rarely/never |

2. Am I comfortable working with people who are a larger size?

| 0 | 1 | 2 | 3 | 4 |
|---|---|---|---|---|
| Often | Usually | Occasionally | Seldom | Rarely/never |

3. Is the dialogue I have with my clients supportive of where they are with their health goals?

| 0 | 1 | 2 | 3 | 4 |
|---|---|---|---|---|
| Often | Usually | Occasionally | Seldom | Rarely/never |

4. Am I aware of all of my client's needs, in addition to concerns about weight or body size?

| 0 | 1 | 2 | 3 | 4 |
|---|---|---|---|---|
| Often | Usually | Occasionally | Seldom | Rarely/never |

5. Are my treatment plans or goals client-centered and based on my client's relational and health goals?

| 0 | 1 | 2 | 3 | 4 |
|---|---|---|---|---|
| Often | Usually | Occasionally | Seldom | Rarely/never |

| Compute the total score on the Weight Bias Questionnaire by summing the questions to give you a total score between 0 and 20. Scores closer to 0 indicate greater self-awareness about issues related to body shape and weight, whereas scores closer to 20 may indicate that the clinicians have further person-of-the-therapist work to do to avoid perpetuating weight discrimination of their clients. | **Total Score** |
|---|---|

Adapted from Puhl & Brownell, 2007.

and blaming words such as "weight," "unhealthy weight," and "overweight" (Puhl, Peterson, & Luedicke, 2012). It is advisable that supervisors take the Weight Bias Questionnaire (WBQ, see Table 39.1) before working with clinicians to ensure they are aware of their own biases on issues of body size and weight.

## Weight Bias Assessment

Before beginning the experiential activities, the supervisor should ask clinicians to complete the WBQ (see Table 39.1).

Supervisors have two options for administering and reviewing the WBQ, based on the setting where the activities will be conducted. If the supervisor is working in a clinical/academic setting where a clinical practicum or period of supervision is taking place, the WBQ should be taken both before and after the activity to provide a measure of change in the clinicians' self-awareness about weight and body size. However, if the activities are being conducted in a one-time lecture or a workshop format, the WBQ can be used as a pretest assessment to provide attendees an idea of where they currently rate with self-awareness on weight and body size. Because of the short-term and time-limited nature of these formats, the WBQ can be used as a tool for self-awareness and to note where improvements and progress can be made, but it should not be applied as a measure of long-term, stable change. In these formats, clinicians will also take this assessment before participating in the activities and will review the results after the activities are complete.

After giving the clinicians an appropriate amount of time to complete the assessment, the supervisor should instruct them to set it aside for further discussion later in the exercise. The first time clinicians take the assessment, the supervisor should inform them that this provides a snapshot of where clinicians are currently at with regard to weight bias. The supervisor should reinforce that the five activities to be conducted soon will provide more insight and opportunity for reflection about clinicians' weight bias.

## Activity 1: Privilege or Oppression Narrative Paper

This first activity is designed to help clinicians examine privilege and potential oppression regarding body size and weight. Supervisors should ask clinicians to write a paper comprising the following three sections:

1. First, clinicians should write a privilege or oppression narrative about their own body size and weight. This section should include an experience from clinicians' lives that demonstrates privilege or oppression, specifically with a focus on body size and weight. Remind clinicians that their papers are a safe space to discuss their issues with body size and weight, regardless of where they fall within the spectrum. The experience clinicians choose may be a specific memory or an overall theme (e.g., "I have been overweight for as long as I can remember"). The events and specific details about how clinicians came to realize they were privileged or oppressed should be explored. Clinicians should describe how their lives have been impacted by such privilege or oppression, both professionally and personally.

2. Next, clinicians should respond to the question "Do individual privilege/oppression narratives affect how the clinicians treat individuals who are overweight versus other clients they may encounter? Why or why not?"

3. Finally, the paper should conclude with the clinicians creating a 10-item list of privileges afforded to nonoverweight individuals based on their body size and weight. Examples of these privileges include items like "When I go to class I do not have to worry about being comfortable in the standard-size desk in my classroom" or "When I shop at a department store, I can be sure of finding items in my size."

## Activity 2: Body Size Media Collage

This activity is designed to examine dominant themes in the media about body image and weight. First, the clinician should construct a collage that uses pictures or words to portray two things: (1) how smaller body sizes are portrayed in the media and (2) how larger body sizes are portrayed. The clinician should describe the themes in the images of the smaller and larger body size individuals seen in magazines, in movies, and on TV.

After completing the collage, clinicians should reflect on the following questions about body size in the general culture:

- How do male and female stereotypes portray the perfect face, the perfect body, and/or the ideal build?
- How do others align with these stereotypes? (For example, do you have overweight friends who act the way the media portrays people with a larger body size?)
- What kinds of problems might these stereotypes cause in relationships?

Once clinicians seem to have an understanding of the effects of stereotypes in general, the clinician should consider the issue in terms of their clients, answering the following questions to understand how these dominant narratives may shape the clients' sense of self:

- How are my clients vulnerable to the stereotypes found in the media?
- How might my clients be influenced by the stereotypes found in the media?
- What would my clients' lives be like if there were not pressures to be thin in the media?
- What might my clients have learned from the media about how weight loss is achieved?
- Based on the media, what are my clients' beliefs about how or why an individual becomes overweight?
- How do body image stereotypes differ for cultural groups outside of the clinician's own cultural group? How do stereotypes differ by gender?

To complete this activity, clinicians should first read the following vignette, and then answer the questions provided. This activity assists clinicians in assessment, while considering the biological, psychological, and social factors that the client may be facing.

> Shay attended her first appointment at the Clinic after being referred by her pediatrician and an emergency room discharge nurse for "self-esteem, suicide, and depression issues." Shay, a 12-year-old, African American female, had a BMI of 32.3 kg/m² and weighed 183.5 pounds. Shay lived part-time with her father, who lived alone otherwise, and part-time with her mother, stepfather, and younger stepbrother. Shay's father lived in a one-bedroom/bathroom apartment, where Shay slept on the couch. Shay's father struggled to maintain consistent employment, resulting in inconsistent access to food and other necessities. Shay's mother and stepfather were both employed and lived in a home in a suburban neighborhood, where Shay had her own bedroom.

> During Shay's intake, she reported "feeling blue" and admitted to thoughts of suicide. There was a past suicide attempt two weeks earlier, when she took a "handful" of prescription pills and was admitted to the emergency room. Shay admitted that she was referred to a psychologist in the past two years after a screening tool suggested she was at risk for depression, anxiety, and suicide. The psychologist suggested lots of ways Shay could change her behavior, but although she tried to do what the psychologist suggested, she couldn't resist the temptations of the unhealthy food available at both of her parents' homes. Her father was reportedly an alcoholic, and Shay would often hoard food in her room to avoid having to run into her father after work when he would start drinking until the early morning hours.

> After several failed attempts to follow the psychologist's suggestions, Shay gave up and decided that since her family and friends were not supportive and "didn't seem to care whether she was big or not," she should not care either. She continued to get bullied at school and felt stretched between both of her parents' households. Things got so bad that Shay reported, "I just thought I would be better off if I didn't have to worry about all of this stuff anymore." When asked to explain what the "stuff" was that she was referring to, she stated, "You know, like my Dad's drinking, not pissing off my parents, my weight, people calling me fat at school, and always having to make jokes about my weight so people will like me."

> Shay continued to express how hard it was for her to control her weight. At her father's house, she was expected to cook, clean, and perform other household duties, while at her mother's she did not have these responsibilities. The differences in households made it difficult for Shay to maintain her grades and have peer relationships, while also trying to make healthy changes to her lifestyle.

> Shay and her mother decided that they should attend weekly therapy sessions. In Shay's individual sessions, she wanted to focus on self-esteem and body image. In the family sessions, she and her mother decided they should work on communication in the family, taking Shay out of the middle of her parents' arguments, and supporting Shay with integrating healthy lifestyle choices into her routines in both parents' households.

After reading this vignette, the supervisor should ask the following questions:

- What are the biological, psychological, and social needs and concerns that Shay detailed, and how would you consider addressing each?

- What role does Shay's family play in her description of her presenting concerns?

- What language does Shay use when she describes her presenting concerns? How does she describe her weight?

- What other professionals might you consider collaborating with, if a release of information can be provided, while working with Shay and her family?

Supervisors should discuss the following questions with clinicians to help them understand weight bias:

- What words do you use with your clients to talk about being an increased weight (e.g., overweight, obese, large)?

- How do you view what is considered attractive for different ethnic groups or genders?

Activity 3:
Client Ethical
Assessment

Activity 4:
Understanding Weight
Bias

- How is weight spoken about in your family-of-origin and support system?
- How do you view the role of religion/spiritual practices in feeding and meals?
- What are your assumptions about how weight loss happens?
- What kind of culture-specific foods and eating rituals are most commonly conducted in your area of practice?

## Activity 5: Clinical Setting Considerations

Have clinicians consider the following questions, in order to gain an understanding of how they could better serve individuals and families who are of larger body size (adapted from Ahmed, Lemkau, & Birt, 2002):

- **Parking and entry to clinical setting:** Is there close parking for clients who may have a difficult time walking extra distances? Are there ramps and handrails? Are door frames and hallways appropriate for larger-size people?
- **Waiting room:** Are there chairs with and without armrests to accommodate individuals of larger body size? Is the room supplied with materials that represent individuals of all body sizes and healthy lifestyles (e.g., magazines, children's toys)?
- **Office staff:** Are office staff members appropriately dressed in clothing that is not offensive to individuals who have a larger body size (e.g., tight-fitting clothing)? Do office staff members demonstrate sensitivity to individuals who are larger in size?

Finally, after completing all of these activities, the supervisor should direct clinicians back to the WBQ. In clinical practicum or supervision contexts that extend over time, supervisors should encourage clinicians to retake the assessment and then address changes in the clinicians' rating of self-awareness about weight and body size, noting both improvements and needed areas of growth. In one-time lecture or workshop formats, supervisors/facilitators should encourage participants to review their WBQ pretests. In both formats, clinicians should be instructed to write down ideas on how they intend to address the lower-rated items in the questionnaire.

# Examples

The activities listed here have been applied in therapy practicums and seminars. Feedback from participants highlights that weight bias is a needed area of training for clinicians. Specifically, clinicians mentioned that the activities allowed them to work through or reduce their own anxiety about working with clients and weight, recognizing implicit weight bias, and challenging their own beliefs about weight. First-year clinicians provided the following feedback on the clinical activities about weight bias:

- It helped to set me up for seeing clients and to talk about some of my anxieties.
- The exercises allowed us to work through some of our fears and anxieties as new clinicians who will likely be working with clients who are overweight.
- These activities challenged me to develop and mature as a therapist, and gain a deeper understanding of my stance on therapy with clients who are struggling with weight concerns.
- I also enjoyed the writing exercise when we were asked to recognize opinions and biases about weight that we may currently have that may be a result of your upbringing and family. This self-reflection allowed me to see that I was not as open-minded as I had thought, and showed me the areas in which I should improve.
- The reflection exercises were very beneficial because you were able to point out and track how your opinions and biases change throughout the practicum.

In addition, the activities have been used in lecture or seminar format. Seminar attendees stated the following:

- The field needs more integration like this. I specifically enjoyed the vignette for a practical example of a case I might encounter as a clinician.

- I learned so much in this session, and feel light-years ahead in my knowledge about weight bias and obesity. As a young MFT student, I found this to be really helpful.

# Measuring Progress

Although weight biases have been shown to have harmful effects on individuals, this form of discrimination often goes unrecognized and is sometimes even culturally accepted. The activities in this chapter are designed to help clinicians recognize their own views about body size and weight and to see weight bias and discrimination from their clients' perspectives. Progress can be measured as clinicians work to eliminate bias from their language, treatment goals, and office environment, all of which helps limit potentially negative interactions with clients and thus aid in successful outcomes. Changes in how clinicians answered the WBQ before and after the activity can also represent a useful way for clinicians to chart their progress.

Overcoming such culturally accepted stereotypes can be a difficult process for some clinicians. After completing the weight bias activities, some clinicians-in-training may still be struggling to progress, which would be evident in use of weight bias language, lack of understanding surrounding weight-related issues (e.g., losing weight, medical diagnoses, influence of family of origin), and lack of attention to clinical setting considerations (e.g., continuing to dress in tight-fitting clothing, lack of sensitivity to different body size individuals). There are additional options for clinicians in training programs who have difficulty overcoming or recognizing weight bias, including options for remediation. First, The Yale University Rudd Center for Food Policy and Obesity has three videos available for free that expose weight bias. Clinicians should be encouraged to watch each video and discuss their reactions with their supervisor, paying particular attention to the points that were most meaningful to them. Clinicians should also reexamine the narrative they wrote in Activity 1 about privileges afforded to individuals who are not overweight.

Second, the supervisor can assign clinicians to write a paper that addresses some or all of the following prompts: What are the causes of obesity (e.g., genetic, biological, environmental, social, and behavioral)? What are positive associations with people who are overweight? How do the media perpetuate weight bias? and Discuss ways you could intervene if you witnessed weight bias happening in everyday life or in a therapy or counseling context. Finally, for clinicians who have witnessed or experienced intergenerational weight bias and discrimination in their family, a weight bias genogram may help them to better understand the root of their own bias and how that bias has manifested over time in their own family. In extreme cases, supervisors may need to refer clinicians for focused counseling to help them deal with the topic.

# Conclusion

Statistics highlight the growing rate of overweight individuals and families in the United States. The co-occurrence of mental health issues in conjunction with increased weight leaves little question that today's clinicians will work with overweight clients and families who are struggling with weight biases and related issues. As clinicians work with clients of varying weights and body types, they must become aware of their biases about body type and weight. It is expected that as a result of this activity, clinicians will explore the potentially negative experiences their clients may have had with weight bias and discrimination in society, allowing them to gain an understanding of these biases and to become more aware of how their language, their clinical setting, and even their clothing can enhance or detract from the therapeutic relationship.

# Additional Resources

Brownell, K. D., Puhl, R. M., Schwartz, M. B., & Rudd, L. (2005). *Weight bias: Nature, consequences, and remedies*. New York, NY: Guilford Press.

Yale Rudd Center for Food Policy and Obesity. (n.d.) Weight bias and stigma. Retrieved from www.yaleruddcenter.org/what_we_do.aspx?id=10

# References

Ahmed, S. M., Lemkau, J. P., & Birt, S. L. (2002). Toward sensitive treatment of obese patients. Family Practice Management. Retrieved from www.aafp.org/fpm.

Andreyeva, T., Puhl, R. M., & Brownell, K. D. (2008). Changes in perceived weight discrimination among Americans: 1995–1996 through 2004–2006. *Obesity (Silver Spring)*, *16*(5), 1129–1134. doi: 10.1038/oby.2008.35

Berryman, D., Dubale, G., Manchester, D., & Mittelstaedt, R. (2006). Dietetic students possess negative attitudes toward obesity similar to nondietetic students. *Journal of American Dietetic Association*, *106*, 1678–1682. doi: 10.1016/j.jada.2006.07.016

Campbell, K., Engel, H., Timperio, A., Cooper, C., & Crawford, D. (2000). Obesity management: Australian general practitioners' attitudes and practices. *Obesity Research*, *8*, 459–466.

Cramer, P., & Steinwert, T. (1998). Thin is good, fat is bad: How early does it begin? *Journal of Applied Developmental Psychology*, *19*, 429–451.

Davis-Coelho, K., Waltz, J., & Davis-Coelho, B. (2000). Awareness and prevention of bias against fat clients in psychotherapy. *Professional Psychology Research and Practice*, *31*, 682–694.

Engel, G. (1977). The need for a new medical model: A challenge for biomedicine. *Science*, *196*, 129–136.

Hassel, T., Amici, C., Thurston, N., & Gorsuch, R. (2001). Client weight as a barrier to non-biased clinical judgment. *Journal of Psychology & Christianity*, *20*, 145–161.

Hoppe, R., & Ogden, J. (1997). Practice nurses' beliefs about obesity and weight related interventions in primary care. *International Journal of Obesity*, *21*, 141–146.

Latner, J. D., Ebneter, D. S., & O'Brien, K. S. (2012). Residual obesity stigma: An experimental investigation of bias against obese and lean targets differing in weight-loss history. *Obesity*, *20*, 2035–2038. doi: 10.1038/oby.2012.55

Liberman, D. L., Tybur, J. M., & Latner, J. D. (2012). Disgust sensitivity, obesity stigma, and gender: Contamination psychology predicts weight bias for women, not men. *Obesity*, *20*, 1803–1814. doi: 10.1038/oby.2011.247

Ogden, C. L., Carroll, M. D., Kit, B. K., & Flegal, K. M. (2012). *Prevalence of obesity in the United States, 2009–2010*. NCHS data brief, no 82. Hyattsville, MD: National Center for Health Statistics.

Petry, N. M., Barry, D., Pietrzak, R. H., & Wagner, J. A. (2008). Overweight and obesity are associated with psychiatric disorders: Results from the National Epidemiologic Survey on Alcohol and Related Conditions. *Psychosomatic Medicine*, *70*(3), 288–297. doi: 10.1016/j.addbeh.2008.08.008

Puhl, R. M., Andreyeva, T., & Brownell, K. D. (2008). Perceptions of weight discrimination: Prevalence and comparison to race and gender discrimination in America. *International Journal of Obesity*, *32*, 992–1000. doi: 10.1038/ijo.2008.22

Puhl, R., & Brownell, K. (2006). Confronting and coping with weight stigma: An investigation of overweight and obese adults. *Obesity*, *14*(10), 1802–1815.

Puhl, R., & Brownell, K. (2007). Weight bias in health care settings [PowerPoint presentation]. Yale Rudd Center for Food Policy & Obesity. Retrieved from www.yaleruddcenter.org/what_we_do.aspx?id=196

Puhl, R., & Heuer, C. (2009). The stigma of obesity: A review and update. *Obesity, 17*(5), 941–964. doi: 10.1038/oby.2008.636

Puhl, R., & Latner, J. (2007). Obesity, stigma, and the health of the nation's children. *Psychological Bulletin, 133*, 557–580.

Puhl, R., Peterson, J. L., & Luedicke, J. (2012). Motivating or stigmatizing? Public perceptions of weight-related language used by health providers. *International Journal of Obesity*, 1–8. doi: 10.1038/ijo.2012.110

Wadden, T. A., & Didie, E. (2003). What's in a name? Patients' preferred terms for describing obesity. *Obesity Research, 11*(9), 1140–1146. doi: 10.1038/oby.2003.155

Wigton, R., & McGaghie, W. (2001). The effect of obesity on medical students' approach to patients with abdominal pain. *Journal of General Internal Medicine, 16*, 262–265. doi: 10.1046/j.1525-1497.2001.016004262.x

# CHAPTER 40

# Dealing With Addiction and Recovery

Fred P. Piercy and Manjushree Palit

## Introduction

There are many ways to learn about addiction and recovery. At its most basic level, learning involves simply memorizing factual details related to certain questions: What are addiction, dependence, and withdrawal? What are the theories of addiction? What are the biological, psychological, and social components of addiction? Where does the family fit in (Fisher & Harrison, 2008)? Understanding, however, involves more than cognitive knowledge. For example, affect is linked to cognition (Immordino-Yang & Damasio, 2007), and in order to fully understand something, it helps for the instructor to connect what is being learned with both the learner's emotions and thinking.

## Rationale

We teach beginning clinicians about addiction and recovery by having them interview recovering addicts and by encouraging them to write a drug/alcohol autobiography. We use these methods to make learning personal and meaningful to clinicians, both intellectually and experientially. Through the interview assignment, clinicians learn what has been helpful or unhelpful to recovering addicts and use this knowledge in their clinical practice to help other individuals whose lives have been affected by alcohol or drug addictions as well as other compulsive behaviors. Through the optional drug/alcohol autobiography, clinicians examine the behaviors of their family and friends and the messages they sent about drugs and alcohol and then reflect on how these behaviors and messages relate to their own drug/alcohol attitudes and behaviors. The optional nature of the assignment allows for choice on the clinician's part; since no one is forced to write a drug/alcohol autobiography, those who do take the task seriously are consequently quite open and committed to the process. Whether optional or not, this assignment pushes the clinicians to learn more about addiction, either from a recovering addict or through the self-reflective autobiography.

## Activity Instructions

The following two activities work together to increase clinicians' understanding of the power of addiction, as well as their own unique histories with drugs and alcohol. These exercises are appropriate for clinicians of all experience levels. It is possible for clinicians to carry out these activities on a self-assigned basis, but they work best when assigned by a supervisor as part of a class, workshop, or other clinical education program. Therefore, the instructions are directed specifically to the supervisors.

After clinicians have completed these activities, we often ask them to discuss the similarities and differences of their recovery interviews in dyads and then within the large group. Likewise, we give clinicians the opportunity to share whatever they feel comfortable sharing about their own drug/alcohol histories, as well as what they learned from writing their drug/alcohol autobiographies. This sharing allows clinicians to hear a range of drug/alcohol experiences and to connect them to their own evolving theoretical, clinical, and personal experiences.

## Recovery Interview Activity

For the interview activity, clinicians are instructed to interview a person who is successfully recovering from an addiction. Most people know such an individual, or know someone who can suggest a willing interviewee. The person should be in recovery and willing to take part in what should be presented as a voluntary interview. We have found that the interview ultimately underlines the strengths and resilience of the recovering addict and empowers him or her in the process, so the experience is usually good for both the recovering addict and the clinician.

This activity is designed to sharpen clinicians' skills in exploring stories about addiction, relapse, and recovery. The activity promotes the understanding that the addict's family plays a crucial role throughout the life of the addiction and recovery process and that the addict is part of the larger family system (Cox & Paley, 2003). Through this interview activity, clinicians begin to understand the interdependence and reciprocity (Guttman, 1991) that characterize many addictive family systems.

Addiction becomes a central organizing principle in the life of addicts, which is difficult for them to change. Many beginning clinicians do not fully appreciate the power of addiction—that is, how addicts' behaviors, needs, motivations, and relationships are all mutually connected through the web of addiction. The family systems perspective provides an understanding of the reciprocal influences at work in addicts' lives and how, through the addiction, relationships develop and are maintained (Dilworth-Anderson, Burton, & Klein, 2005; Elkin, 1984). Many beginning clinicians find it helpful to explore the powerful influence of addiction by listening to the stories of recovering addicts and examining how they make sense of their experiences.

Clinicians can interview a family member, a friend, or a community member who is recovering from an addiction. Through the interview process, the student will explore how the interviewee's addiction started, what kept the addiction going, and family members' and friends' roles in the addiction and recovery process. The interview should focus on exploring the addict's story from the addict's viewpoint. Following are recommended questions as an interview guide:

- Tell me about your life before you quit. How did your addiction start? What was good about the substance you took? What did it do for you? Were there any downsides? If so, what were they?
- Tell me a story about you when you were addicted that illustrates something about your life with the substance.
- How did you try to hide your substance abuse from others? Were you successful?
- Why did you quit?
- How did you quit?
- What role did your friends play in your addiction and recovery? How were they part of the problem? How were they part of the solution?
- What role did your family play in your addiction and recovery? How were they part of the problem? How were they part of the solution?
- What was/is the process of recovery like?
- What was/is the hardest aspect of your recovery?
- What was/is the most helpful aspect of your recovery?
- How did/do you deal with friends or family who were/are still using?
- How do you keep from relapsing?
- What advice do you have for others regarding getting involved with the substance or behavior? What advice do you have on quitting?
- What did you learn from your addiction and recovery?

Following the recovery interviews, clinicians are asked to write a reflection of their experiences of the recovery interview (including illustrative interviewee comments). The following questions are useful in helping clinicians reflect on the experience:

- How did you feel about your interview?

- What will you remember?

- What have you learned from the recovery interview that may be useful in your future work and/or life?

- What theory of addiction did the addict's story most reflect (e.g., the biopsychosocial model, disease model, moral model, habit model)? Why do you think this might be?

- What does this experience teach you about others who want to change compulsive behaviors?

## Drug/Alcohol Autobiography

Marlatt and Gordon (1985) use an alcohol autobiography as part of their relapse prevention work. This activity is assigned on an optional basis and is designed to help clinicians better understand how their families and friends may have influenced their beliefs and behaviors regarding drugs and alcohol. For this activity, clinicians are encouraged to write a paper describing their earliest experiences with drugs/alcohol, including their perceptions of their family's attitudes about drugs/alcohol, positive and negative experiences they had with drugs/alcohol during their life, quitting strategies they have used (if applicable), and expectations about their future relationship with or without drugs/alcohol. To guide clinicians in structuring their autobiographical presentation, McCrady and Niles (1989) suggest clinicians address the following items:

1. First, start your story by reviewing your earliest recollections about drugs and alcohol, addressing the following questions:

   - Did your parents drink or take drugs?

   - Was there a lot of drinking or drug abuse in your household?

   - What messages from family or friends did you receive about drugs or alcohol?

   - What messages did you receive from institutions like your school or church?

   - Was drinking or using drugs considered a grown-up thing to do or an evil thing to do?

2. Second, after examining these primary topics, discuss your own first experiences with drugs or alcohol. If you never got involved with drugs or alcohol, questions to consider include:

   - Why did you choose to avoid drugs or alcohol?

   - What messages kept you from trying drugs or alcohol?

   - Are those messages still alive and well in your life today?

   Alternatively, if you have tried drugs or alcohol in your life, please consider the following questions:

   - How old were you when you first tried drugs or alcohol?

   - Which messages did you listen to and which did you ignore?

   - Did you look forward to having your first drink or taking your first drug?

   - What were the circumstances of your first experience with drugs or alcohol?

   - Did you get drunk/high?

   - How did you feel about this first experience? Were you embarrassed? Proud?

   - Did you or your friends or family think that it was funny? How did your parents react to you? Did you get into trouble?

3. Third, if necessary, review your subsequent experiences with drugs/alcohol by addressing one or more of the following subcategories of questions. If you began drinking or using drugs regularly, consider the following:

- What did your drinking or drug use do for you? (For example, did drug or alcohol use allow you to be more social or better accepted by your friends?)
- Was drinking or using drugs part of dating?
- Did you think that you needed a drink or joint to help you relax after school or work?

If you see yourself as an in-control social drinker or a nonproblem recreational drug user, consider these questions:

- How do you manage yourself as a social drinker or recreational drug user?
- What are your personal rules around your use?
- How much is too much?
- Have you ever exceeded your personal limit? How did you feel afterward?

If you see yourself as a recovering alcoholic/addict, these questions may generate useful responses:

- When did you first realize that drinking/drugging was a problem to you?
- What embarrassing or upsetting things happened?
- How did your drinking/drugging affect your peer or dating relationships, your marriage, your work, your relationships with your children, parents, and/or friends?
- If you used to drink/drug but now abstain, how do you feel about social situations now?
- How do you think others view you now?
- How exactly did you quit?
- What was the most important thing you learned about quitting?
- How have your relationships changed since you've quit?

4. Fourth, conclude your discussion of personal experiences by looking ahead to your future relationship with drugs/alcohol. Questions to consider include the following:

- What role will drinking/drugs have in your marriage and/or significant relationships?
- What rules will guide your use? (For example, how many beers are too many in one evening?)
- What messages about drugs and alcohol do you plan to give to your children? How will you do this?

5. Finally, after responding to all questions on your experiences with drugs or alcohol, conclude your paper by reflecting on what you learned in the process of writing your drug/alcohol autobiography. Consider the following questions:

- What was it like to write the paper?
- What systemic process did you see at work in the development of your own attitudes and behaviors toward drugs and alcohol?
- What decision points or turning points do you see in your drug/alcohol history?
- What addictions concepts or models can you apply to your own drug and alcohol history?

# Examples

The range of addict experiences is vast, yet they can be amazingly similar. Although addicts may engage in a variety of addictive behaviors—abuse of prescription medications, alcohol, illegal drugs, gambling, or extreme weight loss—most addicts describe a period when the addiction met a particular need and created a positive experience. They also describe a time later in the addictive process when they became physically dependent and no longer used the substance to feel good but just to avoid feeling bad. Recovery for most addicts typically involves some sort of planning, connecting to a support system, and employing a new set of behaviors (e.g., AA meetings, athletics, a new job), as well as creating an environment (new friends and surroundings) that supports sobriety and provides the addicts with a focus other than the addictive substance (Fisher & Harrison, 2008; Shaffer & Jones, 1989). Clinicians learn from the addicts how religion, family, friends, and "hitting bottom" all may have played a role in their recovery. Some addicts frame their addiction within a narrative that involves, for example, the disease model, God's hand, redemption, family support, a conscious choice to change a bad habit, or a combination of these. One addict stated, "Getting through the recovery process is easy if you want recovery for yourself and it's not being forced on you." Such narratives and explanatory concepts are important to the addict's recovery and are also helpful for clinicians in training to understand.

Clinicians seem to appreciate the opportunity to reflect on their own drug/alcohol history and are quick to apply their own experiences to their readings on addiction and the family. Following are a few statements from drug/alcohol autobiographies (with changes to maintain confidentiality) that reflect each clinician's unique family and peer environment around alcohol and drug use:

- "When I was a child, my mother used to let me have sips of her drinks whenever she got something, just so I could know what it tasted like."

- "I had friends that smoked pot with me almost every day."

- "My father never attended any of my soccer matches .... He died in jail .... I hate what alcohol did to him and my family."

- "I never really received the message that alcohol was a bad thing, because even when things went wrong because of alcohol, my parents would find a way to blame it on something else."

- "I have not told many people about my past. So, to be this open about it has been both scary and liberating."

# Measuring Progress

Through the recovery interview, clinicians learn about the addiction and recovery process from those they interview. This process gives life to the concepts of addictions and recovery. When addiction concepts are subsequently brought up in the classroom, the clinicians have someone they can connect to these concepts. Progress can be measured by the cognitive knowledge that clinicians learn through the combined classroom-experiential process and through the increased empathy, respect, understanding, and wisdom that is evident in the clinicians' subsequent clinical work with those with addictions. Moreover, clinicians will learn that addiction is a pattern of behaviors that are connected on multiple systems levels and that family and friends can both be part of the addict's problem and can provide the support necessary for recovery.

Similarly, the drug/alcohol autobiography provides experiences that connect addiction concepts to real-life understanding. Clinicians can look at their own attitudes and behavior toward drugs and alcohol and relate them to their family background, support systems, messages they have received, and the theories and concepts they learn in class. These connections make learning more meaningful and ground clinicians in their own experiences. As for measuring progress, this can be done in traditional ways (e.g., tests, essays, papers) and through more reflective means like journals, clinical reflections, small-group discussions, or self-reports.

# Conclusion

In sum, we believe that clinicians learn best when they can experience a concept personally and in a manner that connects with both their heads and their hearts (Piercy & Benson, 2005). We have described two reflective activities to help beginning clinicians learn about the process of addiction and recovery: interviewing a recovering addict and writing a drug/alcohol autobiography. Both learning experiences reflect this dual-focus approach to learning how to bring the subject of addictions to life. We hope that the reader will find these activities helpful as well.

# Additional Resources

Capuzzi, D., & Stauffer, M. (2012). *Foundations of addictions counseling* (2nd ed.). Boston, MA: Pearson.

Fisher, G. L., & Harrison, T.C. (2008). *Substance abuse: Information for school counselors, social workers, therapists, and counselors* (4th ed.). Boston, MA: Allyn & Bacon.

Knapp, C. (1996). *Drinking: A love story.* New York, NY: Delta.

McCollum, E., & Trepper, T. (2001). *Family solutions for substance abuse.* New York, NY: Haworth Press.

Sheff, D. (2005). My addicted son. *New York Times* (pp. 1–10). (Sheff expanded this article into a moving book, *A Beautiful Boy.*)

Smith, J. E., & Meyers, R. J. (2007). *Motivating substance abusers to enter treatment: Working with family members.* New York, NY: Guilford Press.

# References

Cox, M. J., & Paley, B. (2003). Understanding families as systems. *Current Directions in Psychological Science, 12,* 193–196.

Dilworth-Anderson, P., Burton, L. M., & Klein, D. M. (2005). Contemporary and emerging theories in studying families. In V. L. Bengtson, A. C. Acock, K. R. Allen, P. Dilworth-Anderson, & D. M. Klein (Eds.), *Source book of family theory and research* (2nd ed., pp. 35–58). Thousand Oaks, CA: Sage.

Elkin, M. (1984). *Families under the influence.* New York, NY: W. W. Norton.

Fisher, G., & Harrison, T. C. (2008). *Substance abuse: Information for school counselors, social workers, therapists, and counselors* (4th ed.). Boston, MA: Allyn & Bacon.

Guttman, H. A. (1991). Systems theory, cybernetics, and epistemology. In A. S. Gurman & D. P. Kniskern (Eds.), *Handbook of family therapy: Vol. 2* (pp. 41–62). New York, NY: Brunner/Mazel.

Immordino-Yang, M. H., & Damasio, A. (2007). We feel, therefore we learn: The relevance of affective and social neuroscience to education. *Mind, Brain, and Education, 1*(1), 3–10.

Marlatt, G. A., & Gordon, J. R. (1985). *Relapse prevention: Maintenance strategies in the treatment of addictive behavior.* New York, NY: Guilford Press.

McCrady, B. S., & Niles, B. (1989). *The incidence of alcoholism in the general hospital*: Results of a study at St. Peter's. Presented at Department of Medicine Grand Rounds, St. Peter's Medical Center, New Brunswick, NJ.

Piercy, F., & Benson, K. (2005). Aesthetic forms of data presentation in qualitative family therapy research. *Journal of Marital and Family Therapy, 31*(1), 107–119.

Shaffer, H., & Jones, S. (1989). *Quitting cocaine.* Lexington, MA: D. C. Heath.

# CHAPTER 41

# EXPERIENCING THE ADDICTION RECOVERY PROCESS

Angela B. Bradford, Scott A. Ketring, and
Thomas A. Smith

## Introduction

It is estimated that 22.5 million people in the United States abuse or are dependent on drugs or alcohol (Substance Abuse and Mental Health Services Administration, 2010). The comorbidity of substance use and mental health problems requires that practitioners be prepared to treat addiction in its various forms. In addition to drug and alcohol addiction, clinicians increasingly find themselves addressing behavior or process addictions, such as those of sexuality, gambling, computer use, pornography use, eating, and other compulsions.

The broadening of addiction treatment to include substance and behavioral addictions forces clinicians to evaluate personal perspectives associated with this phenomenon. With the high rates of substance and other addictions, almost all clinicians have either experienced an addiction themselves or have had a family member who has struggled with one. These experiences can give a clinician greater understanding of the socioemotional factors related to dependence and the inherent consequences associated with addictions. However, even though many have close relationships with someone who has struggled with addiction, and though they may have an increased understanding of the addictive processes, clinicians are not immune to personal judgment and condemnation. In fact, their personal experiences may contribute to biases that could become an obstacle to providing effective therapeutic services. Unless clinicians have personally engaged in and attempted to cease compulsive behavior, they may not fully understand the nuances of the struggle to overcome an addiction.

## Rationale

Increased personal familiarity with the struggle to overcome addictive behavior can benefit clinicians in multiple ways. First, clinicians can gain greater insight and self-awareness regarding personal biases against addicts and addictive behavior, leading to positive adjustments in attitudes. Second, personal familiarity increases exposure to and understanding of the thought processes and rationalizations made by those struggling with addiction. Finally, clinicians can develop greater empathy for individuals and clients who struggle with addiction if they have personal experience related to addiction work. These benefits may be best gained through an experiential approach that personalizes the experience of trying to overcome an addiction.

This activity is designed to increase self-awareness and to give clinicians insights into their attitudes toward addiction and the process of addiction recovery by allowing clinicians to experience several behavioral and attitudinal factors that accompany addiction recovery. For example, some level of denial regarding the existence or extent of the addiction is usually necessary for addicts to justify their behavior (e.g., "I don't have a problem. Who doesn't like sex?"). In addition, in order to avoid consequences or hide unacceptable behaviors, addicts often commit lies of commission and omission (e.g., saying "I only drank two beers while you were gone last night," when, in fact, she drank four or, when asked how many beers she drank, she answers truthfully that she drank two but omits the fact that the two beers were accompanied by five tequila shots and two marijuana joints). Addicts might stop the addictive behavior but continue to "cheat" by engaging in varying forms of the behavior (e.g., while the addict doesn't play poker at the casino anymore, he participates in office pools and visits the racetrack). If addicts successfully stop doing what they have been addicted to for any length of time, they often find a replacement addiction and engage in many of the same behaviors using a different medium (e.g., "I don't fall asleep drinking anymore, I just smoke a pack of cigarettes daily—a habit developed at AA meetings"). The substitution often leads to relapse into previous addictive behaviors.

Because these attitudes and behaviors (denial, dishonesty, cheating, finding a replacement behavior, and relapse) are all elements of developing and maintaining addictive behavior, recovery can be a long and challenging process. Clinicians with limited experience in addiction recovery may be unprepared to weather these challenges and help facilitate client change. Thus, the experiential training activity should simulate addiction recovery and facilitate experiencing some or all of these attitudes and behaviors. It has been our experience that the level of increased self-awareness and understanding following this activity varies across clinicians. Certainly, the nature of the activity allows for different levels of commitment, difficulty, and success. However, because the level of participation in this activity is self-directed, we have not had any indication that this activity is contraindicated for any type of clinician. In some cases, clinicians have been too ashamed of their perceived failures, so they did not discuss these in the group context; however, because a safe and trustworthy supervisor–clinician relationship existed, they chose to privately disclose specific challenges following the activity, thereby facilitating greater opportunity to process the course of addiction recovery and learn of the quiet and lonely struggle many addicts have.

# Activity Instructions

The experiential activity presented here is developed from a suggestion by Fisher and Harrison (2013) and is focused on eliminating a specific habit or desired behavior for a period of 6 to 8 weeks. The activity instructions are directed specifically to activity supervisors, because it is best conducted in group supervision or in a class setting, where several clinicians (preferably, closely connected) can participate in the activity simultaneously. The greater the collegiality and cohesion of the group, the more closely this activity can mirror the dynamics of overcoming an addiction in the context of a real-life social support system, with its inherent advantages and disadvantages.

Before beginning the activity, clinicians are asked which personal habits would be "the most difficult thing to give up" over the specified time frame and are asked to come to the activity prepared with two or three habits in mind. It is important for supervisors to emphasize that giving up more serious addictions is not necessarily advisable over the course of this activity, because the clinician's personal sense of privacy and personal life need to be respected. Although a participant would be free to give up smoking, other addictions such as eating disorders, sexual compulsivity, gambling, drugs, and alcoholism are more significant. We recommend giving participants clear instruction about the advisability of focusing on these more serious addictions because they are of greater sensitivity and would require more trust and vulnerability than would normally be appropriate for a group supervision setting.

There are five distinct aspects to this activity. First, members of the group complete a sequence of coursework or reading focused on the treatment of addiction. Fisher and Harrison (2013) provide important information on how to assess for substance addiction and begin treatment thereof. Similarly, Bepko and Krestan (1985) provide a fundamental theoretical perspective and model for treating addiction using a family systems approach.

Second, clinicians are asked to choose a behavior or habit they regularly engage in that most closely resembles an addiction. Everyone, *including the supervisor or instructor*, participates in the activity. Common areas of focus are the consumption of substances or products (e.g., coffee or sweets), interpersonal habits (e.g., yelling at children to gain compliance or venting when angry), hoarding behaviors (e.g., keeping promotional freebies, such as multiple computer mouse pads, despite not needing them), compulsive habits (e.g., checking e-mail or social networking sites multiple times throughout the day), or personal attachments (e.g., electronics). The familiar group context is desirable for this activity because, quite often, individuals don't pinpoint the behavior that is most like an addiction for themselves. Some participants are in denial, such as the clinician who tried to convince the group that eating french fries was her guilty pleasure, although group members rarely saw her without a cup of coffee.

Others benefit from the group nature of the assignment because they may lack the self-awareness to identify which of their behaviors are closest to an addiction. For example, one clinician didn't realize she frequently interjected the phrase "you know" when speaking with others and only noticed it after the supervisor brought it to her attention. Another did not realize the role of shopping in her life until her colleagues highlighted that she frequently went shopping and spent money when she felt distressed. A close, familiar group context allows for increased accountability through interaction with peers or friends. In the case of the aforementioned clinician who wanted to give up french fries, she conceded that coffee was her true "addiction" after the group discussion and ultimately interrupted all caffeine consumption. Although collegial accountability is helpful in this process, participants must ultimately choose for themselves the behavior or item that they will eliminate from their personal lives.

Third, the selected behavior is then treated like an addiction from which to recover. The clinicians commit to not engage in that behavior altogether for the designated time frame. Depending on the behavior selected, it might be appropriate to take a more global perspective. For instance, recognizing that coffee was simply the medium to facilitate caffeine intake, the coffee-drinking clinician chose to stop all caffeine consumption for the duration of the activity.

Fourth, once or twice a week, the group members check in with each other regarding their progress and how they are doing emotionally, physically, socially, psychologically, and in any other domains. This mirrors the experience of 12-step meetings or group therapy, in which others who are battling an addiction can provide support and hold each other accountable and in which individuals can talk about their experiences. Many participants may also provide support throughout the week to facilitate the weaning process. Conversely, others, after relapsing in their chosen behavior, may attempt to sabotage others (e.g., holding an Academy Awards party for the entire group when a colleague has given up television). Or, they may use others' weaknesses to rationalize addictive behavior (e.g., "I might overeat, but at least I'm not a drunk" or "She won't stop, so why should I?").

Finally, at the end of the designated period of recovery, the group members reconvene to reveal their successes, challenges, and perceived failures, discussing how or under what circumstances they cheated, whether they adopted any replacement behaviors, and whether they intend to resume the behavior or continue on the path to recovery. It should be noted that as a course assignment, supervisors should evaluate clinicians' efforts to track the addiction process rather than whether clinicians were completely abstinent from their chosen behavior.

# Examples

This activity carries with it the potential for mirroring addiction recovery in a myriad of ways. Addicts often don't recognize or admit they have an addiction. Like addicts whose friends and family point it out and try to convince them of the problem, clinicians often have difficulty identifying something that would be their addiction and do not realize the extent of their behaviors until someone close to them highlights it. One clinician reported, "I was shocked that my [colleagues] were able to identify my addiction—chocolate. Was it really that obvious? I felt it was hardest to actually admit that really was my addiction and decide to give it up."

Clinicians might minimize their behaviors and attempt to give up something that isn't truly their addiction. This process includes varying levels of dishonesty with self and others. Like the addict who is not forthright about engaging in addictive behavior, participants often conceal their behavior out of shame, lack of motivation or commitment, or fear of possible outcomes. In one such instance, a clinician who gave up all liquids except water stated, "I was amazed at the length to which I would go to hide my addictive behavior from my peers. I remember journaling about my experience and planning in excruciating detail when and where I would 'get my fix' and fixating on aspects of what I gave up that wouldn't have even appealed to me before (i.e., 'I can't wait to have a bowl of cereal with MILK!' when I hadn't had cereal in years)."

Like the addicts who cheat and engage in some form of their addiction while in recovery, clinicians also have this possibility and can choose to cheat. This experience increases the likelihood of feeling guilty or ashamed or making rationalizations and excuses. For example, one clinician reported that "'slip-ups' were accompanied by guilt and self-pity. I felt like a failure because I thought it should have been easier." Another, who gave up television, decided it was alright to cheat and watch the Super Bowl because it only occurred once every year, while another gave up television but still watched movies because "movies are not the same as TV."

Sometimes, clinicians will refuse to fully participate. One reported "I refused to give up what my (colleagues) suggested I give up. At that time in my life I was completely unwilling to depart from my spending addiction. I justified and weaseled my way out of giving up the main thing that brought me comfort and control during such a stressful time." The clinicians' level of participation impacts the entire process; however, even at lower levels of commitment or participation, clinicians will still gather important personal information about addictive processes, mental justifications, and challenges in behavioral change. The clinician who refused to give up shopping went on to say, "The exercise forced me to confront my spending/shopping habits, and I brought them up in premarital counseling. I didn't give up shopping for the class exercise, but ultimately I have greatly curtailed my 'shopping therapy' trips."

Once addicts have moved into the stage of recovery in which they no longer succumb to the addiction, they are at risk for finding a replacement behavior. Throughout the activity, clinicians might engage in alternative, yet similarly habit-forming, behaviors in order to (a) distract themselves from the substance or behavior they are avoiding, (b) fill the time that has been left available by stopping the original behavior, or (c) help them cope with the loss of their "addiction." For instance, a clinician who gives up playing video games may fill the time originally spent gaming by surfing the Internet or engaging in another behavior that can become addictive.

Similarly, the risk of relapse is an ongoing concern for most addicts. At the end of this activity, clinicians may also choose to continue life without resuming the prohibited practice or habit. In fact, some do eliminate the behavior and focus on the journey to the point of abstinence, whereas others choose to make adjustments to the behavior (e.g., one clinician wanted to resume eating sweets but planned to be more temperate in the frequency and amount consumed). Still others are eager to resume their addiction and are quite unapologetic about doing so (e.g., one clinician who gave up chocolate was disappointed that an acceptable replacement behavior couldn't be found and happily indulged in a large piece of chocolate cake on the day the activity ended).

Whatever the clinician's decision and response, the activity carries with it the potential of processing what this experience is like for clients who are asked to stop a behavior completely and permanently, without any acceptable reason for relapse. One clinician who gave up ice cream stated, "I was so aware of how often ice cream came up in casual conversation, was advertised on TV, in print, etc. There were regular reminders of what I couldn't have. When I thought about what that must be like for someone struggling with alcohol addiction, for example, and the constant media attention associated with that, it really brought the struggle home for me." The activity also highlights the fact that reading about addiction is a necessary, but almost insufficient, preparation for understanding the processes that exist among addicts. Readings cannot provide the same unique context necessary for changes in cognitions, behaviors, and emotions, nor can they comparably increase clinicians' empathy.

Most importantly, throughout and at the conclusion of the activity, most clinicians highlight their increased self-awareness and empathy for those struggling with addiction. One clinician stated, "The [activity] made me aware of how judgmental I had previously been when thinking about individuals struggling with addictions. It was eye opening and humbling to see that the very weakness I saw in them was every bit as prevalent in me." Another stated, "This [activity] helped me to overcome judgments that I didn't even realize I was making. I knew how addictive substances can be abstractly, not from experience, and it wasn't until I tried to give up something that mattered to me that I developed empathy for those who struggle with substance addiction."

# Measuring Progress

The weekly group meetings are essential for tracking progress made. These meetings are helpful because they provide a context similar to group therapy during which clinicians can complain, report successes and failures, and provide support. These meetings are also helpful because the supervisor has the opportunity and responsibility to highlight how clinicians' experiences mirror those of an addict. Although clinicians can do this on their own, the burden is on the more experienced clinician or supervisor to draw parallels and to use clinicians' experiences as teaching points. As clinicians learn how their own experiences are similar to those of addicts, they have an increased ability to identify previously held beliefs or judgments regarding addiction. They become more adept at recognizing rationalizations, denial, and enabling behaviors in themselves and each other. As they do so, their self-awareness improves and they have the opportunity to reshape their thought processes surrounding addiction.

The group context provides an arena for congratulatory feedback regarding progress made and mirrors the group therapy context many addicts have. However, many addicts build support networks beyond their therapy groups (e.g., family members who attend Al-Anon). Clinicians may similarly choose to discuss their own progress in this activity with their extended support networks. Supervisors can encourage clinicians to tell *close* friends and family about their efforts to change their behaviors, sharing their successes and plans for the future. It is possible that clinicians will want to preface or structure their conversations with information about the assignment. With the goal of helping clinicians increase their own self-awareness, the supervisor should respond to such instances by processing with the clinicians why they would prefer to reveal the motives for their actions to their friends and families, paying particular attention to potential judgments made about habitual or addictive behavior and, therefore, those who struggle with addiction. Whether clinicians choose to provide a context when they share their experiences with their friends and families remains their decision. It has been our experience that most clinicians tell their friends and family about the activity. We should also note, however, that when clinicians develop significantly more understanding and empathy throughout the activity, they are enabled to and tend to share more personal details of their experiences. As is the case with recovering addicts, openness with their extended networks about their struggles and successes is a strong indicator of the clinicians' commitment to the very process they will require of their clients.

# Conclusion

There is a high probability that clinicians will encounter clients with some form of addiction while they practice. In order to become more attuned to client experiences, as well as their own assumptions, it can be helpful—and may be necessary—for clinicians to experience the very process in which they expect their clients to engage. This activity provides a safe and impactful opportunity to do so. Like those of all addicts, individual experiences vary. Some clinicians refuse to participate; others successfully struggle through and overcome a physical addiction. Regardless of the outcome, each experience facilitates discussion and can be used as an important teaching point in helping clinicians increase in self-awareness and other-awareness.

# Additional Resources

Carnes, P. (2001). *Out of the shadows: Understanding sexual addiction* (3rd ed.). Center City, MN: Hazelden.

Fisher, G. L., & Harrison, T. C. (2013). *Substance abuse: Information for school counselors, social workers, therapists, and counselors* (5th ed.). Boston, MA: Allyn & Bacon.

Miller, W. R., Forcehimes, A. A., & Zwiben, A. (2011). *Treating addiction: A guide for professionals*. New York, NY: Guilford Press.

# References

Bepko, C., & Krestan, J. (1985). *The responsibility trap: A blueprint for treating the alcoholic family*. New York, NY: Free Press.

Fisher, G. L., & Harrison, T. C. (2013). The role of the mental health professional in prevention and treatment. In G. L. Fisher & T. C. Harrison (Eds.), *Substance abuse: Information for school counselors, social workers, therapists, and counselors* (5th ed., pp. 1–11). Boston, MA: Allyn & Bacon.

Substance Abuse and Mental Health Services Administration (SAMHSA). (2010). Results from the 2009 National Survey on Drug Use and Health: Volume I. Summary of National Findings (Office of Applied Studies. NSDUH Series H-38A, HHS Publication No. SMA 10–4586 Findings). Rockville, MD. Retrieved from http://oas.samhsa.gov

# CHAPTER 42

# INCREASING SENSITIVITY TO AGEISM

Lori Cluff Schade

# Introduction

Individuals ages 65 and older are rapidly increasing in proportion to the general U.S. population. In 2010, 12.9% of the U.S. population, or 1 out of every 8 persons, was older than 65 (Administration on Aging, 2011). The first cohort from the baby boomer generation will all have reached or surpassed age 65 by the year 2020 (Karel, Gatz, & Smyer, 2012), and by 2030, this demographic of individuals age 65 and older is expected to represent 19% of the population (Administration on Aging, 2011). An aging population experiences significant comorbidities between psychiatric disorders and cognitive disorders (Karel et al., 2012). It is likely that the current cohort of elderly people may be more inclined to seek therapy than any previous generation (Satre, Knight, & David, 2006), making it increasingly important for mental health clinicians to become more familiar with contextual factors related to this vulnerable group (Lambert-Shute & Fruhauf, 2011). Clinicians will need to gain competency in working with families across the generations, as well as understanding unique features of an aging demographic in order to provide effective mental health interventions (Laidlaw & Pachana, 2009). The suggested activity is designed to increase contextual sensitivity to age by increasing knowledge about common stereotypes and encouraging clinicians to develop self-awareness about personal reactions to the elderly.

# Rationale

Although the population is aging, age discrimination exists and is a real barrier for people older than age 65 who attempt to access mental health care services (Blakemore, 2009). Mental health service providers not only frequently have biases toward older people but are often unfamiliar with normative life transition considerations in this age-group, as well as effective mental health care concerns and practices (Myers & Harper, 2004). Traditionally, age and cohort have not been considered as issues of individual diversity in mental health care (Karel et al., 2012). Although many contextual factors are often included in academic curricula for marriage and family clinicians, age is often minimally addressed in marriage and family therapy graduate programs (Lambert-Shute & Fruhauf, 2011). This is potentially problematic because mental health clinicians sometimes present negative conceptualizations of clients who are different from themselves (Roysircar, 2004), despite being frequently presented with clients of various ages, particularly in training programs during which they are not yet specialized.

The term *ageism* was coined (Butler, 1969) as a descriptive term for discrimination and stereotyping related to age, and like other forms of prejudice, it may both overtly and covertly influence individuals' perceptions and attitudes toward a specific population (Ivey, Wieling, & Harris, 2000). Ageism is one form of prejudice that is often even socially sanctioned (Kane, 2004). It is unique in that, in the absence of early death, it is directed toward a group of people to which the perpetrators will eventually belong (Martens, Goldenberg, & Greenberg, 2005). Researchers found that ageism exists in part because the aging remind people of their own mortality, eventual physical deterioration, and eventual loss of cultural worth, because youth-related traits—such as beauty, strength, and productivity—are often tied to cultural value (Martens et al., 2005).

Common beliefs related to older people include that they are inflexible, unproductive, weak, senile, sick, tired, depressed, incompetent, reclusive, and unlikely to change; in other words, older people are viewed as poor therapy candidates (Ivey et al., 2000; Kane, 2004). Even positive stereotypes, such as perceptions that older people are wise, kind, dependable, happy, and have political power and influence, can be problematic by influencing perceptions and expectations in therapy (Kane, 2004). Older people who are well-functioning are often seen as an anomaly (Daniel, Roysircar, Abeles, & Boyd, 2004). In the helping professions, examples of prejudiced feelings toward older adults are evidenced in disrespect, patronizing speech, derogatory humor, and social avoidance (Grefe, 2011).

Evidence of ageism in the mental health profession has also been documented (Kane, 2004; Ivey et al., 2000). In a study to determine the prevalence of ageist attitudes among clinical providers, clinicians were presented with case studies in which the presenting problems were the same, but the ages were altered (Ivey et al., 2000). Clinicians then made evaluations of the presenting cases. Findings indicate that clinicians viewed sexual problems, marital conflict, and substance abuse as more problematic among younger couples compared to older couples (Ivey et al., 2000). In a similar study, Kane (2004) found that clinicians were more likely to recommend psychotherapy to the younger clients as compared to the older clients (Kane, 2004). The author referred to "therapeutic nihilism" (Kane, 2004, p. 769), in which clinicians believe change is not possible for older adults, so they should not treat them therapeutically.

Supervisors can facilitate clinician self-awareness about ageism by both educating clinicians about issues related to an aging population and providing self-reflection opportunities for increasing self-awareness about such issues (Daniel et al., 2004). Another way to decrease negative feelings toward a group of people is to increase contact with members of that group (Grefe, 2011; Daniel et al., 2004). Clinicians can also learn to recognize and face unique emotional challenges that are present while working with older adults—including that the work is often highly emotional because of multiple losses in life, that some older adults can feel hopeless in such circumstances, and that topics discussed with older adults can activate fear in some clinicians who become aware of their own mortality (Lee, Volans, & Gregory, 2003). By exploring ageism in the therapy room, clinicians can improve the quality of their interactions as well as their overall therapeutic effectiveness when treating older clients.

# Activity Instructions

Presented here are experiential activities that have been developed to help clinicians gain greater sensitivity toward older clients and face their own mortality fears as they arise in the therapy room. Previous studies have shown that when student clinicians engage in experiential aging activities, they report that the activities encouraged them to examine their personal stereotypes about aging (Anderson-Hanley, 1999). The activities are suitable for all levels of graduate student therapists and are designed to be introduced and facilitated by supervisors with clinical supervisees. These activities are designed for smaller settings with up to 10 student clinicians. Instructions are directed specifically to the supervisors, and required materials are listed before each activity. The supervisor should have previously established rules with supervisees in the group for respectful handling of personal interactions and emotions that may be elicited from the process. Supervisors should also be sensitive to and be prepared to address emotional reactions that might arise from supervisees during the activities.

## Activity 1: Uncovering Ageist Stereotypes

The activity is designed to help clinicians uncover their own specific biases to increase personal awareness and ultimately increase efficacy in working with older clients. The supervisors will read the two different marital case vignettes (in which two couples of different ages present similar issues in counseling) aloud to the supervisees. The idea is that the issues being presented are the same, but the ages of the couples will vary, so that the supervisees will uncover their internal biases based solely on age differences.

> ***Vignette 1****: Mark and Allison are a couple in their mid-thirties. They have been married for 15 years, have four children living at home, and have struggled financially in recent years due to a weak economy. Mark had been working steadily but lately has struggled to keep a full-time*

*position, which has been a frequent source of conflict between the couple. Allison gets frustrated because Mark works at his home computer a lot of the time. Recently, she found an e-mail that he sent to a former office companion, a female, and she is worried that he might be having an emotional affair. Early in their marriage, when she was pregnant with their first child, he had an affair and confessed to her after it had been going on for six months. They went to counseling at that time. She says she has forgiven him and states that, to her knowledge, he has not had any more affairs; however, she also describes him as frequently flirtatious and explains that ever since finding out about the affair at the beginning of their marriage, she has never felt completely safe with Mark. When she sees him work on his computer, she wonders if he is engaging in online flirting behavior. The couple has not been physically intimate for two months. They tell you that they have always been mismatched in their levels of sexual desire. Recently, Mark has been drinking more frequently, although he claims he does not have a substance use problem, and the couple has had increased conflict.*

***Vignette 2****: David and Judy are a couple in their mid-sixties. They have been married for 45 years and have five adult children who are married. They are struggling financially since inflation has gone up recently, and they have been on a fixed income. David had a job at a local bookstore bringing in extra money, but he lost his job recently, thus reducing their income. Judy works at the local library. She has been frustrated with the amount of time David has been spending on the computer. She found e-mails between him and a former coworker, and she is worried that he might be having an emotional affair. Early in their marriage, when she was pregnant with their second child, he had an affair and confessed to her after it had been going on for a few months. They went to counseling at that time. She says she has forgiven him and states that, to her knowledge, he has not had any more affairs; however, she also describes him as frequently flirtatious and explains that ever since finding out about the affair at the beginning of their marriage, she has never felt completely safe with David. When she watches him work on his computer, she wonders if he is engaging in online flirting behavior. The couple has not been physically intimate for two months. They tell you that they have always been mismatched in their levels of sexual desire. Recently, Judy has been drinking more frequently, although she claims she does not have a substance use problem, and the couple has had increased conflict.*

To begin the activity, inform the participants that you will be reading two case vignettes to them. They are to rate each couple from 1 to 10 in the following areas as you read them:

1. How serious are the issues this couple is facing? (1 to 10)
2. How hopeful are you that this couple can change? (1 to 10)
3. How easy do you think this couple will be to work with? (1 to 10)

After presenting each vignette, ask the student clinicians how their ratings varied between cases. Process how age might have affected their ratings and the way they are thinking about the cases. Consider adding the following questions to the ensuing discussion:

1. What assumptions do you make about the couple's sexual relationship, based on the age of each couple?
2. How does the couple's age influence your feelings about treating the substance use in each case?
3. What assumptions do you find yourself making about whether therapy is recommended?
4. What strengths do you identify in the younger couple that you do not assume for the older couple?
5. What strengths might the older couple possess that the younger couple does not?
6. What biases do you think you might automatically have toward individuals or couples, depending on their ages?

Note that the direction of the discussion can be flexible, but it should always come back to helping supervisees realize their initial biases based solely on age.

## Activity 2: Increased Awareness of Age Stereotypes

Previous research has demonstrated that ageist attitudes are often reflected in the content of birthday cards (Snellman, Johansson, & Kalman, 2012). This activity is designed to give clinicians hands-on experience with specific examples of this form of prejudice and process the meaning behind it. Facilitators should gather an assortment of birthday cards that focus on different milestone age-groups (i.e., where the recipient would be turning 30, 40, 50, etc.). Pass around the birthday cards for the group to examine. Ask student clinicians to reflect on the following questions:

1. What are some of the general differences presented in messages among various ages?
2. What are some cultural attitudes about older people based on the birthday cards?
3. What are some commonly reinforced stereotypes about aging adults?
4. Are the messages primarily positive or negative?
5. As you consider yourself reaching some of these ages, what emotions do you experience?
6. What biases are reflected in the content of the cards?

## Activity 3: Experiential Group Work Activity

Following are a series of experiential in-class activities that are designed to facilitate a class discussion about some of the real physical limitations frequently faced by older clients. The facilitator should come prepared with the following items for use in this part of the activity: rubber gloves with cotton swabs for each finger and thumb, a pair of shoes (with shoelaces), a shirt with buttons, two pairs of nonprescription glasses or sunglasses, petroleum jelly, and earplugs. It is best to prepare the room and set up several tasks that older people complete on a regular basis. Furthermore, the supervisor may choose to conduct one or several of these experiential activities, as time permits. Be sure to adapt the number of materials to the number of supervisees in the group.

- Have rubber gloves prepared with cotton swabs pushed into the fingers to mimic joint stiffness and arthritis. Have the individuals put on these gloves and attempt a simple task like tying a pair of shoes and buttoning a shirt.
- Have two pairs of nonprescription glasses or sunglasses, slightly smeared with petroleum jelly to mimic the effects of cataracts or other vision problems common in aging adults. Have student clinicians put on the glasses and walk from one end of the room to another, negotiating a few obstacles that can be seen but are somewhat obscured by the glasses.
- Have student clinicians put earplugs into their ears to mimic the effects of age-related hearing loss. Have student clinicians attempt to follow verbal directions from someone behind them to complete a task.

Following these activities, lead a discussion about what it was like for the student clinicians to try to complete tasks while physically impeded. Ask participants to explain their experiences, using the following questions:

1. What was it like to struggle when you know you had previously been able to complete these tasks without difficulty?
2. What was it like to have physical limitations while retaining cognitive functionality?
3. Are there any similarities between this activity and the way that elderly people experience the world when their physical abilities become limited, although they still have the same personalities, hobbies, interests, etc.?
4. What unique emotions might follow this experience?
5. How might clinicians approach these issues without stereotyping all elderly people into a category of great physical decline but still remaining sensitive to the possibility that physical decline may be a real factor affecting their ability to function?
6. How does knowledge of physical and possible cognitive limitations affect your attitudes toward older people?

Example                                                                     297

Student clinicians in this assignment are expected to interview two different individuals older than age 65. To achieve the purposes of this activity, interviews should be about 30 minutes long. The point is to gain an understanding of what aging has been like for each individual. Before the interviews are conducted, specific questions can be brainstormed by individual clinicians or by the group as a whole. Questions should be geared around asking people in this demographic about what aging has been like. Sample questions include:

1. What has surprised you the most about aging?
2. What do you think you understand better at your age now than you did 30 years ago?
3. What are you the most proud of in your life so far?
4. What challenges have you overcome in your life?
5. What advice would you give people my age?
6. What do you think people my age misunderstand about people your age?

Shortly after the interviews, students are expected to write a paper addressing the following questions:

1. What assumptions did you make about individuals in this age-group that were not supported by your experiences in the interviews?
2. How were the two individuals similar and how were they different, despite their similar age?
3. In what ways do you share similar characteristics with the interviewees?
4. How has your view of yourself as an older person changed after having completed this interview?
5. When you are the age of the person you interviewed, how will you still be the same as you are today? How will you be different? How do you feel about those changes? What emotions start to surface as you think about it?

This written assignment is designed to promote actual in-person experiences with older people in order to decrease stereotypes and to help clinicians realize how they share similarities even with individuals who differ greatly in age from themselves.

# Example

These activities were conducted with a class of six therapy students in a university setting. All of the activities generated a high level of responsiveness. The student clinicians were able to identify that they did hold negative biases about older clients. In general, they viewed older clients as more inflexible and unlikely to change, thus reducing their hope for therapeutic effectiveness before even meeting with the clients. They also reported believing that the issues were not as serious for older clients. Some of them expressed feeling possible defensiveness toward a perception that older clients would be more dismissive of their professional expertise.

Although the student clinicians were aware of negative biases toward older people in the broader culture, the birthday card activity generated a lengthy discussion about the pervasiveness of negative messages toward aging that permeate society. Several students admitted that they are fearful of the aging process in part because of these messages. The interview activity in this regard was helpful in reducing some of this anxiety. Students reported that in the interview process, they were able to gain appreciation for the depth and wisdom older people have obtained through their many experiences, and that interacting on a more personal level helped them gain positive experiences with an aging demographic.

The experiential activity generated a meaningful conversation about the emotions that older clients might be experiencing. Student clinicians cued into disappointment, frustration, and even shame that aging clients might feel as their physical abilities can be in decline while they remember that they used to complete tasks more easily. In addition, the class identified a potential disconnect if the student therapist thinks he or she has been clear but the client may not have heard or understood something, but tries to fill in the gaps and pretends to go along because of the embarrassment of having to ask the clinician to repeat what he or she has said. They also identified the emotions that might result from being surrounded by younger people who are faster and might seem impatient. Ultimately, this activity generated the most discussion around the need to attune to older clients and attempt to carefully understand and validate their positions.

# Measuring Progress

Progress will be measured by supervisees identifying specific biases they have had toward this demographic. In addition, their abilities to conceptualize plans for recognizing internal bias and dealing with it in the therapy room, as facilitated by discussions with the supervisor, will signal progress. Supervisors can additionally measure progress by asking students to review current caseloads and discuss how previous biases about age might be affecting progress in therapy and how they might improve the quality of their therapeutic relationships and interventions based on increased awareness about biases. This can easily be accomplished by asking for a handwritten assessment of these specific factors. Another option is to ask for an identification of potential age-related biases in future assigned cases. Supervisees can write articulated plans for how they will address personal bias and stereotyping for assigned cases. These written assignments will give supervisors information about the level of insight student clinicians have obtained in the learning process, along with information about their abilities to negotiate these potential obstacles in therapy.

# Conclusion

As the proportion of elderly people in the U.S. population continues to rise, clinicians will likely experience a corresponding increase in the number of elderly people presenting in therapy. Participating in exercises designed to increase knowledge of stereotypes will help student clinicians gain awareness about their beliefs and reactions to this age-group, and will aid them in handling such reactions. The activities listed in this chapter are designed to encourage clinicians to view aging from theoretical, cultural, experiential, and empathetic perspectives. Overall, an increase in sensitivity will help clinicians reinforce the therapeutic alliance, which is fundamental to overall change in any context (Daniel et al., 2004; Roysircar, 2004).

# Additional Resource

Segal, D. L., Qualls, S. H., & Smyer, M. A. (2010). *Aging and mental health*. Oxford, UK: Wiley-Blackwell.

# References

Administration on Aging, U.S. Department of Health and Human Services. (2011). *A profile of older Americans: 2011*. Retrieved from www.aoa.gov/aoaroot/aging_statistics/Profile/index .aspx

Anderson-Hanley, C. (1999). Experiential activities for teaching: Psychology of aging. *Educational Gerontology, 25*(5), 449–456.

Blakemore, S. (2009). Ageism in mental care. *Nursing Older People, 21*(5), 6–7.

Butler, R. N. (1969). Age-ism: Another form of bigotry. *The Gerontologist, 9*, 243–246.

Daniel, J. H., Roysircar, G., Abeles, N., & Boyd, C. (2004). Individual and cultural-diversity competency: Focus on the therapist. *Journal of Clinical Psychology, 60*(7), 755–770.

Grefe, D. (2011). Combating ageism with narrative and intergroup contact: Possibilities of inter-generational connections. *Pastoral Psychology*, *60*, 99–105.

Ivey, D. C., Wieling, E., & Harris, S. M. (2000). Save the young—the elderly have lived their lives: Ageism in marriage and family therapy. *Family Process*, *39*(2), 163–175.

Kane, M. N. (2004). Ageism and intervention: What social work students believe about treating people differently because of age. *Educational Gerontology*, *30*, 767–784.

Karel, M. J., Gatz, M., & Smyer, M. A. (2012). Aging and mental health in the decade ahead: What psychologists need to know. *American Psychologist*, *67*(3), 184–198.

Laidlaw, K., & Pachana, N. A. (2009). Aging, mental health, and demographic change: Challenges for psychotherapists. *Professional Psychology: Research and Practice*, *40*(6), 601–608.

Lambert-Shute, J., & Fruhauf, C. A. (2011). Aging issues: Unanswered questions in marital and family therapy literature. *Journal of Marital and Family Therapy*, *37*(1), 27–36.

Lee, K. M., Volans, P. J., & Gregory, N. (2003). Attitudes towards psychotherapy with older people among trainee clinical psychologists. *Aging & Mental Health*, *7*(2), 133–141.

Martens, A., Goldenberg, J. L., & Greenberg, J. (2005). A terror management perspective on ageism. *Journal of Social Issues*, *61*(2), 223–239.

Myers, J. E., & Harper, M. C. (2004). Evidence-based effective practices with older adults. *Journal of Counseling and Development*, *82*(2), 207–218.

Roysircar, G. (2004). Cultural self-awareness assessment: Practice examples from psychology training. *Professional Psychology: Research and Practice*, *35*(6), 658–666.

Satre, D. D., Knight, B. G., & David, S. (2006). Cognitive-behavioral interventions with older adults: Integrating clinical and gerontological research. *Professional Psychology: Research and Practice*, *37*(5), 489–498.

Snellman, F., Johansson, S., & Kalman, H. (2012). A pilot study of birthday cards as vignettes: Methodological reflections on the elusive everyday ageism. *International Journal of Humanities and Social Science*, *2*(7), 21–33.

# CHAPTER 43

# HELPING CLINICIANS DEVELOP END-OF-LIFE AWARENESS

Michael N. Humble, Melinda W. Pilkinton, Kilolo Brodie, and Jennifer L. Johnson

## Introduction

Chronic illness and dying are interrelated topics that clinicians are rarely exposed to during their graduate education and training (Csikai, Herrin, Tang, & Church, 2008; Pomeroy, 2011). Graduate programs tend to focus on the earlier part of the life cycle (e.g., birth, young adulthood, parenthood), giving very little attention to end-of-life issues (e.g., coping with an elderly parent who is ill and dying or struggling with the death of a young parent or child). The exploration of this challenging clinical topic can help clinicians become more sensitive and clinically prepared for issues related to illness and death while also becoming more clinically aware of their own unresolved grief issues in their families of origin.

In hospitals, clinicians typically make rounds alongside other medical professionals in a care management team that can include physicians, nurses, respiratory therapists, chaplains, and other ancillary personnel. Ideally, clinicians will develop a good rapport with physicians so they can work collaboratively during the diagnosis of a terminal illness, physically and emotionally demanding treatment, and end-of-life care decisions in order to better help clients and families. Student clinicians should be prepared to recognize and to respond when a team approach to end-of-life care becomes unbalanced (e.g., when the roles of healthcare team members are not clear to either the team members or to the family). This misbalance can also occur when physicians mistakenly ask clinicians to deliver the "bad news," sharing a terminal diagnosis that they are reluctant to give to their patients (Deja, 2006). Inexperienced clinicians who do not fully understand their own scope of practice may not recognize that medical diagnoses should always be given first by medical professionals (Dybicz, 2012; Hopps & Lowe, 2008) or in accordance with established hospital policies involving the use of treatment teams (Deja, 2006).

Because some clinicians may have less experience with or acceptance of end-of-life issues, we recommend that they work through their feelings regarding death anxiety, apprehension within medical settings, discomfort with terminally ill patients, and other relevant issues while still in the safer context of regular supervision and mentoring (Simons & Park-Lee, 2009; Werth, 2002). In preparing student clinicians or beginning therapists to work in the healthcare field, it is important to help them develop the skills needed to effectively and empathically practice in the context of end-of-life clinical encounters (Hales & Hawryluck, 2008; Pollens, 2012).

## Rationale

Although it is impossible for student clinicians to gain exposure to all possible clinical issues in the classroom, it is important for educators to aid student clinicians in developing clinical skills through their field placements, clinical internships, and volunteer experiences. Yet, unless beginning clinicians are placed in hospitals or hospice clinical settings, they will have very few opportunities to encounter end-of-life clinical issues and may not practice the skills needed for working with terminally ill patients and their families. Although role-playing does not replicate these difficult real-life clinical encounters, it is helpful because it can facilitate developing clinical skills related to loss (Mooradian, 2007; Willadsen, Allain, Bell, & Hingley-Jones, 2012). In fact, role-playing and simulations may be the student clinicians' only exposure to these important topics before interacting with real clients in a field learning experience (Moss, 2000).

# Activity Instructions

This learning activity includes role-playing a scenario in which a patient receives a terminal diagnosis from his or her physician while a student clinician is present. The clinician does not know beforehand that he or she will be required to provide all of the emotional support to the dying patient, and in each scenario the physician leaves right after the diagnosis is given. As a pedagogical modality, role-playing can be difficult for both participants and facilitators unless they have established a strong working relationship and some level of rapport. Therefore, it is recommended that this exercise be used later in the training program or supervised working environment after all parties are more familiar and comfortable with one another. This purposeful delay in implementing the activity allows all parties to know one another better. The facilitator is able to shape the role-play to target students' specific weaknesses, and students are more at ease around the facilitator.

In order for student clinicians to fully engage in this training exercise, we recommend that instructors make the role-play as realistic as possible (Dennison, 2011). In the cases described as follows, the training exercise was team-taught by several clinical instructors with expertise in the areas of grief and loss. Current literature suggests that instructor-delivered role-plays or simulations often provide a better training experience for student clinicians compared to peer-to-peer role-playing (Mooradian, 2008). In our classes, some of the instructors are actively involved in playing various roles while other instructors are designated observers and recorders/graders of student clinicians' clinical performances.

Although a hospital setting can be time-consuming to create, it is helpful to replicate the hospital environment as realistically as possible. During our classes, we create a hospital bed by arranging tables in front of the classroom with pillows and blankets. A water pitcher and a glass sit on a desk that serves as a bedside table. A laptop with a screensaver of a heart monitor (free screensavers can be found online) is placed on a chair next to the patient. We also utilize tubes/IV lines and bedpans (donated by hospice facilities). Using only one overhead light helps mimic the atmosphere of a hospital room. Furthermore, the noise of hospital monitors and activity is replicated with sound apps. These can be downloaded for free on most smartphone devices.

During the role-play, one instructor acts as the patient while another instructor is the physician. The physician is seated approximately 5 feet away from the patient when the physician is called out of the room (he or she will move behind the student clinician, out of view). The student clinician who just completed the exercise is also present, but he or she is also placed out of sight of the student clinician.

All of the clinical vignettes were designed to resemble real-world clinical encounters in which the student clinician and physician enter a patient's room together to discuss either a new diagnosis or the worsening of a chronic condition. During the role-plays, the physician is unexpectedly paged out of the room after giving the diagnosis because of an emergency situation with another patient in the hospital, an occurrence that is familiar to medical clinicians.

Before starting the exercise, student clinicians are paired off and told to come to the classroom on a staggered schedule, in roughly half-hour increments. When each pair of student clinicians arrives, they are given an envelope containing one of two clinical vignettes and are given 5 minutes to review the vignette and 15 to 20 minutes to interact with the simulated client.

Following are the two clinical vignettes that we have used in our classes:

### Vignette 1: Sheila

*You are covering the post-op floor as a clinical intern when you run into Dr. Smith, an oncologist whom you have known for about a year. He asks for your help with a difficult case, and you agree to his request. Sheila, a 36-year-old Latina, was admitted to the hospital six days ago with vaginal bleeding. Upon further examination, it was discovered that Sheila had multiple uterine cysts. Sheila had been experiencing symptoms for approximately six months prior to admission. Sheila lives with her husband, Adam, and their two children: Susan, 4 years old, and David,*

*10 years old. Sheila works part-time at Walmart, while her husband works the night shift at a local steel mill. They relocated to the area 5 years ago when her husband was offered the job at the steel mill. The closest family on Sheila's side is her sister, who lives 500 miles away.*

*Pathology reports have been received after examination of the tissue samples, and the diagnosis is cancer, stage IV. Furthermore, a computed tomography (CT) scan has revealed masses in her lungs and liver. Dr. Smith believes that these are also cancerous and is planning to recommend palliative care. You enter the room with Dr. Smith; the patient is alone, alert, and resting comfortably. Dr. Smith explains the procedures, tests, and the overall prognosis. Sheila looks at both you and Dr. Smith with a blank stare. Dr. Smith is then paged overhead for a code blue in the ICU (if possible, the instructor acting as the patient can play a prerecorded code blue message on his or her smartphone). The physician leaves the room quickly (at this point the instructor acting as the physician takes his or her place behind the student), leaving you alone with the patient. What do you do next?*

## Vignette 2: George

*You have recently been assigned to the critical care unit after working at Memorial General for two years. The critical care team has a full-time physician who is shared with the stepdown unit. George, a 38-year-old male, was admitted 5 days ago with shortness of breath and a high fever (104.5 degrees). George was intubated quickly and put into a medically induced coma to make him more comfortable. After talking to the nurses, you discover that George has not worked for two years because of multiple illnesses. These illnesses were the result of a compromised immune system, as George was diagnosed with human immunodeficiency virus (HIV) when he was 25. George tried numerous holistic treatments prior to seeking Western medical help. Physicians prescribed combination antiretroviral therapy, a potent blend of at least three active antiretroviral medications commonly known as "the AIDS cocktail," but the side effects were perceived by George as too intense for him to tolerate for any length of time; thus, he stopped taking the medications when the side effects became bothersome to him. Further complications with medication compliance were evident because of George's inability to obtain health insurance and his placement on a waiting list for the state AIDS Drug Assistance Program (ADAP). George did not initially qualify for ADAP based on his income, and the medications were extremely costly for him.*

*Upon admission to the hospital, George's physician, Dr. Chang, ordered a viral load test (to show how much HIV is in his system) and a CD4 test (to determine how many immune helper cells are in his system and help establish when antiretroviral therapy should be initiated). Both tests showed that George had little immune system functioning. The physician also ordered HIV resistance tests to determine whether George would be able to use any of the available medications; because of his issues with medical compliance, however, he has developed resistance to all current medications. Dr. Chang noted that because of resistance, a drug combination with the current medications available would not be feasible.*

*George was extubated yesterday and began to inquire about his health. Dr. Chang has requested that you (the clinician) accompany her as she delivers the results of the tests and recommends hospice for the patient when he is ready for discharge. You accompany Dr. Chang into the room and listen as she explains the results of the tests to George. Just as George begins questioning Dr. Chang about his treatment options, she is called out of the room by the nursing staff to attend to a patient who has fallen and is unconscious in the hallway outside of the patient's room. Dr. Chang rushes out of the room with a quick call to you over her shoulder that she will be back in a few minutes. You are standing at the patient's bedside as he looks at you and asks, "What should I do?"*

As part of the role-play, the patient could request water or ask the student clinician to sit on the bed beside him or her. Following the role-play, the instructors should explain that clinicians must always ask the nurses or certified nursing assistants for permission before taking any action with a patient, because the patient may be restricted from liquids for medical reasons ("nothing by mouth" or "NPO"), or the nursing staff may be measuring input/output, etc. Additionally, as patients could be at high risk for infection, clinicians are often not allowed to touch a patient's bedding and other items. This feedback will prompt student clinicians to think about the ramifications of a simple request for water and will also encourage discussion about the importance of clinicians' scope of practice, not only in hospitals but in all clinical settings.

Other questions the patient could ask during the role-play include:

- Am I going to die? What are my chances?

- Should I create a will/advanced directive with you right now?

- What should I say to my family? How should I tell my children? (These questions apply to the vignette with Sheila.)

- I have not been to church in a long time; will I go to heaven? (We hope most student clinicians will engage somewhat with this question, but it is important to remind them that outside spiritual support, such as the hospital chaplain, is available. In some instances, we have specified that George is a Jehovah's Witness and rejects blood transfusions. This serves as an additional learning opportunity for student clinicians.)

# Examples

This real-world role-play allows instructors to assess how well they are preparing student clinicians to deal with a variety of practical, legal, and ethical issues. As part of this assessment, a debriefing takes place immediately following the role-play, in order to help students to process their existing emotions. In our experience, the debriefing can evoke many intense emotions in student clinicians, such as personal despair for the patient, shock and anger toward the physician for leaving the room, and anxiety about statements they feel they should have made or did make. Most student clinicians note that they did not feel prepared for the quick turn of events, because they arrived only planning to enter the room with the physician, provide some encouragement to the patient and offer resources, and then depart. They did not expect to encounter feelings of transference or countertransference during the role-play.

During the debriefing session, the student clinicians typically note the unnerving nature of entering their classroom and having it look like a hospital room. This unsettling feeling is compounded further for most students because they were surprised at the suddenness of coming to class, receiving the envelope with a vignette, and walking into what was their *regular* classroom where they find their professor covered in sheets hooked up to an IV. Many students speak of a visceral feeling of "wanting to leave the classroom" or "needing more time" but also knowing the clock was ticking in terms of how much time they had to do the assignment. Most state that they did not feel that they grasped the clinical situation quickly or effectively enough to apply their theoretical knowledge to the interaction with the patient. Student clinicians always tell us that they wish they had been more prepared and performed better, but they have also expressed unanimous appreciation for the opportunity to participate in the activity. All have been able to grasp the connection between this suddenly assigned exercise and the fact that their real-life clinical work can be equally unpredictable.

# Measuring Progress

This exercise has one follow-up component in the form of a written paper that measures progress in three core areas (critical thinking, rapport/clinical style, and theory). This paper also allows students to process the 5-minute debriefing session that includes the student clinician, the patient, the physician, and the student clinician who completed the training exercise. The paper is loosely structured and is typically due the week following the role-play, while emotions are still easily accessible

The first section of the paper is graded for critical thinking, where we look for references to in-class presentations as well as the current clinical best-practice standards. Student clinicians are instructed to first describe the medical issue of the patient whom they worked with during the role-play. This includes a medical overview of the condition, including the latest advances in treatment (or lack thereof). An extensive review of the literature associated with the medical condition is assigned for two reasons. First, this investigation helps ground the clinicians, providing them a context for what the physician knew about the medical condition used in their role-play. We have found that this helps the clinicians understand, with more clarity, the difference between, for example, stage 1 cancer and stage 4. Second, we want student clinicians to describe whether having this medical knowledge beforehand would have changed their chosen clinical intervention.

Next, student clinicians are asked to write about the actual interaction between the clinician and the patient (rapport/clinical style portion of the paper). This includes the use of empathy, scope of practice, and the legal and ethical issues encountered during the role-play. This section allows for demonstration of specific interventions as well as the important discussion of scope-of-practice issues (such as helping the patient who requested water but who was prohibited from having any liquid by mouth).

The final part of the paper involves student clinicians writing a critical analysis of any theoretical lenses they used, or wished they had used, with the patient. This is an important aspect of the paper as clinicians begin to integrate their theoretical lens (e.g., CBT, motivational interviewing, strengths perspective theory) with the specifics of clinical cases. This section also includes a dissection of the debriefing section and what students took away from that interaction. In this section, student clinicians are asked to discuss and process the topic of death anxiety and consider possible tools to help address it (e.g., individual counseling, volunteering with hospice).

# Conclusion

This end-of-life role-play provides students with the opportunity to apply their clinical skills learned in the classroom to a simulated real-life hospital situation. The exercise is built to help clinicians with the topics of grief and loss, as most students who leave graduate programs state that they would like more training in this area. By utilizing this exercise, facilitators can help train clinicians to be more at ease when working with the dying process in their clinical practice.

# Additional Resources

Chabner, D. (2011). *Medical terminology: A short course* (6th ed.). St. Louis, MO: Saunders.

Johnson, J. L., & Grant, G. (2004). *Casebook: Medical social work*. New York, NY: Pearson.

Lewis, D., O'Boyle-Duggan, M., Chapman, J., Dee, P., Sellner, K., & Gorman, S. (2013). 'Putting words into action' project: Using role play in skills training. *British Journal of Nursing*, *22*(11), 638–644.

# References

Csikai, E. L., Herrin, C., Tang, M., & Church, W. T. (2008). Serious illness, injury, and death in child protection and preparation for end-of-life situations among child welfare services workers. *Child Welfare*, *87*(6), 49–70.

Deja, K. (2006). Social workers breaking bad news: The essential role of an interdisciplinary team when communicating prognosis. *Journal of Palliative Medicine*, *9*(3), 807–809.

Dennison, S. T. (2011). Interdisciplinary role play between social work and theater students. *Journal of Teaching in Social Work*, *31*(4), 415–430. doi: 10.1080/08841233.2011.597670

Dybicz, P. (2012). The ethic of care: Recapturing social work's first voice. *Social Work*, *57*(3), 271–280.

Hales, B. M., & Hawryluck, L. (2008). An interactive educational workshop to improve end of life communication skills. *Journal of Continuing Education in the Health Professions*, *28*(4), 241–255.

Hopps, J. G., & Lowe, T. B. (2008). *Comprehensive handbook of social work and social welfare, Volume 1: The profession of social work*. Hoboken, NJ: Wiley.

Mooradian, J. K. (2007). Simulated family therapy interviews in clinical social work education. *Journal of Teaching in Social Work*, *27*(1/2), 89–104.

Mooradian, J. K. (2008). Using simulated sessions to enhance clinical social work education. *Journal of Social Work Education*, *44*(3), 21–35.

Moss, B. (2000). The use of large-group role-play techniques in social work education. *Social Work Education*, *19*(5), 471–483.

Pollens, R. D. (2012). Integrating speech-language pathology services in palliative end-of-life care. *Topics in Language Disorders*, *32*(2), 137–148.

Pomeroy, E. C. (2011). On grief and loss. *Social Work*, *56*(2), 101–105.

Simons, K., & Park-Lee, E. (2009). Social work students' comfort with end-of-life care. *Journal of Social Work in End-of-Life & Palliative Care*, *5*, 34–48. doi: 10.1080/15524250903173884

Willadsen, A., Allain, L., Bell, L., & Hingley-Jones, H. (2012). The use of role-play and drama in interprofessional education: An evaluation of a workshop with students of social work, midwifery, early years, and medicine. *Social Work Education*, *31*(1), 75–89.

Werth, J. L. (2002). Incorporating end-of-life care into psychology courses. *Teaching of Psychology*, *29*(2), 106–111.

# About the Editors

**Roy A. Bean, PhD, LMFT**, is associate professor and program director of Marriage and Family Therapy Programs in the School of Family Life at Brigham Young University in Provo, Utah. He has presented nationally and internationally and is the author of more than 30 peer-reviewed articles and book chapters, an edited book, *A Practice That Works: Strategies to Complement Your Stand Alone Therapy Practice*, and a variety of other lay audience papers. He is an approved supervisor, as designated by the American Association for Marriage and Family Therapy (AAMFT), and serves as a co-principal investigator for the Flourishing Families Project, a research study dedicated to identifying the characteristics that help youth flourish emotionally, academically, and socially. His research and clinical interests include parent–adolescent relationships, particularly those in ethnically diverse families, and culturally competent family therapy.

**Sean D. Davis, PhD, LMFT**, is a licensed marriage and family therapist, AAMFT approved clinical supervisor and fellow, and associate professor in the California School of Professional Psychology, Couple and Family Therapy program at Alliant International University, in Sacramento, California. He is a frequent national and international presenter and has published several peer-reviewed articles and three books, including *Common Factors of Couple and Family Therapy: The Overlooked Foundation of Effective Practice*. He serves on the editorial board of the *Journal of Marital and Family Therapy*. He maintains an active private practice and focuses his research and writing on common factors of successful therapy.

**Maureen P. Davey, PhD, LMFT**, is a licensed marriage and family therapist, AAMFT approved clinical supervisor, and associate professor in the College of Nursing and Health Professions, Department of Couple and Family Therapy, at Drexel University in Philadelphia, Pennsylvania. She is a frequent national presenter and is the author of more than 40 peer-reviewed articles and book chapters. Her program of research focuses on how different relational and cultural contexts contribute to the experience of health disparities. She has conducted mixed-method clinical research studies focused on developing culturally relevant interventions for minority cancer patients and their families and training providers to use more family-centered approaches to care. She currently studies ethnic and racial minority families in which a spouse, parent, and/or school-age child is coping with a physical illness.

# ABOUT THE CONTRIBUTORS

**Tohoro Francis Akakpo** is an assistant professor in the social work professional programs at the University of Wisconsin—Green Bay. He teaches Small Groups and Family Facilitation Skills in the BSW program and Practice Competence in Diverse Community and Advanced Research Application of Social Work Practice in the graduate program. His research and practice are focused on adolescent sex offender treatment and mental health, and other issues of concern to African immigrants.

**Yudum Akyil** is an adjunct professor at Bilgi University in Istanbul, Turkey. She also works at private clinics with individuals, couples, and families. Dr. Akyil's research interests include the person-of-the-therapist issues, intergenerational value transmission and social change, and parent–child relationships. She is a cofounder of the Couple and Family Therapy Association in Turkey.

**Anna Andrews** is a student in the marriage and family therapy master's program at Texas Tech University in Lubbock. Her clinical interests are in Christian couple and family therapy and addiction and recovery.

**Harry J. Aponte** is a family therapist known for his writings and workshops on the person-of-the-therapist, spirituality in therapy, therapy with disadvantaged and culturally diverse families, and structural family therapy. Dr. Aponte was a staff member and teacher of family therapy at the Menninger Clinic in Houston, Texas, as well as director of the Philadelphia Child Guidance Center.

**Alane Atchley** is currently pursuing her master's degree in marriage and family therapy at Texas Tech University in Lubbock. Her clinical and research interests are sexual assault and addiction.

**Alyssa Banford** is an assistant professor at Alliant International University in San Diego, California. She has been supervising master's-level clinicians in the University of Connecticut marriage and family therapy training program since 2011 as an assistant professor-in-residence. She has experience in individual, group, and live supervision.

**Andrae Banks**, MSW, is a licensed clinical social worker at the Durham County Department of Public Health, North Carolina. His interest areas include total wellness, health disparities, obesity, diabetes, poverty, political genocide. and macrolevel intervention.

**Kristyn M. Blackburn** is a family science doctoral student at the University of Kentucky in Lexington. She researches couple and family therapy as well as couple processes.

**Anna I. Bohlinger** is a doctoral student in the family social science program at the University of Minnesota in Minneapolis. Ms. Bohlinger's clinical and research foci include family dynamics and resilience in adolescent nonsuicidal self-injury and family resilience.

**Angela B. Bradford** is an assistant professor of marriage and family therapy at Brigham Young University in Provo, Utah and an AAMFT approved supervisor. She researches the mediators and moderators of change in couple interventions, and her clinical work focuses on treating individuals and couples who have experienced trauma, severe relationship trauma and distress, sexual dysfunction, and sexual addictions.

**Andrew Brimhall** completed his master's degree in counseling psychology at Alliant International University's California School of Professional Psychology in Mexico City. He provided therapy services in Mexico City to orphans and high-risk youth populations. His areas of interest in research include LGBTQ adolescent issues, adoption practices and outcomes, and multinational/multicultural social justice.

**Kilolo Brodie**, PhD, MSW, is an assistant professor at California State University Stanislaus. She has been teaching for five years. Dr. Brodie's research interests include Down syndrome, families of color, and racial inequalities.

**Venessa A. Brown** is an associate provost and professor of social work at Southern Illinois University Edwardsville. Her research and practice has focused on child welfare, domestic violence, and international child and family practice.

**Paul Burke** became lead trainer and team leader in a private-practice training company that specializes in facilitating the development of Motivational Interviewing (MI) skills following a 22-year career in providing individual and group treatment in a variety of outpatient and residential settings for persons with mental health and addictions issues. He is a member of the international Motivational Interviewing Network of Trainers (MINT).

**Karen L. Caldwell** is a professor in the Department of Human Development and Psychological Counseling at Appalachian State University in Boone, North Carolina. She has taught marriage and family therapy, counseling, and expressive arts therapy to graduate students for more than 20 years, and her current research foci include mind-body interventions for mental health as well as integrative health coaching.

**Kimberly A. E. Carter** is an assistant professor of social work at Southern Illinois University Edwardsville. Her research and practice have focused on family mental health and healthcare disparities. She also has an extensive background in program development, evaluation, capacity building, strategic planning, and organizational cultural competence.

**Karina A. Chandler-Ziegler** is a doctoral student in the couples and family therapy program at the California School of Professional Psychology (CSPP) at Alliant International University in Los Angeles. She holds an MFT master's degree from CSPP. Karina has provided therapy services to dual-diagnosis prison parolees in transitional housing. She holds a certificate in liberation psychology and assists the crisis and trauma course at the CSPP Los Angeles and Mexico City campuses.

**Adam M. Clark** is a doctoral student in the human development and family studies program, College of Public Health and Human Sciences, at Oregon State University in Corvallis. His research interests include parent–child relationships and the development of prosocial outcomes in children.

**Kathy Cox** is an associate professor at the School of Social Work at California State University, Chico. She previously worked as a licensed practitioner, a clinical supervisor, and an administrator in the field of children's mental health. She is the coauthor of *Self-Care in Social Work: A Guide for Practitioners, Supervisors, and Administrators* and currently teaches a variety of courses in social work practice, research, and practicum.

**Jaclyn D. Cravens** is an assistant professor in marriage and family therapy at Alliant International University, San Diego. She has experience providing supervision for master's students. Her research interests are in the Internet and relationships, juvenile justice populations, and social justice issues. Jaclyn has presented at local and national conferences on the Internet and relationships and social justice.

**Norja Cunningham** will be graduating in 2013 from Antioch University New England, in Keene, New Hampshire, in the marriage and family therapy doctoral program. She has experience working with children and families utilizing trauma-focused cognitive-behavioral therapy and experiential family therapy models during individual, sibling, family, and group therapy. Ms. Cunningham has supervised and taught courses to master's-level students at Antioch University New England and Central Connecticut State University in New Britain.

**Ally DeGraff** is a student in the marriage and family therapy master's program at Texas Tech University in Lubbock. Her clinical foci are in military family systems, financial therapy, and addiction and recovery.

**Elisabeth E. Esmiol**, PhD, is an assistant professor and the director of clinical training in the Department of Marriage and Family Therapy at Pacific Lutheran University. Her research interests include effectiveness in training and supervising marriage and family therapists in areas of contextual awareness and integrating client feedback.

**Shari Galiardi** is the former director of service-learning at Appalachian State University, in Boone, North Carolina, holds a master's degree in Educational Leadership from Miami University, and worked in the field of community service and service-learning for 18 years. In addition to developing a successful domestic service-learning program in the Appalachian mountains, she developed service-based opportunities for students in Wales, India, Ghana, and South Africa, while assisting faculty with designing similar programs all over the world.

**Bob Gillespie** is an assistant professor and clinical supervisor for the Edgewood College marriage and family therapy program in Madison, Wisconsin. He co-leads a narrative therapy study group with Julia O'Reilly and has presented internationally on mindfulness.

**Armando Gonzalez-Cort** is an adjunct faculty member in Alliant International University's couple and family therapy program. His interests include international education and helping families maintain a family member's major weight loss.

**J. Christopher Hall** is a licensed clinician and an associate professor of social work at the University of North Carolina Wilmington, where he co-directs the Strengths Collaborative. His teaching areas include advanced master's clinical practice and field courses. His area of focus is the research, teaching, and practice of collaborative clinical practices that are supported by positivist concepts of empirical evidence and postmodern ideas of reciprocal collaboration (yep, it can be done!).

**Noah Hass-Cohen** is an associate professor and program director of the marriage and family therapy and art therapy program at the California School of Professional Psychology at Alliant International University in Los Angeles, California. A licensed marriage and family therapist, clinical psychologist, and registered art therapist, she incorporates expressive arts–based experientials in her teaching.

**Cody Heath** is currently a student in Texas Tech University's marriage and family therapy program. His interests include working with LGBTQ populations and increasing cultural, educational, and therapeutic practice awareness concerning these populations.

**Barbara Couden Hernandez** is the director of Physician Vitality and a professor in the School of Medicine, Loma Linda University, in Loma Linda, California. She has been a registered nurse for more than 30 years. She formerly served as the director of medical family therapy activities in the Department of Counseling and Family Sciences at Loma Linda University when this chapter was written.

**Ana M. Hernandez** is a doctoral candidate at Drexel University in Philadelphia, Pennsylvania, in the Couple and Family Therapy Department, where she is currently completing her dissertation, which focuses on the role of discrimination, racial identity, and parental racial socialization on self-esteem and depression among Latinos. Ana received her master's degree in marriage and family therapy from Syracuse University in Syracuse, New York.

**Monica Higgins** was a high school English teacher for three years and returned to receive a master's degree in counseling. Her area of interest is to help raise awareness around the sensitive diversity issues present in the schools and elsewhere.

**Melinda Hohman**, PhD, LCSW, is a professor at the School of Social Work, San Diego State University, San Diego, California. Dr. Hohman teaches courses in substance abuse treatment, research, motivational interviewing (MI), and social work practice. Dr. Hohman has published numerous articles about substance abuse assessment and treatment services and women's issues in this area. She has been a member of the Motivational Interviewing Network of Trainers (MINT) since 1999, training community social workers, child protection workers, probation officers, and addiction counselors across Southern California.

**Alexander L. Hsieh** is an assistant professor in the California School of Professional Psychology, Couple and Family Therapy program at Alliant International University, in Sacramento, California. His research and clinical interests include marital and parent-child relationships, particularly among Asian American families.

**Mary C. Hufnell** is a clinical psychologist and an assistant professor in the Department of Counseling at Gallaudet University in Washington, DC. Her clinical, teaching, and research interests include diversity and multicultural identity, the use of mindfulness in clinical work, family systems, psychological assessment, learning and attention deficit disorders, clinical supervision, and the use of popular films in teaching clinical diagnoses.

**Michael N. Humble**, PhD, LCSW, is an assistant professor at California State University Stanislaus. He has been teaching for five years. His research interests include HIV/AIDS, rural social work, and clinical practice.

**Jennifer L. Johnson**, LCSW, is a full-time lecturer at California State University Stanislaus who has practiced in multiple settings. She recently co-wrote and administered a grant in order to reduce suicide and mental health stigma on the college campus.

**Elizabeth King Keenan** is a professor of social work at Southern Connecticut State University in New Haven, where she teaches social work practice, theory, and field seminar courses. She has extensive agency and private-practice experience and has supervised graduate- and doctoral-level clinicians for more than 10 years. Dr. Keenan's clinical interests include common factors and the use of evidence in clinical practice.

**Scott A. Ketring** is an associate professor of marriage and family therapy at Auburn University in Auburn, Alabama, and an AAMFT approved supervisor. He researches the role of the therapy alliance in therapeutic change, and he provides trauma-focused therapy to individuals and couples and treats couples who are experiencing severe relationship distress.

**Lana Kim** is an assistant professor of marriage and family therapy in the Department of Sociology, Anthropology, and Criminal Justice with Marriage and Family Therapy at Valdosta State University in Valdosta, Georgia. She formerly completed a research assistantship at the Loma Linda University School of Medicine, Medical Simulation Center, where she collaborated with Dr. Barbara Hernandez to develop and pilot the methodology presented in their chapter.

**Karni Kissil** is an adjunct faculty member in the couple and family therapy department at Drexel University in Philadelphia, Pennsylvania. She has a private practice in Jupiter, Florida, where she works with individuals, couples, and families. Dr. Kissil's research interests include the person-of-the-therapist, the impact of chronic illness on the family, and the impact of immigration and acculturation on the clinical work of foreign-born therapists.

**Chandra Lasley** is a doctoral student in the marriage and family therapy program at Kansas State University in Manhattan, Kansas. Her research and clinical interests include therapy with minority populations, especially those of Asian or multiethnic origins, and intimate partner violence.

**Bethany Luna** is a student in the marriage and family therapy master's program at Texas Tech University in Lubbock. Her clinical interests are in LGBTQ family systems, addiction and recovery, sexual offenders, and athletes.

**Peggy McIntosh**, PhD, is Associate Director of the Wellesley Centers for Women at Wellesley College in Wellesley, Massachusetts. She is also founder and co-director of The National SEED (Seeking Educational Equity and Diversity) Project on Inclusive Curriculum. The SEED Project is the nation's largest professional development project for K–16 teachers spanning all grade levels and all subject areas. Its aim is to prepare teachers to lead their own professional development seminars with colleagues on making curricula, teaching methods, and school climates more multicultural, gender-fair, and inclusive of all students, no matter what their backgrounds may be.

**Tai Justin Mendenhall** is an assistant professor in the couple and family therapy program, Department of Family and Social Sciences, at the University of Minnesota, Minneapolis. His clinical and research interests center on family coping with chronic illness, working within interdisciplinary teams in response to mass disaster and trauma, and compassion-fatigue prevention and recovery.

**Lisa Vallie Merchant** is a marriage and family therapy doctoral student at Texas Tech University in Lubbock who has experience working with victims of domestic violence at a women's shelter. Her research interests are in improving services to victims in domestic violence shelters and understanding how violent couples desist from violence.

**Rebecca Mirick** is a clinical social worker with an MSW from the School of Social Work at Boston University in Boston, Massachusetts, and a PhD from the School of Social Work at Simmons College in Boston, Massachusetts. She is currently a Visiting Assistant Professor in the School of Social Work at Salem State University in Salem, Massachusetts. She has worked in the field of social work since 2000, working in a residential school, an outpatient mental health center, and a residential facility for adjudicated youth.

**Kathleen Nash** is an adjunct professor and clinical supervisor in the couple and family therapy program at Drexel University in Philadelphia, Pennsylvania. She is currently pursuing a doctorate in marriage and family therapy with a specialization in medical family therapy. As a contextual family therapist, Kathleen's clinical work focuses on families of children with autism spectrum disorders, childhood trauma, and bereavement. Kathleen also presents regional seminars for corporate managers and their teams on balancing family and work.

**Kerri E. Newman** is a master's student in the marriage and family therapy program at Texas Tech University in Lubbock. Her clinical interests are in parent–child relationships and bereavement counseling.

**Alba Niño** is a doctoral candidate in the Couple and Family Therapy Department at Drexel University in Philadelphia, Pennsylvania. Her clinical work has centered on immigrant Latino families, couples, and individuals. She is also interested in many aspects of the person-of-the-therapist, including training, supervision, and the experiences of immigrant therapists in the United States. Other interests focus on attachment and emotion-focused approaches in marriage and family therapy.

**Julia O'Reilly** is currently in private practice and supervising interns and residents at the Family Center, the clinical training facility for the marriage and family therapy program at Edgewood College in Madison, Wisconsin.

**Manjushree Palit** is a doctoral candidate in the marriage and family therapy program in the Department of Human Development at Virginia Tech in Blacksburg, Virginia. Her research and clinical interests include couples, families, and illness, sexuality, and intimacy. Ms. Palit is presently interning at the Houston-Galveston Family Institute in Houston, Texas.

**Trent S. Parker** is an assistant professor at the University of Kentucky in Lexington. He has worked in a variety of clinical settings, including a women's shelter, a juvenile justice center, and community mental health centers. His research interests include understanding the role of empathy in therapeutic processes.

**Rebecca Partridge** holds a graduate degree in marriage and family therapy from Pacific Lutheran University in Tacoma, Washington. She is a member of AAMFT and a clinical therapist at NAVOS Mental Health Solutions in Seattle, Washington, where she integrates self-awareness and client feedback in her work with children, adolescents, and families. She formerly worked at the PLU Couple and Family Therapy Center and as a research assistant with Dr. Esmiol.

**Haley V. Pettigrew** is a master's student in the marriage and family therapy program at Texas Tech University in Lubbock. Her clinical and research interests are in intimate partner violence, foster care children and their family system, and addictive parent–child relationships.

**Binh Pham** is a doctoral candidate in the marriage and family therapy program at Antioch University New England in Keene, New Hampshire. Ms. Pham is a clinician at Southwest Counseling Solutions in Detroit, Michigan. She provides therapy for at-risk children and their families. She supervised and taught master's-level marriage and family therapy students at Antioch University New England in 2009–2010. Ms. Pham's research and clinical interests are refugee trauma, intergenerational trauma, domestic and international issues, and interracial couple/family relationships.

**Fred P. Piercy** is a professor of marriage and family therapy in the Department of Human Development at Virginia Tech in Blacksburg, Virginia. Dr. Piercy's areas of scholarship include family therapy education, family therapy for substance abuse, HIV social science research and prevention, couple education, and qualitative research.

**Melinda W. Pilkinton**, PhD, LMSW, is an associate professor and program director at Mississippi State University. Dr. Pilkinton has more than 25 years of clinical practice experience in multiple social work settings. Her research interests include LGBTQ, social work and the military, and PTSD.

**Keeley J. Pratt** is an assistant professor in the couples and family therapy program in the Department of Human Sciences at Ohio State University in Columbus, an independently licensed marriage and family therapist, and an AAMFT approved supervisor. Her research focuses on family-based treatment for children who are overweight or obese. She has presented at local, national, and international conferences and has authored articles and book chapters about child and adolescent family-based obesity treatment, medical family therapy, and supervision in healthcare settings.

**Karen Rich** is a faculty member at Marywood University in Scranton, Pennsylvania, and has studied police officers' interventions with rape victims, interdisciplinary collaboration between victim advocates and police, policewomen's experiences on rape cases, and the coping strategies of disabled crime victims. She is currently researching college students' approaches to sexually assaulted friends. A clinician for 15 years, she has counseled survivors, co-victims, and perpetrators of sexual assault.

**Bridget Roberts-Pittman** is an associate professor in the Department of Communication Disorders and Counseling, School, and Educational Psychology at Indiana State University in Terre Haute. She completed her PhD at Indiana State University in counseling psychology. She has more than 15 years of clinical and supervisory experience and holds a designation of AAMFT approved supervisor.

**Elizabeth Rodriguez-Keyes** is an assistant professor of social work at Southern Connecticut State University in New Haven, where she teaches practice, theory, and field seminar courses. She has been a practicing clinician for 20 years and has been providing supervision for 15 years. Dr. Rodriguez-Keyes' research interests include clinical supervision, teaching with technology, and synchronous learning.

**Lori Cluff Schade**, PhD, is a licensed marriage and family therapist and an adjunct professor at Utah Valley University in Orem. Her research and clinical interests include emotionally focused couples and family therapy, applied to a variety of clinical presentations.

**Dana A. Schneider** is an assistant professor at Southern Connecticut State University in New Haven, where she oversees the practice sequence for the undergraduate social work program. She has been a practicing clinical social worker for 18 years and has a special interest in contemplative practice and pedagogy.

**Kami L. Schwerdtfeger** is an assistant professor of marriage and family therapy in the Department of Human Development and Family Science at Oklahoma State University in Stillwater. Dr. Schwerdtfeger is a licensed marriage and family therapist (LMFT) in Oklahoma and an approved supervisor and clinical member of the American Association of Marriage and Family Therapists (AAMFT). Dr. Schwerdtfeger's clinical and research specialization is in the areas of trauma, posttraumatic stress, and posttraumatic growth and resilience in couple and family systems.

**Thomas A. Smith** is an associate professor of marriage and family therapy at Auburn University in Auburn, Alabama, and an AAMFT approved supervisor. His research and practice have focused on divorce and stepfamily issues, and he has consulted as a supervisor in community mental health settings for more than 25 years.

**Sara A. Smock Jordan** is an associate professor of community, family, and addiction services at Texas Tech University in Lubbock. Dr. Smock Jordan is the developer of the Solution Building Inventory, has completed outcome and process research on Solution-Focused Brief Therapy (SFBT), and is actively involved in SFBT's growing recognition as an evidence-based practice. In addition, she is on the board of the Solution-Focused Brief Therapy Association (SFBTA), serves on SFBTA's research committee, and is a founding member of the organization.

**Phillip Sorenson** is a student in the marriage and family therapy master's program at Texas Tech University in Lubbock. Mr. Sorenson's clinical interests are in military family systems and families within family businesses.

**Sue Steiner** is a professor at the School of Social Work at California State University, Chico. She has taught community and organizational practice and social welfare policy for 20 years and has worked and consulted in a variety of public and private organizations. She is a coauthor of both *An Introduction to the Profession of Social Work* (4th edition) and *Self-Care in Social Work: A Guide for Practitioners, Supervisors, and Administrators*. Her current research focuses on teaching effectiveness, self-care for helping professionals, and community development through the use of alternative currencies.

**Jayme R. Swanke** is an assistant professor of social work at Southern Illinois University Edwardsville. Her research and practice have focused on areas of addiction and recovery, child welfare, and the use of digital technologies (e.g., blogging) as a form of social support for families of children with autism spectrum disorders.

**Rachel Tambling** is an assistant professor at the University of Connecticut in Storrs. She supervises master's- and doctoral-level clinicians in the marriage and family therapy training program. She specializes in group live supervision, including the use of reflecting teams and Greek chorus. She regularly provides individual and group supervision to trainees.

**Stephanie Trudeau-Hern** is a doctoral student in the couple and family therapy program of the Department of Family Social Sciences at the University of Minnesota in Minneapolis. Her clinical and research interests include caregiver well-being, family coping with chronic illness, end-of-life issues, and provider self-care within collaborative healthcare teams.

**Cecily R. Trujillo** is a master's student in the marriage and family therapy program at Texas Tech University in Lubbock. Her clinical interests are in couples' emotional attachment and families with children in a juvenile justice system.

**Thomas Veeman** has worked clinically for Northwest Youth Corps as a job skills and leadership coach for teenagers and as a wilderness therapy field supervisor serving teen and young adult clients for the ANASAZI Foundation in Mesa, Arizona. He currently works as a consultant for corporate team building and intercultural communication while completing a master's degree in international counseling psychology at the California School of Professional Psychology at Alliant International University in Mexico City.

**Anna M. Viviani** is an assistant professor in the Department of Communication Disorders and Counseling, School, and Educational Psychology at Indiana State University in Terre Haute.

She completed her PhD in counselor education at the University of Iowa and is an approved clinical supervisor through CCE/NBCC. Her research interests include violence against women and children, trauma-related grief, practice issues, and counselor preparation.

**Jeni L. Wahlig** is a doctoral student, adjunct faculty, and supervisor-in-training in the marriage and family therapy program at Antioch University New England in Keene, New Hampshire. Ms. Wahlig's clinical and research foci include same-sex couple enrichment and mental and relational health in the LGBT community.

**Monique D. Walker** is a doctoral candidate in the Couple and Family Therapy Department at Drexel University in Philadelphia, Pennsylvania. She is now completing her dissertation, tentatively titled *How Black LGBQ Youths' Perceptions of Parental Acceptance and Rejection Are Associated with their Self-Esteem and Mental Health.*

**Jason B. Whiting** is an associate professor in the MFT program at Texas Tech University in Lubbock. His research is on the distortion and denial process that occurs in violent and abusive relationships. He also has an interest in mindfulness interventions and qualitative research.

**Larry D. Williams**, PhD, is an assistant professor of studies in the child and family services concentration in the School of Social Work at North Carolina Central University in Durham, North Carolina. His research focuses on the areas of HIV and AIDS, power and oppression affecting African-Americans and oppressed populations, health disparities of minority populations in the juvenile and criminal justice systems, and resiliency in minority families.

**Senem Zeytinoglu** is a doctoral candidate in the couple and family therapy program at Drexel University in Philadelphia, Pennsylvania. She works in a community mental health clinic with individuals, couples, and families in Philadelphia. Her research interests include cleft lip palate and families, medical family therapy, person-of-the-therapist issues, and trauma in minority populations.

# Author Index

# SUBJECT INDEX